CW00767562

Saint Petersburg

Saint Petersburg

Sacrifice and Redemption in the City
That Defied Hitler

SINCLAIR McKAY

PENGUIN
VIKING

VIKING

UK | USA | Canada | Ireland | Australia
India | New Zealand | South Africa

Viking is part of the Penguin Random House group of companies
whose addresses can be found at global.penguinrandomhouse.com.

Penguin Random House UK,
One Embassy Gardens, 8 Viaduct Gardens, London SW11 7BW

penguin.co.uk

Penguin
Random House
UK

First published 2025

002

Copyright © Sinclair McKay, 2025

The moral right of the author has been asserted

Set in 12/14.75pt Bembo Book MT Pro
Typeset by Jouve (UK), Milton Keynes
Printed and bound in Great Britain by Clays Ltd, Elcograf S.p.A.

The authorized representative in the EEA is Penguin Random House Ireland,
Morrison Chambers, 32 Nassau Street, Dublin D02 YH68

A CIP catalogue record for this book is available from the British Library

ISBN: 978–0–241–74131–3

Penguin Random House is committed to a sustainable future
for our business, our readers and our planet. This book is made from
Forest Stewardship Council® certified paper.

To my ever-inspirational father, Peter

Contents

List of Illustrations

Operation Barbarossa and Leningrad Siege positions,

FINNISH
OFFENSIVE

*Gulf of
Finland*

Kronstadt

LENINGRAD

Oranienbaum

Strelna

Nevskaya

R. Neva

Uritsk

Pulkovo

Krasnoe Selo

Pushkin

Kolpin

GERMAN
OFFENSIVE

Gatchina

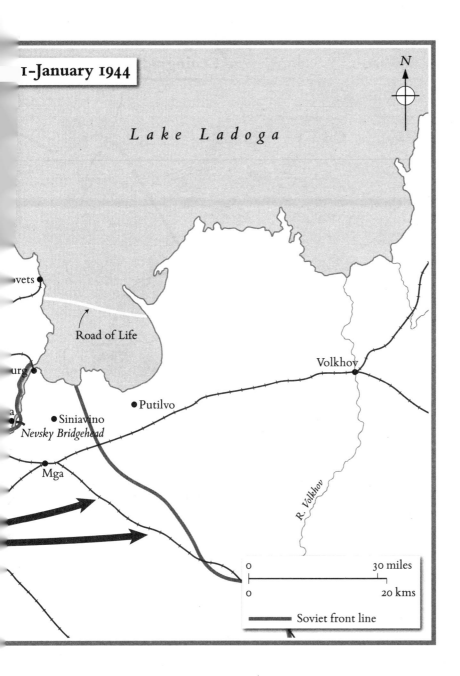

1–January 1944

N

Lake Ladoga

Road of Life

Volkhov

...vets

...urg

Putilvo

Siniavino
Nevsky Bridgehead

Mga

R. Volkhov

0		30 miles
0		20 kms

Soviet front line

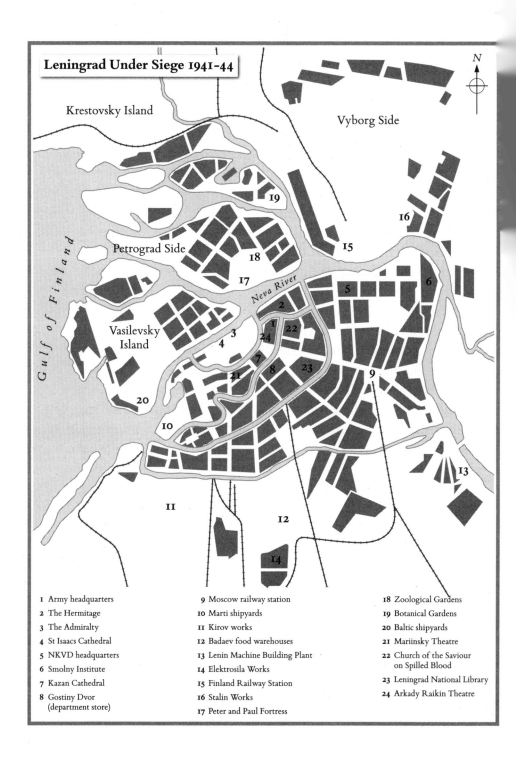

Leningrad Under Siege 1941-44

Krestovsky Island

Vyborg Side

Gulf of Finland

Petrograd Side

Neva River

Vasilevsky Island

N

1 Army headquarters
2 The Hermitage
3 The Admiralty
4 St Isaacs Cathedral
5 NKVD headquarters
6 Smolny Institute
7 Kazan Cathedral
8 Gostiny Dvor
   (department store)

9 Moscow railway station
10 Marti shipyards
11 Kirov works
12 Badaev food warehouses
13 Lenin Machine Building Plant
14 Elektrosila Works
15 Finland Railway Station
16 Stalin Works
17 Peter and Paul Fortress

18 Zoological Gardens
19 Botanical Gardens
20 Baltic shipyards
21 Mariinsky Theatre
22 Church of the Saviour
   on Spilled Blood
23 Leningrad National Library
24 Arkady Raikin Theatre

Preface

A silent silver English winter's morning, deep in a leafless valley. The village road was metallic with frost. I was meeting my acquaintance from St Petersburg at a limestone cottage. On the doorstep, both she and I were curiously guarded. And throughout that morning, as we spoke in the bright quiet room overlooking the garden, she never smiled. But then, that was one of the details of the life that she remembered, growing up in the city that is now St Petersburg but was then called Leningrad: the absence of smiles. It was not to do with hostility, or even unhappiness, but simply that a smile had to be authentic and had to be earned. There had to be trust.

My acquaintance from St Petersburg seemed suspicious about my motives, but also curious. I was there first because I was eager to learn more about the city. That much was natural, and she was proud: who would not want to hear about the astonishing baroque architecture, or the rich poetry of Alexander Pushkin; of violent revolution and bloody assassinations; of composers who held the world still with pleasure, and ballet dancers who taught that world new possibilities in the art of movement? Saint Petersburg is a city of the imagination – yet it is also grounded in a grubby reality: colourful rococo facades, spires and domes, planted upon islands, fretted through with snaking rivers and canals, facing less exalted districts of hulking concrete brutalism. Perhaps more than London, it is a city that has been shaped and influenced by its own storytellers.

But that was not my chief reason for visiting my acquaintance. I was there partly for advice on the city's less explored byways and history; and also about its archives. This was because of one vast and terrible event that had taken place within living memory. In Britain, talking about the Second World War comes naturally and easily: partly because even though the country was bombed and its cities set ablaze, the vast majority of its people didn't suffer the trauma of invasion. The war that I had been brought up on as a child in the 1970s was a matter of comic-strip morality, of unimpeachable heroism versus icy Nazi sadism. For my acquaintance from St Petersburg, the Second World War brought to mind quite different associations.

For her, it was the Great Patriotic War, or Great Fatherland War. This was the conflict that had broken over her family like a terrible thunderstorm in the summer of 1941, when Hitler's forces, over three million men, launched an invasion of eastern Europe and Soviet Russia that covered thousands of miles and led to the obscene slaughter of literally uncountable numbers of people. My acquaintance's parents had been children at the time of the calamity.

From the autumn of 1941 to the beginning of 1944, Leningrad – on the north-western edge of Russia, where it borders Finland and the Baltic states – and its population were effectively encircled by Wehrmacht forces. Throughout, the Germans bombed the city; they fired shells at it; but much more pressingly, they severed all the transport arteries and veins. It was, for a time, impossible to bring in any meaningful supplies of food.

This was the siege of Leningrad: a murderous act that outshadowed any other siege in history, from the ancient walls of Carthage to the blood-soaked blockades of the Thirty Years War. It cannot be viewed solely as military history because it was intended as civilian extermination. Leningrad had been a city of some two and a half million. These people began to starve as, day by day, the most commonplace food ran out, and the bread rations shrank and dwindled. Then the snows came. Electricity faltered. There was not enough fuel for domestic fires. Temperatures plunged to minus 43 °C. Starving bodies had to cope with the most acute, knife-like cold. The diorama of suffering, and the sheer scale of it, was – and remains – almost impossible to comprehend.

The hunger by itself brought the most terrible suffering. As bellies began to swell, and limbs began to stiffen, dreams were cruelly filled with fresh, hot, dripping meat and buttery potatoes. All this as the bombing shattered windows and snow swirled into the apartments. Death came in stages: wheezing weakness; then dreadful pain and intestinal torment and self-soiling; then lethal, staring apathy. Flesh darkened: even the blood became too apathetic to move properly.

The creeping cold induced visions, and people knew that once the visions started, they would never more awake to the real world.

The numbers of the civilian dead were so enormous – anywhere between 800,000 and over a million, in the space of just one starvation winter from 1941 to 1942 – that there was not enough ground in the city to accommodate them. The dead had to queue to be buried. Some corpses were furtively stolen before they could be lowered into mass graves, robbed by those on the furthest, darkest edges of desperation. It has been observed that the numbers who perished in Leningrad almost outweighed the entire total of British and American troop deaths in the Second World War. Those who survived this ordeal saw the dreadful extremities of human nature: the moral abyss of war and the amoral struggle to survive.

My acquaintance's father had been a boy in that hell. I was not so presumptuous that I was asking her directly about family personal experiences: I was there to find out more in a wider sense, especially about what happened to those in the city afterwards, and how those memories had been preserved. But my acquaintance was watchful: how could anyone wish to hear such things? These were not stories to be swapped as though in some pub reunion. They touched on the deepest nerves of family, loyalty and love. My acquaintance gave the impression that no matter how much the wider story of the siege of Leningrad formed part of world history, these were stories that were to be guarded.

But more: this was about violation. A proud city had been deliberately, calculatedly, plunged into degradation: civilization and culture, art and intellect reduced to bestial squalor. The debate has been threaded through the life of the city since: how should this story be framed for the generations to come? Leningraders were initially labelled heroes: the term *blokadniki*, used to describe all those who had been through it, was intended to suggest pride, like a verbal medal. The term and the sentiment still stand, but the ordeal was akin not to a military operation but to mass torture: a vast atrocity. Victims are not necessarily always heroes, and the suggestion of heroism can diminish the horror that was inflicted upon them. Remembrance usually implies silent reflection, but there anger still burns bright.

This appears to be an attitude shared in part by Russia's leader, Vladimir Putin, himself born in post-war Leningrad in 1952 to parents who had themselves suffered atrociously. Putin would have had an older brother – Viktor – were it not for the fact that, as a toddler in spring 1942, Viktor had died of starvation. Putin himself was born into a city of mass graves. When we consider the nightmare that Putin is, at the time of writing, insistently inflicting upon a fresh generation of parents and children in Ukraine – the nightly bombing, the torture, the abductions – it is impossible not to wonder how much his own mental landscape has been formed, or perhaps malformed, by the generational repercussions of trauma.

Throughout Putin's prosecution of this bloody modern conflict, he has made constant neurotic references to what he perceives as a latent Nazi history in Ukraine: is this a cynical propaganda move or some insanely paranoid reflex that reflects his true fears about western Europe and NATO? Those who have not experienced invasion might sometimes struggle to understand the profound insecurity of those who have. There is another historical echo here, though, harking back to a mistake that Stalin also made: Russia's modern-day belligerence has led its northern neighbour Finland to abandon its own neutrality and join the Western alliance of NATO. The last time Finland and Russia were implacably opposed, with borders firmly sealed, was in the Second World War, and throughout the siege of Leningrad. Were it not for the will of the Finnish military in 1941 – itself hardened by ferocious Soviet aggression in the Winter War between the two nations in 1939–40 – there might have been the slender chance of another supply route into the starving city. As it was, the Finns taunted any Red Army soldiers they saw with a simple cry: 'Russki! Bread! Bread!'

The blockade of the city was finally lifted in January 1944; a year later, the Red Army stood victorious over the destroyed Nazis. Yet would it ever be possible for surviving Leningraders to feel properly, heedlessly secure again? My acquaintance from St Petersburg had been brought up there in the 1970s, when it was still Leningrad, deep among the gaunt tower blocks of its smog-smirched suburbs from where the city's splendours could be reached only via tram and metro. Her environment was one of concrete, and of schools and institutions and housing estates with numbers rather than names. Life had an intense flavour, especially for the young. But that also meant that there were elements to be savoured, and to be held with pride. From a very early age, her own musical aptitude had been spotted: and as her schooling progressed, she was given the most concentrated musical education.

There was richness there too in her 1970s childhood: frequent trips to the theatre and the opera. My acquaintance's parents were assiduous about grafting their reverence and their gratitude for beauty: and the Leningrad authorities in general encouraged this. The city continued to glitter with a worldwide name for dance and music. And how could it not? This was where Mussorgsky and Rimsky-Korsakov, Prokofiev and Shostakovich had been nurtured. It was the home of the Kirov Ballet. And in addition to this was the heritage of the great writers and poets, sensitive to the city's curious and *unheimlich* atmosphere: Alexander Pushkin, Nikolay Gogol, Fyodor Dostoevsky, the young Vladimir Nabokov – and the extraordinary modernist poets Osip Mandelstam and Anna Akhmatova. Peter the Great – the Tsar for whom the city was built – famously envisaged it as Russia's 'window on to the west'. A window may be gazed through in either direction, but what the Tsar and all the city's artists and musicians also appeared to be conjuring was a city that itself lay upon a spiritual borderland. This was not just a matter of east and west but also more fundamental distinctions: in the summer, the borders between day and night dissolved, leaving the sun suspended on the horizon; in the winter, the day brought little but darkness. Similarly there was a blurring of the border between land and sea. In 1824, a cataclysmic flood inundated St Petersburg, and from that point a constant sense of insecurity about the city's very foundations, and about its permeability, remained. The city, always prone to flooding, was sometimes depicted as an Old Testament ark, floating on hostile waters.

Then, with the war and the siege, there came the most horribly porous border of all: that between the living and the dead. As the silent snows fell on deserted embankments and bridges, starving men and women alike sank slowly to their knees and lay down to die. Occasionally passers-by might check them: tiny pulses indicating that the sufferers had not quite yet crossed the line. Yet even on the living side of that borderline, death was intimately close.

There was so much I wanted to know. Those who had wished to had contributed diaries and memoirs and small, telling objects, first of all to the city's specially dedicated Museum of the Defence and Siege of Leningrad. This museum had opened in 1944, as the siege was lifted. It sparked the instant, terrible wrath of Stalin, and that anger was directed at the civic authorities, some of whom would later be executed. It was considered 'ideologically impure'. The museum smacked of exceptionalism – had not other Soviet cities suffered too? – as well as inadvertently underscoring the story of Stalin's own incompetence. (Exceptionalism – a form of pride – was Petersburg's founding sin. The city had long been resented by other Russians for its perceived intellectual and artistic superiority, as well as its overt European bias in its grandest architecture and art and music.) But the people continued across the years to contribute diaries and memoirs to other archives in the city. It wasn't until the late 1980s, as communism crumbled, that the siege exhibits were reassembled in that original museum, a nineteenth-century house close to the Fontanka river and Peter the Great's Summer Palace. It is still there today.

Chiefly, my acquaintance from St Petersburg seemed electrically aware that history is not an abstract, airy pastime there: it is alive and urgent and sometimes dangerous. Successive regimes have all been intensely sensitive to how events are remembered. For the other extraordinary thing about St Petersburg is that throughout its 300-odd years of existence – from the moment that slave labour started raising palaces of stone from frozen swamps, straight from the imagination of a world-spanning emperor, and through to its cultivation of beauty and art and colour – its history has always coursed with blood.

To understand the siege of Leningrad – an ordeal that was in its own way unique in history – it is also necessary to understand the people who moved through this rich maze of elegance and poverty, of industry and commerce, of crystalline light playing on the icy

Neva, of the dark winter fogs through which real and fictional murderers and maniacs have walked. The siege was not the only time the people had suffered: the citizens had been through years and decades of oppression and insecurity, and the stones of the streets held memories of generations of bloodshed. And more vitally today, it is intriguing to grasp the intense duality of the city: the soaring aestheticism and that ever-present sense of the uncanny – not least because it might hold the key to how we think of Vladimir Putin. Here is a man seeking to reorder the world, and his own place in history and time. He has been fixated upon Russian nationalist certainty. But the city from which he came remains on those weird and beautiful and sometimes terrible borders.

1.   The World Will Tremble

The pale sun at midnight made romantics of them all. The firmament was jade, streaked at the edges of the horizon with amber; and the people of the city, in great numbers, walked by the steep granite banks of the rivers and the canals, gazing at the dream-like light glittering on the waters. Every summer equinox, it was tradition – a solid point of continuity in a revolutionary world – that brought the citizens out to promenade, to laugh, to seduce one another, to eat salty *minogi* (lamprey: an eel-like fish) and sip warm *kissel* (a creamy concoction of mashed summer berries and cornflour), to absorb the wonder of the sky. These were people who had always enjoyed the city's reputation for the eerie. It was part of the romanticism. There was little in their world on that night of 21 June 1941 to disturb them.

The war in Europe that had been raging for two years was far away. As the fires of Nazism engulfed the continent, with Russia's old enemy Britain standing alone against the inferno, the people of Leningrad had the security of a Mephistophelean peace pact formed between their rulers and Hitler – the Molotov–Ribbentrop Pact. In addition to this, the recent war with their immediate neighbour Finland – fought just a few miles outside the city's northern boundaries – had been decisively won. Russia had a firm non-aggression pact with Nazi Germany. Hitler may have conquered and terrorized the west of the continent as far as Poland, but that land had been divided with the Soviets.

Earlier that day, there had been one solitary warning chime: the Leningrad edition of *Pravda* had reported a puzzling build-up in the numbers of German troops on the borders of the Baltic states, although it had not drawn any conclusions from this menacing development.

That non-aggression pact had been intended by its two signatories to last at least five years. Hitler was fighting Britain; Stalin had no wish for Russia to be pulled into the conflict. But Hitler had never made any secret of his aims. In his 1920s autobiography and prospectus *Mein Kampf* he wrote: 'We terminate the endless German drive to the south and west of Europe and direct our gaze towards the lands in the East . . . if we talk about new soil and territory in Europe today, we can think primarily only of Russia and its vassal border states.'

In June 1941, those 'vassal border states' numbered Estonia and what is now Belarus. And on the brink of invasion, Hitler and his forces were about to bring unprecedented bloodshed and horror to those lands. Hitler's idea of German *Lebensraum*, or living space, was a conceptual idea of a reordered Nazi Europe that would stretch all the way to the Ural mountains. Along the way, there would have to be extensive ethnic cleansing. The Jewish populations of eastern Europe were marked for total extermination. The Roma were also to be wiped out. The Slavic peoples – viewed by the Nazis as so dirty, so primitive – were to be turned to new enslaved purpose. Hitler dreamed of the oil riches of the Caucasus. He had studied the illimitable agricultural bounty of the vast land of Ukraine. Moscow was to be conquered.

And so was Leningrad. That it was a glittering architectural jewel, an historic and unique city of islands and ideas, amid the beauties of the ice-cold waters of the north, mattered nothing to him. The Russian people and the Soviet leadership – which in the eyes of Hitler and his lieutenants was a Jewish cabal – were only to be preserved if they could serve the Reich in some way. The Nazis had studied recent episodes in the Soviet conflict with Finland – the way that the vast Red Army was initially humiliated in deathly forests by the tiny but nimble and determined Finnish forces. Stalin's armies – ill-equipped, badly trained – had prevailed only through sheer weight of numbers. The Nazis had concluded that the Red Army was weak, disorganized and demoralized. They believed that the people of a city like Leningrad would be simply, and swiftly, overcome.

When the Nazis gazed upon Leningrad, there may have been subconscious associations with its gilded aristocracy, murdered by revolutionaries not twenty-five years earlier; there might have been an idea that the city was populated with artists and dancers and poets – what the St Petersburg ballet visionary Sergei Diaghilev referred to as 'water-colours on a Friday afternoon'.[1] The Nazis might also have thought of the city's industrial workers: factory floors filled with men who had been raised as agricultural workers but chased from the land by Stalin's rigid programmes of collectivization. But more fundamentally, there seemed to be an icy dismissiveness, which would become more horribly apparent over time: the city – in their eyes – was just another mass of humanity in a backward, brainwashed Bolshevik realm. The exquisite art and architecture, the sensibilities of all those performers and writers, did not find even the tiniest echo of appreciation. There was no initial apprehension on their side that the people would be difficult to conquer and dominate.

Yet despite the ostentatious beauty of the city – or at least the beauty of its facades, frequently concealing less alluring interiors – its people had already been hardened ever since 1917; the wake of the Russian revolution had brought nothing in the way of peace but instead periods of sharp hunger and pain and fear; stability was a luxury that had been afforded to none of its citizens. By that midsummer night of 1941, the bubbling optimism of its young people – from the students to the engineers to those working in the ever-mightier factories – was in itself a remarkable thing: quite apart from the shadows of war, the Stalinist regime itself had been capriciously cruel. No one – not even the most valued talents – had been safe from the terror it sought to inspire.

All in Leningrad were familiar with the term 'taken'; this was the terse way that news of a friend or relative being arrested by the secret police, brutally interrogated, thereafter consigned to the distant frozen hells of the Gulag labour camps, was communicated among them. Someone who very simply went missing during the night? 'Taken'. Poets arrested not because of their own verse, but because of friendships they had once enjoyed years beforehand with figures now deemed to be dissidents? 'Taken'.

Yet the generations of the city had found ways to accommodate and live with constant insecurity and watchfulness. The young that night were blithe. 'These were White Nights, and we were just sitting on the bench, singing and having fun,' recalled Yevgeniya Aluf, who was a teenager at the time. 'Someone was playing the guitar.'[2] Young Leningrad couples – some of whom had just finished exams at the city's technical schools – were sauntering along the embankments. Many young women were in their finest dresses; many of the young men in suits. The aim was not to suggest any sort of formality, or even grandeur, but rather sophistication. 'There was no more night . . . dusk dragged on, grey, blue, mauve, ashy, pearly, brighter and brighter . . . they met with ghostly smiles.'[3] And this world for them was full of promise.

Natalya Uskova, a teenage student, was contemplating a forthcoming family holiday in Kyiv and daydreaming of its 'fragrant acacia'.[4] Moisei Frid was that night relaxing after having finished his first year at the Leningrad Shipbuilding Institute. This had been the culmination of what he described as a wonderful education – a 'classical education in literature, mathematics and history' in a school on Tchaikovsky Street that occupied 'a former manor house'. Leningrad had a centuries-long naval tradition, founded, along with the rest of the city, by Peter the Great, and in his younger years Frid had been mesmerized by 'maritime affairs and shipbuilding'.[5] That sense of heritage, and of overlapping centuries, was everywhere. The great shipyards lay a little to the south, cranes reaching into the pale sky. But turning back to the islands in the centre, here was a city that pulsed with colour under that undying sun: not just the rich white and turquoise of the vast Winter Palace, or the earthy ochre of the houses and theatres in Mariinsky Square, but also those houses and apartment blocks in the more ordinary streets: the art deco mosaics that pulsed on the exterior of the Nikonov apartment block, the rich grass green of the eighteenth-century Evmentyev House, immediately facing the Fontanka river. This particular building was a lurid source of local stories of the supernatural. At its centre was an unusual rotunda (that is, a circular space bordered with pillars). This rotunda was said to be the secret meeting place for Masons: sometimes even for Satanists. It was also said that there was once a very young man who, in the dead of one night, spent just fifteen minutes alone in that rotunda. When he emerged, he was elderly.

This latter legend, one of a textured seam of uncanny tales of Petersburg, played on the city's own sense of being slightly removed from the normal ebb and flow of time. The grander buildings were not haunted in the traditional sense, but rather had the ability to imaginatively transport Leningraders into earlier eras. 'The different periods of the Empire had thus marked the streets with imposing structures which might make you dream at night of the tombs of the Pharaohs of a Theban dynasty,' wrote Bolshevik novelist and poet Victor Serge.[6] But blended with that sense of displacement was also the hallucinatory perception of a city poised (impossibly) upon water, always on the edge of inundation. 'The lowlands of the city . . . seem to hover between sea and sky, so that one expects to see them fade into the void,' wrote another White Nights observer, the Marquis de Custine, in the summer of 1839. 'Can this be the capital of a vast empire, this scrap of earth that one sees shimmering against the water like froth carried on the flood', the horizon indistinguishable between 'the whiteness of the sky and the whiteness of the river'?[7]

Despite the roil of revolution, and the vast socially engineered changes that had followed, the bones of the old city (built from 1703 by Peter the Great in part upon the buried bones of slave labour – 'He who with a will unbounded/ A city on the marshland founded'[8]) had remained stubbornly immutable. In 1941 the Bronze Horseman – the statue of Tsar Peter – still stood sentinel overlooking the Neva. All Leningraders were familiar with the nineteenth-century Alexander Pushkin poem in which a humble clerk, Yevgenii, driven to madness by the flooding of the city that carried off his love, curses the Horseman – only to see the Tsar's statue come to life, jump down from the pedestal, horse and all, pursuing him through Petersburg streets, hoofs clattering on cobbles, finally killing him through fear. This was how the exercise of modern Stalinist power still felt to many in the city: impulsive, wrathful, verging on the preternatural in terms of the all-seeing surveillance state and its merciless judgements.

Elsewhere, the extraordinary early nineteenth-century edifice of the Kazan Cathedral, with its sweeping colonnades and mighty dome, all intended to mirror the splendour of St Peter's Basilica in Rome, continued to dominate the skyline of Nevsky Prospekt, the city's main boulevard, which itself glittered with the light of modernism. 'Oh, do not trust that Nevsky Prospekt,' wrote nineteenth-century novelist Nikolay Gogol. 'All is deceit, all is a dream . . . the whole city turns into thunder and glitter . . . and the devil himself lights the lamps expressly in order to show everything off in an unreal guise.'[9] The devil had no interest in the most arresting religious construction: just a few hundred metres north on the Griboedov Canal, on one of the city's central islands, loomed the prospect of the extraordinary Church of the Saviour on the Blood, which had been built to commemorate Tsar Alexander II on the spot where his assassination occurred in 1881. Under that green midnight sky, the golden and enamelled shine of its nine onion domes could still be discerned, though the more intense colours that striped around them, the exuberant blues and lemons, were dulled. The church had been barred and bolted since 1932. The old Russian Orthodox faith had not been welcome in this new age of rational socialism. Yet many walkers on that White Night who glanced at it felt a secret, invisible tug of a long-buried impulse.

Elsewhere, there were some insomniacs who found these White Nights unsettling, lying naked and sleepless. Others found there was a kind of emotional dislocation, that 'nocturnal gestures, thoughts, sentiments, objects that are born only in the secrecy of darkness, and that the night jealously guards and protects in its dark bosom, can be seen in full daylight'.[10] Yet this was at heart a deeply sensual city: Leningrad Philharmonic woodwind player Edith Matus recalled cheerfully how the city's orchestra at that time was a seething sexual roundelay.[11] Elsewhere, the stiff grandeur of the Hermitage Museum and the city's other dustier institutions, were remembered by *Lolita* author Vladimir Nabokov – himself a teenager in pre-revolutionary St Petersburg – as being ideal for mid-morning sexual encounters when there were very few people about: 'There we would seek the quiet back-rooms, the stopgap mythologies nobody looked at.' He particularly recommended 'a certain hall on the ground floor, among cabinets with scarabs, behind the sarcophagus of Nana, high priestess of Ptah'.[12]

These midnight Leningrad promenaders on 21 June 1941 were also moving through a modern, knowing city which, even under communism, had never completely thrown off its ingrained habits of commerce. From the great store of Gostiny Dvor – an elegant eighteenth-century construction, marigold-yellow and colonnaded, in which might be found furs and furniture, and which had originally been akin to a Middle Eastern bazaar – to the more demotic stalls and bars of Sennaya Square, the old hay market, at which could be found everything from haberdashery to cuts of meat to the poets' bookshop on the wide, bright Nevsky Prospekt, here was a vision not so much of materialism but rather of culture. Since the revolution, the grander apartments and homes were communal, living spaces sometimes divided between families with arrangements of hanging blankets.

The interiors of these apartment buildings could be surprisingly large, rambling and maze-like: the exterior doors would open on to stairwells that would lead to corridors, and passages that would lead into apartments that would themselves lead into other apartments deeper within the building. In many cases, this had been one of the effects of revolution, the city's grander homes now made available to all sorts of different households, with sometimes squalid results. But this was also a feature of the city that stretched further back into the Tsarist regime of the nineteenth century: dark corridors twisting to reveal obscured rooms, labyrinths leading up and down to further shadowed nooks and apartments, and sometimes gathered around deep courtyards. But many of these households – whether they occupied an entire apartment, or the corner of a formerly grand high-ceilinged drawing room – still had antique samovars, fine china, Persian rugs and solid furniture passed down from grandparents. Life was socialist but the past, in all its aesthetic pleasure, was quietly honoured too. Even the most chaotic of communal apartments had books and maps. Fifteen-year-old Yura Riabinkin lived with his mother and younger sister in a communal apartment close to the centre of the city. There was a large sofa, for reading on. He had received commendations at school for his close studies of nineteenth-century Russian military history, but on Sunday afternoons he could be found reclining and gripped by Alexander Dumas's *The Three Musketeers*. The people of Leningrad were proud to understand themselves through a love of books, and of theatre, as well as the more rarefied opera and ballet. The city's central library, a great repository of not just the finest Russian works, but everything from first editions to the writings of Catherine the Great, was an ever-popular focal point.

Yet here also was a city with two sorts of skyline, indicating the sharp duality in its nature: those walkers strolling across those bridges might have gazed upon the golden spire that punctuated the Peter and Paul fortress, or from the green grass of the Field of Mars to the vast dimensions of the Winter Palace. But moving in other directions, the towers and the chimneys silhouetted on that pale midnight sky belonged to the majestic citadels of industry: the Kirov Plant, the Bolshevik Plant, the Red Banner Factory, the Stalin Works, each daily issuing huge quantities of dense smoke that rose into the air and then, in the autumn and winter, would transform into greasy fog. In 1941, there were still large numbers of labourers, relatively fresh from small villages, who were living in vast dormitories close to these works: part of the city's ongoing housing crisis. And as much as Leningrad revelled in its art, its heart lay in those factories, which were producing tanks and planes and armaments.

There was also an extensive industry of academia: not just all the teachers in the university and the colleges, but also the historians and archivists who studied and cared for the treasures of the Hermitage Museum (oblivious to the Nabokovian sexual thrill-seekers) and the city's rich archives. One such senior archivist, Georgii Knyazev, in his mid-fifties and wheelchair bound, was transported with intellectual excitement on that day of 21 June. Deep in Uzbekistan, a team of Leningrad archaeologists had just opened Gur-i Amir, the tomb of the legendary fourteenth-century conqueror Tamburlaine (or Tamerlane). The aim was to exhume his sarcophagus, and to use modern scientific techniques to reconstruct what his face and his frame would have looked like.

All this would form part of a grand new exhibition amid the splendour of the Hermitage. It was a Leningrad archaeologist called Mikhail Gerasimov who had gazed upon the black sarcophagus in Uzbekistan, levered it open and then held within his hand the skull of the great warrior.

The pleasurable, popular shiver of unease that came with such a venture had echoes of the opening of the ancient Egyptian tombs. It was said that Tamerlane's mausoleum bore written warnings upon its walls. 'When I rise from the dead,' one was said to have proclaimed, 'the world will tremble.' Then there was the rumour of another inscription, which when translated read: 'Whoever disturbs my tomb will unleash an invader more terrible than I.'[13]

It was said that a number of local Uzbeks had enthusiastically amplified the idea of a curse, that Tamerlane would reach through the centuries to wreak vengeance for this desecration. The Leningrad edition of *Pravda* made note of this with a measure of dry amusement. 'Certain superstitious types believe spirits of the dead exercise power beyond the grave,' noted their correspondent. 'They will no doubt make much of this exhumation.'[14]

On the evening of 21 June 1941, Leningrad had been alive with the flower of German music. At the Kirov Theatre, there had been a performance of Wagner's opera *Lohengrin*. On this, the day before the Molotov–Ribbentrop Pact was terminated, such a towering emblem of German culture was still relished. Even as it was performed, Luftwaffe bombers, just a few hundred miles to the west, were preparing to bring shock and death.

But perhaps the seeds of the tragedy to come for Leningrad had in part been sown by Stalin in the years before. That unending midsummer night in 1941 had been an unusual moment of ease in the city; those huge numbers of young people promenading had not seen what their parents had seen. They had not experienced the same hunger, nor tasted the same sleepless dread. The city's older residents understood horribly well the brittleness of existence. During the previous decade, thousands upon thousands of them had been targeted by their own rulers: purges that would extinguish not only life, but also experience, knowledge and wisdom. In Petersburg tradition, hell was sometimes depicted as being composed not of fire but of the deepest, blackest ice. It was this to which the people of Leningrad were soon to be condemned. On that warm night on the edge of an unfathomable ordeal, those young promenaders had no sense of just how acutely vulnerable they were; yet at the same time many Leningraders had already had a foretaste of the hell to come. They understood very well about fear.

2. Time and the Bolsheviks

In July 1918, just months after the Bolshevik revolution, the city's old nobility – Tsar Nicholas II, his wife and their children – had been slaughtered in a frenzy of bayonet and bullet in a floridly wallpapered basement in Yekaterinburg. Back in St Petersburg, now called Petrograd, their exquisite palaces in and around the city were being repurposed by the revolutionaries: the Alexander Palace at Tsarskoe Selo, some thirty miles south of Leningrad, had been turned into a museum – time held in suspension – so that the ordinary people could gaze upon the obscene wealth and luxury that their oppressors had enjoyed. By the 1930s, this museum had been quietly closed; it appeared that it had been creating rather too much sympathy for the young Romanov family and their violent fate.

That political violence had been pulsing outwards to the wider population in the intervening years, darkening the lives of countless citizens. Closely following the revolution and Lenin's negotiated armistice in the Great War, shattering the Tsarist empire, came savage civil conflict: Bolsheviks and so-called 'White Russian' counter-revolutionaries inflicting medieval barbarities upon each other, and upon ordinary people, who were also targeted in Bolshevik-sponsored secret police terror. In Petrograd one correspondent from *The Times* described in 1921 the city's 'privation, gloom and despair', of how its people resembled 'gaunt skeletons'.[1] Food was so scarce as a result of conflict that 'starving dogs' were 'leaping at pedestrians'. 'Even the women of pleasure, who crowded the gaily lit streets before the revolution' had 'vanished'.[2]

With Bolshevik rule finally consolidated, the city's restoration to peace was not wholly trusted: in the early 1920s, art historian Nikolay Punin confessed to his diary: 'One quality of revolution – life gets to be a risk.'[3] In every apartment block, on every factory floor, there were Party officials, watchful and hostile, alert to any potential expression of counter-revolutionary dissidence. It was not uncommon for ordinary people to be arrested seemingly out of nowhere, even to be imprisoned, all upon the testimony of a single official. The sense of 'life becoming a risk' had to be internalized by all. Fear was part of the texture of the city. Yet it had been so since the time of the Tsars, and their own cohorts of secret police. 'Thus from the Finnish marshes the city will show you the site of its mad way of life as a red, red stain,' wrote Petersburg novelist Andrei Bely poetically at the turn of the century. 'As you journey through our immense Mother-land, from the distance you will see a stain of red blood rising into the dark-coloured night.'[4] He referred to Petersburg as 'Gehenna' – the realm of damned souls. Elsewhere, the city's great nineteenth-century chronicler Fyodor Dostoevsky wrote, in his novel *Demons*: 'Life is pain, life is fear, and man is unhappy. Now all is pain and fear. Now man loves life because he loves pain and fear.'[5]

And by the 1930s, the people of Leningrad were being taught anew that even in a modern world, ordinary individual lives could be ended upon a whim, without warning or reason, by the authorities. There was a pitch-dark joke circulating throughout the city in the middle of that decade. It was inspired by the extraordinary and frightening spectacle of faithful Communist Party members being hauled out of their beds in the darkness of the early hours, dragged to a freshly built detention centre close to the banks of the Neva and then frequently never being seen or heard of again. They had been 'purged'. The joke went like this: the secret police – the NKVD – are knocking hard on an apartment door. There is a quavering voice from within: 'Who's there?' 'It's the NKVD,' bark the arresting officers. 'No, no, you've got the wrong apartment,' cries the voice. 'The Communists live upstairs!'[6]

That former detention centre still stands today, on the busy and upmarket Liteyny Prospekt (Putin himself operated from there in the 1970s), and is still used for intelligence purposes. The building – a rectilinear eight-storey proposition of beige and darker granite – is popularly known as 'Bolshoy Dom' (or 'Big House'), and in the 1930s it was the modernist headquarters of the NKVD. All cities have an element of sharp duality: apparently well-to-do elegant streets and

the unseen darkness behind their facades. In the 1930s, Petersburg/
Leningrad elevated this duality to a form of urban philosophy: seeing
and yet not seeing. Thus it was that 'Bolshoy Dom' was understood –
in its constructivist sophistication, contrasting with the ornate,
proud Moorish-influenced nineteenth-century apartment blocks
that neighboured it – to be a place of fear. But the eyes of the citizens became trained to flicker away from it, as though it was not
there. And when they could not do so, the building became the subject of another dark urban quip, referred to as 'the tallest building in
Petersburg', the joke being that most of its 'height' was buried deep
underground in the form of many rumoured subterranean levels of
interrogation chambers and cells.

The Stalinist Great Terror of the 1930s, which would sweep across
the vastness of the Soviet Union like a firestorm, is still the subject
of layered debate, focusing on cities like Leningrad. As we shall see
presently, the frenzy actually began there in the winter of 1934: triggered by a political assassination that sparked a nationwide spasm of
paranoiac accusations and counter-accusations followed by a programme of mass murder. It would also create consequences in the
years ahead that would sharpen the horror of the city-wide ordeal
to come at the hands of the Nazis. Yet here is the psychological con-
undrum: for all the many thousands of Leningraders who would be
imprisoned, sentenced to slave labour, tortured and executed, did
these purges create a wider sense of dread in each and every one of
their fellow citizens? In other words, how was it possible – in the
wake of bosses, of colleagues, of friends, of neighbours, of families
being removed and disappearing – for any semblance of normal life
for *any* citizen to continue? How could the people of Leningrad find
any kind of accommodation with the constant prospect of sudden
random assault and death? Yet, on the face of it, they did.

The routines and rhythms of life had an outward appearance of
stability. Neighbours, colleagues and their children rose each morning and made ready for the day's tasks. Their samovars – ornate
copper or brass containers, frequently ornamented with intricate
engravings, used for boiling water for strong tea – were fired up
with charcoal. They caught noisy, busy trams from long streets of

six- and seven-storey apartment blocks, across the city's bridges to the islands that lay in the historic centre. The traffic was directed by men and women in stark white uniform. The office workers – men in shirts and ties, women in dresses – milled along wide pavements, in the streets around the unusually pretty nineteenth-century stock exchange (white and grey and grandly pillared, in the Greek revival style, on the very edge of Vasilyevsky Island). The industrial workers further to the south marched through the gates of vast factory complexes – assembly halls on the scale of medieval cathedrals, mazes of pipes like long metal viscera. And to feed these workers, the city's industrialized bakeries, staffed by women in headscarves and dungarees, daily processed tons of flour and dough in swirling masses, great gulping machines producing neat loaves and bread sticks.

Elsewhere, the city was being advertised to progressive tourists in western Europe. It was a beacon of socialism (the modernist poster for the 1934 'Leningrad Festival of Music' was dominated by a jazzy-looking double bass).[7] Visitors were drawn by attractions such as the Mariinsky Ballet (later to be the Kirov Ballet), which, under Agrippina Vaganova, was staging innovative work such as *The Red Poppy* (the scenario involving Soviet sailors arriving at a Chinese port run by 'British capitalists') and *The Flames of Paris*, a production set around the French Revolution. '[It] reflects the spirit of our times,' said Vaganova. 'The liberation of the oppressed – that is, class warfare – carried out by the French people . . . awakens the revolutionary fervour of the audience.'[8] Under Vaganova, new, brilliant ballerinas such as Natalya Dudinskaya were learning their art: the ferocious traditional discipline layered with new demands that dance should exalt 'socialist realism'. Yet the beauty and the romance abided. These dancers still celebrated first nights at the Astoria Hotel on St Isaac's Square – an elegant establishment that had briefly been a 'hostel' for the Petrograd Soviet of Workers' and Soldiers' Deputies, but had reverted (partly for the sake of foreign visitors) to its former hospitable spirit. For Leningrad's domestic ballet audiences – the authorities had sought to widen the appeal of this theatrical art – these were nights in the rich dark of auditoriums when the underlying fear might be forgotten.

One curious point about that fear: Leningrad was, by the 1930s, a city with a notably young population; almost a third of the citizens were under the age of twenty. And, conversely, a striking proportion of those who were taken through the night were almost always older than forty. In this sense, it is possible that fear was rationalized with the natural optimism of the young: an assumption that the system wanted the best for all. Writer Joseph Berger observed that those who had been arrested were thought of as 'victims of a misunderstanding which sooner or later would be cleared up'.[9] Elsewhere, in overheard conversations, Leningraders were reported to have said of the round-ups that 'when wood is cut, splinters fly',[10] meaning that the consolidation of revolution and socialist life was a struggle that would produce inevitable victims. Other overheard sentiments included 'the state has a right to defend itself' and also that 'errors were possible',[11] but that these could never be blamed upon Stalin himself. Perhaps in this way the broader population of Leningrad – with their routines of work, of trips to the cinema and the theatre, of walks in parks filled with statues – rationalized what would otherwise seem to have been the ultimate expression of irrationality.

Not all the victims were Communist Party members. For instance, Veronika Viktorova worked at a port a little way outside the city. The NKVD men came for her at night, accusing her of espionage. It's possible that her real crime was being Polish, rather than native-born Russian. The sentence: death by firing squad. Elsewhere in the city, an experienced boilermaker called Georgii Sorokin, who worked at the Kronstadt Marine Plant, found himself accused of sabotage. It is possible that the factory's productivity levels had fallen. For this alleged transgression, the sentence was also death by firing squad. A saturnine and thoughtful-looking accountant called Kanon Krasovsky heard the midnight hammering on his door: his apparent crime was also one of espionage and he too was to face the bullet.[12] These were among many thousands of Leningraders who throughout the mid to late 1930s were to find the state that they served turning upon them with savagery. Their neighbours would have heard their arrests, and subsequently noted their echoing, silent absence.

Yet, once noted, those neighbours tried to live their own lives normally. The city was certainly still filled with innocent pleasures. Although the grander restaurants like Palkin, close to the Anichkov Bridge, had closed down (its once-renowned cabarets, dances and concerts replaced with a vast cinema called Titan), the streets of Leningrad were now dotted with *stolovaya* – unfancy but nourishing cafes and canteens that served the fundamentals of beetroot soup, buckwheat and 'herring under a fur coat'. (Depending on taste, this still-popular dish can be, for some, a culinary trial – the herring concealed beneath layers of carrots, beetroot and egg with a texture unnervingly close to trifle). There were still family outings. Across the wide Neva from the Winter Palace, and located in a park behind the Peter and Paul fortress in the Petrogradsky district was (and still is) Leningrad Zoo, which throughout the 1930s was building a reputation not merely as a repository of captured wildlife but also as a semi-scientific concern where species were bred. The zoologists in those years had had particular success with their captive polar bears, welcoming some forty cubs into the world. Parents and grandparents took their children to the zoo almost religiously. There was a stall selling syrupy drinks in flavours ranging from cranberry and cherry to jokey zoo-themed 'fresh hay'. The poet Olga Berggolts, or Bergholz – a well-known Leningrad figure, with bobbed blonde hair, a steel-trap gaze and an enigmatic smile – recalled a moment in the 1930s when her father, a military doctor, insisted upon taking her there once more – even though she was in her twenties, and a busy Party functionary. He had wanted to remember the innocence of their original visits years earlier. Berggolts was initially reluctant – she noted the melancholy autumn morning that 'smelled not like the city but of cool fall earth' – but to cheer her father up, entered into the spirit, affecting wonder at the hyenas, the tigers and the venerable elephant whose name was Betty.[13] Betty had an impressive trick: if a coin was thrown into her enclosure, she could locate it with her trunk, pass it to a keeper and 'buy' a carrot as a reward.

In the years to come, Berggolts and her father would suffer terribly, both at the hands of the authorities and throughout the ordeal of the siege. And that zoo would – in the days of siege – fill some Leningraders with an intense anguish for the suffering animals that they barely felt for their neighbours. The innocence of the animals, and the unchanging nature of the institution, had made it something of an unconscious psychological haven. The zoo was an Edenic sanctuary.

There was also some curious solace to be derived from the city's historic architecture – monuments to continuity in a world where nothing else seemed stable. Though the contextual meaning of the more emblematic sites – the expanse of Palace Square with its red granite Alexander Column, framed to the north by the famous and ornamented turquoise splendour of the Winter Palace and to the south by the butter-yellow facaded General Staff Building, with its vast crescent sweep and spectacular arch – had changed through the years.

Before the 1917 revolution, Palace Square stood at the centre of a capital, and at the heart of an empire. By the 1930s, Leningrad was no longer the capital (Lenin had moved it to Moscow immediately after the uprising) and the reality of Soviet empire-building was not admitted or acknowledged. But the rich architectural beauty remained seductive, and it was cared for. The art historian Nikolay Punin had been interested in the repainting of many of those grand facades, which glowed in a range of colours from candy pink to pale tangerine. But by the 1930s, Leningrad was also fast embracing the new aesthetics of the twentieth century. To the south of the city, near the docks, lay the Putilov Works, a mighty factory complex – and close to that lay the Gigant bathhouse, a multi-storeyed concrete sauna and bathing centre, used by many thousands of workers a day.

If the wet cold cells of the secret police in the 'Bolshoy Dom' were harbingers of pain and death, the hot moisture of the modernist Gigant *banya* was intended as the reverse: a determined Bolshevik effort at physical regeneration, and at creating the socialist ideal of the New Man, enjoyed not just by a privileged few in the icy countryside, but by the urban masses.[14] Here, in Gigant, the workers, segregated by sex and mingling in unselfconscious nakedness in steam-filled rooms, and in pools with fountain jets, were made clean and renewed: as they bathed, the intention was that their deposited undergarments would be taken away and laundered. The undergarments they received back at the end of the process were very often not their own. The system was something of a lottery. This was of no matter: just as the communal apartments broke down old ideas of family privacy, so the *banya* dissolved personal physical boundaries, with shyness regarded as a form of exceptionalism, and individual bodies joining the undifferentiated mass.

The Leningrad Bolsheviks were also keen that minds should continue to be nourished. Closer to the centre, near the Narva Triumphal Arch (a sea-green edifice of copper and stone topped with statues of rearing horses, built in 1814 to commemorate Russia's triumph over Napoleon), 1930s Soviet constructivist architects created the Gorky House of Culture. Behind its stark, severe exterior lay a cinema, a theatre, a library and a concert hall, designed and built with trade union money, aimed at uplifting the lives of the workers. (In the darker years to come, with the city held in the death-grip of siege, the Gorky House of Culture would remarkably never close its doors; the structure remains today.)

There were cafes and 'Houses of Technical Studies': severely rectilinear apartment blocks with shared kitchens and living areas, promoting the virtues of communal existence. Yet for Leningraders walking through the city – the winding canalside paths bordered with ornamented terraces and spanned with delicate pedestrian bridges (among them the Bank Bridge, with its nineteenth-century winged lions on the abutments, their paws rubbed smooth in the superstitious belief that to do this would bring wealth), the glow of the golden dome of St Isaac's Cathedral, the earthier streets of the newly built Serafimov housing estate, in the south-west of the city, with low-rise white-exterior apartment blocks – these prospects, in the early wet autumns and stygian foggy winters, still echoed other times. Helplessly drunken men would still fall insensible in the middle of the road in front of cabs and then pick themselves up, insisting tearfully that nothing had happened, as they had done in the nineteenth century. There were still barges on the canals, and these still froze solid come hard, dark December.

★

Even though the Russian monarchy had been extinguished, post-revolutionary Leningrad was still striated with stubborn class distinctions that were less to do with material wealth and more with sensibility: the distinctions between, for instance, highly educated electrical technicians and displaced agricultural workers newly arrived at factories. And there were other, newer, nobles in the city; they did not have titles or inherited wealth but they had privileges all of their own. The revolution had started a new cycle of time, the Soviets impatient to remould human nature so that it – and future events – could soon be shaped with scientific precision. But old patterns and archetypes, and even forbidden dynastic impulses, recurred. In the eyes of many workers (as anonymous letters of complaint from factories showed), Leningrad's pure socialist society had simply produced a new generation of nobility with Tsarist power: the Party leaders of the city, many of whom had smart new multi-bedroomed apartments with oak staircases in a modernist block (elevated on pillars in case of flood) called Leningrad City Council First Residential House, facing the Karpovka river.

Chief among the new nobles was a lynx-eyed man, portly, with a taste for luxury. His name was Andrei Zhdanov. In years to come, he would be most associated with a 'doctrine' that forced all the artists of the Soviet Union – from its greatest musicians to its lightest science-fiction adventure story writers – to follow his strictures on what they might and might not dare to create or imagine in this Soviet world. Under his eye, absurdities such as classical composer Sergei Prokofiev reworking a ballet based upon Shakespeare's *Romeo and Juliet* to give it a happy ending, on the grounds that the couple were 'young, strong, progressive people' working against an oppressive bourgeois generation, became possible.[15] Even the senior Kremlin commissars found this risible: tragedy was restored.

But Zhdanov would also be the emblematic leader of Leningrad as the horror of the blockade began in 1941; and as hundreds and thousands of his fellow citizens starved, his own undiminished ruddy plumpness would be a constant source of dissident gossip.

Zhdanov, born in Mariupol, Ukraine, in 1896, was an art lover, a pianist, a literary critic and an alcoholic. Even Stalin, himself deeply partial to overpoweringly strong liquor, had advised him in vain to stick to fruit juices. Zhdanov's political ascendancy had been shrouded in one mystery: how a man with no conspicuous talent for administration could have thrived. Yet he possessed the great strength of lacking qualms: he would be personally responsible for staggeringly long lists of Leningrad death orders. And in an era of grimly unsmiling Bolsheviks, Zhdanov's manner was comparatively urbane. (He was given to bouts of wheezy laughter, for example.) Next to the overwhelming darkness of figures such as secret police chief and serial rapist Lavrentii Beria, Zhdanov appeared to be a moderate. He combined iron ideological correctness with an intermittent warmth that made him seem recognizably human. It had helped Zhdanov immeasurably that he had been an early unquestioning adherent to the authority of Stalin in the 1920s when other rivals had clamoured for power. But there was more than this: the two men were, in a sense – as far as anyone could be in that Bolshevik arena – friends. Stalin regarded him as a fellow book lover, an intellectual. By the 1930s, he and Stalin were close enough to holiday together. In time, Zhdanov's son Yuri would be married to Stalin's daughter Svetlana. In this sense, Zhdanov was little different from a medieval baron arranging a marriage between his offspring and the king's. And had time woven its tapestry a different way, Zhdanov would have been Stalin's eventual successor in the 1950s. His name would have been known across the world. But as it was, his rule over Leningrad – a city shadowed by faded grandeur and artistic pride – reflected his personality best.

Zhdanov was a man of profoundly bourgeois education and background (one of the very few such permitted in Stalin's circle); his father had been a school inspector. When Zhdanov had been pulled into the First World War in 1914, it seemed to radicalize him; by 1915, he had joined the Bolsheviks. By 1917, the year of revolution, he was chairman of the Bolshevik Committee in the town of Shadrinsk, in the shadow of the Urals. As attempted counter-revolution and vicious civil war broke out, he was swift to join the fight as a political commissar in the Red Army.

By the mid-1920s, he was Party secretary in the ornate, richly coloured city of Nizhny Novgorod, on the banks of the vast Volga. Sitting in the centre of European Russia, and on the confluence of the Volga and the Oka rivers, the city had long been a pulsating trading centre. In the days of Lenin's New Economic Policy, which sought to bring some stability after a war of barbarity and frequent outbreaks of intense sadism, cities such as Nizhny Novgorod began to find a new kind of life. Yet that life was still founded upon the absolute power of the Party; and the efforts to cement socialist philosophy were unyielding.

The collectivization of agriculture – the seizing of farms from 'kulaks' and transforming of the land into a series of vast communes which began in the late 1920s – was one of the revolutionary policies that Zhdanov had a zeal for. The result, in his own homeland of Ukraine, was mass death on an almost unimaginable scale – the Holodomor: a famine entirely man-made, and which left starving families scrabbling desperately in the soil for scraps of roots to eat.

Like Stalin, Zhdanov was wholly unmoved by the catastrophe that unfolded across that shadowed country: the commissars moving in to execute 'kulaks' and others suspected of hiding grain; the villages filled with men, women and children, bellies distended, unable to stand. Also wholly disregarded were the stories of cannibalism; the children who looked upon the bodies of their dead parents as meat; the parents who looked upon their babies in the same way.

By 1934, at the 17th Congress of the Communist Party, plump Zhdanov was ushered on to a wider, more brightly lit stage when he was relocated to Moscow to serve as Secretary of the Central Committee. Stalin was watching him closely; Zhdanov's moment for a greater responsibility lay close. It would be the result of violent death.

Throughout the late 1920s and early 1930s, the city of Leningrad had been under the administration of Sergei Kirov. Kirov was a friend of Stalin's who had taken part in the abortive 1905 revolution, who had spent the last years of the Tsarist regime in and out of prison as an open Bolshevik, and who had fought hard in the ensuing blood-soaked civil war. In time Kirov was appointed First Secretary of Leningrad, based in an elegant suite of panelled offices in the eighteenth-century Smolny Institute (another building with a butter-yellow facade, this one originally intended for the education of aristocratic young ladies and commandeered by Lenin in 1917). The nightmarish results of collectivization – the famine and the food shortages – had hit Leningrad and other cities hard. There was severe rationing and malnutrition.

It was in the frozen darkness of 1 December 1934 that the assassin came. Kirov's offices were on the third floor. Leonid Nikolaev, a Party member, had somehow gained entry to the heavily guarded institute.[16] (In the mirror maze of Stalinist history, in which lurid conspiracy theories compete with equally lurid reality, some accounts have it that this was possible because the Kremlin had directed that security around the Smolny be relaxed.) In his bag Nikolaev carried a revolver. Kirov had a bodyguard; but that bodyguard was some distance away when Nikolaev materialized on the third floor. Kirov was shot in the head at point-blank range and died immediately. His assassin then attempted to take his own life: pointing the revolver at his own temple. Yet somehow he missed, or slipped, or faltered. At this point, he lost consciousness; when he revived several hours later, he was in custody.

This murder had lit the most terrible fuse. First, the authorities ensured that public mourning for Kirov attained a form of Orthodox intensity. He was 'the truest son and outstanding leader' of the city. 'Kirov can never be torn from our hearts,' proclaimed one city newspaper. 'Until the end of our days we will remember your life and struggle, Comrade Kirov!'[17] The accounts of Sergei Kirov's final hours were to attain a form of bathos that – according to historian Matt Lenoe – found an answering echo of morbid laughter in a great many Leningraders, who had grown immune to the hysteria of propaganda.[18] According to Kirov's biographer, his final day on earth was instead supposed to be one of celebration. He asked his wife Mary when he had last enjoyed a birthday. She had replied: 'All right – you shall have cabbage dumplings tonight and some specially strong tea. I'll brew it myself.' Kirov then moved in to kiss her. And he said: 'You know, my dear, great things are afoot. Bread rationing is coming to an end and we can have a "birthday" every day.'[19]

Some more cynical Leningraders, hardened by years of hunger and repression, were openly wondering if the assassin himself had been prompted to act out of malnourished despair. This was a sentiment that found no place anywhere either in official coverage or in the speedy and bloody quasi-trials of not only the assassin himself but also an array of 'political opponents' who were deemed either to have inspired or aided him, or who themselves simply wanted to see Sergei Kirov dead.

This, then, was the start of the great purges – Stalin's Terror, a tide of interrogations, torture, slave labour and executions that would come to engulf the lives of many, many thousands across Russia. And it began in Leningrad.

Hundreds of prisoners already in the city's jails – many of them political – had apparently been 'named' by the assassin; within days, they had been shot in the back of their heads. Politicians deemed not wholly favourable to the regime were either murdered or sentenced to many years within the Gulag system – there was a prison colony a few hundred miles to the north of Leningrad where the labour was lethally intensive (everything from sub-zero-degree railway construction to logging, on starvation rations of buckwheat and potatoes) and the frozen climate often deadly.

And as the denunciations began spreading like some nightmarish forest fire, implicating ever wider circles of Leningrad society within the plot to kill Kirov, the man selected as his replacement stepped forth. Andrei Zhdanov was poised to take control, from within that suite of offices in the Smolny Institute.

Was Kirov murdered on the secret orders of Stalin? Was there – as alleged by later Soviet leader Nikita Khrushchev in 1956 – a shadowy plot involving NKVD agents?[20] Was it possible, as suggested elsewhere, that Stalin had been pricked to paranoia by Kirov's apparent popularity with the people, scenting in this a possible future threat to his own rule? The argument rages because, as has been noted, Kirov's assassination was in many ways a key historical moment comparable to the Reichstag fire of February 1933. On the back of Kirov's death, many thousands more were doomed to die over the coming five years, among them the country's most experienced military commanders and officers, who might have brought their expertise to bear against the growing threat from Germany.

And presiding over this was a man who – ironically – sought to impress himself upon Leningraders above all as a cultural visionary. In 1934, Andrei Zhdanov had been addressing the question of how all artists should strive to follow the precepts of 'socialist realism'. Their aim, he declared, should be to 'depict reality in its revolutionary development'. This aim was to be 'combined with the ideological remoulding and education of the toiling people in the spirit of socialism'. Their visions had to be made to cleave close to that of 'the toiling people' and to Stalin himself. 'Comrade Stalin has called our writers "engineers of the human soul",' he told the first All-Union Congress of Soviet Writers a little before he rose to power in 1934.[21]

But now began the engineering of truth and mortality. Among Zhdanov's first victims were a class known by some as 'Leningrad aristocrats'. These were people whose chief crime was to have been descended from some of the grander St Petersburg families: from nobility to rich merchants. If, for instance, Vladimir Nabokov, the son of a wealthy St Petersburg official, had chosen to stay on within the city after the revolution, he would have been among those picked out as being as treacherous as Kirov's assassin. Among these 'aristocrats', some 11,000 people were placed upon a list by Zhdanov and the city's NKVD officials by the beginning of 1935.

The 'aristocrats' were perhaps fortunate; they were to be banished to the raw wilderness, as opposed to simply being shot. As old a tradition in that city as any other, banishment would none the less for some be a death sentence. To survive being sent out to the Gulag, to forced labour colonies in the east or in the Arctic north, required great powers of physical endurance. The work undertaken in such conditions, from mining to logging to digging canals, frequently proved fatal.

Also immediately targeted were associates of veteran Bolshevik (and former Leningrad overseer) Grigorii Zinoviev. In the tangled, tortuous days around the final illness of Lenin in 1924, Zinoviev had sided against Stalin. Upon the dictator's triumphant ascendancy, he had been suspended from the Party. Zinoviev went in desperate supplication to Stalin and was allowed back in, but since the late 1920s he had been a permanent focus of suspicion. The murder of Sergei Kirov was the trigger for a long-awaited revenge: Zinoviev was decreed to have been complicit in Kirov's killing and sentenced to ten years in prison. Moreover, anyone who had been friends with Zinoviev, or had simply had a casual association, also suddenly found themselves on Zhdanov's list.

Such a fire, once started, was not easily extinguished. Those lists of the damned grew in length. Along with the shop managers, customs controllers, farmers and construction managers there was even a urologist. The charges were usually 'sabotage' and sometimes 'espionage'. There was a chain reaction of other 'unveilings': more plots, more traitors, plots within plots, plotters reaching out to one another. Was there anyone at all who could be trusted?

Zhdanov was not apparently inflamed with rage or malice; he was simply looking at names on long lists and signing them off, signalling his approval for those on it to receive bullets in their hearts or heads. This, perhaps, was the late recoil of revolution and civil war; a society that had been founded on so much bloodshed needed yet more blood sacrifices to keep it pure. (There was also an element of ethno-nationalism – Poles and Lithuanians who had settled in Leningrad were dragged, bewildered and terrified, from their homes at midnight, to face death for no reason that they could discern.) In this sense, too, Zhdanov's alcoholism may have been a factor, blunting the natural nausea that a clearer-headed official might have felt.

He was also adept in finding a range of secret enemies close to home. In 1936, he turned his gaze on to Leningrad's own secret police, the city's NKVD, and on to the man who himself had overseen the execution of Zinoviev, as well as the deaths of some 12,000 political prisoners who had been sentenced to the Gulag slave labour squads constructing the White Sea Canal. That man was Genrikh Yagoda, a hatchet-faced director of the NKVD. Until the end, Yagoda imagined that Stalin would show clemency. At his show trial he made an emotional appeal, invoking Stalin's name and crying out: 'I appeal to you! For you I built two great canals!'[22] His echoing voice found no answer; he was taken out and executed immediately.

Throughout the horror, Zhdanov had contrived to remain impassive even as the officials closest to him were picked off. In 1937 they came for Ivan Kodatsky, a former Leningrad shipyard worker who, in the wake of the revolution, had risen through the Party, eventually becoming chairman of Leningrad City Council in 1931. What possible charges could have been laid against such a figure? He was accused of 'participation in a counter-revolutionary terrorist organization'. The trial, such as it was, found him guilty: the executioner's bullet found its target weeks later. Even some older revolutionaries who had dedicated their lives in St Petersburg/Leningrad to the Bolshevik ascendancy were vulnerable. One such was Dora Lazurkina, born in 1884. In pre-revolutionary days, she had worked in a match factory, and had then become a teacher. By the turn of the century, she had absorbed Marx and was a keen follower of Lenin, whom she met, and she took the word into workers' educational circles in St Petersburg, from the Baltic shipyard to the Putilov factory. Through the 1920s and 1930s she had risen in Party prominence in appreciation of her fine faithful work.

Zhdanov abruptly consigned her to hell. Her crime: she had spoken up in defence of Ivan Kodatsky. Zhdanov was icily honest with her: 'This will not end well for you,' he told her.[23] First, her husband was arrested and subjected to interrogation so brutal that he died. The security services insisted that it was suicide. Then she was tried and sentenced − aged fifty-three − to five years of 'exile' (another term for banishment to a penal slave colony). This was for 'participation in a counter-revolutionary organization'. Two years later, as she struggled with life in a barracks set in a wilderness, the sentence was arbitrarily increased: a further eight years in the labour camps. Zhdanov's dire prediction, however, was ultimately confounded. Following the death of Stalin, she was released in 1955 and then − in that mirrored world of continual disorientation − she was wholly exonerated and rehabilitated. She was awarded the Order of Lenin in 1956. She died in 1974 aged eighty-nine, her remaining years shadowed with night-time horrors: her sleep filled with recurring nightmares of torture.

As the Terror reached its zenith, some 19,000 Leningraders had been sent to their deaths: random, homicidal twitches. At no point did Zhdanov appear to fear for himself, or his wife Zinaida or his son Yuri (at that point a teenager). By March 1939 he was a full member of the Politburo (and attracting the hostile attention of rivals such as Georgii Malenkov). Zhdanov was not alone in his devotion to the purge; his deputy, too, was ruthless in preparing those lists of names, and of assembling the charges of sabotage and treachery.

And this deputy, like Zhdanov, would find his own name enhanced for a time when faced with the nightmare of the siege.

Aleksei Kuznetsov was a handsome, open-faced man with a young wife and two children (a daughter and a son). His own rise within the Stalinist regime had been in some ways admirable: born some 200 miles south of St Petersburg in 1905, and leaving school to start working in a sawmill in the small market town of Borochi just after the revolution, Kuznetsov had been swift to join the All-Union Leninist Young Communist League, or Komsomol.

His intelligence, combined with his complete loyalty to the cause of Stalin, ensured his rise within the Party, and in time he became a protégé of Zhdanov. This youthful figure had quickly found a place by the early 1930s serving on various Party committees across the city of Leningrad – building a knowledge of its industry and its workers, of their lives and of their political views. According to historian Richard Bidlack he was, in this sense, more attuned to the city and its people than was Zhdanov.[24] What seems most striking now is the distance between the family man photographed holding his children close and the icy bureaucrat who without qualm sent so many to a violent death. Kuznetsov was a sane man; how did he rationalize mass murder? 'No matter how bizarre or disgusting,' wrote historian Stephen Kotkin in an examination of the Terror, 'at some level it "made sense" . . . [which is] why so many people could and did participate in a process that often led to their own undoing.'[25]

Paranoia and survivalism were built into the system. The world that Kuznetsov understood was that of industry – from heavy machinery to timber mills – and economic targets. If these targets were not being met, how to explain the failure? There were certainly outbreaks of corruption, of illegal strikes, of embezzlement carried out by management, of workers absenting themselves from the production line. Yet there was also duplicity on a higher level: output figures and financial spreadsheets being falsified, conspiracies between factory management and local Party officials, so that in reporting their results back, both would escape the cold scrutiny of Moscow and the NKVD.

But many of the targets set were impractical; some impossible. Sometimes local officials and factory workers would help one another to try to present themselves as perfectly efficient; but equally, in this tense and nervy atmosphere, there were desperate outbreaks of accusation and counter-accusation, as individuals sought to save themselves from NKVD torture, and from death or exile. Thus factory managers were no longer merely on the fiddle: they were 'terrorists'. Workers slinking off to warm themselves by canteen stoves were no longer shirkers: they were instead 'wreckers'. Output that failed to match targets could be pinned on 'wreckers', who were now actively seeking to undermine the revolution.[26]

The accusations inflated: even Leningrad economists could now be labelled 'terrorist Trotskyite-Zinovievite counter-revolutionaries' if their published academic papers failed to agree completely with the theories approved by Zhdanov and Kuznetsov.[27] At the height of the Terror in the mid to late 1930s, thousands of Leningraders – guilty perhaps of little more than a perceived torpor – had been labelled in this way. What made it possible for the eminently sane Kuznetsov to believe all this? Perhaps it was simply that this was the world he had grown up in. Young people like himself joining the workforce for the first time were not merely apprentices but passionate cadre comrades. Revolution was a flame that had to be kept burning, and the wider world was filled with saboteurs who sought with all their power to extinguish it.

Naturally, this philosophical framework was able to accommodate the most startling contradictions. Towards the end of the great purges, with many thousands of people either in their graves, or close to them in the icy wastes of the slave colonies, it became apparent that the Terror itself was imperilling the revolution: in industry, in the military, so much experience and expertise had simply been exterminated.

Thus it was in 1938 that Kuznetsov was able to write, with no apparent dark irony, to a freshly appointed local NKVD chief a memo stating that the security services had simply been too zealous, and that this now had to be rectified. 'The NKVD in the republic [of Karelia] has slaughtered all of our cadres,' he wrote, as though this was somehow inexplicable. 'And you need to introduce some order.'[28]

As the violence of the Terror spread through the city – the NKVD agents muscling their way into apartments, finding their intended victims dry-mouthed with fear – Kuznetsov was the man deputed to maintain a correspondence with the frightening figure of Lavrentii Beria, long a rival of Zhdanov. It was deemed better that any communication between them be indirect: Beria was burningly envious of Zhdanov's ease with Stalin. This was not merely a question of Beria's own ultimate ambitions; it was also the sense that the man who finally ascended to the summit would lose no time in having his rivals dispensed with. Even before the war, those internecine tensions were rising.

Zhdanov spoke often of eliminating capitalism; but just how true was his own dedication to a Soviet life? It was said of him and his wife that their Leningrad apartment was filled with fancy and luxurious material possessions. Yet that was not completely unusual: those grand old apartments, even if divided into communal living spaces, remained filled with beautifully made nineteenth-century furniture, the walls hung with tasteful watercolours and oil paintings. Many women retained the rich furs that had been passed down through generations. And there was still some distance between these high-ceilinged apartments looking out over pleasing prospects of canals and squares, and those more roughshod tenements outside the centre of the city, close to the mighty industrial works that dominated the southern skylines.

The gentleman Bolshevik Andrei Zhdanov was, by 1939, a full member of Stalin's Politburo. As Europe was fast sliding into the chasm of war, and Stalin was secretly plotting a shock alliance, Zhdanov would be at the centre of ruthless military efforts to ensure Russia's security, part of which would involve bloody conflict with the nation on Leningrad's borders.

But the purges of the 1930s – which Zhdanov by 1939 declared should be 'abolished' because the aim to 'eliminate capitalist elements' had been achieved and also because the process had been 'co-opted' by 'hostile actors' to persecute the innocent – had had a corrosive effect that neither Zhdanov nor Stalin nor anyone else in the surviving Soviet hierarchy had anticipated.

From among the vast ranks of the Red Army, three of its five most senior marshals along with 220 of its highest-ranking officers had been executed. Altogether, 36,761 officers were murdered. These had been men of experience and expertise who had both knowledge and skill, their talent thoughtlessly erased. As the winter of 1939 approached, that particular branch of the purge would come to have the most terrible and humiliating consequences out on battlefields of northern snow: a conflict that would have the further effect of turning a once-neutral neighbouring state into a confirmed enemy, one that was at first implacable and then, by the time of the horror of the siege, lethal.

3. The Haunted Forests

Comrade Stalin had been impatient for a war with his neighbour, Finland: he had to dominate that nation, and its people, and compel their loyalty. This was partly because, as the Nazi ascent in Germany brought Hitler's menacing ambitions in eastern Europe completely into focus by the late 1930s, Finland's potential as an invasion route was making the Kremlin anxious. There was also an almost involuntary imperialist twitch: Finland had once essentially belonged to Tsarist Russia. Its independence was recent, its government reactionary and, to Bolshevik eyes, politically sinister. 'It was demonstrably flirting with Hitlerite Germany,' wrote Nikita Khrushchev years later. It appeared to be doing so by 'following policies hostile to the Soviet Union'.[1] Given the tiny size of Finland's population, its defiance was impertinent.

All Soviet Russia required was a spark of provocation to launch an invasion in so-called 'defence'. And so Stalin's forces engineered a blood-smeared lie in the form of a bellowing, blossoming ball of white, orange and black in the snow-covered forests of the Karelia region to the north of Leningrad. On 26 November 1939 an explosion occurred at a Soviet Red Army sentry post in a village called Mainila. 'Four dead, nine wounded, in an attack by the Finnish army', declared the Soviet reports: an impeccably executed 'false flag'. Russia now had an excuse to embark upon a conquest that it expected would be achieved in a matter of days. It was grimly wrong.

According to Aristotle, one of the rules of tragedy is that the punishment suffered by the flawed hero should be proportionate. In Russian literature, tragedy always tended to be crueller: rather than kings and princes being laid low by the fates, it was ordinary people who were the victims – frequently in foggy St Petersburg streets, assailed by the deadly consequences of their weaknesses and observed by pitiless onlookers. Joseph Stalin himself was impatient with classic stage tragedy: Hamlet's problem, he thought, was quite simply that he was weak-willed. Stalin's own fundamental tragic flaw – quite apart from his psychopathic indifference to suffering – was that he believed he stood as an emblem of good: that 'Stalin', as a public construct, was there to improve the moral condition of humanity, and that any who dissented were evil. This was not politics: it was atavistic ritualism. In the last five years, murder had piled upon murder as Stalin and his deputies sought to purge and cauterize heretics from their new faith. The consequences – the punishment – would be visited upon ordinary people.

In November 1939, war came once more to Leningrad. This war was intended to be modern and technologically advanced. Every general since the invention of gunpowder has thought the same, but war remains as ungovernable as weather. In this instance, Soviet confidence was driven in part by the incredible research and development that had taken place in Leningrad's cavernous factories throughout the 1930s. The age of the cavalry, of animal vulnerability, had passed; this was the era of the tank. The city was now one of the largest producers of weaponry in the world. Stalin's Russians were being taught to take patriotic pride in progress. The price of this progress had been oppression for some: Leningrad's industrial workers were forced to meet ever more gruelling quotas from ever more anxious managers, a few suffering ever harsher punishments for transgressions such as unauthorized absence. Yet among those workers there was never a perfect uniformity of opinions or outlooks. And others found that the city offered many consolatory distractions.

In 1939, Leningrad's cinema audiences – who had been enjoying a blend of comedy dramas (*Girl With a Temper*, featuring the madcap adventures of a female farm manager in Moscow), charming fantasies (*The Golden Key*, a reworking of Pinocchio) and the reissued slapstick of Charlie Chaplin (much beloved) – had also been engrossed in a heavy industrial saga entitled *The Vyborg Side*, a drama focusing on one of Leningrad's factory districts, detailing the workers' rise from the cruel oppression of Tsarist days to the enlightenment of proletarian rule, as seen through the eyes of young hero Maxim (who in this film also begins to master Leningrad's banking system).[2] Among young Leningraders, the world that they now had was the world as they thought it should be: a city of light, and of learning. Their parents had suffered in the years after the 1917 revolution, but by autumn 1939, Leningrad – the wide avenues clanging with the bells of turquoise-and-cream liveried trams, with piles of newspapers being sold on every corner, with bakeries selling fat pastries – was once more itself: confident and proud in its culture and art. Bertha Gutkina was sixteen years old and she ached to learn the piano. Her parents – her father held a senior position at the Elektrosila Plant, her mother was an accountant at the Institute of Fine Mechanics and Optics – arranged for an upright piano to be carried up to their fifth-floor apartment, where the teenager received lessons from a tutor. She was, she recalled, quite the 'little lady'.[3] But this was the opposite of snobbery. The city was serious about inculcating beauty: even on the edge of war.

In the countryside not far north of the city, the false-flag explosion that splintered a timbered village would set in train a series of bitterly violent battles, resulting in enormous numbers of casualties and the forced evacuation of around 400,000 Finns, their homes often devoured by fire. This short but bloody conflict – the Winter War – would have the most terrible repercussions. Not just for the Finns, and for the villagers of the Karelian Isthmus, but also for their Leningrad neighbours. In earlier decades, Petersburgers had casually traversed that Karelian border of pine forests for trade, for holidays, for pleasure, and the people had regarded one another as close cousins. The psychological – as well as physical – barrier that the war would build would never be fully lowered.

The foundations of the tragedy had been laid in part by Vyacheslav Skryabin, a man who had studied in St Petersburg. Square-headed with a brush-like moustache, in his younger years he had attended the St Petersburg Polytechnic (and shared peeling-wallpapered digs for a short period with a young Joseph Stalin) before the flames of the 1917 revolution were lit. Skryabin later adopted the name Molotov. *Molot* was Russian for hammer; this seemed to him appropriate for a new age of proletarian industry and steel, and for the ruthless annihilation of enemies within and without. In May 1939 he had become the Soviet Union's minister of foreign affairs. Molotov and Stalin had watched pensively as Nazi Germany had acquired Austria in 1938 and then Czechoslovakia in March 1939. There was no state secret about Hitler's intentions towards the lands that lay east of Germany; Hitler had written about them himself in the 1920s in his testimonial *Mein Kampf.* It was necessary for the Soviets to believe that his larger ambitions could be forestalled.

By summer 1939, Molotov was in the final stages of hammering out a non-aggression agreement with the Nazi foreign minister Joachim von Ribbentrop. It was finally ratified on 23 August. It contained a secret protocol: an agreement that both Nazi Germany and the Soviet Union had 'spheres of influence' that – in this state of 'non-aggression' – neither power would seek to challenge or overthrow. The old kingdom of Poland, which itself had a couple of centuries earlier commanded territories beyond its land, and which more recently had fought bitterly with the Soviets, was to be broken in two: the Nazis to possess the west and the Soviets to have the east. Soviet Russia was also understood to have claim to the Baltic states: Latvia, Estonia and Lithuania.

Also in that sphere of influence was Russia's neighbour, Finland, a source of tremulous paranoia to Stalin since the inception of his rule. The independence of Finland was more than an irritant: there grew the fear that these lands might be used as a conduit through which Germany might attack Leningrad and advance into Russia.

Throughout the nineteenth century, Finland had essentially been a part of the Russian empire: ceded by the Swedish, it became a Grand Duchy supervised by generations of Tsars. It was permitted a certain amount of autonomy but it was the domain of its larger neighbour: a country overseen by the magnificence of St Petersburg.

The First World War, which had dissolved so many empires (and during which Russia's royal family was overthrown) was Finland's opportunity. It proclaimed its proud independence. Initially, Lenin and his Bolshevik revolutionaries were in principled agreement: this was Finland's constitutional right. But the inter-war years generated paranoid tensions.

Moreover, there was mineral wealth and rich timber in those illimitable Finnish forests, resources that Russia felt it had a claim to. (In this sense, Putin's invasion of Ukraine has profound echoes: the Kremlin citing territorial security, but its target also being rich in rare-earth resources vital to advanced technology. Additionally, like Finns, Ukrainians for the most part have a broad sense of their own national identity.) There were also small islands in the Gulf of Finland of great strategic importance in keeping some control over the Baltic Sea. Stalin wanted these. There was a deep historical compulsion too: the never-ending irony of anti-imperialist Communists seeking to re-establish old imperial borders.

Just days after the Molotov–Ribbentrop Pact was ratified, the Nazi forces staged their own more infamous false-flag 'attack' upon their own forces in Poland in the final days of August 1939: the prelude to bloody Blitzkrieg and invasion and conquest. Precisely two weeks later Stalin gave the order for the forces of the Red Army to roll swiftly and brutally across the flat landscape of Latvia and Estonia (preparing them for life under Bolshevik rule) and seize the east of Poland.

Pressing Soviet weight upon their Baltic sphere of influence, Stalin and his commanders now gazed more steadily at Finland. First came the intimidation of 'negotiations'; a party of Finnish politicians were invited to Russia to hear Molotov's demands for certain parts of their country's territory: the Russians wanted the border on the largely uninhabited Karelian Isthmus moved some miles to the west; there was also a demand for the Finns to dismantle their careful fortifications. The aim, in part, seemed to be to increase the distance between Leningrad and Finnish territory; a wider buffer to protect the historic city against unexpected attack. In these 'negotiations' was also the dainty pretence that the Soviets would offer other parts of Karelia back to Finland in exchange, namely the regions of Repola and Porajärvi. There were also stipulations concerning those small islands in the Gulf of Finland – possible sites for Soviet naval bases – and a small peninsula that might serve the same purpose. Throughout all of this, the Finnish team treated their opposites with grave respect, and reported back to the Finnish parliament.

In Leningrad – unbeknownst to the Finns – the internationally renowned composer Dmitri Shostakovich had been summoned to Party Headquarters in the elegant Smolny Institute. Just a few years previously, the composer had feared for his own life, having provoked Stalin's displeasure (as we shall see later). But on this occasion, he received a most unusual commission: to compose a special Finnish suite. It was to 'celebrate' Finnish folk song and melody, and also to underscore just how closely related Finnish and Russian music were: a conjoining of artistic souls. Shostakovich was speedy and the work – a medley of traditional themes and folk songs – was indeed uplifting. Among the pieces was a song entitled 'The Strawberry is a Red Berry', set for a baritone voice and based upon an old Finnish tune.[4]

What the composer did not know was that the intention was for the music to be performed by the Red Army as they triumphantly entered Helsinki.

The diplomatic 'negotiations' were merely a Soviet dance: a display of power combined with a richly cynical sense that, in international eyes, Stalin and the Soviet leadership were treating Finland with the utmost fairness and grace. But as the Finns waited in expectation of further talks, the Soviets were moving into their next deadly phase.

On 30 November 1939 the fire poured from the skies above Helsinki as a Soviet bomber raid on the Finnish capital brought vaulting flame to a city frozen in the deep blue and silvery white of early winter. This was 'retaliation' for the smaller nation's recalcitrance. The Finns were grimly prepared: bomb shelters had been built and gas masks issued. Thanks to distrust of Stalin, civil defence had been active for the past five years. Some shelters had been carved into rock, others carefully constructed in basements. One entire hospital in the city had been sited underground. The loathing of Stalin's Soviet regime had been sufficiently intense for the sparsely populated state also to invest in searchlights and anti-aircraft guns. (In countries with dense urban centres, such as Britain, where it was warned that 'the bomber will always get through', such precautions were understandable. It was more striking in somewhere like Finland.) The morning before the incendiaries fell, the Soviet planes had first dropped leaflets bearing messages for the citizens: 'You know we have bread,' read one. 'Don't starve. Soviet Russia will not harm the Finnish people. Their disaster is due to the wrong leadership. [Chief of Defence Carl Gustaf Emil] Mannerheim and [Prime Minister Aimo] Cajander must go. After this peace will come!'[5] Later that evening, the bombs came instead: some 600 of them rained down upon the city. The effect upon some streets was infernal: tall buildings sliced wide open, vast flames billowing from within.

Just as Dmitri Shostakovich was under intense pressure to compose music that would exalt the Soviet system, Leningrad's other dedicated craftsmen – the workers and engineers and technicians – had been readying themselves for war. Since the beginning of the 1930s, there had been mighty armaments factories to the south and the east of the city centre. Production lines stretched out into the distance, high ceilinged, with huge windows bathing them in light. Some of these echoing workshop floors had been initially dedicated to the mass development of a very specific kind of tank: the T-26. This was closely based upon a British design from Vickers-Armstrong: a Soviet delegation that had visited England in 1930 concluded that these compact vehicles would be perfect for Russia. A gifted young Leningrad technician called Semyon Ginzburg was impressed by the lightness of these new-generation tanks, their cross-country manoeuvrability and various other key features including their water-cooled machine guns.[6] He and his team began a programme of not only mass production – some 12,000 tanks would be built over the course of a decade – but also mass experimentation.

In test firings, Ginzburg's prototype T-26 tanks were hit with storms of searing bullets: a trial to see how the lightweight armour, ideal for nimbleness and speed, stood up to repeated punishment. Ever newer incarnations, up to the T-34, featured more powerful single cannons, plus the addition of machine guns. For the occupants – the whitewashed interiors punctuated with telescopic sights and cylinders of ammunition stowage – there was an ever-wider array of weaponry that might be deployed. There were experiments with flame-throwers; tests with multiple machine guns; powerful searchlights so that the tanks might prowl the battlefields at night.[7] The operators were consistently aware of one vital piece of equipment that they prayed they never had recourse to: fire extinguishers. The claustrophobia of tanks was bad enough, but the idea of these tiny cabins being penetrated by flame was terrifying.

The Soviet assumption was that Field Marshal Mannerheim's Finnish forces – numbering around 340,000 and possessing just 32 tanks against the Soviet Union's 6,500 – would capitulate within days when faced with the unstoppable force of the Red Army. But there had been a failure of intelligence. The Finns had been quietly training their young men, without anything quite so obvious as conscription. These thousands of trainees had, for the last couple of years, been acquiring a range of skills specifically adapted to their country's unique landscape.

Blood was to be spilled amid Karelian forests of light birch and thicker pine, of spruce and alder, of sphagnum moss and deep bogs and deep clear water. Back in the nineteenth century, in the time of the Tsars, the area had enjoyed a tremendous vogue among outdoors-loving citizens of St Petersburg as newly constructed railways carried them across the border. Yet it was not the sort of terrain suited to the most modern military transport: in most parts, the roads were rudimentary and sparse. A warning note was sounded by Red Army commander Kirill Meretskov, who would later become a key figure in the desperate fight for Leningrad. He saw potential dangers. 'The terrain of coming operations,' he advised, 'is split by lakes, rivers, swamps, and is almost entirely covered by forests . . . the proper use of our forces will be difficult.'[8] Elsewhere, journalist John Langdon-Davies observed that 'every acre of its surface was designed to be the despair of an attacking military force'.[9] In and around Leningrad, stretching up into the northern forests, and far beyond, along a frozen border of some 830 miles, the attacking forces had been assembled and distributed: some twenty-one battalions totalling around 450,000 men (and the numbers would later rise steeply to 750,000). Here for the first time could be seen the fruits of Leningrad industry at war: the newest tanks, deployed in this freezing landscape.

The Finns soon learned, however, that it was more than possible to halt and disable these mighty vehicles. There was a pleasing note of mordant wit in the naming of one particular extemporized weapon that remains with us to this day: the Molotov cocktail. The name was inspired darkly by the Soviet incendiary bombing of Helsinki: Molotov, facing an indignant world, cynically lied that the Soviet air force was dropping not bombs but food parcels. The Finnish army, when devising this liquid bomb composed of petrol and tar, named it the Molotov cocktail as it was the 'perfect drink' to accompany Molotov's generous gift of 'dinner'.[10]

And there was already established the Mannerheim Line, named after the Finnish Chief of Defence; this chain of concrete bunkers spanned the isthmus from the Gulf of Finland in the west to Lake Ladoga in the east, a distance of some thirty-five miles. Construction had taken place in the years after the Great War, as Finland had declared independence. The bunkers themselves, concrete redoubts half concealed amid trees, and amid mounds of moss, were relatively durable. Soviet intelligence was perfectly aware of them, but there also seemed to be a sense that there were still gaps in this defensive line that could be exploited.

And yet they could not: or not initially, at any rate. It was here, in November 1939, that the Red Army commanders began to realize that they were facing men who were implacably determined to defend their land. The Soviets had calculated that tank charges – the heavy vehicles rumbling and blasting towards lines of lightly armed infantry – would be crushing. But it became apparent that the reverse was true. In such a landscape – trackless, wet, spongy – tanks were not so easy to manoeuvre, and the Finnish troops – at first concealed before appearing seemingly out of nowhere – became adept at countering the charges, rushing among the vast vehicles first with Molotov cocktails (the flames making visibility difficult for the tank occupants) and then courageously getting close enough to jam the tank tracks with logs.

Not all the young recruits to the Red Army were so enthusiastic. 'Once I finished my initial training as a young soldier, the Winter War broke out and we were immediately sent to the front,' recalled Yakov Elner. 'It was frightfully cold. I hated it from the get-go. In general,

I didn't enjoy being in the army. From the very first time when I was handed a wooden spoon and it smelled like herring, which I couldn't stand, I didn't want to serve in the army.'[11] Very soon, as an infantry soldier, he was riding on the outside of a tank. 'The tank was weak,' he recalled, 'got stuck in one spot, [then] hit a tree.'[12] He and his comrades escaped lightly with minor injuries. For the crews of other tanks, getting stuck was a more severe proposition: because of structural weaknesses in the riveting, it was possible for the flaming fluid of Molotov cocktails to penetrate to the interior, causing larger fires and hideous burns. By this time, Finland's leading drinks manufacturer was turning out industrially vast numbers of these bottled bombs, the cloth fuses attached to their necks. Opportunity also arose when internal fires reduced visibility for the tank crews: opening the vehicles' hatches made them intensely vulnerable to further fiery attack.

The Mannerheim Line consisted of more than just concrete shelters and pillboxes: there were also deep trenches and booby traps. Each trench had to be attacked individually, which meant that each tank had to be accompanied by other troops and engineers lending support in the effort to break through. Any soldier in the open was consistently vulnerable to attack. The casualties began mounting.

It was not long before the snows and the ice arrived; and with them, the most dramatic temperature drops seen in the region for decades. For this eventuality, again, the Finnish troops had long been making their preparations. They had been issued with white camouflage capes and uniforms, rendering them virtually invisible from a distance against the snowy ground and the birch trees.

In addition, their solution to the transportation problem was ingenious: utilizing reindeer-drawn sleighs rather than jeeps or tanks. Even if it meant that supply lines were more stretched – there was only so much weight the beasts could pull – here was a means of moving across a hostile winter landscape without breakdown and also, brilliantly, in near silence. Other Finnish soldiers took to skis, propelling themselves with slick speed across the frozen snow.

Among their number was a sniper who would become known to his comrades as 'The White Death' – a man called Simo Häyhä, who could lay claim to having personally picked off approximately 540 Red Army soldiers, and often not in full daylight but rather in the turquoise shades of northern winter afternoons. (Impressively, he lived to the age of ninety-six, dying in 2002.)[13]

There were other sharp innovations in the Finnish army: specially constructed small log cabins, superheated to become saunas (there are startling photographs of naked Finnish soldiers gleefully peering out of them, surrounded by the wider snows).[14] Like the *banya* in Leningrad, the aim was to maintain and improve health. Also out in those woodlands were vast steaming cauldrons, filled with thick meaty stews: the Finnish forces were kept well nourished against the knife-keen cold.

By contrast, in this realm where the dark now had dominion over the day – the winter hours of light fitful and short – the Red Army troops were extraordinarily ill prepared. Their uniforms, standard issue, made no concession to the intense below-freezing temperatures; and when moving across snow-covered plains, the deep green and browns of those uniforms made them the starkest imaginable targets.

Nevertheless, advances were made, and the Finnish civilians who dwelled in the towns and villages of these forests suffered horribly at the hands of the invaders. Thousands were forced to pack up their life's belongings, loaded on to sleds, as shells and rockets fell indiscriminately and homes disappeared in the cruelty of flames. (It was in this atmosphere of terror that Finnish author Tove Jansson began writing what would become her internationally beloved children's stories about the Moomins. The first, *The Moomins and the Great Flood*, which she started in 1939, featured Moomintroll, a furry white hippopotamus-like creature, walking through a sinister and fantastical forest – 'here and there giant flowers grew, glowing with a peculiar light like flickering lamps, and further in among the shadows moved tiny dots of cold green' – and meeting weird, soulless strangers in the shape of the Hattifatteners.[15] Jansson was explicitly projecting her nauseous anxieties about the war on to a fantasy realm that she conjured so that her characters might find safety and home.) One reason the Finnish army fought back with such intensity was that they understood the blank remorselessness of the Red Army as an exterminating force.

Perhaps one of the most emblematic moments in the conflict was that which became known as the Battle of Raate Road. Taking place some 400 miles north of Leningrad, and close to the frontier between Finland and the USSR, here was where the Red Army understood just how unyielding the Finn defenders were. Its build-up began in the early days of December 1939. The Soviet 163rd Rifle Division had captured the territory of Suomussalmi, an area chiefly noted for large numbers of reindeer, and a preponderance of lakes. But that division thence found itself cut off from other Red Army forces, with the Finn defenders beginning to encircle them.

It seems barely conceivable now that so few Finnish troops – around 6,000 or so, facing some 25,000 Red Army soldiers – could have been responsible for death on such a scale. On that snow-covered road, bordered with heavy pine, there was burned-out tank after burned-out tank; and in that air of seemingly pure ice, the corpses froze as they fell: one Soviet soldier lay as though suspended in time, his arms reflexively covering his face, his fists clenched, his legs drawn up slightly, and his eyes still wide open.[16]

This was deep in December, and it was only the start; as the new year dawned, the Battle of Raate Road – four Finnish divisions fighting against the Red Army's 44th Division – began in its full bloody earnest. The Finns had set up roadblocks laced with mines, and machine-gun nests in snowy woodland hollows, manned by white-suited teams with heads and necks swaddled in thick fur. The more the Red Army tanks tried to push through, the more they came under fire, their occupants burned. Mighty as the 44th Division was, the Finnish troops, scattered through those trackless haunted forests, and moving with stealth, calculated means of splitting up the Soviet units into manageable numbers as they themselves progressed in lines along woodland floors, and picked them off ruthlessly. The Red Army troops had little fuel, and even less food. Many of the men were suffering terribly from hunger; many of them were almost literally paralysed by the cold. With temperatures again plunging to minus 40°C, frostbite became endemic: blackened toes and extremities, the necrosis spreading. There were other terrible considerations of a sanitary nature: how to defecate in frozen latrines without risking more exposure to the cold than necessary.

As the historian William Trotter wrote: 'The Soviet soldier had no choice. If he refused to fight, he would be shot. If he tried to sneak through the forest, he would freeze to death. And surrender was no option for him: Russian propaganda told of how the Finns would torture prisoners to death.'[17] Yet even without their intervention, the cold itself was a form of torture: veins thrumming with electric shocks of pain, the gangrenous ravaging of fingertips and noses.

The forests were now punctuated with the perfectly preserved bodies of the recently killed; many would lie in the same positions until the first thawing breezes of spring. In a matter of several days, the small but agile Finnish force had destroyed an entire Red Army division, its tanks moribund and silent on that snowy woodland road. The number of Soviet casualties was running into many thousands – some estimates suggest 9,000 fatalities in this battle alone. The Finns had also – to their bemusement – captured a large number of musical instruments. There is a photograph of a Finnish soldier holding a tuba: this was intended as part of the orchestra that would sweep into Helsinki and perform Shostakovich's freshly composed suite.[18]

There were other battlefields – half a million Red Army soldiers were probing the northernmost parts of that border, and the snows of Lapland were bloodied in a series of military confrontations. Another vulnerable point was the coastal road that wound around the edge of the mighty Lake Ladoga, in the east of Finland.

And the world had not been silent; the League of Nations – an international body established in the wake of the First World War to promote and maintain peace (and the forerunner of today's United Nations) – condemned the invasion, pronounced that it was illegal, and expelled the Soviet Union from its ranks. There were international supporters of Finland who yearned to spur its armies on, and for the shrewdest of strategic reasons. Partly these involved access to the riches of natural resources: the iron-ore fields of neighbouring northern Sweden, which the Nazis and the British alike had been eyeing as potential vital supplies. But there were also, for some, moral considerations too. In January 1940, Winston Churchill, then First Lord of the Admiralty, was viscerally horrified by the Soviet incursion. His loathing of Bolshevism ran through his very bones. 'Finland shows what free men can do,' he declared. 'Everyone can see how Communism rots the soul of a nation, how it makes it abject and hungry in peace and proves it bare and abominable in war.'[19]

Certainly in Leningrad, the Winter War was making life uncomfortable: as the air turned to ice, and as the snows fell, shortages of oil and coal led to power cuts. These spells of frozen darkness – in a city that had come to cherish its own electric modernity, 'the gift of Lenin' – were disconcerting. Those raw, unlit nights were felt especially harshly in the newer tenements and workers' barracks in the suburbs that had been built to accommodate the many new arrivals from the countryside, who barely had five square metres of their own space: intermittent electricity, no running water.

There were other effects, some obvious, others less so. Rationing of food brought its own sense of insecurity, even in a city already used to food shortages (in the early 1930s, famine in Ukraine, the Urals and Kazakhstan, the result of Stalin's Five-Year Plan to eliminate landowing 'kulaks', had its own repercussive effects in Leningrad); but owing to military casualties, the city's medical supplies were also depleted, and the authorities never quite got around to addressing the shortfalls.

The war had also made extra demands upon the workers: teams of engineers had to join soldiers in those Karelian forests to help with repairs. By deep December, with news of continual Finnish attacks difficult to suppress, a new mood of insecurity swept through Leningrad: were they all on the edge of the same precipice as the rest of Europe? What kind of war was this where the Red Army seemed to be thwarted by small numbers of Finns? Out of this came the first suggestions of a city preparing itself for the possibility of greater trials: the lateral thinking that led to Leningrad's engineers dealing with fuel shortages by identifying nearby areas rich in peat that could be cut and burned. Factories developed their own integral power plants and generators.

Yet however many triumphs they had scored, the Finnish government and army – with their comparatively minute forces – knew that their surprise victories could only be fleeting; that the Red Army – seemingly infinite in weight and numbers – would absorb what had happened, learn what it had to do and then counter-attack with greater force.

It did so in February 1940, as the worst ravages of the winter were passing. Now the Red Army was better prepared, the men finally issued with white camouflage uniforms and properly trained. Their numbers were ever greater: a renewed push through the Karelian Isthmus met with Finnish forces that were now short of ammunition, and also at the very brink of exhaustion. The Red Army thrust through in other regions too: even legendary figures such as The White Death could not hope to succeed against these better-armed multitudes.

'I was a tank commander and sometimes a gunner,' recalled Henrikh Dudnik, who would later be among those fighting to defend Leningrad. 'All the crew members knew how to perform every task in the tank. I could easily do the job of gunner, or mechanic, or radio operator.' His young cohort – Dudnik was then just nineteen years old – had been more sharply prepared. 'We had universal skills,' he said.[20]

Throughout all of this, the Finnish government had kept channels open in the hope of finding other means of halting the inexorable Soviet advance. By February and March 1940, they were calling for an armistice. The fact was that Stalin also needed this conflict to be brought to a conclusion. The defeats inflicted upon the Red Army – some 127,000 soldiers killed – had brought him international embarrassment. The images of wrecked tanks and exulting Finnish soldiers had made the Red Army and its High Command seem lumbering, clumsy and dense. Which it was, the Stalinist purges having murdered so many of its finest minds.

And this in turn increased Russia's vulnerability: who else might be noting the worn-down state of the Red Army? In March 1940 a ceasefire was agreed, and the territory that the USSR had acquired for itself exceeded its original demands. A number of industrial areas in the east of Finland were now under Soviet control, and the Karelian Isthmus, so bitterly fought over, was now also in Stalin's domain. There was certainly – or so it seemed at the time – far greater security for the exposed city of Leningrad. The border with Finland was now very much further away.

That security was illusory, however. The Finns had been shown the snarling face of Stalinism. No alliance or friendship could now ever be possible. Just a little over eighteen months later, that hostility would mean that one conceivable route of salvation for Leningrad would be closed off: borders sealed, and no chance of any supplies being smuggled through by sympathizers.

This tremulous period of war had found Leningrad's chief political authorities wanting: Andrei Zhdanov – amid his other administrative deficiencies – was no military planner. This man would soon be trying to mitigate the most nightmarish human catastrophe, but his own capacity for empathy was as limited as that of his friend Stalin.

In the meantime, Leningrad factory life became even more rigid. Yet those who were not 'gentleman Bolsheviks'[21] – the workers, the *rabochie*, who populated those factories – might have had a sense none the less that they were part of another kind of tradition. In the dark days to come it would be they, paradoxically, who would enjoy comparative privileges in industrial complexes such as the Bolshevik Plant and the Stalin Works.

The proudest of St Petersburg's historic industrial concerns – a foundry that in time became a citadel, surviving war, revolution and the passing decades, and still a presence in the city today – was the Kirov Plant (once the Putilov Works, renamed in 1935 in honour of the assassinated city leader). Its factory floors and testing areas, its furnaces and chimneys, the roads and the railway lines that led to and from it, formed a metropolis within a metropolis. The lives of those who worked within it could be taken as barometers of the political situation outside its high walls. This had been the case since it was first opened in 1801. At its inception, it was the St Petersburg Iron Foundry, and it had been established using the expertise of a Scottish engineer called Charles Gascoigne (there has been a curious affinity between St Petersburgers and

Scots across the years; for example, the great nineteenth-century writer Mikhail Lermontov was of Scottish descent).[22] Russia's industrialization was slow; unlike the compact British Isles, this was a prospect of countless thousands of square miles of steppe, forest and tundra. And the foundry itself, though manufacturing cannonballs and other items of weaponry for St Petersburg's military and naval establishments, suffered fluctuating fortunes. But in 1868 a Russian engineer – Nikolay Ivanovich Putilov – acquired it, and set to work on a transformative vision. This involved bringing the railways to this illimitable land.

The factory was renamed the Putilov Works, and his high-quality steel rails, made to a stress-bearing design of his own invention, proved brilliantly successful (unlike rails imported from Britain). Russian rails had fiercer climate conditions to withstand; Putilov gave them strength. He went further than this too: as an industrialist, he had a paternalist vision of the ideal factory citadel, and how its workers' productivity might be maximized. It involved a range of benefits and facilities: an in-house pharmacy, a school, a hospital, a well-stocked library and a canteen serving nourishing food. Such comforts were not common, either in the poorer districts of nineteenth-century St Petersburg or in the city's other factories.

By the 1890s – when young Vladimir Lenin was moving through the city, collecting and amassing knowledge of the injustices and hardships and inequalities that workers faced – there was already a flavour of profound change in the air. That was the very cusp of the electrical revolution. The mighty German firm Siemens, which was beginning to illuminate Europe from Berlin to London, established a huge plant in St Petersburg. There were other citadels of smoke and furnaces, too, such as the Semyannikov Works, heavy with the manufacture of everything from ironclad battleships to steam locomotives.

As well as inaugurating mass production, another kind of life was taking shape among the workers at around that time. Lenin's wife-to-be, Nadezhda Krupskaya, was among a group of women bringing education to illiterate men. She ran an 'evening Sunday school' at one factory; here, she would meet with her students not just in the quieter hours of Sunday, but also two evenings a week. She and they were assiduous about maths, and about Russian literature and Russian history. Like good missionaries everywhere, she and Lenin were also obviously keen to bring a new gospel: that of Karl Marx. In order to summon a socialist future into corporeal reality, the workers would have to arm themselves with knowledge. The appetite was there not just for the basics, but also for everything from philosophy to geology to theology. There were many men asking themselves if it were possible for a world to outgrow its old God. The evening Sunday schools were there to assure them that a faith in man and his own revolutionary progress shone brighter and more truly.[23]

And just as St Petersburg was the city in which the first spark of the Russian revolution took hold, it was from within those same sprawling industrial plants that the raw human power to effect this change came. This included the Siemens factory, which after the revolution as the renamed Elektrosila (meaning Electric Power) Plant, under state control, became an almost idealized centre for bringing the Soviet vision to life. It was here that the huge turbogenerators were made for the 1920s programme of hydroelectricity, drawing power from the flowing waters of the mighty Dnieper and Volkhov rivers. (The Elektrosila Plant would remain at the centre of Soviet industrial dreams well into the 1970s, as it began the shift from hydroelectric to nuclear power.) The Putilov became the Red Putilovite Plant, and the workers and the engineers now turned their hands to the modernization of agriculture: it became focused upon a new generation of domestic tractors. This was technology that changed the face of the land (and in so doing, also upended the lives of millions who had previously been devoted to that land).

There was a corresponding darkness too amid the progress: that brutal push towards collectivization in the late 1920s and early 1930s which brought entirely human-made famine to millions out in the country, that same starvation and violence conversely forcing once-agricultural families to find a new life in the city and then to be bound by a form of industrial enslavement.

When the population of Leningrad started growing dizzyingly in the wake of that catastrophe, the city authorities neglected to pay much attention to the fact that vast new numbers of workers and their families would need to be housed. There were men who arrived from the countryside – half-starved, in ragged clothes, essentially refugees – who were easily employed amid the metalworks and the timber mills and the smelting furnaces. But home for many of them would be barracks: long dormitories in roughly built constructions with primitive heating from central stoves and no running water. In some cases, this was only a slightly more civilized version of the prospect facing those sent to the Gulag.

A little later, the authorities would try to balance these hardships with facilities never before seen. There is a marvellous propaganda photograph from 1937 depicting the 'daycare of Elektrosila factory': portrait of five small children in a warm and cosy room with plants, all gathered round a little table, lit with a lamp, upon which is a storybook. On a vacant chair, the children have been joined by a large teddy bear.[24] By this stage – Stalin's Terror having had the effect of removing so many men from the city to suffer penal servitude – plants such as Elektrosila were having to persuade women (and young mothers) that they too could work among the turbines and the generators.

Such vast numbers of workers could not be expected to maintain any sort of uniformity about their attitude to the factory, or about the way that they were being treated. Even in the days of the Terror, the workers of Leningrad found ways of expressing discontent. Party Secretary Zhdanov's office was – over the years – in receipt of hundreds of letters, some anonymous, but all scrupulously filed. These ranged from complaints about food shortages to accusations of malfeasance against factory managers. There was an acute sense of a divide: there were the ordinary workers, who saw themselves as a separate class from the *vozhdi naroda* – that is, 'officials', senior Party figures, and 'Jews'. (Anti-Semitism was never far from the surface in the city, as we shall see later.)[25]

Many of these workers looked at the ruling regime with an intelligent cynicism. A. I. Ugarov, a former Leningrad City Committee secretary, observed the sour response when the newspapers were filled with 'parades, clamour, boasting, glorification of leaders and toadyism'.[26] These same newspapers would insist in their reports that workers 'listened with great love to the Party Secretary's speech'. Ugarov pointed out that 'this is obviously fake and distorts our relationship with workers'.[27]

On those production lines, some of the labourers who were old enough to recall the Tsarist regime now considered that 'workers were slaves and remain slaves'. There was a grim continuity: where once there was a ruling royal family, there were now the Communists, who had become the 'nobility', their lives gilded in different ways.[28]

In 1940, after the Winter War and in the months before the siege, factory labourers were being monitored – and punished – as never before. Their productivity and attendance rates were noted down by management in work booklets. Any worker wishing to change jobs would have to present that booklet to their new employers. Skipping work – taking an unauthorized day off – was made a criminal offence in 1940. The same went for persistent lateness. The punishments were harsh: short periods in local prisons or labour camps, where the prisoners would be forced to work for no pay. It might have been thought that the penalties were so horrendous that no factory workers would ever dare risk them.

Yet some tried bravely to raise voices in protest, even if they were too frightened to use their own names. Another anonymous letter sent to the Smolny Party HQ picked up this theme of the rupture between the rulers and the ruled, and of the lessons that such a chasm might teach. Zhdanov, the letter writer claimed, was 'a leader without the people'. 'It's bad you are never at factories and in the districts,' the letter continued. 'There's no need to fear the workers but you must come to us at the factories. The Tsar was afraid to come to the people and they killed him.'[29]

Nor – as mentioned – were these workers uniformly urban in background. The city's population had grown by about a million throughout the 1920s and 1930s. Former country dwellers had also brought with them some of their old skills. Near their badly built tenement apartment blocks on the southern outskirts, some found bare patches of land that they organized into allotments and gardens cultivating root and winter vegetables. There was a sense within a city that had already seen so much hunger that this kind of self-reliance might be worth hanging on to.

A different sort of resilience was necessary for the working families gathered together in the city centre's communal apartments: living spaces formed within the once grand homes of Petersburg merchants and politicians and nobility. A high-ceilinged drawing room in one such house might accommodate a couple of families of four; there were large dining rooms that could host several families, divided by sheets or fabric on lines. Corridors became bed-spaces; kitchens and bathrooms were shared between as many as eleven families. Doors no longer signified privacy: personal borders became porous in these dwellings. Noise – the crying of infants, repetitive gramophone music, drunken abuse, even 'games of Tiddlywinks' – had to be tolerated for the sake of sanity. This was a life in which personal possessions also crossed those borders into wider ownership; ornaments and bric-a-brac going missing, acquired by neighbouring families. Conversely, there were some who found comfort amid the bustle: Anna Novikova was seven years old when her father died in 1930; her mother was a pharmacist who did not have much time to attend to her daughter. But in their communal apartment, 'the neighbours loved me and helped me out', as she recalled.[30] And they – as well as her mother – encouraged her education. Come the blockade, she would be playing a courageous role on the medical front line; her qualifications, though, would be acquired from the Ulyanov Electrical Engineering Institute.

There was also an idea that these communal dwellings might help free women from traditionalist drudgery, though quite how was never explained. They didn't. In all of this, men, women and children had to devise means of nurturing interior lives: through reading or writing journals. In the siege days, the issue of food storage would become combustible.

A stubborn sense of preserving individuality also persisted among the many poets and writers who were so central to the city's identity. But as the next chapter will show, these artists were just as vulnerable as workers to the calculated cruelty of the system.

4. 'Flung myself at the hangman's feet'

The other women wondered at her: this elegant figure in fine – though old and frayed – clothes. They knew her: the proud slender profile, the eyes that held depths of melancholy, were famous. And yet, among all the other women, she stood outside the high red-brick walls of the city's Kresty prison every day for eight months in 1938, hoping to pass messages and food through to the prisoners within.[1] She was Anna Akhmatova, and she was Russia's greatest poet.

Over the past few years, her life had been maliciously dismantled piece by piece by Andrei Zhdanov: publications banned, work denied, income stopped. Now, behind those prison walls lay her young son Lev, arrested on absurd charges of anti-Soviet activity and being systematically tortured. Zhdanov hated Anna Akhmatova purely because he could not control her poetic voice. She conveyed interior passions and rich insights that could not be framed within the Soviet version of the truth. She would not yield up her artistic freedom, simply because she couldn't. This war on truth had been foreseen.

'Those two in Paradise were presented with a choice,' wrote her old friend the visionary St Petersburg novelist Yevgenii Zamyatin of Adam and Eve. 'Either happiness without freedom – or freedom without happiness; no third choice given. They, the blockheads, chose freedom – and so then . . . after that they pined for fetters.'[2] But the poets had no choice: their passions could not be synthesized, or blended with ideology that they did not feel. 'Only in Russia is poetry respected – it gets people killed,' said Osip Mandelstam, another of the country's extraordinary verse-makers. 'Is there anywhere else where poetry is so common a motive for murder?'[3] In his case, the words were prophetic.

But in this most self-consciously literary city, the poets were as vital as the much-cherished classical musicians and the incredibly

disciplined dancers. And beyond persecution, it would be their words
that the city authorities looked towards to bring comfort and inspiration when the darkness rushed in. In 1941, their freshly composed
work would be broadcast on loudspeakers throughout the streets as a
means of keeping the heart of the city beating strong. It is difficult to
imagine anywhere else on earth where verse would be understood by
the authorities as having the power to shape living reality.

And curiously, the persecution that writers suffered was part of
a cycle of artistic abuse that stretched back through the decades.
Literary artists of St Petersburg – no matter how brilliant, how
renowned – had long been condemned to exile, and imprisonment;
torture and death. Those who chose freedom over happiness always
met with the grimmest punishments. Yevgenii Zamyatin – whose
1921 science-fiction novel *We* piercingly evoked a totalitarian surveillance state – was himself loathed by the Bolsheviks and was
forced to flee into exile. He had notable antecedents. The intense
nineteenth-century novelist Fyodor Dostoevsky – whose frequently
dark works had explored the shadowed recesses of St Petersburg, and
its sometimes murderous, feverish passions – had himself endured
a spell in one of Russia's notoriously harsh prisons. He later used
the experience for his semi-autobiographical *House of the Dead* – an
extraordinary exploration of the psychology of captivity, and the
accumulation of harsh empty years. That was an era when prisoners
were frequently flogged so severely, with so many dozens of strokes,
that they had to be hospitalized in prison wards – their shredded, la-
cerated backs so intensely painful that all they could do was stand still,
or walk very slowly, trembling in silent trances.[4] By Soviet times, the
floggings had been replaced by tortures that took more technocratic
forms, as Gulag prisoners were exposed to skin-blistering heat, lethal
cold and semi-starvation in the course of their labours.

In more recent times, the aforementioned Osip Mandelstam –
who had earned an international reputation for his poetry by the
time he was twenty and who, as a leading light of the Acmeist literary movement, had been at the heart of St Petersburg's vibrant
modernism – was himself subjected to ultimately murderous ordeals.
Under Stalin, writers had to hew close to what the regime defined

as reality: the glorious advancement of human nature itself, under Soviet guidance. To do otherwise was to risk being silenced. Fear sometimes inspired a kind of love. There were writers of that period who dreamed of meeting Stalin; who yearned to converse with him. But Mandelstam, whose individuality was 'counter-revolutionary agitation', was repelled by Stalin, a 'soul strangler' with 'fat fingers'.[5] The poet composed – though never wrote down – a satirical 'Epigram to Stalin' and declaimed it to a small inner circle of friends. One must have betrayed him. He was arrested by the NKVD and tortured; his friends, including fellow poet and novelist Boris Pasternak, desperately intervened.

Pasternak received a heart-clenchingly frightening telephone call from Stalin himself. There are some fourteen different versions of what passed between the tyrant and the poet, from Kremlin files to literary memoirs. But the essence was that Stalin – knowing the terror he inspired – was seeking an opinion from Pasternak of Mandelstam's talent. And would Pasternak say that he was friends with Mandelstam? 'Poets rarely make friends,' Pasternak was said to have replied, scenting a trap that would see him dragged off for interrogation as an associate. 'They usually envy one another.'[6] Stalin was (again, apparently) displeased: he told Pasternak that – if the positions had been reversed – he hoped he himself would have been a better friend to Mandelstam than Pasternak had proved.[7]

Mandelstam and his wife first suffered exile, to a town in the Urals. But the purges intensified and Mandelstam at last was condemned to a forced-labour camp at the eastern edge of Russia in 1937; he died two months after arriving.

And the story of his Petersburg associate Anna Akhmatova – stretching from the last days of the Tsars to her 1960s salons with European philosophers in modern Leningrad – was perhaps the most emblematic of those years of trauma. In 1941, on the edge of the siege, she was walking the city's streets in threadbare clothes, gaunt and hungry. As the citizens passed this pale, coughing figure on those grand canalside streets, their eyes were cast down or to one side at the spectacle that she presented. In previous years, she was imperious; the regime had been fixated upon humbling her through fear.

Akhmatova, born in 1889 near Odesa, had from a very early age an acute sense of her family's heritage, and of its nobility. The line of her ancestors, she once asserted, could be followed back to Genghis Khan. There had been princesses in this family; pieces of exquisite jewellery fashioned with diamonds and emeralds endured as the generations that held them rose, then withered and died.[8] It was when she was a baby that Akhmatova's parents made the move north to Tsarskoe Selo, just outside St Petersburg; and despite the violent maelstroms of the years to come, that city remained her spiritual and artistic home.

It was while she was still at school, aged fourteen, that she met Nikolay Gumilev, seventeen years old and himself an aspiring poet. Art crossed borders; the world of these young Petersburgers was large. While Akhmatova, leaving school temporarily, returned to Odesa and Sevastopol, Gumilev went travelling, from Armenia to the south of France and thence to a period of study at the Sorbonne in Paris. Soon Gumilev would be joining with other Russian poets to start a journal called *Apollon*, which across the years would prove very influential. As both he and Akhmatova returned to St Petersburg, he renewed his efforts to make her his wife. Very suddenly, in 1909, she finally capitulated.

There was a cellar club in those days before the first war. It was called the Stray Dog Cabaret, found beneath a grand nineteenth-century apartment block on the corner of Italianskaya Street. Here, under these low-vaulted ceilings, with the walls brightly coloured with abstract friezes, young women and men gathered to drink, to smoke and to listen to poetry. It was here that Akhmatova gave recitals of her work, while getting to know fellow poets such as Mandelstam. She had poems published together with that of fellow literary eminence Alexander Blok, with whom she was rumoured to have had an affair. Published poetry led to volumes, and her fame was spreading beyond the city. There were journeys to Paris too, where she formed a friendship with the artist Amedeo Modigliani.[9]

Marriage to Gumilev brought a son, Lev. Gumilev was then drawn away by the drums of war, in that innocent summer of 1914 when the young men across an entire continent imagined a coming conflict that would be pure and full of honour. It also happened by then that their marriage was essentially over, both Akhmatova and Gumilev seeing other lovers (St Petersburg was and remained a city that had an easy and natural sensuality). The war swiftly became a charnel house. And she was there in the cold streets of February, in 1917, when centuries of Tsarist rule were overthrown. 'This granite city of fame and calamity,' as one of her lines ran.[10]

Then came October, and the profounder revolution, with its concrete promise of violence and blood. Akhmatova had been intensely sensitive to the suffering in the trenches of war – many of her poems had dwelled upon it. The suffering was nowhere near any kind of end; the violence of the Red Guards – and the subsequent Red Terror – was as unstoppable as a storm. Added to this, civil war brought hunger and disease to renamed Petrograd. It was around 1918 when her marriage to Gumilev, long ailing, finally expired. They would be permanently sundered by the new regime. In the wake of the 1921 anti-Bolshevik Kronstadt sailors' rebellion – itself an expression of the Civil War – the authorities, seeking to cast blame and to spread terror, alighted on the city's artists. Gumilev was among those rounded up in 1921 by the secret police, betrayed by an artist friend who had been tortured. Gumilev was accused of sedition and counter-revolutionary plots, charges of which he was almost certainly innocent – though it was true that he had monarchist sympathies and had expressed loud scorn for 'half-literate Bolsheviks', which had been noted. The eminent writer Maxim Gorky wrote directly to Lenin in a plea for mercy.[11] By the time Lenin had granted a reprieve, it was too late. Gumilev, among many others, had been executed.

This was the shadow that was to loom over Akhmatova's life, and the life of their young son. 'There is an ominous knock behind the wall,' as one of her verses ran.[12] There was more: the new regime, in its Marxist purity, had little time for 'intimate domestic' poetry; it did not serve the greater ideals of society. Akhmatova – a poet of genuine widespread popularity whose volumes had found thousands upon thousands of homes, and who had been open about her bourgeois heritage – would find herself pulled down, degree by degree. She was identified as one of the 'aristocrats'. Publishing houses would close their doors to her; her past work would be placed under an official ban; her son Lev would find himself locked out of university; and even as friends such as Pasternak offered comfort, the world would grow colder. She found work as a translator of approved authors: Victor Hugo was among those she brought to a Leningrad readership.

Her endurance was not that of a martyr, and certainly not that of a fool. She knew at every step that those in power viewed her malevolently. But her essential strength also made her attractive to others. There was a brief marriage to another poet, Vladimir Shileiko, then an intense relationship with the art historian Nikolay Punin – one that would persist on and off through the darkest days of terror and then of siege while she was living in the House on the Fontanka, or the Sheremetev Palace. This was a bright eighteenth-century baroque confection that – in revolution – had been turned into one of the city's grandest flat shares. Another poet, Fyodor Sologub, saw to it against official hostility that Akhmatova was granted a threadbare pension of sixty roubles a month. Other friends gave her clothes to replace the ripped dresses that she was habitually wearing in public.

There could be no peace, and when Stalin's Great Terror came in the 1930s, her son Lev – forever suspect because of his executed father – fell victim. To the despair of Akhmatova, Lev was arrested by the NKVD in 1938 and she was denied all contact with him. Life was held in the most gruesome suspension, Akhmatova standing outside Kresty prison in those daily queues, helpless, her anguish immeasurable. 'Seventeen months I've pleaded for you to come home,' she wrote in one of the many forbidden verses that had to be memorized by her friends in case they were caught in possession of her work. 'Flung myself at the hangman's feet./ Oh my terror, of my son.'[13] A twist of additional cruelty was that Lev – sentenced to be deported north, and forced to labour on the White Sea Canal – had no way of knowing of his mother's vigils. The authorities refused to tell him. With their connivance, he formed the idea that she had abandoned him, and his love for his mother soured.

And as the Terror swept through the city like a wall of flame, even her lover Nikolay Punin found himself being denounced and arrested and subjected to the soul-withering routine of interrogation. The random reason for suspicion? A keen photographer, he had used a new kind of camera flash when taking a picture of a family dinner: he had joked to the guests that it was akin to a death-ray, and could have been used to assassinate Stalin.[14] It was only a matter of hours before the NKVD came for him. Through all this, Akhmatova knew every single day that the Damoclean sword was glinting above her head.

Yet there were also those who – even when treated cruelly – were enraptured by this new world; and theirs were the voices that would be broadcast across the city in the coming siege. The most fervent desire of Olga Berggolts was to write the perfect Soviet book. She had fought hard to attain the faith; to weave it into her soul. Poetry was her unstoppable passion but she wanted the purity of her vision to uplift the Motherland, and the revolution. She yearned for ideological cleanness.

This young woman, blonde and delicate of feature, born in 1910, was not completely blind to the occasional nonsense that this new way of life threw up. 'I looked at our house: it was the most absurd house in Leningrad,' she wrote of her collective dwellings in a modernist 1930s construction. 'Its official title was the Engineers and Writers House Commune.'[15] Because of its unusually shaped radical architecture, this building became known locally as 'the Teardrop of Socialism'.[16] It had been established as a cooperative that would do away with 'the old way of life', which in essence meant 'kitchen' and 'nappies'. Instead, there was a communal dining room, a communal nursery, a communal living room with 'incredibly small room-kennels'.[17] Yet life for its women still ineluctably snapped back to kitchens and nappies.

But in her wider ambitions, Berggolts never lost the dream of writing 'the Essential Book': the text that would exalt and lift up society as a whole. 'At its foundation the Essential Book rests on a single, all-encompassing and clear feeling, that is, on the foundation of our great idea, which became all five human senses, and it integrates them by means of the writer's special artistic sense,' she wrote, transported by rapture. 'The Essential Book openly and truthfully displays the formation, maturation and ripening of this idea-feeling – or put another way, of the communist worldview and the person's view of life; it reveals his struggle – with circumstances, with himself, with remnants of the past within him and around him, with enemies, with opponents and sometimes even with friends.'[18]

In a curious way, this is the sort of self-examining prose that might have been written by a nun in a convent cell: the effort to take that faith deep into the heart. She mused on 'the internal, spiritual world of our person', and of how the writer faces 'no higher or more noble task' than capturing the core of the 'public-spirited person'; and then, as a result, 'the effective transmission of the personal, spiritual and life experience acquired in the whole people's struggle for the creation of the new just society'.[19]

But that regime also turned viciously on Olga Berggolts. In 1928 she had married Boris Kornilov, and her first daughter, Irina, was born not long afterwards. Her second child, Maya, tragically died before her first birthday. Then, in the mid-1930s, as the great purges engulfed countless innocent lives, the shadows at last overtook her completely. Irina died aged seven, and before Olga had a chance to recover from this trauma she was arrested. The reason? A meeting some years previously with a flinty Bolshevik literary critic called Leopold Averbakh – who himself had ended the careers of other writers for their lack of communist rigour. The time came when the regime judged Averbakh himself insufficiently deferential: he was shot. Olga Berggolts had met him only once. That was enough.

She was pregnant when the secret police came for her. The treatment she received was that meted out to men and women alike: cold wet cells, enforced sleeplessness – and beatings. She had nothing to confess. This was of no interest to her captors. Guilt was predetermined: and in 1937 she remained in that dark prison for seven months. The stress and the injuries destroyed her pregnancy: her third child was stillborn – a death sentence placed on a baby within a womb. How, then, was it conceivably possible for her faith in Bolshevism to be maintained in this dark world?

In the years that followed, she rationalized her political adherence thus: she thought back to that day in 1924 when news of Lenin's death came through. She and her friend Valya had stood numbed with shock in the cold. The teenager suddenly confessed to her friend: 'I have to tell you a terrible secret. I haven't believed in God for a long time already. You know, Valya, he doesn't exist.'[20] Valya knew. They both at that point vowed to join the Komsomol. 'And since then,' wrote Berggolts, elliptically alluding to her nightmare ordeal at the hands of the NKVD, 'this has given me the strength, despite all the misfortunes, to live fully, to live with all my being – this belief that I didn't break my sworn adolescent oath, the consciousness that I belong to the Party, fused with Lenin's name.'[21] By 1941 it appeared that the Party had at last recognized her unswerving loyalty, despite the horror of that stillborn child. She had been rehabilitated. Her poetry – and the faith that pulsated through it – might yet be of use to her fellow citizens.

In this, she would be joined by another, Vera Inber: Inber's own distant family connections to the reviled Trotsky might have been enough to have her killed. She was spared. Already, her talents had been harnessed in the most terrible ways: avowedly proud to be a 'Soviet writer', she was among a group led by Maxim Gorky who had in the early 1930s visited the construction site of the notorious White Sea Canal, and who had then contributed to a book detailing the wonders of this vast engineering project, with a workforce of convicts, where the tundra was shaped to Stalin's will.[22] At no stage in these observations was it noted that these political prisoners were slave labourers with no choice in their fate, and that the death toll among them was enormous. She also made an enthusiastic journey to Uzbekistan, where she documented the lives of female silk workers. She was happy to proclaim in a general sense that communism had boosted the cause of women's equality. There was a streak of determined optimism within her. She addressed a Soviet Writers conference, telling her fellow artists that there had to be more happiness in their literature.

And Vera Inber also had some international cachet by the time of the purges: as other writers were being pulled from their homes, she was permitted to make a limited speaking tour of neighbouring Scandinavian countries. Those who met this 'short slim woman, lively, dark and charming', were impressed by her vivacity.[23] She was middle-aged but taken for a thirty-year-old.

She was also radiantly alive to the beauty of Leningrad: not merely the graceful architecture set on cold water, but also prospects such as the city's botanical gardens, opposite which she lived, and which she would gaze upon as the nightmare of the siege descended. 'The trees are preparing themselves for autumn,' she wrote. 'Already the leaves are gold and scarlet and what a riot of colours there will be in September! From the balcony we can see a huge glasshouse filled with palm trees, there are green lawns and avenues.'[24] In the fight for survival, even the most beautiful landscapes would come to mean nothing. But Leningraders would remain adept in seeking out spiritual succour.

5.   New Gods and Old Believers

Stalin was a jealous god. His image – reproduced on vast banners, hung from Leningrad public buildings, the eyes unreadable, pock-marks smoothed out, the moustached lips nearing a smile – was there to supplant older faiths. He was more than a man: he resembled the elements themselves. 'Like the sun, you have illuminated the expanse,' wrote Dagestan poet Suleiman Stalsky. 'Live like the sun, live for a hundred years!'[1] His chosen name, meaning 'man of steel', deliberately evoked Ossetian folk legends from his own lands, of supermen made of iron.[2] Stalin was a protean figure bestriding a vast land conjured visually in futuristic terms: mighty pipelines stretching and snaking to the horizon, gigantic dams feeding epic hydroelectric plants. He literally brought power to the people: let there be light. Upon his birthday, thousands upon thousands of gifts were sent: offerings, some from ordinary workers genuinely impelled to please him and even perhaps to be noticed by him. It was noted by one cynical city-dwelling woman that the requirement to praise Stalin was 'akin to thanking God for our daily bread'.[3] In Leningrad, there were also banners around the city featuring Andrei Zhdanov – an archangel stationed near Stalin's heavenly throne. These images were modernist icons: echoes of Russian Orthodox piety. That was the faith that Stalin had tried to expropriate, and he wanted its former traces, the images of the old saints, obliterated.

But those old saints were remarkably persistent. They were there within the interiors of the churches. Framed with rich blues and golds, they gazed down upon the people, even when the authorities had made every effort to stop those people looking up. This spark of the old faith, the twitch upon the thread, would be vitally important to large numbers of Leningraders during the blockade.

Throughout the 1920s and 30s, the people had been told that Christianity was a lie: that they and generations before them had been following fairy tales. The method chosen was violence: some 80,000 'Russian Orthodox clerics, monks and nuns' across the nation were murdered.[4] They could not forsake their faith; the Communists could not tolerate any belief whose standards were higher than their own moral code.

Churches were closed; seminaries were shut down. Schools were forbidden to give any kind of religious education, nor could there be any prayers offered or hymns sung or any other token of Russian Orthodoxy exhibited. The intention was that religion would simply be suffocated; a younger generation that knew nothing of God would not be open to the temptation to turn to Him.

Yet Christianity was also an idea, and how does anyone go about completely killing an idea? Moreover, the repression of religion in the early 1930s was in part linked to the brutality of collectivization: both the land and the people had to be remoulded. There was, felt some, 'too much interest in the Russian soul'.[5] Religion had to be expunged because it spoke of a 'shameful backwardness';[6] the primitive belief in supernatural intervention had to be replaced with the diamond light of pure Soviet rationalism. The 1920s saw a new movement burgeoning, one that grew enormously throughout the 1930s: Soyuz Voinstvuyushchikh Bezbozhnikov – the League of the Militant Godless. In Leningrad, as with the rest of the country, it had bases everywhere: factories, offices and most particularly threaded throughout the city's schools and universities. The chief targets for recruitment were the young. And in a darkly amusing inversion of Christian missionaries, these Militant Godless would be sent out among believers, in the city and out into the countryside too, to preach the virtues of non-belief. 'Struggle against religion is a struggle for socialism!' ran the League's chief creed.[7] Given this was a national movement, there was a newspaper, *Bezbozhnik* – Atheist – edited by veteran Bolshevik Yemelyan Yaroslavsky, whose fervid non-belief had been noted back in the early 1920s by Molotov – that was published in languages from Azerbaijani to Uzbek and also Yiddish.

As with any of the religions that it sought to counter, the League found itself becoming splintered into factions and sects, some arguing that religious believers were dangerous class enemies, others favouring more subtle education as opposed to punishment for faith. Nikolay Bukharin, a Marxist cultural theorist and politician, suggested ferocity: religion should be murdered 'at the tip of a bayonet'.[8] Others pressed for the old methods of religious education to be replaced with dialectical materialism (which might have felt like a form of murder to some). To a limited extent in Leningrad, this appeared to work with the very young: they learned dialectical materialism like a catechism: something to be absorbed deeply, and also to be tested upon.

This was the movement that eventually made the mass murder of priests and other clergy possible in the purges of the 1930s (though this did not quite have the purity of traditional religious persecution – every other stratum of society was targeted for this cruelty too). But it also led to some extraordinary moments of the darkest comedy. It was necessary for members of the League, for instance, to enter churches in order to confront and reason with the believers within. However, before so doing, they had to solemnly affirm to each other that they were not in fact secretly planning to worship themselves. The suspicion that their fellow atheists might in fact be harbouring a furtive belief in God haunted many League members, who may have been troubled by their own private stirrings or flurries of faith.[9]

Before the murderous 1930s, the contemplative religious life – slowly being strangled – none the less fascinated some prominent Leningraders. The literary critic Nikolay Punin (by that time immersed in his long common-law marriage with Anna Akhmatova) was beguiled by an institution that lay in the heart of the city: a splendid eighteenth-century citadel of white and pale blue attached to the Smolny Cathedral. This was the Smolny Convent. According to some accounts, it had originally been built for Elizabeth, daughter of Peter the Great: upon learning that she would be denied succession, she opted instead to become a nun, forswearing a colourful love life with a Ukrainian Cossack called Aleksei Razumovsky. (Though the wheel of fortune turned swiftly – the immediate successor, Ivan VI, was deposed and Elizabeth acceded with some triumph to the Russian throne in 1741 – with Razumovsky back on the scene and all the while construction work on the exquisite convent continuing.) The last remaining nuns at the Smolny in the 1920s were distrustful of roaming secular visitors. 'By chance we succeeded in getting beyond the front gates,' Punin wrote in his diary in the high summer of 1925. 'We walked around the church and went out into the garden . . . It is abandoned, wonderful . . . The church was locked, the glass was broken in many places and the colours were faded and peeling. Silence and emptiness.

'All evening I heard the captive voice of this ghost of White Nights,' he continued. 'Then we walked out into the square, which was overgrown with camomile.'[10]

There was that aesthetic sense of fascination with earthly decay and enduring spirituality: precisely the sort of sentiments that the younger rationalists in the Party were seeking to extinguish. (This sense was sharpened as he also visited the Sheremetev Convent at Borisovka near Belgorod: 'The crosses have been torn off the churches, and every kind of violence has been committed,' wrote Punin. 'They mock the nuns in every way . . . They cut out the eyes of the icon of St German.')[11]

Belief was one thing: a bourgeois weakness for beauty was another. And the additional element of religious temptation in Leningrad was the majesty and splendour of so many of its churches. Quite apart from the hypnotic colours and superb art within the Church of the Saviour on Spilled Blood, there were sites such as the magnificently baroque Church of the Kazan Mother of God, the Cathedral of Saints Boris and Gleb and also the richly detailed Church of the Dormition (known as Saviour on the Haymarket, a location that had formed part of the landscape of Dostoevsky's fiction). In the case of the Saviour on Spilled Blood – and also of the imperious Kazan Cathedral, both in the heart of the city – the authorities worked to repurpose the structures as museums. The exhibits – and the careful labelling – were intended to portray religion in primitive anthropological terms. In the case of other churches, the authorities were in some cases in favour of demolition.

But here was an aesthetic quandary for Leningrad's intelligentsia: even in Stalinist times, as modernist architects constructed exciting new industrial works, flats, and even bathhouses, it was held by many that the city's eighteenth-century religious architecture none the less stood as monuments to Russian artistry and industry: architecture that did not speak of a shameful backwardness but rather of ingenuity and creativity; a sense of beauty that did not cast any scornful shadows on the city's newer Soviet buildings. Those glittering domes, those rich blue intricate mosaics, those vaults and buttresses and vast arches suggested not only God and the saints, but also a certain brilliance of engineering that could in its own way be inspiring. Thus it was that structures such as the great rounded baroque mausoleum at the Church of the Kazan Mother of God evaded the bulldozers and the pickaxes.

Nor could the religious impulse in Leningrad's individuals be so easily extinguished; and for a time, the authorities relented. In 1936 an article was added to the updated Soviet Constitution that appeared to guarantee 'freedom of religious worship'.[12] This carried particular weight in Leningrad, where the religious diversity, even amid the uniformity of Stalinism, was remarkable. As well as Russian Orthodox and Jewish worshippers, there were 'Lutherans, Baptists and Seventh Day Adventists'.[13] There was also a mosque. (In addition to all these was the presence in the countryside of the Old Believers: a sect of the Orthodox faith that had rejected seventeenth-century reforms and held fast to older rituals and beliefs, from chanting to immersive baptisms. By tradition, they despised Petersburg, with its wide variety of sin: even the painting of portraits was forbidden in their religion. But they were regarded by nineteenth-century Petersburg artists such as the composer Mussorgsky as being 'authentic Russians'.[14] Recent years have seen greater respect being shown to Old Believer communities.)

In Tsarist days, there had been some 500 Orthodox churches in and around St Petersburg. By the mid-1930s, only around fifty of these were left; and following the apparent loosening of strictures on 'religious worship' in that updated constitution,[15] the city's authorities none the less determined to shut down all remaining churches: the crowds that gathered before and inside them were in some ways a regular rebuke to their own earthly dominion. Moreover, the last terrible waves of the Great Terror claimed more church personnel as its victims, including 'psalm readers'.[16] The Leningrad purge of religion could hardly have been more thorough. And yet the flame continued to burn.

It was found flickering in a late 1930s nationwide census, for instance, when 57 per cent of respondents nationwide declared themselves believers in the Orthodox faith. And here perhaps was a crux, for while the city's powers could move against the great physical structures of churches, they could not systematically enter every single home. And vast numbers of these dwellings, some with more elderly residents, had heirloom icons in the corners with lamps in front of them – the large eyes of the saints believed to be quite literally windows into heaven.

And in the matter of fairy tales, it was true for some – especially those who still had a foot in the countryside – that Russian Orthodox beliefs were sometimes commingled with more pagan superstitions. By 1941 there was a tacit and grudging acknowledgement from the Kremlin that perhaps – if closely regulated – there might still be room in this world for the old God.

But while private icons and incense, hidden from the public gaze, might just about have been tolerated, one of the city's most distinguishing aural characteristics was silenced ruthlessly by the Stalinists: the bells of old St Petersburg – which had hung in the belfries of all the grand cathedrals and all the Orthodox churches (and of which the deep, rich clangour had been commemorated in a symphony by the Petersburg-educated composer Sergei Rachmaninov) – were torn out. For Orthodox believers, this was as much an act of blasphemy as the tearing up of holy books: according to the priests, the music of the bells was quite simply the voice of God. As the eyes of icons were windows through which Paradise could be glimpsed, so the bells were the sound of the Creator speaking directly to the faithful.[17] The music was symbolic of the trumpets that would sound on Mount Sinai when the day of the Final Judgement was at hand. For the Communists, such ideas were unendurable, and unlike in the French revolution, when bells were removed and yet kept intact, the bells of the Soviet Union were instead beaten and broken and melted down and turned to industrial purpose. Symbolically, some of the grander examples would become tractor parts.[18] (Osip Mandelstam used the bells of St Petersburg as an emblem of stability and sanity; their removal could only mean derangement. 'Someone has pulled the bells/ out of the blurred tower.')[19]

Russian Orthodoxy was not the only religion practised in the city. Still present on the island of the Petrogradsky district, just across the Neva from the centre of St Petersburg, is the large mosque that was originally built in 1913, at a time when St Petersburg had a small but active Muslim population of about 8,000. The minarets reach fifty metres into the sky and the interior features hypnotic deep blue and turquoise mosaics.[20] Possibly because there were so many fewer worshippers involved, the Leningrad regime did not fully focus its anti-religious campaign against Islam until the late 1930s, after the flood of the great purges had swept through the city. It was only in 1940 – as the war with Finland was underway – that the city's authorities banned services in the mosque. Then, as the city's crisis began in 1941, the building would be turned to an entirely different purpose, though unlike so many Orthodox structures it was not threatened with demolition.

There was also the Grand Choral Synagogue, along with a few others dotted throughout the city. Ever since the Tsarist days (a time elsewhere in the Russian empire of terrifying pogroms, from Kyiv to Warsaw though, strikingly, not in St Petersburg) the Jewish population here had always been relatively high compared with many other Russian cities. By 1939 there were some 200,000 Jews in a population of nearly three million. 'Jews were well represented in several professions, including law, medicine, teaching, journalism and retail trade,' noted historian Richard Bidlack.[21] And to an extent, there was assimilation. Yet anti-Semitism was always present, even if it did not take the form of murderous violence erupting on the streets. Hatred of Jews was 'the most common form of expression of ethnic hostility in Leningrad', wrote historian Sarah Davies.[22] It festered on factory production lines, where some workers were heard to exclaim that Jewish people used ruses to avoid having to do hard manual jobs: instead, it was said, they insinuated themselves into the more comfortable managerial positions. They were also 'constantly identified with a ruling elite, which included Party members, state servants and the Soviet intelligentsia'.[23]

There was perhaps also an element of truth in the idea that there were large numbers of Jewish artists and writers in Leningrad: yet no one could surely deny the glowing lustre of the talent that had taken them to those positions. The Grand Choral Synagogue, built in the late nineteenth century, had spoken of a certain rising confidence: it embraced a fusion of Moorish, Baroque and Byzantine styles.

Before the outbreak of the Second World War, the city authorities were actively considering turning the entire synagogue into a children's theatre. Those same authorities might have argued that they were not motivated by anti-Semitism; that they were equally keen to extinguish all the lights of the Christian faith. They might even have pointed to secular instances when they sought to punish the more egregious and demotic outbreaks of anti-Jewish feeling in the city. In 1929 there was an intriguing trial in Leningrad. The accused were the residents of a communal tenement block and the charge was harassment and persecution of their Jewish neighbour, Sonya Chaevskaya, who was alleged to have 'lost her mind' as a result of their repeated menaces.[24] 'Her neighbours were in the habit of standing in her doorway at five in the morning,' went one report. They were shouting: '*zhidovskaya morda*', a hideous term roughly translating as 'kike face'. In addition to this, they blocked her from access to the building's sole source of running water.[25]

There could never be any justification, but one explanation for that and other localized outbreaks of anti-Semitism was that it arose from former agricultural workers, used to dwelling in monocultural communities, and unable to adjust to the differences that they found in urban life.

Faith took different forms. It did not always need churches. 'We were raised in Soviet times,' recalled tank regiment recruit Henrikh Dudnik, who was based just outside the city in Pushkin. 'The young people were all patriotic. I made an inscription on my tank that read 'For the Motherland'.[26] His faith was in technological progress. Elsewhere in the Red Army was a brilliant general – an artillery expert – called Leonid Govorov. The day would come when he would be key to Leningrad's future, and it would be at that time that his own Russian Orthodox faith would suddenly be manifested in a crystalline light.

The city itself – whether as Leningrad, Petrograd or St Petersburg – had always had a faintly pagan undertow as well: encouraged by popular stories of men haunted by doppelgängers in those thick Baltic fogs, or the feverish pacing of Dostoevsky's Raskolnikov in *Crime and Punishment*, witnessing silent suicides from canal bridges. The numinous and eerie atmosphere of the city's thoroughfares – 'Petersburg streets . . . turn passers-by into shadows; while Petersburg streets turn shadows into people', as author Andrei Bely observed[27] – might have been a psychological symptom or reflection of instability and insecurity. This, after all, was the city which sparked a revolution that would echo around the world.

6. The Blood of Saint Petersburg

The people saw nothing strange in the mingling of beauty and death. Perhaps this was an element in their unusual resilience. St Petersburg's history, the city's very foundations, had been shaped by violent events through the centuries. It was as if the rich splendour of the palaces, the glow of the theatres, were underscored by a continuous insistent sense of mortality. Violence was hardly unique to Leningrad as a city; yet it was unusual in forming so vivid a part of its historic understanding of itself. This extended to assassinations, to mutinies, from a dismembered Tsar to a gothically slaughtered shaman, and thence to revolution and all its agonizing aftershocks. It was a city of unusual, sometimes uncanny passion. This was natural, and this was life.

The bloody end of one of the city's most emblematic figures – Alexander Pushkin – was taught to all of Leningrad's children as a lurid example of courage and stoicism. They were taught about the white snow starkly blotched with crimson, the blood issuing from Pushkin's side, so hot that the snow hissed. The greatest writer in Russia – one of the world's greatest – had been shot. Yet even in his agony, he somehow managed to pull himself upwards, pull his pistol from the snow and fire back, wounding his opponent.

This had been in a duel in 1837. By 1941, Pushkin and his work and his death were being reframed as part of a new nationalist morale-building exercise. The gunshot that ended his life was one of a series of historic incidents that were to be understood as symbolizing endurance and suffering. And thanks to Stalin, Pushkin – a writer with direct African lineage who delighted in his own 'African strangeness' – had been elevated almost to the status of a secular saint. Pushkin was born in 1799 and lived his life under the alternating displeasure and favour of the Tsar. And his work was frequently suffused with an element of the macabre. He was St Petersburg's first prominent example of what the critic George Steiner called 'conscience under despotism'.[1]

His best-known work, *Eugene Onegin*, a novel in verse form, first serialized, then published in full in 1833, evoked a world that must have seemed dazzlingly alien to his later twentieth-century Soviet readers. Onegin is a wealthy St Petersburg dilettante who forms an intense friendship with a young poet called Lensky and subsequently, in a tragic series of events, involving the sisters Olga and Tatyana, kills Lensky in a snowy pre-dawn duel. 'The poet stops/ And silently his pistol drops,' wrote Pushkin. 'He lays a hand, as in confusion/ On breast, and falls. His misted eyes/ Express not pain, but death's intrusion./ Thus, slowly, down a sloping rise/ And sparkling in the sunlight's shimmer/ A clump of snow will fall and glimmer.'[2]

The doomed romanticism of duels haunted Russian culture in the early nineteenth century. Impulsive Pushkin had himself been in thirty such encounters (despite their illegality), ultimately without shots being fired. But his death at the hand of French officer Georges d'Anthès (who was serving in the Russian Guard) in February 1837 was gruelling and strung out. The scene itself might have been a remarkable reminder of *Onegin*: the starlit pre-dawn Petersburg sky, the snow in the darkness of that forest clearing. But as the duel got underway, romance turned to visceral nightmare. D'Anthès fired first, and the bullet entered Pushkin's lower abdomen. It passed through his intestines but failed to exit through his back. In the initial shock, he was able to grab for his dropped pistol, wipe the snow off it and take aim at his opponent. The bullet caught d'Anthès in the arm; the wound was slight.

It was clear, however, that Pushkin was in a serious state. Friends carried him back to his apartment near the Winter Palace; a doctor was summoned. The bullet could be felt under the flesh of his back. Pushkin was told that there was nothing that could be done. He made ready for death, sending word to Tsar Nicholas asking for forgiveness and also beseeching that his wife be looked after financially. The request was granted. Pushkin's final night was one of horror: the bullet, having burned through so much soft tissue, caused peritonitis and he spent his last hours in agony. By morning, he was dead.

Pushkin had had his revolutionary enthusiasms. The writer had backed the so-called Decembrists. These were army officers – educated, aristocratic – who loathed the Tsarist system of serfdom. They rose up in St Petersburg on 26 December 1825, but their number was insufficient for the revolt to depose Nicholas and they were all rounded up, with many being sent into Siberian exile. Pushkin's fervent support, conveyed in letters to Decembrist friends, earned him the Tsar's anger and a long period down south in the Caucasus, but also a place in Russian revolutionary tradition.

This was duly noted by Stalin, who had always admired and never abjured Pushkin's work. And as Soviet Russia in the twentieth century squared up to the fresh prospect of war, a heated conversation on a Leningrad train in the late 1930s illustrated where Pushkin stood in the Soviet imagination. There had been a sing-song at the end of the carriage: an old Russian folk tune (of the type that had not been encouraged by the Soviet regime, on the grounds of its backward-looking nostalgia). It prompted one man to tell the group: 'You sing well, but it's old stuff – he who thinks of the past is a fool.'

'But he who forgets the past is a bigger fool,' responded another.

The first complainer felt he had to explain his ideological stance. 'But you're wrong in saying that,' he told the singer. 'We need cheerfulness for our new way of life and look what you're doing. You're resurrecting the past. Forget the past.'

The singer could not agree: 'What about Pushkin?'

The complainer was only too pleased to explain. 'Pushkin was an isolated case,' he said. 'Pushkin managed to foresee our time way back then and stood for it. He was an exception.'[3]

'Pushkin is ours!' went the official declarations in 1937, on the hundredth anniversary of his death.[4] After years in which his work had been comparatively neglected, Stalin – who had profounder reading tastes than many might have credited him with – was anxious that Soviet Russia should celebrate and embrace a literary hero who could be viewed as a genius on the level of Dante or Goethe or Shakespeare. 'It is only in a country of socialist culture that the name of the immortal genius is surrounded with ardent love,' the proclamation continued. 'It is only in our country that Pushkin's works have become a treasure for all people.'[5] There was a vivid socialist realist poster: a boy and a girl, seated, smiling, with a copy of Pushkin's collected works before them.

Elsewhere, the memory of violent attempted revolution – the repeated echo through the years of the Decembrists and those who followed them – was also inherent in the fabric of Leningrad's most startling architectural monument: the Church of the Saviour on Spilled Blood. This was both a temple and a curious shrine to murder. It was built from 1883 onwards, on the precise site where in 1881 a revolutionary faction apprehended the coach of Tsar Alexander II and succeeded in assassinating him. Their aim had been to overturn the monarchy, yet the results of their actions were instead to bring further oppression, paranoia and state brutality to the streets of St Petersburg for decades to come. There was a direct line of continuity between the revolutionary socialist faction that plotted the assassination and the granite-eyed officials in Stalin's time who in their turn sought to destroy all counter-revolutionaries.

That faction, formed in 1879, was called Narodnaya Volya (The People's Will), and concentrated its activities on the poorer streets of St Petersburg. Its members – women and men alike – were intellectuals and happy to proclaim that they sought to create terror within the heart of the ruling establishment. Theirs was not a movement of words: they were instead dedicated to direct action. Any of their number killed while carrying out attacks would be termed martyrs.

Out in the countryside, the serfs had nominally been freed; their 'emancipation' had come in 1861. To this end, Alexander II had been seen as a reformer. But the members of Narodnaya Volya could look west across Europe and discern that this was a modernizing, industrial world: Russian peasants, no matter how emancipated, were still living in conditions closer to the fourteenth century than the nineteenth. They might no longer have been the property of the landowners, but they were still used as though they were.

Narodnaya Volya looked at the peasant villages and saw within their lives the possible seed of socialism. Without the dark shadows of the landowners looming over them, they would have structures of equality: the peasant commune, an organic and natural way of life, untarnished by the vampiric demands of aristocracy and capitalism. And so it was – paradoxically – within the teeming streets of St Petersburg, near the reeking Sennaya Square hay market, that ideas of 'land and liberty' began to take a grip within this secret society (at a time when there was no shortage of socialist secret societies elsewhere within the city). 'The People's Will' was to be exerted with bombs.

From the group's inception, its target had been Alexander II himself. Killing the Tsar, they theorized, would be the catalyst for the speedy dissolution of the entire Russian aristocratic system. Its Executive Committee – among whom were Andrei Zhelyabov (a legally trained travelling activist) and Sofiya Perovskaya (a young aristocrat whose father had been the military governor of St Petersburg) – met frequently to fathom how the assassination might be carried out.

On 13 March 1881 the group was ready. It was Nikolay Rysakov who stood ready with the first bomb, wrapped in a handkerchief. A red-haired twenty-year-old engineering student, Rysakov was prepared to give his life to take that of the emperor. He threw the bomb under the carriage as it passed. It detonated; one of the Cossacks riding behind the carriage was caught up in the blast and died immediately. A baker's boy, standing nearby, was badly injured. But the Tsar's coach had suffered only minimal damage. In the moments of shock and silence that followed the blast, the Tsar emerged from the vehicle. Rysakov called out to one of his comrades for help but was seized immediately by the Tsar's retinue.

The vicinity was filled with potential killers and Alexander's entourage implored him not to leave the shelter of the coach but, possibly in shock, he could not resist going to look at both the injured and the apprehended Rysakov. The Tsar was asked how he was. 'Thank God I am unharmed,' he said.[6] It was in this moment of vulnerability that the man regarded as the world's first suicide bomber stepped forward.

Ignacy Hryniewiecki – like Rysakov a young engineering student in St Petersburg, but himself descended from minor Polish nobility – had been preparing for this moment for a long time. He knew that, for the plan to succeed, he would have to be close enough to be taken apart in the resulting explosion himself. The night before he had written a final testament: 'Alexander II must die,' he proclaimed. 'He will die, and with him, we, his enemies, his executioners, shall die too . . .

How many more sacrifices will our unhappy country ask of its sons before it is liberated?'[7] The emperor had just given thanks to God. 'It is too soon to thank God yet,' declared Hryniewiecki.[8] Raising both arms, he then smashed his own bomb down at the Tsar's feet.

One bystander was killed immediately, some twenty others badly wounded. The Tsar crumpled to the ground. His legs were shattered – flesh and bone beneath the knee had been shredded. His abdomen had also been punctured. His face was a mass of blood. His assassin lay by his side, also mortally injured. As the Tsar's retinue gently bore him up, he was able to tell them: 'Take me to the palace. There I will die.'[9] And as they hurriedly transported him back to the Winter Palace, his killer was taken to an infirmary.

The Tsar was carried to his study, to where an Orthodox priest was summoned to perform the last rites. His suffering was brief; not much more than an hour after the explosion, he passed away upon his couch. His killer lingered a little longer in his final throes. In vain, officials sought to interrogate the young man; either through flickering consciousness, or through extraordinary defiance, he would not answer any of their questions. None the less, the network was being swiftly uncovered.

When rounded up, the various members of Narodnaya Volya – young women and young men alike – faced hostile trials. Five of the men were taken to regimental parade grounds where they were shown a mass gibbet: they were all to be hanged together in public. One other young woman who was part of the group – Hesya Helfman – would have faced the same fate were it not for the fact that she was pregnant. Instead, her sentence was commuted to exile and forced labour – as it turned out, itself a form of prolonged death sentence. She would eventually succumb to illness and her baby daughter would die not long afterwards.

Instead of dissolving the structure of the Russian aristocracy, with its cruelty and tyranny, the assassination brought to St Petersburg a prolonged period of fear as the new Tsar's secret police instituted a surveillance state. And there arose in the centre of the city the Church of the Saviour on Spilled Blood. As well as being an aesthetic marvel, it also contained a literal shrine to the Tsar, and the very stones upon which his blood had spilled. The church's exterior was a fantasia of Old Russia, based closely upon the seventeenth-century Yaroslav churches. The outer walls were decorated with heraldic symbols, each denoting a different region of that vast land. The extraordinary onion domes – striped turquoise and cream, or dotted with other colours, were created using vitreous enamel. There was a golden onion dome too, which glittered and flashed on the city's skyline. Within the church – and its intricate, wall-covering mosaics of saints and icons – there was a floor of richest Italian marble. Above the exact point at which Alexander was mortally wounded was a canopy fashioned from jasper, topaz and the mesmeric blue of lapis lazuli. And deep within this blazingly colourful interior lay the shrine: a ciborium, so-called, where the original pavement upon which the Tsar's blood had poured was preserved, not after being moved there but having had this astounding structure built all around it.

Late nineteenth-century St Petersburg became, for so many, a city of suspicion and fear, monitored by a secret police force called the Okhrana and punctuated with random outbreaks of state-sanctioned violence. As the city's industry expanded, and as ever-larger workforces were drawn from the wide countryside, so too grew up a teeming subterranean culture of dissident groups publishing forbidden leaflets and newspapers with the aim of kindling revolt. Aleksandr Ulyanov – the brother of Vladimir Lenin – was hanged in St Petersburg in 1887, accused of conspiring to assassinate Tsar Alexander III.

Vladimir was at that stage seventeen years old. He had come to the city to study law. It was in St Petersburg that his deeper, more passionate research revolved around his discovery of Marx. He graduated, and thence immediately slipped into St Petersburg's shadowed realm of hermetic activist groups, distributing leaflets among the vast workforces at the city's factories and foundries. Yet – as he must have known from the fate of his executed brother – he himself was being shadowed. In 1895 the authorities acted upon his sedition, and he was arrested and convicted. His sentence: three years in exile in the tundra of Siberia. Also sentenced was Nadezhda Krupskaya, noted earlier for having introduced large numbers of workers to after-hours education. This had involved more than mathematics and literacy. She too was condemned to Siberia, and it was there that the relationship between the pair bloomed.

Back in St Petersburg, the icy brutality of the authorities was intensifying, and so too were the tensions in the factories. There had been strike actions throughout the last years of the nineteenth century, and they had had some success. Employers had to guarantee a measure of safety amid vast plants filled with dangerous machinery; in the 1890s, there came the eye-rubbing success of limiting the working day to a maximum of eleven and a half hours. But the negative side of these victories was an ever more hostile political and imperial establishment.

Then, in the frozen December of 1904, the mighty Putilov Works had been the scene of a vast walk-out: a strike that had left the proudly electrified city without power in the twilight snows. The industrial action had been sparked by the firing of six workers who had belonged to the Assembly of the Russian Factory and Mill Workers of the City of St Petersburg.

By the early weeks of 1905, amid city-wide bread shortages, that mass sense of resentment was growing further. One of the figures at its centre, attempting to harness and direct the energy of all the anger, was an enigmatic Russian Orthodox priest with a charismatic manner. Father Georgii Gapon was – curiously – at the heart of the Assembly of Factory Workers. A striking figure with long dark hair, Gapon had been organizing factory labourers for some time. He was a source of especial fascination to skilled engineers and mechanics: he in turn relished recruiting literate men, who knew their Russian classics inside out, who would then preach his word to colleagues who had yet to taste this finer education. There were demands that the Orthodox father had to make of the Tsarist regime: in a petition that he drafted with elegance, these included a further reduction in the length of the working day to eight hours, improved wages and improved working conditions. These in themselves might not have been regarded as an existential threat to the regime, but the cleric was also calling for votes for all, and for those votes to be directed towards a meaningful parliament.

This manifesto, or petition, had been crafted within his own headquarters and, although its ambitions were a blast of modernism, its essential form would have been recognizable hundreds of years previously in Russia: humble petitions submitted to the Tsar with a plea that he look upon them with favour.

And Gapon was careful to let the St Petersburg authorities know how the petition would be presented: a procession, or march, through the city to the Winter Palace on 22 January 1905, in order that it might be put before the Tsar himself. Unfortunately, the day before the planned event, the Tsar had left for his nearby residence at Tsarskoe Selo. No one in authority saw fit to tell the Orthodox priest, but those same authorities had ensured that large numbers of mounted soldiers were posted around the Winter Palace. The fear that more intense unrest might be sparked was pervasive.

On the snowy morning of 22 January, just before dawn when that snow was silver blue under the wide, cold skies, Gapon's workers began to assemble at key points in St Petersburg. Yet a chasm had opened up between these thousands of workers – there were suggestions that as the dawn gave way to day, they had been joined by many tens of thousands of other citizens – and the 10,000 or so troops who were ordered to halt their progress before the square of the Winter Palace.

The ever-swelling numbers of people marched forward ineluctably, and now, at various points near the Winter Palace, as they tramped through the snow and along the banks of the steel-grey Neva, they were faced with troops pointing guns and bayonets at them. One group, following Father Gapon, were assembling around the Narva Gate, a triumphal arch of stone that had been built to commemorate Russia's victory over Napoleon. It was here, on that frozen January morning, that the first shots were fired; what then followed throughout the day was an irrational whirlwind of bloodletting; for many other St Petersburgers, walking the city on an ordinary winter shopping day, there was now a spectacle of death: mounted Cossacks slashing flesh with sabres. Several hundred people lay dead, bleeding in the snow. This day marked the first stage of the gradual unravelling of Romanov rule.

As Father Gapon, now a very obvious target for the secret police, was helped to flee the city by the writer Maxim Gorky,[10] the flame of revolution was kindled from Moscow to Baku. What then followed was a months-long nationwide series of industrial strikes: serious and crippling, cutting power, halting railways, closing factories. Tsar Nicholas II would initially only go so far as to describe what became known as 'Bloody Sunday' as a very 'sad day'.[11] But the industrial stoppages were intense, and portended worse for the regime, and for a while he felt forced to compromise. He promised some form of functioning Duma, or parliament. At the same time, however, the secret police extended their grip of paranoid surveillance and torture. The lever had been pulled, the shades drawn back: light had flooded in upon the nature of Russia's autocracy. The chances of any future demonstration of workers crying 'God save the Tsar' were vanishingly unlikely.

It was the workers of St Petersburg who had changed the nature of Russian reality. The Tsar was no longer the godhead. By the time the wider conflict of global war came a few years later, only the most iron-headed conservatives could believe that he was.

Among the multitude of fissures and ruptures created by that global war, the renaming of Russia's capital city was one of the more arrestingly symbolic developments. Petersburg was too Germanic (the city, incidentally, had long been a second home to a thriving German community), and so the more emphatically Russian 'Petrograd' was adopted instead. The miseries of the war – the wet, freezing trenches a thousand miles from the sometimes romanticized images of the Napoleonic conflicts a hundred years earlier – were pulling the young men of the city into a conflict that appeared to have no fathomable conclusion other than annihilation. The rechristened Petrograd was still busy with vehicles and commerce, but all activity was being pointed towards the war effort. There was exhaustion, and a sense that violence and death were being visited upon millions of families for no easily discernible reason other than a miserable effort to merely survive.

★

In this city, poised on the border between a modernist future and a feudal past, it would not take much for the smouldering embers of revolution to flame once more. It was fitting – given the city's hallucinatory legends and stories – that Petersburg's monarchy should be fatally weakened by an unsettling figure who was a fusion of corrupt politics, sexual promiscuity, arcane religion and – to onlookers – an element of the supernatural.

His nickname was Grisha. For some years, this mendicant figure – robed, long-haired, piercing-eyed – had been fulfilling the role in St Petersburg of 'holy fool'. Holy fools (or 'fools for Christ's sake') were Russian religious men – descended perhaps from very much older Byzantine traditions, and a distinct feature of the medieval Russian landscape – who had not been conventionally ordained and who were yet invited into aristocratic households to provide mystic guidance. The reason they were accepted was that their provenance stretched back to Paul and the Corinthians: the Corinthians, measured in their faith, contrasted with Paul, who stood outside polite society. 'We are fools for Christ's sake, but you are wise in Christ. We are weak, but you are strong. You are held in honour, but we in disrepute.'[12] The Pauline 'holy fool' was thus understood as frequently seeming mad, impetuous and filthy. Holy fools might be drunks; they might engage in acts of startling transgression. Yet it was in their ungovernability that their paradoxical religious wisdom lay.

Such figures had been chronicled by Tolstoy, whose own family had played host to such a man. They survived as archetypes well into the twentieth century, even as the landscapes and estates that they haunted were suffused with the bright rays of electricity. But the man known as Grisha – who had spent his earlier life tramping from monastery to monastery, and then from grand estate to grand estate – had risen to the very heights of St Petersburg society.

As the war ground on, Grisha – better known then and now as Grigorii Rasputin, the 'mad monk' who was actually neither of these – was firmly enveloped at the very heart of the regal imperial household of Tsar Nicholas and his wife, Alexandra. Born in 1869 in Siberia, Rasputin had originally worked on a farm; he had married, and fathered three children. But in 1892 he had taken himself to a monastery. He did not receive holy orders, but none the less had transformed into an unorthodox holy man. Thus began his career of travelling from estate to estate, offering spiritual succour. By 1906, he was in St Petersburg.

Rasputin was not the royal household's first holy fool: they had seen many such men. Yet from the start the imperial couple considered him different and were bewitched. It would not be long before the Tsarina was asking him for spiritual advice on a much wider range of affairs, including politics and the governance of the country.

Rasputin famously maintained the tightest hold over Empress Alexandra because of his apparently supernatural ability to counter her son Aleksei's haemophilia. As with many other holy fools, Rasputin led a life of sharp duality, seducing smart society women and drinking prodigious quantities of spirits. This is what was expected of such a figure. What was not expected was for him to loom increasingly large over the political decision-making of the Tsar, especially during a grinding, horrifying war in which Russian casualties – by 1916 nearing five million – were on a scale beyond comprehension.

It was a St Petersburg aristocrat, Prince Felix Yusupov, who was married to the Tsar's niece, who conceived the idea of murdering Rasputin. Partly it was motivated by outrage and vengefulness, but it was also to do with a keen perception that the Tsar's rule was on the edge of a precipice. And the legend of Rasputin's assassination was burnished by Prince Yusupov's later account; he suggested that he had helped to slay a demon.[13] This in turn added an extra layer to the mysterious reputation of St Petersburg. According to Yusupov, Rasputin, invited to the Moika Palace in the midwinter darkness of 30 December 1916, and sitting among a group of nobles, was first served with cakes accompanied by great quantities of decanted wine. The cakes and the wine were heavily infused with potassium cyanide, the expected effect of which would be speedy paralysis, asphyxiation and agonizing, breathless heart failure.

The scene became instantly famous for its gothic intensity: the glaring-eyed holy fool devouring the cakes and wine, his hosts looking on . . . and their anticipation turning to astonishment (and superstitious horror) when it became apparent that the poison had had no effect. Yusupov called in desperation for the Grand Duke's revolver and shot Rasputin at close range several times. And yet still he would not die. Yusupov, who wrote an account of these extraordinary scenes in 1927, recalled: 'This devil who was dying of poison, who had a bullet in his heart, must have been raised from the dead by the powers of evil. There was something appalling and monstrous in his diabolical refusal to die.'[14]

Ultimately, it fell to some of the younger aristocrats to overcome the still mighty Rasputin, to bear him outside. From there they conveyed him all the way from the palace to the River Neva, and in the ice-black of that midwinter night the mad monk was consigned to the freezing waters, from which his corpse was recovered not long afterwards.

A matter of weeks later the world was watching, as on a camera obscura, the bloodshed of the revolution as the Romanov dynasty was deposed. Next to the five million or so lives that had been extinguished in the grim trenches of Europe, what fascination could 'anarchy' on the streets of Petrograd in February 1917 hold for those outside Russia? But it was that very suggestion of anarchy that disturbed: if it could happen there – in the city of Peter the Great – then where else might such disorder manifest? The establishment of the Provisional Government, led first by Prince Georgii Lvov and then by Alexander Kerensky, suggested a new equilibrium, and it had the support of the Mensheviks, the Marxist party that had split with the Bolsheviks over the pure form that revolution should take, and which led the Petrograd Soviet, representing the city's workers, throughout much of that year. But the First World War continued, Russian soldiers carried on fighting, and in Petrograd there was hunger: food was in pitifully short supply and it appeared to many as though revolution had changed nothing.

The October 1917 triumph of Lenin and the Bolsheviks over the Provisional Government – coming after weeks of unease and random violence in the city (looting, men psychopathically firing volleys of bullets randomly into crowds and thereafter being lynched) – was better understood to the wider world as pivotal. Blood might have been shed, but here it had purpose, and drama, and heroism, in sharp contrast to a war being fought across dead European landscapes. 'The revolution screamed like a newborn baby,' wrote Olga Berggolts, who as a seven-year-old girl was transfigured by the shifting of the world.[15] 'Here it is, the revolutionary city in its time of troubles, hungry, depraved, frightened, absurd, emergent, powerful and drunk,' wrote Nikolay Punin in his diaries before it became clear that Lenin and the Bolsheviks were about to secure power. 'The revolutionary Nevsky Prospekt; the capital of a great people in a time of troubles.'[16]

Revolution unfolded, and the wider world stared on as the majesty of the Winter Palace was stormed – or opened up at last to the workers, depending upon perspective. On 7 November, as the cruiser *Aurora*, which was anchored on the Neva and under the command of Bolshevik naval personnel, trained its guns upon the eighteenth-century walls of the Palace, those within – the remnants of the Provisional Government – prepared themselves for submission. Some, in the course of exiting the building, found themselves facing Lenin's Red Guards with guns cocked. The Bolsheviks had already found a way in. 'The Maximalists [as the Bolsheviks were also termed] have occupied the Winter Palace and the premises of the Army General Staff in Petrograd,' reported the correspondent of *The Times*.[17]

Other newspaper correspondents hinted darkly at the fate that awaited many of the women soldiers loyal to the government who were taken down to the lower floors of the Winter Palace. There were bullet-ridden casualties around the building. At a time of such global violence, how would it have been possible for the new Soviet regime not to have been infected with the same contagion?

Yet for the modest quantity of blood that was spilled in the streets and at the Winter Palace among Red Guards and the troops defending what scraps remained of the Provisional Government (Kerensky having fled), there were even greater quantities of vintage red wine flowing down the roads – the consequence of the palace's cellars being discovered, and the liberation of a seemingly unlimited supply of Château d'Yquem, taken outside the walls and splashed around in the icy streets. The established order of things had been inverted, and the residents of Petrograd were witnessing a spectacle that was unfolding like street theatre.

But as Menshevik Julius Martov observed: 'the monster tasted hot human blood';[18] and after a post-revolution assassination attempt on Lenin in 1918, so began the Red Terror: a mirror image of Tsarist terror, with the same paraphernalia of forbidding prisons, torture with truncheons and whips (official floggings had stopped but the barbarity would continue when it came to the interrogation of counter-revolutionaries), execution and flame-consumed corpses. Now the Bolshevik secret police, the Cheka, were instituting a blood-hunt of perceived anti-Bolsheviks. 'As for the rest, we have nothing to say to them,' observed Lenin's close comrade Grigorii Zinoviev. 'They must be annihilated.'[19] The annihilation would become mutual: four years of nationwide civil war, piling atrocity upon atrocity.

Meanwhile, the revolution itself was restaged as real theatre several years later, in 1920: *The Storming of the Winter Palace* was re-enacted, this time with over a hundred dancers, as well as actors and innumerable extras, all this time outside the walls of the Palace. This celebration was revolution as *son et lumière*. Its purpose in part was education but it also reflected an innate theatricality in the very personality of the city itself; the exquisite architecture of Peter the Great's vision had largely defied a political earthquake that should have levelled it. These were structures that spoke not of equality, but rather of an intense aesthetic superiority. It was very soon after the Bolshevik revolution that Petrograd ceased to be the capital of Russia; Lenin moved it instead to Moscow. But there was a certain defiance in the city's historical grandeur.

The years between internal revolution and a second global conflict brought little peace; but there was a new generation of children being born in what was now Leningrad who knew nothing but the socialist world; for them – the girls and boys who studied, who enrolled in the city's many technical schools, who were assiduous about attending to their contemplation of dialectical materialism – there was no disorder, but rather progress. By the summer of 1941, with the carefully landscaped parks and gardens flourishing and full of lilac blooms, and the old men seated at tables outside in the grander squares, playing chess, Leningrad was also the city in Russia that had held hardest to its great theatrical traditions. And even with the shadow of atrocity moving closer, and the deeper darkness of Stalin's cruelties still lingering, one of the great traditions of resilience – laughter – was still, incredibly, thriving.

7. 'Life has become merrier'

For the soldiers based on the plateaus and in the forests around the city in the spring of 1941 – many quite young, and still adjusting to the shock of hard training – there were the expected preoccupations: sex (and the unavailability thereof, aching yearnings confessed to diaries); monstrous commanding officers and their elaborately sadistic routines and rituals; and the vacant hours in cold tents and foxholes. But there was also an unexpected appetite among many: for laughter. The absurdities that sometimes emerged in training (Leningrad-based Yakov Pikus recalled learning anti-aircraft-gun techniques by being made to fire at a sort of intestinal tarpaulin pipeline being drawn high through the sky behind a plane, which he came to find compulsively amusing)[1] could render men helpless with mirth. When the war got underway, this vein of mordant comedy would be addressed in print with the hugely popular creation of Vasilii Tyorkin, a fictional everyman Red Army soldier (his adventures written in instalments by Aleksandr Tvardovsky), who even through the toughest ordeals of combat contrived to be wry and witty.[2]

But this need for laughter extended to civilians too. Perhaps surprisingly, in Leningrad, comedy and social satire had thrived even through Stalin's Terror. It would continue to do so. And the leading comedian in the city – by 1941, nationally famous and renowned – was Arkadii Raykin.

He had seduced and mesmerized audiences with a variety of stage characters who caricatured bureaucrats and other minor authority figures. And as the horror of the siege began, Raykin would be among those artists who would be active on the front line, performing for the navy and in the city. In the coldest and most despairing of days, it would be colleagues from his theatre (when Raykin was performing for troops elsewhere) who on one occasion contrived to bring some semblance of comfort to small children by giving them home-made Christmas gifts and tinsel. In a wider sense and, incredibly, given all that the citizens were facing and had already endured, there was a continuing appetite in the city for silly merriment.

Raykin was compared by his admirers to Charlie Chaplin – quite a compliment in Chaplin-adoring Soviet Russia. But in one respect he was rather more remarkable: here was a comedian who somehow had managed to navigate the intense and hostile surveillance of the great purges. He poked fun and satirized; but this was an age when one misplaced joke might result in reports being made to the secret police, with death following swiftly. Arkadii Raykin – and his performances at the Leningrad Theatre of Comedy – somehow appealed not only to workers and managers but also to the political authorities, up to and including Stalin.

There was a dazzling duality here. On the one hand, everyone in this society was keenly aware of the proximity of violence and death; everyone knew that – regardless of how carefully they behaved – they could be the next occupant of that wet cell. Yet there was also laughter: deep, unforced, even passionate. Film comedies such as *Volga-Volga* (1938) were loved. And in Leningrad, there was a theatre dedicated to comedy, and to what we might term music-hall entertainment. (Interestingly, it was at such an evening of comedy performed by Arkadii Raykin and his colleagues in the late 1930s that Vladimir Putin's mother and father first met.)

Even now, Raykin is revered in Russia, for the other crucial point about comedy is that it is founded upon truth; and that the laughter it produces is in some ways beyond governing. It might have been expected that a paranoiac totalitarian like Stalin would fear good comedy for this very reason; that he might have dreaded its power to undermine through ridicule. Yet Raykin was granted licence to, in a literal sense, act the fool.

Raykin – in common with Chaplin and Buster Keaton – had the soulful, expressive eyes of the clown who could conjure a variety of emotional responses other than simple crude laughter. Born in Riga in 1911, he and his family came to what was then Petrograd in 1922, and during his teens the young man realized that theatre was his calling.

His film debut came in 1938, in a production called *Fiery Years*, followed closely by *Dr Kalyuzhnyy*. But his lustre gleamed brightest on stage, and in the wake of the Leningrad purges he was settled as the head of the Leningrad Theatre of Variety and Miniatures. Based in a converted eighteenth-century former inn that had previously played host to a marionette theatre, he offered not just comedy but popular music too. If the city soared aesthetically in terms of ballet, opera and classical music, then Raykin's theatre offered entertainment that provided its own rich emotional satisfaction.

The performances – farce, popular music, thunderous melodrama – all had to fit within a notional schema of Soviet realism. Yet Raykin was developing comic characters who found an answering sympathetic echo within his audiences. Soviet satirist Mikhail Zhvanetsky later observed that Raykin 'was the only one who wasn't afraid to say a bit more than the rest'.[3] It was this sense of comic daring – sketches involving managers and officials making life vexatious for the ordinary people – that would give succour to Leningrad throughout the war.

But it wasn't just Raykin; even in Leningrad's darkest days, there was a generalized understanding that laughter was acceptable. Stalin himself – throughout the more murderous excesses of his reign – declared without apparent irony: 'Life has become happier, life has become merrier.'[4] In this vigorously policed cultural climate, there were those even at the time who sought to analyse the roots of this humour, and of what was really prompting the laughter. Philosopher and literary critic Mikhail Bakhtin, himself persecuted by the regime and sentenced to exile from Leningrad to Kazakhstan in the 1930s, was fascinated by the duality of darkness and comedy. He had a 'theory of the innocuous carnival', that 'all the acts of the drama of world history were performed before a chorus of the laughing people'.[5]

This was noted in Leningrad in the 1930s. 'To live here is like being on a bus,' one unnamed city wit observed. 'Half are sitting and half are shaking.'[6] Here, 'sitting' carried a double meaning, being a slang term for incarceration. A little later, the following exchange was overheard. 'How are you doing?' one man asked of another. 'Like Lenin,' was the reply. 'Unfed and unburied.'[7] (Lenin's corpse, yellow and wax-like, had been preserved and on display in his Moscow mausoleum since 1924.)

There was nothing foolish in this laughter; quite the reverse. In a world where language was patrolled viciously, the involuntary laugh revealed the truth. As another critic, Mikhail Ryklin, put it, laughter was 'one of the multiple expressions of the ecstasy of terror'.[8] It could not be helped; it could not be suppressed. Laughter, as Bakhtin judged, was also about 'overcoming fear'.[9]

Stalin and his deputies were intensely aware of the power of humour; they sought in some ways to control and to guide and manipulate it. At those vast and sombre Party sessions, heavy with carefully weighed speeches, Stalin understood that jokes might be deployed in order to put enemies in insultingly small perspective. Whether talking of Nazis or of internal Party figures who seemed resistant to his innovations, Stalin's speeches would be peppered with iron sarcasm, and each sarcastic comment was dutifully greeted with waves of laughter from the assembled listening apparatchiks. 'They were also taught to laugh at that enemy,' wrote historian Natalya Skradol, because 'to make something ridiculous means hitting the very centre of life. Laughter is cheeky, laughter is blasphemous, laughter kills with poison arrows.'[10]

Humour was not Stalin's natural mode of discourse, but he was capable of mordant, dark jokes. In 1936, as the bodies piled up across Russia, there had been a wild rumour in western Europe that Stalin himself had died. One Associated Press reporter decided – with a little chutzpah – to write to the leader himself to ask if it were true that he was no more. Stalin was amused enough to reply. He 'had indeed departed this earthly realm', he told the reporter, and had 'no wish to be disturbed in the next world'.[11] Again, with humour comes an unintended glint of truth: a leader who had worked so remorselessly and icily to liberate his people from the bonds of religious superstition could not help envisaging and referring to 'the next world'.

Leningraders also craved the nourishment of music; and would be desperate for it in the days to come. In residence was Dmitri Shostakovich, a Leningrad composer who had forged a mighty international reputation by the early 1930s, and whose career and very life had been imperilled shortly afterwards. His 1934 modernist opera *Lady Macbeth of Mtsensk* – depicting nineteenth-century Tsarist oppression – had made a big impression overseas. But it was in 1936 that his wheel of fortune turned. Stalin and Molotov attended a performance of the opera in Moscow: Stalin's displeasure with it – and with its atonal modernism – led to a series of sharp criticisms in the state newspaper *Pravda*. There was a special conference of the Moscow Union of Composers: lesser talents gathered to denounce Shostakovich and his experimentation. Nikolay Chelyapov, as president of the Union of Soviet Composers, outlined the accusation of formalism:

> Every composition should be considered formalistic in which the composer fundamentally does not have as his aim the presenting of new social meaning, but focuses his interest only on inventing new combinations of sounds that have not been used before. Formalism is the sacrifice of the ideological and emotional content . . . to a search for new tricks.[12]

This would be crushing enough in a free society; within the bounds of murderous totalitarianism, it was terrifying. The path back to favour had to be negotiated with great care: the 1939 Finnish suite, those evocations of old folk tunes, was acceptable. But in what sense were they honest art? Shostakovich's great St Petersburg contemporary Sergei Prokofiev – who had spent time abroad, in France and America, and who had actually returned quite willingly to Stalin's new Russia – became accordingly more watchful. Apart from his *Romeo and Juliet* misstep, he seemed naturally attuned to the 1930s move back to more traditional Russian harmonies. The authorities wanted them so that the children of the new Soviet age might have their love of homeland rekindled, and thus be better prepared to defend it. This meant reconnecting them to the emotional melodies that their grandparents had danced and wept to, from Leningrad to Tashkent.

But there was an even simpler reason for Stalin's harsh dismissal of any music that seemed jarring or difficult or even highbrow. His daughter Svetlana wrote of the music that Stalin kept close by his own side. 'In one corner [of his sitting room], there was a record player,' she recalled. 'My father had a good collection of Russian,

Georgian and Ukrainian folk songs and didn't recognize the existence of any other kind of music.'[13] As Victor Seroff noted, Stalin
also preferred the music hall for public performances because there
was 'a more intimate atmosphere in which the music was an accompaniment to drinking and dining. He was bored by symphonic
and chamber music. He disapproved of such long compositions
for solo instruments as concertos and sonatas, deeming such works
'anti-democratic'.

Sergei Prokofiev wanted to find a middle way through this thorny
landscape: he told friends he did not want to compose variations of
old Russian drinking songs. (There was also a danger that simply
using old folk tunes might sound horribly parodic.) But while Shostakovich was in part rehabilitated by his evocation of Finnish folk
music as an ornamental accompaniment to the Winter War, Prokofiev, almost by instinct, found the form that would most please the
leader: the medium of film scores. And there was one film project
in particular that he would approach with great passion. The great
Leningrad director Sergei Eisenstein – himself not long rehabilitated
after a period of official disfavour – was, with war looming, attacking a suitably grand theme intended quite specifically to inspire the
workers in the fight to come.

The film would be *Alexander Nevsky* – an historical epic set in the
thirteenth century, detailing the searing battles of Russia's first great
heroic figurehead against the armies of the Swedish Teutonic cru-
saders. Prince Alexander of Novgorod faced them across the surging
waters at the Battle of the Neva. There was a later attempted invasion
from the Teutonic hordes, and Alexander was recalled to lead the
defending forces at the Battle of the Ice on Lake Peipus. A diabolical
and savage enemy swooping in from western Europe was defeated by
the strength of a Russian 'taller than the others', with 'a voice like a
trumpet',[14] who would have the courage to vanquish this demonic
foe: a perfectly fitting subject, so it seemed, in 1938.

And apart from the marvellous medieval imagery – Eisenstein
himself taking care to avoid any accusations of snobbish 'formalism' – the film, as enjoyed by huge numbers of Leningraders, boasted
Prokofiev's rich and dramatic music. There was no experimentation

here (and certainly not any inclination to recreate the religious chants of the thirteenth century, which would have sounded as strange and dissonant as the most extreme modernism). Instead, there were colourful themes and moving choral interludes (one passage, 'Arise, People of Russia', is as uplifting as the title suggests, and the baritone voices heard in 'Lake Pleshcheyevo' are haunting). There might have been those who would argue that Prokofiev's score would not have sounded out of place in the late nineteenth century in any concert hall in Europe – but it was there primarily to work upon the deeper passions of the audiences. Like the film itself, it had a striking sincerity.

The layers of Leningrad art and culture – from the fraternizing poets to those designing the costumes for the quick-change comedians – were also freighted with the historic weight of ballet. Dance was as integral to the city's idea of itself as the grandest eighteenth-century architecture. The city's founder, Peter the Great, had introduced ballet not as some means of entertainment, but rather as a quasi-philosophical proposition: here on stage, in all its discipline and spectacular physicality, would be an expression of what humanity itself should be striving towards. The dancers were tested to their limits, their performances intended to elicit not merely applause but also profound meditation and reflection.

By the nineteenth century ballet was firmly embedded as part of the aristocratic culture of St Petersburg life, but the theatres also featured a number of cheap seats – rough wooden benches lining the galleries – in the expectation that working men would also seek this form of artistic nourishment. Under the Russians, any idea that dance could be fey or dainty was crushed: here was military precision and a certain remorseless brutality in training. In 1909, the art form was exported to become one of St Petersburg's most notable gifts to the world: the Ballets Russes was established, not in the frozen north but rather amid the sensual pleasures of Paris. The company was conceived and led by Sergei Diaghilev, who for many years had been an intrinsic figure in the cosmopolitan artistic circles of St Petersburg – one of a group who called themselves the 'Nevsky Pickwickians'.[15]

Diaghilev, the son of an officer, was no dancer himself; but he had a raptor's eye for the finest art, music and literature, and a compulsion to bring Russian art into western Europe. A striking figure, distinguished by a streak of white in his hair, Diaghilev was first an art and music connoisseur, moving between Paris and St Petersburg. But then his eye fell upon the St Petersburg Imperial Ballet, and he conceived – with associates in dance – a means of fusing exquisite, innovative music, beautiful avant-garde sets (some later designed by Picasso) and dancers who themselves would be giving revolutionary performances. The Ballets Russes – a company that would travel from Paris to cities across the world – would come to symbolize a certain idea of Russianness: the pursuit of beauty, but with a hard, uncompromising edge.

Soon came lauded success (and some notable commercial failures when the productions were deemed that shade too modern), and Diaghilev's association with Igor Stravinsky conferred a form of immortality: the 1913 production of *The Rite of Spring* is still regarded as one of the great artistic turning points – an evocation of paganism and sacrifice, blending sometimes deliberately disorientating choreography with dissonant, atonal music: the hot shock of modernism.

It was natural that this artistic fire should also burn bright in St Petersburg, even though after the revolution Diaghilev himself, presenting as he did the very image of bourgeois decadence, would no longer be welcomed by the authorities. The Imperial Ballet Company, which since the last years of the nineteenth century had been based in the city's Mariinsky Theatre (its productions of the Tchaikovsky ballet *Swan Lake* were renowned internationally), was itself a temporary victim of Lenin's revolution. At first, the new regime associated ballet with the deposed ruling class; within two years, however, it was recognized that the form was a strength that might be utilized to the credit of socialism.

In 1920 the Mariinsky was resurrected as the State Academic Theatre of Opera and Ballet. And following his assassination in 1934, the greatest tribute was bestowed upon Sergei Kirov when the ballet company was renamed after him. The Kirov Ballet was as luminous an idea in the global imagination as the former Ballets Russes. Fyodor Lopukhov was the dancer at its helm up to the siege of Leningrad and beyond. With most artists struggling to interpret what was meant by the term 'Soviet realism', Lopukhov was in some ways ahead of the game. In 1924 he and his company had staged a production entitled *Red Whirlwind*, a balletic re-enactment of the 1917 Bolshevik triumph. The narrative loosely involved the Bolsheviks and Red Guards represented by dancers performing strongly assertive moves, as opposed to the bourgeois element who were indicated by means rather more fey. Dancers also performed the roles of the working classes, who vanquished the White Russian armies, as well as capitalists.[16]

This and other productions were regarded within both Leningrad and wider Soviet society as the highest art, and there were dancers under Lopukhov who would later take the benefit of his experimental approach out into the wider world. One such was Georgii Melitonovich Balanchivadze, who eventually emigrated to America as George Balanchine and whose ballets staged in New York are still performed and are the subjects of admiring books.

The company and its theatre glowed at the heart of Leningrad life throughout the horrors of the purges, its dancers revelling in the opportunity to perfect their art. And that life continued to pulse not only until the Nazis encircled the city in 1941 but, incredibly, throughout the ordeal as well. The authorities, scenting the immense propaganda value of the Kirov Ballet, would make hasty plans to have many of them evacuated to safer regions. (In this respect, they were elevated to the same level of importance as the city's aircraft and tank factories, which would also be earmarked for transportation deep into the east.) But, crucially for the morale of its inhabitants, there would also be a number of dancers and musicians, divas and divos who would remain in the city. The Leningrad Philharmonic in particular would come to be held before an astonished world as the most amazing symbol of Russian life, art and soul in the darkest pit of human experience, as we shall see. But the citizens as a unified whole would also face the coming calamity with a steely directness that was itself unnerving.

8. 'Germany has declared war on us!'

In the early hours of 22 June 1941 – in that flickering pale-blue half-light, half-dark of the northern summer night – millions of ordinary people across eastern Europe and Russia were condemned to death. The sentences would be inflicted at different times – some immediately, some later – and in varying nightmarish ways. But the executioners were coming. Fifteen-year-old Leningrad school-boy Yura Riabinkin, living in an apartment block with his mother and younger sister, had a form of presentiment on the night that the German invasion was launched. He was woken intermittently by some unidentifiable 'buzzing', which could well have been his imagination, and in the twilight of that White Night he got out of bed, went to his window and silently watched the luminous skies.[1] It wasn't until the day dawned properly that he learned that the course of his future – the courses of uncountable futures – had been violently changed.

The Nazi attack on Russia had been launched. Theirs was a front line that extended over one thousand miles from one sea to another – the Baltic in the north, the Black in the south – while directly before them lay the green plains of the Baltic farmlands, the vast Pripet marshes and the dark mass of the Carpathian mountains. Three million German soldiers – together with Romanian, Hungarian and Slovak troops – were ranged along that line. The sheer scale of such a deathly array – the 3,700 tanks, the 7,000 artillery pieces, the 3,000 aircraft armed with bullets and bombs – was unprecedented. The technology was modern yet the principle was ancient and awful and stretched back to the beginning of warfare. The mighty Timur, immortalized by Christopher Marlowe as Tamburlaine (whose tomb had been entered only a couple of days previously) would have understood. And the savagery of the approaching conflict – the lives of so many millions of civilians torn to obscene shreds – would come to be compared by the Wehrmacht's General Gotthard Heinrici to the Thirty Years War of the seventeenth century. On that apocalyptic morning, the pre-dawn skies along Russia's borders from eastern Poland to Romania flashed and boomed and echoed with the guttural roar of artillery. Hitler's reasons for declaring war, thin and cynical, included subversion and an alleged conspiracy with Britain. 'Do you think we deserve that?' said Molotov to the German ambassador.[2] Stalin, who had been apprised of the news in Moscow, slowly sat down, looking (according to Marshal Zhukov) 'pale' and 'bewildered'.

And like the shock wave from the impact of a meteorite, news of the invasion swiftly rippled to Leningrad. It was met with varying degrees of bewilderment and disbelief. Red Army conscript Henrikh Dudnik was stationed not far from the city. That morning, he happened simply to be washing his feet, and his foot-wrappings, by the riverbank. 'It was announced we were at war,' he recalled. 'The sentry came running and told me war had started. I laughed.'[3]

He, like his comrades, had no reason to anticipate that the Molotov–Ribbentrop Pact would be torn apart in the blink of an eye. 'What war?' Dudnik remembered saying.[4] Certainly the Red Army High Command had been preparing for a day when war would come; Stalin's defence commissar Marshal Semyon Timoshenko had been among those studying war games, and considering ways that the German serpent might be beheaded before it struck. Yet the timing of that strike was wholly unexpected. Partly this was to do with inconsistent briefings, but also simply to do with Stalin's personal belief, communicated downwards, that the Germans would not attack yet. A few years later, Soviet defence minister Marshal Georgii Zhukov would recall that when 'the war broke out, the majority of our mechanized corps and divisions were still in the state of being formed and trained, as a result of which they entered battle weakly equipped and in a poorly organized state'.[5] They had not been helped by their own internal decimation during the years of the Stalin purges.

'It was a beautiful day,' recalled Elya Gendelevich, who was in Leningrad studying medicine as the invasion, code-named Operation

Barbarossa, began. She and her friends gathered to hear the news. 'Everything turned upside down, the sun darkened, and it was difficult to fathom what was happening.'[6] Elsewhere that morning, in the thick, richly scented woods that lay outside the city, one young physics student was taking a stroll with a friend, and noticed that everyone they passed looked anxious and drawn. They soon found out why. 'It was surreal,' the student said. He and many thousands of others would in the coming days be swept up as conscripts in the desperate military effort to repel the invaders, facing the enemy with barely a lesson on how to fire a gun. Some of those not destined to be shot or burned or dismembered in explosions would be taken prisoner, and that too would be a death sentence, though of a markedly crueller and slower kind.

This was the start of an invasion upon whose axis the future of the world would tilt. For the peoples of eastern Europe – and particularly the Jewish populations – the fiery genocidal nightmare would be all-consuming. For the people of Leningrad, the ordeal would change their very conception of human nature, and its darkest limits.

When General Werner Marcks of the Wehrmacht was studying the maps in 1940 – all the wide rivers, the roadless forests, the vast marshes – he did not yet know the code name of his Führer's carefully planned operation. The German invasion of Russia had originally been mooted by Hitler for the autumn of 1940; wiser voices around him suggested that it was foolish to tempt the old enemy of the Russian winter. Hitler was impatient for expansion, and though it was clear that a successful invasion of Britain was not feasible at that stage, it was imperative that at least Bolshevik rule be eradicated. The invasion was then reset for spring 1941. By then, it had its secret name.

For Field Marshal Wilhelm Ritter von Leeb, and possibly some of the vast numbers of troops who were gathered in bases in East Prussia and German-occupied Poland, the name might have produced some satisfying martial resonance. 'Barbarossa' was the appellation of an extraordinary twelfth-century German ruler, Frederick I, Duke of Swabia, crowned at Frankfurt, who rose to become Holy Roman Emperor. Barbarossa was a figure who combined courage with perspicacity: a fearless fighter who also had the skill to weave together the then 1,600 disparate states (some too tiny to figure properly on maps) that comprised Germany, as well as imposing a rule of law across the wider continent that countered the mighty power of the Papacy in Rome. *Barbarossa* was an Italian term meaning 'red beard'; for Frederick was a rufous-haired warrior, tall and broad, wise as well as courageous on the battlefield. 'His eyes are sharp and piercing, his lips delicate . . . his whole face is bright and cheerful,' wrote a provost called Rahewin not long after Frederick's death. 'His teeth are even and snow white in colour . . . Modesty rather than anger causes him to blush frequently.'[7]

As emperor of lands stretching across Europe towards the eastern edge of Christendom, he had a deftness both with sword and with intelligent diplomacy. He and his forces were pulled into the Third Crusade against Saladin, with whom he had once forged good relations. It was through this that he met his end: drowned in the swollen River Saleph (now the Turkish Göksu river) near Antioch in 1190. Almost immediately legends arose that the emperor had entered a twilight realm, neither quite alive nor quite dead. That he lay sleeping, among many of his knights, deep within the hollows of the Kyffhäuser mountains in Thuringia, southern Germany, awaiting rebirth and Germany's new glory.

The plan invoking his name had a trident-like shape: three spearheads with different targets. Army Group South would be focused on piercing through to Ukraine and the city of Kyiv, and thence deep into the Caucasus region in order to secure its valuable oil resources. Army Group Centre would strike through to Smolensk, and from there to Moscow. By driving a military stake through Russia's political heart, the Nazis could begin the work of repurposing these vast lands and all their peoples so that they would be subordinate to the German settlers who would arrive after victory.

Finally, Army Group North's initial objective was the conquest of Leningrad by way of blazing through the Baltic states – lands that had only very recently been annexed by Stalin's Russia – and securing the north of the country. Subjugating Leningrad, with its vast military factories and workforces, would sever Russia's armament supply chain.

Von Leeb spent time studying the obstacles he and his forces would meet: the wide, powerful rivers to be crossed before Soviet defenders could blow up bridges, the forested plains with their rudimentary roads. As with Ukraine in the south, there was intelligence that a significant proportion of the populations in Estonia and Lithuania would celebrate the advent of the Nazis, and their chance to shrug off the iron grip of Soviet ideology.

The field marshal, despite being sixty-four years old, had been summoned particularly by Hitler to command Army Group North; he was one of the men who in 1940 had divined the best means of powering through the Maginot Line, thus bringing about the capitulation of France. Von Leeb had known nothing but soldiering all his life. Starkly bald, with a knife-sharp gaze, he had as a young man fought in China at the time of the Boxer Rebellion at the turn of the century.

This had been an especially ugly war: a foreshadowing of the mass atrocities that would seep across the century. The 'Boxers' – highly organized young Chinese rebels known more properly as the Society of Righteous and Harmonious Fists – began a campaign of resistance to Western influence and Western plunder. They had been so named because of their intense skills in the martial arts. What started out as a blaze of violence against various Christian legations in cities across China soon became a larger, more determined effort through violence to expel the foreigners. But the countering forces responded with a more murderous intensity, presenting the atrocities they inflicted as theatre. An eight-nation alliance that included Germany invaded China and countless thousands of Chinese men were subjected not merely to execution, but to terrible public spectacles of torture, including 'standing strangulation'.

In this procedure, the prisoners would be bound within wooden struts, and their heads placed through cangues – planks with holes, like medieval stocks, but held horizontal with the victim standing, the wooden block fitting around the neck. There would be supports beneath the feet to take the pressure off the neck. One by one, at a pace of the executioner's choosing, the supports would be removed, so that at last the victim's body would be supported only by the neck. Death by asphyxia, sometimes hideously slow, would follow.[8]

The conflict also saw dreadful outbreaks of mass rape of Chinese women – one of the oldest and most traumatic of war crimes, leaving shadows over entire lives. In the context of this war, any notional Prussian military ideals of 'honour' and 'nobility' were reduced to obscene jokes by such depravity. At the end of it all, the Western powers demanded reparations – vast quantities of Chinese silver. Those who fought there, including young von Leeb, had seen carefully calculated atrocities and knew that these, rather than fine sabre charges, were the true reality of war.

In the inter-war years, von Leeb had continued his career with the German military; and even if he was a throwback to the world of the kaisers, he was not some old-fashioned imperial romantic with chivalric ideals. Nazi methods were not a shock to him. And as he looked out in 1941 from those East Prussian headquarters, he cannot have been under many illusions about what his troops were about to inflict upon eastern Europe. As well as the 18th and the 16th armies, plus a panzer group, von Leeb's forces would also be accompanied by an SS Totenkopf – Death's Head – division.

The key, once more, was speed, and when Operation Barbarossa was launched, the progress of the vast armies as they began their 500-mile advance across eastern Europe was astounding. In the north, von Leeb first had to negotiate mighty natural barriers: the River Neman and then, deeper within Latvia, the wide, fast-flowing Dvina. As the territories had been annexed by the Soviets in 1940, Red Army tank corps were positioned along these routes: in bursts of fire and blazing steel, initial encounters were short and bloody, and young German troops – many of them experiencing their first taste of front-line action – who were following the advance parties through this green and gentle landscape, witnessed the reality of death, even as they dealt it. Those they faced were also young, and often hopelessly ill prepared, and yet the young Soviet soldiers in their final moments defended themselves with a kind of dislocated delirium. 'They fight like madmen,' observed General Heinrici. 'They never give up.'[9]

In that warm, humid summer, the air above the sandy roads was sometimes made cloying by smoke and the smell of burned flesh.

Those marching along would see their first bodies by the roadside: Red Army soldiers, torn and mangled.

What was striking in these initial battles was the fact that the Soviet tanks – the fruit of years of research and manufacture in the vast Leningrad plants – were technically superior to the German vehicles. Models such as the KV-1 and KV-2 had terrific armour plating designed to make them both impregnable and unstoppable. In other, slightly more southerly regions in the early days, those tanks did succeed for a time in holding back the German onslaught: some of the forces under General Georg-Hans Reinhardt were surprised by the materialization of Red Army beasts such as the T-34 and their lethally effective guns. 'Half a dozen anti-tank guns fire shells at him [a T-34], which sound like a drumroll,' read one Wehrmacht report. 'But he drives staunchly through our line like an impregnable prehistoric monster . . . It is remarkable that Lieutenant Steup's tank made hits on a T-34, once at about twenty metres and four times at fifty metres, with Panzergranate 40 (calibre 5 cm) [anti-tank rounds] – without any noticeable effect.'[10]

But a little to the north, the oncoming German forces were nimbler and cleverer at tricking the Soviet tank drivers into advancing across open ground towards unsuspected German heavy artillery. When faced with shelling from relatively close range, not even their armour plating could save these metal behemoths. And as the hot, verdant countryside became punctuated with the carbonized remains of their crews, von Leeb's armies pushed on towards the Dvina.

There were other smart moves: Oberleutnant Hans-Wolfram Knaak led a special unit within the 8th Panzer Division: he and his men moved far ahead of their main forces, dressed in Red Army uniforms and conversing with anyone they met along the way in fluent Russian. Their objective was to seize bridges before the Soviets could shatter them with dynamite. Broadly, this stratagem was not always successful; the real Red Army managed to blow up other bridges, leaving the Germans to construct less satisfactory pontoon replacements.

There were communities and towns in Lithuania where the invading German forces were greeted by some locals with celebration; the resentment of Soviet annexation had been intense, and there had been civilian uprisings in the town of Kaunas and the capital, Vilnius. Even before the Wehrmacht had appeared on the horizon, men in Kaunas had turned on the few Red Army troops to be found there; some were even disarmed and taken prisoner. Here and in Vilnius, the rebels also took over the radio stations and the newspaper offices. They were convinced that the Nazis would ratify their break for independence. They could not have been more dramatically wrong.

Even as these dissidents honed their idealized plans for government, the distant bass drone of approaching Luftwaffe bombers filled the air with their own grim reality: Lithuanians would be allowed no agency. They would be lucky to remain alive. Towns and communities across the country were targeted from the skies with the intention of wiping out all and any Soviet airfields. On the first days of Operation Barbarossa, the civilian casualties had already risen into the many thousands. Looting also began immediately, those hoped-for Wehrmacht liberators seizing eggs, cheese, chickens and, worse, possessions: furs and family valuables. No civilian food or private property was safe; these young Wehrmacht soldiers were little different from their seventeenth-century forebears in the Thirty Years War.

And in the giddy exhilaration of the first hours of the attack on 22 June 1941, it will have seemed to von Leeb and all those serving under him that the way to Leningrad, as well as to Moscow, was clear. It had been heavily drummed into German soldiers that the Soviets – despite their ingenuity in blowing up roads and bridges in their retreat – were inherently weak because theirs was in essence a corrupt Jewish system. In this twisted logic those same soldiers were being told to envisage themselves as freeing the Russians from a hateful regime.

On the morning that the first of three million German soldiers began their advance towards Russia, the Leningrad schoolboy Yura Riabinkin – who despite his disturbed night had yet to hear the news, and who had some free time during his summer holidays – decided to spend the day at the Pioneer Palace. This was a spectacular eighteenth-century colonnaded edifice, elegant and glowing white, which had formerly been the Anichkov Palace and, like the Smolny

Cathedral, built especially for the Empress Elizabeth. Now it was a centre for many dozens of extra-curricular Leningrad youth clubs, offering everything from sports training to specialized lectures. (This one had been partly the brainchild of the city leader Andrei Zhdanov; in the Stalinist years, the broader idea of 'pioneer palaces' spread right across the Soviet Union.)

Riabinkin, on that hot sunny morning of 22 June, was intent upon joining his fellows at the institute's chess club. Upon leaving his family's apartment, he 'noticed something peculiar. At the gateway to our building, I caught sight of the caretaker with a gas mask and wearing a red armband on his sleeve,' he wrote in his diary. 'The same thing at all the other gateways. The militiamen had their gas masks with them and there was even a radio broadcasting at each of the cross-roads. Something told me that a situation threatening the city had been declared.'[11]

Yet in the way of a teenager intent upon his chess, Riabinkin walked on to the classical prospect of the Pioneer Palace. It was relatively early; there were only one or two other boys there. But as more arrived, the news started to spread. One boy told an assembled group that he had heard that German bombers had attacked Ukraine at four in the morning; that there had been bombs dropped on Kyiv and Odesa. That boy also told his fellows that Molotov had announced on the radio that Russia was now at war with Germany.

'Well, I simply sank down, stunned,' wrote Riabinkin. 'This was some news! And I hadn't even suspected anything of the kind! Germany! Germany has declared war on us!' His mind flickered back to the caretakers earlier that morning. 'That's why they all had their gas masks.'[12]

Dazed and disorientated, the boys then went on to play several games of chess, uncertain of what else at this stage they ought to be doing.

Similarly, a group of twenty-four freshly graduated students from the Leningrad Institute of Fine Mechanics and Optics had decided to celebrate with a sunshine-filled day promenading in the grounds of the Peterhof – the extraordinary eighteenth-century palace with its vast classical facade of white and peach, its landscaped water-courses and fountains and its golden statues. For these students, the lavish aesthetic spectacle of the palace complemented their bright and limitless optimism – a rich backdrop for a day of dreams. As soon as the students arrived, however, they saw the loudspeakers being erected: a state announcement of some importance was about to be made.

'People said that Molotov was about to speak,' recalled Samuil Hedekel. 'We didn't know what was going on.'[13] Then the loudspeakers crackled into life: a pronouncement that would be heard all the way across Leningrad, through a hundred different loudspeakers. Molotov 'announced the beginning of the Great Patriotic War', said Hedekel. In the immediate aftermath, he and his fellow graduates – shocked and disorientated – continued 'strolling around' the vast Peterhof gardens. 'We didn't know what war meant,' recalled Hedekel. 'In the evening, when we were getting ready to leave Peterhof, we saw soldiers digging trenches.'[14] Very suddenly, the reality punched home; and Hedekel and his friends would shortly be pulled into the military as well.

In the meantime, the older adults in the city were reacting in their own ways to the news and to Molotov's grave announcement of the Nazi ground invasion and of the bombing attacks: some had made their way to the city's banks to withdraw their savings, presumably for some in the hope that they would be able to use it to leave the city to travel deeper into Russia (the railway booking offices from the city's Moscow station, from which the rails pointed south and west, instantly assumed a frantic character; there were families with relatives in more southerly regions in and around Ukraine and deeper within Russia who imagined that the Nazis would not get so far – but from the very start of the invasion, railways were naturally being prioritized for official evacuations and exclusive military use). And there was a surge of shoppers to grocery stores: an effort – rather like the initial cash hoarding – to stock up on some staple non-perishables. Given all that so many citizens had been through in the preceding years, the initial response to Molotov's address was comparatively mild. In addition, there were few initial questions about why it was Molotov – and not Stalin – who was addressing the nation. It would only be as the days crept on that Leningraders – disturbed by Stalin's complete silence – would start to wonder where the leader was.

Elsewhere in the city, there were huge outbreaks of patriotic fervour and enthusiasm. The same afternoon that the panzer tanks were engaged in their remorseless push east, some 2,500 workers at the Leningrad shipyards Ordzhonikidze and Zhdanov immediately volunteered to join the army or the navy. This was also the case in various factories right across the city.

The authorities in all these institutions were listening out very carefully for any suggestions of dissidence: among the labourers, there were many conversations about quite how the Soviet leadership could ever have trusted the pernicious Nazis in the first place. But in those hours following the announcement of war, this was perhaps understood as legitimate bewilderment at the ruthlessness of an ally that had suddenly turned enemy.

Amid this new civilian fervour to join the military effort, Leningrad's social season of White Nights – a time of studied elegance and grace – was still in full swing. And even as Molotov's announcement echoed in the hearts of all Leningraders, there were two particular scheduled performances that sat uncancelled on the playbills of the Kirov Theatre. (The Mariinsky Theatre had been renamed in 1935.) One was an anniversary gala for a veteran ballerina called Yelena Lyukum. She 'had rehearsed so that this would be the icing on the cake of her career', recalled fellow dancer Natalya Sakhnovskaya. 'She planned for it to be her last performance, a farewell, and a triumphant end to her stage career.'[15]

The finale was scheduled for the night of 23 June. Such was the breathless shock of the declaration of war – and the absence of any immediate public statements from Stalin compounded that sense of unreality – that the theatre, the performers and their audiences numbly carried on. No one thought to cancel because they had not been told to. Yelena Lyukum's swansong performance went ahead, the audiences still flocked to it and the evening was deemed to be a great triumph. One adjustment had to be made for the new circumstances, however: rather than being joined on stage in adulation by celebratory colleagues, Lyukum instead had a rather more discreet leaving party backstage: now was clearly not the time for visible and ostentatious enjoyment.

There were those immediately following the announcement on that hot morning of 22 June who felt another sort of pang: the prospect that this war with the Nazis would endanger Leningrad's rich scholarly and intellectual life. The director of the Archives of the Academy of Sciences was Georgii Knyazev. He had been particularly gripped by the news that had come the previous day that Timur's tomb in Uzbekistan had been opened. 'I never did manage to find out the details,' he complained wistfully in his diary. 'Military events pushed the information about the archaeological excavations in Samarkand into the background.'[16]

None the less, he was intrigued by what he saw as the symmetry of the living and the long-distant dead:

How everything in the world repeats itself! In the fourteenth century, Timur, or Tamburlaine, conquered India from the Ind to the Ganges, and Persia, Syria, Turkey and southern Russia. And now comes another one – the upstart Hitler – who has gone far beyond Timur the Lame in bringing so much suffering both to his own people and to all other peoples, to the enslaved and the humiliated as well as to those fighting against his hellish regime.[17]

For those in the factories and electrical and chemical plants in and around Leningrad, the Soviet regime itself was increasingly, grimly, demanding: penalties for even a few minutes' lateness might include a spell of forced labour. Yet the numbers of Leningrad offenders in those months before the war was remarkably – and oddly – high. It has been pointed out that, in some cases, the 'shirker' was anything but: a mother, for instance, trying to care for a sick child and having to take time off to do so.[18] Drunkenness might well have been another cause; but while alcoholism is, of course, an illness, the act of drinking could also sometimes have its roots in a sense of conscious defiance of authority.

A letter sent to the Leningrad edition of *Pravda* from an anonymous disaffected worker in the Stalin Metalworks in early June 1941

1. The stunning portico of the Hermitage Museum, held aloft by mighty Atlantes sculptures. In the city's darkest hours, the museum itself was seen as a source of spiritual strength.

2. Sennaya Square, Saint Petersburg's historic hay market, as represented in a nineteenth-century painting and evoked darkly on the page by novelist Fyodor Dostoevsky. During the hardest days of hunger during the siege the square would be at the centre of the trade in unidentifiable flesh.

3. The main staircase of the Winter Palace/Hermitage, photographed in the early 1960s. Novelist Vladimir Nabokov noted the surprising erotic allure of the city's museums for young couples.

4. Hermitage Bridge – the oldest in the city, its original form dating back to the eighteenth century – stands on the Winter Canal, and in the months of fog and cold frames Petersburg's curious and eerie sense of timelessness.

5. The Winter War between Russia and Finland began in November 1939. Stalin and his deputies were convinced Finland would be subjugated in days. They were dramatically wrong.

6. By January 1940 Red Army casualties were in the hundreds of thousands; corpses froze as they fell, remaining where they were until the thaws.

7. Leningrad First Party Secretary Andrei Zhdanov (*left*); unlike outwardly flintier Soviets, Zhdanov had his jocular side. But he was instrumental in sparking Stalin's Terror, condemning thousands to death. In the 1930s he enjoyed a warm friendship with Stalin, sharing family holidays with the leader. His son was to marry Stalin's daughter.

8. Aleksei Kuznetsov, pictured in the 1930s, was Zhdanov's deputy; comparatively young, he brought initial terrifying zeal to the purges – before understanding that they were decimating Leningrad industry. He and Zhdanov were present throughout the years of siege, trying to hold the civic realm together.

9. Lenin's arrival at the city's Finland station at 11 p.m. on 3 April 1917 on the 'sealed train' was the spark that lit the fire that would become Bolshevik revolution. But in this later painting of the occasion there was a crucial addition: the presence of Stalin – who wasn't there – behind him.

10. The city above all prided itself upon its poetry and love of books. During the lethal siege, the city's central library remained open for all readers – civilians and soldiers – seeking escape (pictured here in 1941).

11. The moment that haunted Russian literature: the nation's greatest poet, Alexander Pushkin, fatally wounded in a Petersburg duel in 1837, his blood hissing on the white snow.

12. Leningrad was a mighty city of industry: by the early 1930s, the Kirov Works and the Putilov Works were extraordinary citadels, building tanks and aeroplanes as well as vast hydroelectric turbines. The evacuation of these plants took precedence over the human population.

13. One of the greatest of Russia's twentieth-century poets, Anna Akhmatova in part embodied the artistic spirit of the city. She was sadistically persecuted by the authorities, but her voice would be broadcast on public speakers to the besieged citizens.

14. As Stalin's Terror began in the mid 1930s, claiming the lives of thousands of Leningraders torn from their homes in darkness, the city's artistic life continued to flourish. International visitors relished the aesthetic splendour without glimpsing the fear beneath it.

15. In the wake of revolution, the Bolsheviks had initially dismissed ballet as a bourgeois art form. But in the 1920s, they soon saw the value of the Mariinsky – later the Kirov – Ballet as the highest expression of Soviet art.

16. The Church of the Saviour on the Blood – built in 1881 to commemorate the assassinated Tsar Alexander II – was a deliberate fantasia of old Russian architecture. The religion-hating Bolsheviks never quite knew what to do with the building.

17. The interior – a dizzying kaleidoscope of colour and orthodox imagery – presented a challenge to Stalin's League of the Militant Godless.

complained of terrible living conditions, of workers so packed into barrack-style accommodation that there could be as many as forty in one dormitory. The writer also protested that large numbers of consumer goods were not available, that the wastage of material at various sites was prodigious and that drunkenness was endemic. The authorities might have thought it was the cause of inefficiency, but it might well have been a nihilistic riposte to a life where there seemed nothing much better to do.

Those workers who sought to emulate the Stakhanovite ideal – impossible increases in productivity, ever-lengthening hours spent on automated lines – will have also seen something that might not have been quite so apparent to their less-involved fellow citizens: that the vast industry devoted to military hardware and technology would make the city a key target for any invading force. This went especially for sites on the outskirts of the city: the flat countryside of the region made it conducive for Soviet aeroplane runways. The NKVD had seen to it just weeks before war came that their armies of slave workers – political prisoners – were laying out and building no fewer than eleven runways at separate sites throughout the area.

The delivery target was September 1941: from here, whole new fleets of Soviet fighters and bombers could be launched westwards. Yet by June 1941, the planned complex of airfields and hangars was nowhere near completion.

When Operation Barbarossa came, the Luftwaffe took immediately to the skies, heading east. The partially built air bases made pitifully easy targets. Within hours, Luftwaffe bombers reduced them to smouldering ash. The same was true of some 1,000 Soviet planes that were in hangars near the border, turned to sunburst balls of white flame in a matter of moments.

The vulnerability of Leningrad was felt in other ways too. The people of the city had been deprived of food before, and they knew how pervasive and pernicious the effect of that hunger was. During the non-aggression pact with Germany, Russian grain was still being sold to the Nazis in return for machinery and technical parts; there was never much in the way of surplus. These were not trivial matters. After the revolutionary civil war, and after the repercussions of collectivization, and after seemingly endless rounds of rationing, the people of Leningrad already knew with a pang how even the most basic staples – foods fried in fresh butter – could become bitterly unattainable luxuries.

And the wider point about worker absenteeism and disobedience was that by the summer of 1941 – and the moment when all of Leningrad understood the terrible storm that was approaching – there was not perfect ideological purity. There were a few who – when looking between the Communist authorities and the German fascists – were equivocal about which was worse. There were some others (strikingly, in a city with such a large Jewish population) who felt that the Nazis were perfectly right in their loathing of the Jews. All, though, were expecting to hear the voice of their leader: for Stalin to point the direction forward. Yet Stalin remained silent.

9. Safeguarding the Treasure

Finally, Stalin spoke. No one had any explanation for his bewildering absence, and by the time he was ready to address his people on 3 July 1941, he was talking about a war that the citizens of Leningrad had already started fighting.

It had been almost two weeks since the roiling shock of invasion. In all that time, the great leader had said not a word. Leningrad's city-wide network of public loudspeakers had instead been exhorting the people not to turn their radios off. The authorities had started confiscating domestic sets in apartments, replacing them with small speakers connected to the city's main radio station, to minimize the chances of dissident or enemy broadcasts being heard – 'We had a round black radio speaker,' recalled Sofiya Mirskaya, who was then a Leningrad schoolchild aged ten. 'It gave us information from the Soviet Information Bureau and Olga Berggolts read her poetry'.[1] On 27 June, Andrei Zhdanov received an anonymous letter from a Leningrader: 'Where is he?' it demanded, referring to Stalin. 'We have never seen him on the podium in Leningrad. What, is he afraid of his own people? Let him go up to the loudspeaker so that the people hear the voice of the one about whom so much is sung.'[2]

Six days later the leader's words, slightly guttural, echoed through the city. There were those who thought there might be something wrong with him; they detected a 'gurgling' noise, as though water were being poured. His voice, tenor-pitched, sounded a little strained. All knew better than to speculate too openly. But the intense oddness of his disappearance from view at the start of an invasion was none the less hanging in the air.

'Comrades, citizens, brothers and sisters, men of our army and navy!' he began. 'My words are addressed to you, dear friends.' The familiarity was striking, especially given the terror he had inflicted over the past few years. The address that followed was also notable for being remarkably straightforward, even if it was garnished with the inevitable propagandized untruths about enemy losses. 'The perfidious military attack by Hitlerite Germany on our Motherland, begun on 22 June, is continuing,' Stalin said. 'In spite of the heroic resistance of the Red Army, and although the enemy's finest divisions and finest air-force units have already been smashed, and have met their doom on the field of battle, the enemy continues to push forward, hurling fresh forces to the front.

'Hitler's troops,' Stalin continued, 'have succeeded in capturing Lithuania, a considerable part of Latvia, the western part of Byelorussia and part of western Ukraine. The fascist aircraft are extending the range of their operations, bombing Murmansk, Orsha, Mogilev, Smolensk, Kyiv, Odesa, Sevastopol. Grave danger overhangs our country.

'How could it have happened,' he went on, addressing the question that would have been most pressing to his audience of millions, 'that our glorious Red Army surrendered a number of our cities and districts to the fascist armies? Is it really true that the German-fascist troops are invincible, as the braggart fascist propagandists are ceaselessly blaring forth?'[3]

The question of invincibility was addressed in the context of conquered western Europe: the subjugation of France, of the Low Countries, the swallowing of Austria and Czechoslovakia and Poland. The people of Leningrad had, the year previously, been reading intensive accounts of the Luftwaffe Blitz on London, written by eyewitness Russian correspondents.

But Stalin was ready with lessons from Russia's past, even if occasionally he had to manipulate that past a little. 'History shows that there are no invincible armies and never have been,' he declared. 'Napoleon's army was considered invincible but it was beaten successively by the armies of Russia, England and Germany. Kaiser Wilhelm's army in the period of the First Imperialist War was also considered invincible but it was beaten several times by Russian and Anglo-French troops,' he went on (neglecting to dwell on how Russia's war ended) 'and was finally smashed by the Anglo-French forces. The same must be said of Hitler's fascist army today.'[4]

The most unsettlingly honest response to Stalin's address came from the Leningrad-based children's writer Daniil Kharms. This distinctive and disorientating figure – tall and dandyish in English tweeds, emulating Conan Doyle's detective Sherlock Holmes, with blazingly intense eyes and a pugnaciously fixed jaw – had for many years stood at an angle to the regime, like a secular version of a Tsarist holy fool, theorizing lubriciously about Soviet sexual fantasies and habits (pouring scorn on 'passionate' as opposed to 'sensual' women – the former grabbed any part of their partner's body without any consideration, paid insufficient attention to their partner's genitals, and were too intent on speedy orgasm)[5] and satirizing the new social norms. Kharms's entire adult life had been spent – through the medium of absurdist poetry, and through extraordinary, innovative stagecraft – trying to bend the shackles of Stalinist rule. He had already suffered for it: a spell of imprisonment in a camp in eastern Ukraine in the early 1930s, after which his adult material was banned and children's books left as his only creative outlet. Now his anarchic, ungovernable voice had apparently bellowed the truth as he saw it: at least, this was according to the security forces of the NKVD, who claimed to have evidence of Kharms declaring: 'The USSR lost the war on its first day. Leningrad will be either besieged or starved to death. Or it will be bombed to the ground, leaving no stone standing.

'If they give me a mobilization order,' he was said to have continued (and it is more than possible that he did say this, given his lifelong trajectory of declaiming his own artistic truth to friends and impromptu audiences), 'I will punch the commander in the face. Let them shoot me, but I will not put on the uniform and will not serve in the Soviet forces, I do not wish to be such trash. If they force me to fire a machine gun from rooftops during street-to-street fights with the Germans, I would shoot not at the Germans, but at *them*, from the very same machine gun.'[6]

In August 1941, Kharms would be removed to Kresty prison's psychiatric unit. This meant – unusually – that he was spared execution (though death would soon find him by other means).

Yet even if the vast majority of Leningraders, who had already spent the last few days under a burning sun helping to dig the first anti-tank trenches around the outskirts of the city, had been inspired by the words of Stalin, there was none the less a fresh alertness to the novel nature of this conflict: it was without any question total war. Everyone was a combatant. Stalin's address was also quite candid about this – and about the ultimate aims of Operation Barbarossa:

> The enemy is cruel and implacable. He is out to seize our lands watered by the sweat of our brows, to seize our grain and oil secured by the labour of our hands. He is out to restore the rule of the landlords, to restore tsarism, to destroy the national culture and the national existence . . . to turn [the people] into slaves of German princes and barons . . . the issue is whether the peoples of the Soviet Union shall be free or fall into slavery.[7]

As with Churchill's encouragement to 'fight on the beaches', there was an exhortation to the people not merely to put all industry and agriculture on a total war footing, aiding the Red Army in every way imaginable, but also to begin a campaign within occupied territory of espionage and sabotage, harrying the fascist foe at every step. This was no time, he warned, for cowards or traitors; they, and those who believed and spread 'false rumours', would be hauled up before military tribunals. The punishment did not need spelling out.

'Comrades, our forces are numberless,' declared Stalin. 'Side by side with the Red Army many thousands of workers, collective farmers and intellectuals are rising to fight the enemy aggressor.'[8]

In those first few hours of war, the city's factories had been bustling with men and women volunteering for military service. There seemed little heed of what this might actually entail: civilians stepping forward to fight, if necessary, alongside fully trained Red Army comrades. It also seemed as though the volunteer spirit was genuinely spontaneous, as opposed to being subliminally encouraged: a relief to Zhdanov's authorities, monitoring anonymous notes of dissent.

Similarly, the sheer speed with which some half a million Leningraders – about a quarter of its working-age population – immediately drafted themselves into building fortifications was dazzling. By 27 June 1941, men and women alike – sixteen to fifty years old in the case of males, sixteen to forty-five for females – were being posted for defensive work on top of their regular manufacturing shifts. This meant either civil defence – fire-watching, building shelters – or manual labour out in the countryside. The proud poet Anna Akhmatova instantly volunteered for night-time fire duties, patrolling roofs for incendiaries, as did many eager teenagers. All these civilians were already facing the front line.

There was an expanse of rich green landscape – dotted with birch trees and glinting with the onion domes of undemolished churches – some 220 miles south-west of Leningrad that stood on the borders of Latvia and Estonia: initially, huge numbers of workers – the emphasis was on younger people rather than experienced factory engineers – were transported daily to work in shifts digging out huge trenches as tank defences and building pillboxes and other fortifications. The work was not only arduous – unyielding sun-baked earth, no shelter from the heat, muscles straining and pulling after a day on the production line – but it was very obviously hazardous too. The skies above droned with the approach of Luftwaffe fighters; in the distance to the west could be heard the deep booming echoes of artillery. Those Luftwaffe pilots could not have had clearer targets: as well as soldiers, any civilian labourers who could not take evasive action in time were pierced with bullets.

The wounded were returned to the city; the hospitals immediately began to feel the strain. Young women – some of whom themselves had been out in the country helping to construct defensive lines – were now also conscripted into nursing and ambulance driving. They had to adjust very quickly to the sight of deep purple wounds, of sprays of blood; they had to learn paramedical skills at extraordinary speed. 'We washed the bandages at night because we didn't have enough,' remembered Bertha Gutkina, who was seventeen years old at the time. 'We washed and dried them so that in the morning we could take them all to the bandaging room.'[9] This was not the life that she had been brought up to expect: the previous months had been filled with piano lessons. Now in the space of just a few days, her father was dead – a heart attack at the depot as he was overseeing the rail evacuation of Elektrosila technical equipment to Tomsk. And without any chance to grieve, both mother and daughter, left in their communal apartment, were thrown into the vortex of defensive work.

A little closer to Leningrad itself was the Luga Line (Luga was both a river and a small town about ninety miles south of the city), which also saw the frantic preparation of defences. But out in the country-side the workers had a foretaste of the struggle to come: not only the outbreaks of strafing from German aircraft that were growing ever more assertive in the skies above, but also woeful supplies of nutritious food to keep them going.

In those first days of war, the city's older children had an important part to play as well. It was understood very quickly that Leningrad would have to be adapted to face the onslaught of bombing. Shelters would have to be constructed and the grander, more ornate buildings would have to be camouflaged. 'We cleared the roofs,' recalled Leonard Polyak, who was then seventeen. 'Removed any extra wooden partitions from the roofs. We dragged buckets full of sand up there. Water, too, to prevent fires spreading from incendiary bombs.'[10]

Yura Riabinkin – the teenager who had spent the first hours of war in a fugue-like daze of chess games – was also swift to adapt to this new world. On 26 June he was back at the Pioneer Palace, this time up early to report to the youth centre there. He and his chess-playing friends were quickly organized into work teams, and Riabinkin was sent to a building site next to the Kazan Cathedral. 'I worked from eleven in the morning till nine in the evening with a break for dinner,' he recalled in his diary. 'Both my hands got calloused and had splinters in them. I lugged planks, dug holes in the ground, sawed and chopped wood – all sorts of things to be done. Towards the end my arm began to ache so much that I could not saw any more.'[11]

Yet with the brilliant – and universal – earnestness of all bright teenage boys, Riabinkin was determined not to let fatigue mar his intellectual contribution to war spirit. He had begun reading *Virgin Soil* by Ivan Turgenev – one of the nineteenth-century classics that had, after many years of proscription, at last been enfolded into the bosom of the Stalinist regime. Concerning Aleksei Nezhdanov, a young, disaffected St Petersburg man ('Spies everywhere! Oppression, lies, betrayal, deceit!')[12] who accepts the role of tutor on a distant country estate and who is then inevitably sucked into local feverish political movements, this was a work that blended sharpness and humour with genuine raptures about the illimitable landscapes of the mother country.

In the days just before the war, one of the most popular films showing in Leningrad was a Soviet comedy entitled *Anton Ivanovich is Angry*. In some senses, it was a typical Leningrad subject: the Anton Ivanovich of the title was a musician of such purity that he would only ever play music written by J. S. Bach; his daughter, attending a music conservatory and falling in love with a young composer, enraged him by composing operettas. Could the gulf between their tastes ever be bridged? Come the outbreak of war, Bach's Germanic identity cast his oeuvre in quite a different light; moreover, Leningraders in those immediate days of alarm and fear had other things to think about than escapist comedy cinema. But the poet Olga Berggolts recalled vividly how the posters for the film remained up in that period, and of how the idea of an 'Anton Ivanovich' and his 'anger' took on a whole new dimension: 'The idea unwittingly arose of a real, living person, very kind-hearted, who, not understanding everything and fiercely desiring people to be happy and good, with anguish was becoming angry at people for all the needless, absurd and awful suffering.'[13]

This was also a time, further back from the creeping line of the German assault, when Sergei Eisenstein's epic film *Alexander Nevsky* – swiftly pulled from cinemas in 1939 for diplomatic reasons in the wake of the Molotov–Ribbentrop Pact – was now speedily re-released. Along with Stalin's appeals to historical defeats of Germany, the war with the Teutonic Knights was now seen as an invaluable morale-booster.

Hearts were often more fearful than bellicose; mothers were looking at their small children and bursting into helpless tears. There were rumours that the Germans would start using chemical weapons. In those first few days, much thought was also given to the prospect of evacuation. For many parents with children no more than five or six years old the idea was agony: a child labelled, bundled on a train with countless others and transported unquantifiable distances to the east. But everyone had seen the newsreels of the infernos caused by the Luftwaffe in the west.

By 26 June word was spreading that the authorities were beginning to load up some 'factory machinery' on to trains, and that certain parts of military production lines were to be relocated far further into Russia. The authorities were also beginning to reserve trains for children. The evacuations were about to begin.

Lidiya Okhapkina and her husband were beside themselves with distress, as her diary records:

On 28 June, we sent our son off. Poor little fellow, he was only five years old! I had got his clothes ready for him and had marked every item, stitching his first and last names in thread. While I was dressing him that morning, I was wondering when I would next have to dress him. And I was abruptly overwhelmed by alarm and anxiety as to when I might ever see him again – what if he were lost all of a sudden?

She could not help sharing her fears with her husband, and when she looked at him she saw that 'there were tears running down his cheeks'.[14]

The first of the children were being assembled in their classroom groups; many would be taken to the city's Moscow station, and from there they would be guided on to trains by female Party members who sat on Education Executive Committees. Those trains in some cases would be pointing south towards the Novgorodskaya region. Within a matter of days, the evacuations would be hit by panic and chaos: the advance of the Wehrmacht, and the pressure from its ever-increasing bombing raids, were not foreseen by the authorities. As we shall see a little later, the intense confusion – with a new emphasis on bringing evacuated children back to Leningrad – would create an extra layer of anguish for parents.

There was a different sort of protectiveness about the city's literary and artistic treasures, but those who oversaw them felt the danger – of invasion, of bombing – with an intensity that they had not perhaps expected. Georgii Knyazev, director of the archives at the Academy of

Sciences, had spent the first few days of the war in emergency meetings with colleagues. How best to protect and hide the city's intellectual heritage? He met with the director of the archives at the Institute of Russian Literature. This, in so many ways, was the real beating heart of the old St Petersburg: the 'manuscripts of Pushkin, Lomonosov, Lermontov, Turgenev, Dostoevsky, Tolstoy and others',[15] as Knyazev noted. These were original, and irreplaceable; and they were also obviously fragile. Yet in those early days, all staff could do to protect them from the hazards of flames and fumes was to fill the archive chambers with barrels of water, and have fire hoses ready nearby. In addition to that were a number of sandboxes. The prospect was chaotic and – in the context of delicate paper and ink over one hundred years old – acutely worrying.

And yet throughout this, routine work continued also: even for the intellectuals. Knyazev found sleep difficult in those first few nights, imagining the drone of approaching war. But in the day, he wrote, 'I took some students on an excursion and delivered a lecture to them with great panache.'[16]

And what could be done with the city's monuments? In the case of the Bronze Horseman, legend had it that as long as the statue stood on its pedestal of red granite, the city would never be conquered. The Communists were apparently as much in thrall to the old superstitions as their Tsarist predecessors. The statue was swiftly surrounded with sandbags and a wooden shelter built around it, an extemporized house of planks. Before long, many of the city's other statues – such as the 'horse tamer' sculptures on Anichkov Bridge – were removed and buried in places of safety in parks and gardens. Elsewhere, parties of teenagers from the Pioneer Palace had been set to work on the golden dome of St Isaac's Cathedral, attempting to cover it completely with grey material to make it less identifiable from above.

The expectation of the city being bombed heavily was based in part upon all the news coverage of the London Blitz the previous winter. The authorities issued gas masks to residential wardens. And as well as the instructions about papering over every window, there were also first-aid posts established. Citizens needed no encouragement to check their own supply of bandages and iodine. Residents in apartment blocks, gathering in associations, discussed their resources for dealing with burns.

A blackout was ordered: no lights to be shown in the city after dark, either in the streets or peeping from homes. The authorities had also begun distributing special blue-shaded light-bulbs, the ghostly illumination of which would not be detectable from the air. They also made reading difficult; and faces illuminated by them acquired an ethereal character.

Elsewhere, at the Hermitage, the vast museum that was home to countless works of art and sculpture, the tension was multiplied many times over. Yet curiously – perhaps because of the years of paranoia that Stalin's Terror had brought in the 1930s – here was one of the city's institutions that had begun planning for apocalyptic catastrophe as early as 1937. And even throughout the fragile two years of the 1939–41 Molotov–Ribbentrop Pact, museum director Joseph Orbeli had been studying the logistics of packing up over a hundred vast galleries of treasure and thence removing them from the building to places of greater safety.

There was also the matter of the grand palaces that lay on the outskirts of the city in their exquisitely landscaped gardens: Tsarskoe Selo and the Peterhof Palace, as well as other grand houses that had been repurposed by the Soviets (some as children's homes). This was a question not only of art, but also of historic furniture, of extraordinary tapestries rich in colour and detail, mosaics dating back to the eighteenth century, their craftsmanship still luminous in reds and golds and blues. There was little doubt that the aim of the Nazi armies would be to loot these treasures and take them back to Germany. The Hermitage and all the assorted works would have to be transported as far into the heart of Russia as could be managed; but where would be most suitable not only to preserve but also to cherish this irreplaceable aesthetic hoard?

Orbeli seemed to have had some form of premonition several years before the invasion (and indeed before the outbreak of war in western Europe). To this end, he had quietly started to sequester huge numbers of crates from various sites around the city. He also managed to commandeer vast quantities of packing material: from Old Masters to marble, there was a science to preservation.

Intriguingly, according to historian Lane Bailey, Director Orbeli was so intensely secretive about all this that no one in the higher offices of the Kremlin knew of his plans. In fact, there was a moment right at the start of the German invasion in that summer of 1941 when those close to Stalin specifically ordered that the Hermitage and its works should not be evacuated; that nerves should be held. The reason apparently was that if the people were to see the city denuded of its riches, the blow to morale would be terrible.[17]

Just as quickly as these commands were issued, they were rescinded. The treasures of the Hermitage, and of the former Tsarist palaces, were to be loaded on to special trains and taken to Sverdlovsk (Yekaterinburg), in the shadow of the Ural mountain range. The prospect was this: over half a million different works of art, each in its own specially protected container, obsessively catalogued so that not one piece could go missing. The task was gargantuan: had Orbeli not already secured a head start by preparing the specially labelled crates and boxes, there would have been the most unholy panic.

Even so, it was still a time of high anxiety. Two full trains – starting at the Moscow station and heading south – had been earmarked for this responsibility and the date was set for 1 July. This could only be the start – two trains could carry only a fraction of the Hermitage's priceless masterpieces. The security was intense, police and soldiers on watch as canvases and sculptures were carefully loaded aboard long goods wagons. As well as the art, there was one carriage set aside for a platoon of specially appointed guards who would keep watch as the train made its slow journey across the vast plains. Each train would also be equipped with one flat-bed carriage upon which was mounted an anti-aircraft gun.

In overall charge of this extraordinary cargo was one of Orbeli's deputy directors: Vladimir Levinson-Lessing. Lessing, a forty-eight-year-old originally hailing from Estonia, had been selected as the guardian of the Hermitage in exile. It was he who would have responsibility for ensuring that the works would be perfectly preserved in Sverdlovsk, far from the perceived range of any Luftwaffe bombers. In fact, it was a city so deep within the Russian interior that it was closer to Kazakhstan than to Moscow. There was an art museum there established back at the turn of the twentieth century, which also had within its precincts buildings that dated back to the eighteenth century.[18] But nothing could match the scale or the opulence of the Hermitage and, in any case, the exiled treasures were not for show: this was about safekeeping.

Back in Leningrad, another shipment of around three-quarters of a million art works – again, all packed and ready to go – were scheduled for a train that would leave a couple of weeks later. Yet this still left more than a million dazzling artefacts within the echoing and vulnerable grandeur of that great institution. And, as with the city's human treasure, that potential escape route was being closed off with a nightmarish speed.

In those days of summer, Orbeli and his large team of helpers – volunteers as well as staff had been drafted in for the vast task of moving everything from room-sized paintings to gilded historical Tsarist carriages out of immediate danger – had been spurred on by a single-mindedness about their duty. When it became apparent that transportation routes were being severed, they would also start to understand that their duty was graver: to stand sentinel, and never desert the institution, as though the Hermitage were the soul of the city itself.

An even more pressing evacuation looked as though it was coming closer just weeks after the shock news of invasion. No matter how wrenching it was for parents to face the idea of having their very small children taken from them, there was another sense that they had to be entrusted to the Party and the state. But in the dense mists of confusion that accompanied the German attack, some of those initial evacuations – by train and by bus – were accidentally to become harrowing journeys deeper into the heart of war. By trying to keep the little ones safe, the authorities in some cases were inadvertently sending them towards more terrible danger.

One town that had been fixed upon as a destination for the youngest evacuees was Demyansk, in the Novgorod region. It was deep in the rich countryside, and lay almost exactly halfway between Leningrad and Moscow. A Party official, Mariya Vasilyevna Motkovskaya, had been sent ahead with a couple of colleagues to ensure that the town and its people were ready to receive around 5,000 children, some of whom were of nursery-school age. There seemed few practical difficulties: housing billets were made ready, the logistics of making space in classrooms were settled.

So when the trains set out from Leningrad – tense mothers waving off tearful (or cheerful) children – there was an initial sense of optimism that their destination would be a secure refuge. What had not been anticipated, however, was the nightmarish speed of the German advance into the Russian countryside.

A force of Wehrmacht paratroopers had made a landing just thirty miles west of Demyansk; the battles were fierce and both sides were facing torrential summer downpours. The Red Army had begun to pull together a more determined resistance. But almost as soon as these thousands of children arrived, it appeared that they would have to be moved on again – re-evacuated, this time with many of Demyansk's children, to new destinations further east. The result, recalled Motkovskaya, was harrowing in terms of the distress of the smaller children. Newly settled in welcoming households, they were then corralled by fearful adults into whatever transport could be found in that atmosphere of panic.

Buses and coaches were summoned to ferry huge numbers of small children to a railway station at Lychkovo. This, as it happened, was the recent epicentre of the attempted German advance. On that day, the powder-blue skies above were criss-crossed with the vapour trails of Luftwaffe bombers and Soviet fighters. Motkovskaya got to the town, and to the railway station, and discovered a terrible scene: one teacher in a school building, surrounded by a vast number of frightened children screaming at each explosion as bombs fell nearby. Many of the children were crying for their mothers: the sole teacher was almost paralysed in the face of such mass distress.

There was a train ready at the station: a chance to pack as many of the scared children on as possible. But the station itself was frighteningly vulnerable, and as the children were being helped into the carriages, Luftwaffe bombs were blowing craters into the surrounding ground. The sheer ruthlessness shocked Motkovskaya – to her, it was perfectly obvious that the German pilots above could see the small children swarming around the station, and that these same children were being deliberately targeted. Some had been wounded elsewhere by shrapnel: the train out was their chance to get medical treatment back in larger towns. This attack on helpless infants revealed to her the truest face of the enemy: her hatred was molten white and almost beyond the power of words.[19]

But the flight of the children continued: numbers were now heading for Kirov, a very pretty city even further east than Moscow, and on the way to the Ural mountains. Many other children, however, were caught in eddies of adult confusion: some because they were injured, some because of railway logistics, were instead returned to the city from which they had first been evacuated: Leningrad. One mother had had the chance to accompany her daughter out: on the train back, they got caught up in the most terrible attack.

The train, recalled the mother, had not been far out of Mga, a small settlement a short distance outside Leningrad, when the unholy booms began. Everyone on that packed train – children and adults – had been travelling for the best part of three days, and they were already disorientated. When the bombing came, it was hideously quick, but the instincts of the adults were razor sharp. The explosives seemed to hit the carriages one by one in lightning succession. The train was instantly full of broken corpses. In the grim dark, parents scrambled to cram their children under the seats, and they sought to cover them with coats and blankets as extra protection. Following the attack, the air rang with silence; but then there were efforts to get out of the smouldering carriages.

Children and adults alike had to drop from the train on to the stony trackside in the deepening murk of twilight. The noise of firing from the sky saw children being thrown down into ditches near the tracks for protection, faces down in the earth.

Yet back in Leningrad in those hazed, disorientated summer days, there was, curiously, for a while some semblance of stability. While the sense of approaching menace could not be dispelled, or the sense that Leningrad was soon to be strangled by renewed Finnish aggression, there was, among some, a striking insouciance.

The weather – so warm and fine – meant that in their lunch breaks, older workers from offices were gathering in squares and parks, bordered with fine houses and apartment blocks of ochre, yellow and pale green, setting up tables and playing dominoes and chess. The sounds of the city were still familiar: the trams, which had not yet been requisitioned for military purposes, were still clanging up and down the wider streets, and those small children who had not been evacuated were scampering around playfully in the larger squares as their teenage siblings shovelled at great mounds of deposited sand, filling hessian sacks. There was, according to academic Georgii Knyazev, one especially striking smell in the air: that of smouldering, burning peat.[20] Huge quantities of the stuff were being cut from the earth in the countryside to the north of the city: fuel for when the seasons turned and the thin, blade-like winds began to scour the streets – a lesson from the Winter War.

The people were not yet imprisoned; but the city already felt acutely vulnerable and isolated. In addition to anticipation of chemical attacks from the skies, there was a sense that the war was a terrible incoming tide: the violence and the slaughter that the Germans were bringing with them had swept through central Europe and would soon be lapping at the edges of the city. There was a double vulnerability: for the violence came not only from the Germans, but from rather closer neighbours too.

10.   World Without End

The Green Man – or the Borovoi, or the Metsavana – was still invoked by some in Leningrad: a childhood apparition of fable, a malign figure who dwelled in the dark forests and who would seek to lure the unwary away from their path. The superstition had been brought to the modern city by the older people who had once lived under wider skies, in landscapes of pine and linden and silent rivers. Like St Nicolas the Wonderworker, and the other painted Orthodox icons with their piercing gazes, the Green Man, despite being a pagan hobgoblin, was treasured: he was part of the tapestry of folk identity that not even the most determined Stalinist could erase. By the summer of 1941, when the Soviet occupiers of the Baltic states were seeking to destroy what they could before the territory was seized by the Nazi invaders, the dense forests of those lands took on a whole new form of life. And when it came to the simplest questions of sustenance for Leningrad – supplies of dairy products, of meat – the anarchy in those Baltic forests would contribute to the slicing of those lifelines, and to the terrible descent into mass hunger.

Just eighteen months earlier, the Soviet annexation of the three countries in the wake of the Molotov–Ribbentrop Pact had created seething, desperate pockets of resistance: in Estonia, for instance, some 10,000 men – ranging from politicians to schoolteachers – had massed in the forests. This was not mere ideological protest: in the space of little over a year, the Stalinist security forces had rounded up many thousands of intellectuals and civil servants in Estonia, Lithuania and Latvia, and had had them sent to the deathly wildernesses of Siberia. They had been enslaved, and their chances of surviving the crushing forced labour and the overcrowded, stinking tubercular barracks were slender. So the Soviet occupation of the region was not a passive weight, simply milking the lands of their resources: there was a real viciousness and hatred there too.

The Brothers of the Forest, as they became known, were armed: they were concealed deep within wooded labyrinths and surviving on woodland game. Hideously, it seemed to them that the Nazis had handed them an opportunity. When the bloody cacophony of Operation Barbarossa was launched, these guerilla fighters were prepared to wage their own particular war. While much of the occupying Red Army was busy trying to halt the Nazi advance head on, the partisans took on its thin remnants in the town of Tartu. The resulting terrible battle went on for two weeks, the Soviets eventually forced to retreat (albeit at some cost, the NKVD managing to kill some 300 townsfolk as it pulled out).

Such outbreaks of impromptu resistance – former civic leaders forced into outlaw life in dense forests – were repeated across Latvia and Lithuania too. In all cases, there were many among these white-collar warriors who wanted most keenly simple independence: freedom both from the brutish oppression of Stalin, but also from the colonizing ambitions of the Nazis. But the result of the Soviet occupation was that resentment was stoked to such a level that the Nazis were initially considered welcome liberators.

They were, of course, nothing of the sort. Any scorched-earth horrors that the retreating Stalinists had inflicted were soon to fade next to the savagery that the Nazis' enthusiastic death squads would bring to cities like Tallinn and Riga. The Germans enacted a credible impression of a liberating force: there were German generals who understood the locals – in terms of Nazi racial hierarchy – to be themselves very close to German racial stock, for example. And so, in that high summer of 1941, as the German tanks rolled across those plains, the Brothers of the Forest emerged into the open, whereupon they were forcibly disbanded.

For these lands too were intended for new generations of Nazi farmers. They would no longer belong in any sense to the people who had flickeringly imagined that the Nazis might allow them some kind of independence and freedom. For them, the planned future would involve at best servitude, at worst (and more likely) starvation. Hitler – like Stalin before him – understood very well the use of hunger both as a means of control and as a genocidal weapon.

The General Plan for the East was partly about grabbing its resources and its fuel, but more particularly about harvesting its food, first for German soldiers and then for the German people. What was left after that could be distributed to subdued Soviets, and then Soviet prisoners. It could also be withheld from them.

'Few Germans doubted our ultimate triumph, but many wondered about the duration of the struggle and the price of final victory,' recalled Wilhelm Lübbecke, a German conscript with Army Group North, many years later. 'Almost no one questioned the morality of a crusade to destroy Soviet Bolshevism, but there were some like me who shared practical misgivings.'[1] But in this, he was subsuming one of the chief Nazi goals, to which Leningrad's sizeable Jewish population was intensely alert: that of the open and methodical killing of Jewish civilians. In the summer of 1941, in Latvia's cities and towns, the Nazi Einsatzgruppen 'action squads' had begun by rounding up any Jews they termed 'Communist' – Jewish men at first, then also women and children.[2] Some groups were very simply taken out of the towns, driven to nearby forests, shot and then buried in mass graves. Children and women were crowded into large barns and held there for weeks before suffering the same fate.

The murderous orders were camouflaged as the suppression of dissent and resistance. But the disguise was contemptuously thin: the Nazis moving through these Baltic states were simply identifying Jewish people and slaughtering them in ever larger numbers. While partly this was the psychosis of war, it also formed the spine of the Nazi philosophy and worldview. Warfare was the face that this lethal frenzy wore, but the Nazis would have made it happen by any means. Throughout their training, and through all their active service, German soldiers were taught that the Jews were a sickness in the world, an infection that had to be burned from the land. This was the darkness moving towards Leningrad: an army without pity, a front line that stretched for many hundreds of miles and a force that appeared to be devouring all before it.

It was not only the Germans who were advancing. On 25 June Finland had declared war upon the Soviet Union following a pre-emptive Soviet bombing raid on the country. Loathing had been coursing through the Finnish government ever since the Winter War of 1939–40, and the Finns – determined to recapture the forest territory that they had lost a couple of years beforehand – now had their excuse to invade. And, like the Germans further south, they faced a Red Army that was floundering and in disarray.

There is a currently popular phrase hurled around in political disputes: 'the right side of history'. It is usually the mark of imbecilic populism, suggesting a fairy-tale world of moral absolutes. Yet the relationship of Finland with the Nazi regime from 1940 through to the end of the war did raise some stark questions. And it also created some remarkable anomalies.

The Finnish state's decision not only to ask for help from Hitler's Germany – a supply of armaments – but also to actively offer to work alongside it was certainly a moment of moral horror. By 1940, when the Finnish government was provided with some arms and intelligence from Berlin, the true murderous nature of the Nazi regime was hardly any kind of secret. The German takeover of Norway that year – Wehrmacht troops flooding into the country, entire villages set ablaze, the puppet regime of Norwegian fascist Vidkun Quisling aiding and abetting the persecution of the country's tiny Jewish community – was enough alone to indicate the truth.

Yet the Nazi relationship with Finland did have some curious elements. And in Finland, that relationship came to be known by some as an example of 'driftwood theory' – that as a small player without any kind of real agency, Finland was as helpless as driftwood caught in the tides of a mighty ocean;[3] that what happened was less about intentional cooperation and more about the forces of geopolitical gravity. Finland wanted to be free of the Russian threat. Britain, under attack itself, was in no position to help. Late in 1940, the Germans indicated to the Finnish government that they themselves would be moving against the Bolsheviks – and that they would expect the cooperation of the Finnish army.

No official treaty was signed; Finland did not publicly join the Axis. But it was regarded by Hitler's inner circle as an ally none the less. Hitler spoke in his declaration of the 'Finnish freedom fighters' who stood alongside 'the heroes of Narvik' at the 'edge of the Arctic Ocean'.[4] As well as the German troops coursing through Finland, the Finnish army itself comprised almost half a million men. One of their specific aims was the recapture of the Karelian Isthmus, that rich land of timber and ice-cold lakes. The Finnish soldiers were anticipating – in the wake of the Winter War – that vast numbers of Soviet troops would be stationed in the region. There were, however, considerably fewer than they had estimated – some five divisions, numbering around 45,000 men.

This assault, then, from the north, seemed swift; under those endless (and to some, enervating) sunlit summer nights – and with the help of hardware and fighter planes supplied by the Nazi regime – the Finnish forces once more began laying waste to the Red Army; once more, the forests filled with charred corpses. The ill-preparedness of the Soviets in this sector mirrored the collapse and confusion taking place right across the Baltic states.

These were the forces that were now advancing towards Leningrad from the north, the Finnish soldiers not quite in full alliance with the Nazis yet marching alongside them as comrades.

There were other irregulars allied with the Wehrmacht: soldiers drafted from Franco's Spain formed the Blue Division. As the German tanks roared and bulldozed across endless plains and marshes, and skirted vast cold lakes, and as Wehrmacht troops marched into tiny Russian villages, these other soldiers followed. One such Spaniard referred to 'a landscape of nothingness';[5] another wrote mockingly in his diary of communism: 'We see here "equality" and "paradise". Every person is barefoot, scarcely clad, and unaware of the most basic personal hygiene. The people, as they call the workers, live in wooden huts.'[6] Corporal Tessier was accompanying a German division as it moved through from Lithuania across the Russian border in that bloody summer. 'We began to see the authentic Russians,' he wrote, 'dirty and impoverished. The villages and the homesteads look completely wretched. The Russians were all beards and tall boots. The dirty houses must surely be full of parasites. The gates of Soviet paradise open before us.'[7] And this also demonstrated with what terrible ease it was possible to start seeing other people as less than human. Even the Spanish soldiers, with their rumoured compassion, were staring at people in villages as though they belonged to another species.

This was a land where labourers tried – often unsuccessfully – to hide food: roadsides punctuated with the ribbed bodies of dead horses. In that summer, the skies above frequently bulged with growing storm clouds; and when the rains came, they were prodigious. Dust-tracks that had served as roads became swamps of dark mud. The air was electric and heavy and the smell of dead animals carried across farmsteads. The long marches began to cast an uncanny spell on the invaders, as Wilhelm Lübbecke recalled:

> Battling both stifling heat and thick clouds of dust, we plodded countless miles. There were few breaks from our march, except for the occasional chance to hitch a lift on one of our company's horse-drawn vehicles. After a while, a kind of hypnosis would set in as you watched the steady rhythm of the man's boots in front of you. Utterly exhausted, I sometimes fell into a quasi-sleepwalk. Placing one foot in front of the other in my state of semiconsciousness, I somehow managed to keep pace, waking only briefly whenever I stumbled into the body ahead of me.[8]

The Germans, and those who marched with them, were meeting the Soviet Russians for the first time. There had been a long tradition in Germany of caricaturing so-called Slavic people, and these inevitably involved stereotypes to do with brutishness, low intelligence and primitive tastes. So it was that the young Wehrmacht soldiers, often drawn from brightly lit cities, confronted with the pre-modern rural life of Belorussian, Ukrainian and Russian villages, thought they were seeing a confirmation of all that they had been taught. Even though the mass atrocities did not begin immediately – the systematic rounding up and killing of Jews, the burning of entire villages – the attitudes that made them possible were already fixed.

And the Wehrmacht invasion of the historic city of Novgorod in August 1941 would – as well as being nightmarish for those civilians – bring a moment of fresh dread for the citizens of Leningrad when the news came through. For while other conquests were equally ghastly – the submission of Kyiv, leaving the way open for the Nazi domination of Ukraine and Crimea – Novgorod, a city of great beauty, also had the most intense symbolic value.

It was where, seven centuries earlier, Prince Alexander Nevsky had faced the forces of the Teutonic Knights and defeated them. Now darker forces swept over this place of ancient onion-domed cathedrals and grand nineteenth-century civic structures. In that August of 1941, the destruction was intense: much of the city's older architecture was bombed and shelled.

Fire and bombardment had also disfigured the city of Smolensk, and the landscape all around it. Battle here roared throughout the summer days and nights of 1941 from July to the beginning of September, the Soviet Red Army forces slowly encircled and then trapped in ever-constricting pockets by lethal panzer divisions. Hundreds of thousands of Red Army prisoners were taken and, again, the symbolism was frightening. Hitler's armies were flooding across the Luga and the Dnieper, rivers understood as boundaries between worlds for centuries. That those Nazi armies had no concept of the world that they had entered made no difference.

'You can't afford to be soft in war,' one soldier wrote to his wife back in Germany. 'Indeed, you have to be pitiless and relentless.' Then he added: 'Do I sound like a different person to you?'[9] In rapidly secured victories, there was certainty in the ideological purity of what they were doing if not in its morality. One soldier, Wolfgang Kluge, wrote: 'Men die daily, and daily rise from the dead.'[10] The killings had to be justified in terms of war itself being a cleansing process through which purer, newer souls would emerge. Among some of these soldiers, though, there had already been an intimation of another kind of unease, triggered by the landscapes that they had already crossed: the thick, trackless forests, the lush green valleys, the distant shores glimpsed across wide, silent, fast-flowing rivers; then the expanses of the steppes, horizons that lay flat and infinite. The truly alien part of this invasion was the nature of the land itself. They could not know or feel it as those who lived here knew and felt it – that when gazing to the east, they were gazing at a land that might as well know no end, a land that ran halfway round the world.

These were men who were accustomed to borders, and to populous country. For those who marched thousands of miles with unwavering confidence, there must have been flutters of bewilderment about where the marching was to stop. On top of this, there was simple topographic disorientation. 'In our advance northward, we began to be increasingly hindered by both the worsening roads and intensifying resistance from Soviet rearguards,' recalled Wilhelm Lübbecke. 'Our advance was also complicated by maps showing main roads and highways that simply did not exist. Beyond problems with a lack of accuracy, there were also few maps to go around.'[11]

The incessant agony of suspense had been building in Leningrad throughout that late summer, as the city's life had become geared towards shoring up defences and trying to fathom the logistics of evacuating children and women. The Party apparatus was drafting citizens for their sessions of manual labour in the surrounding countryside, digging through the heat-hardened earth to create trenches and tank traps. As well as available men up to the age of sixty, women along with children aged ten and older would now also receive their instructions to report either to designated bus stops or to the Moscow station; from there, they would be ferried by coach or rail into those flat, wooded landscapes that ringed the city, and their shifts of heavy physical work would span the entire day. These days were fraught with the absolute certainty of danger when the warm summer skies filled once more with the bass humming that foreshadowed the appearance of Messerschmitt fighter aircraft, strafing the people below. Huge numbers were bloodily wounded. Equally huge numbers, their organs burst by burning bullets, died where they lay. Their corpses were taken back to the city, where the pressure upon the gravediggers started to grow. They too were feverishly excavating that dry earth on a scale not seen since the 1919–21 Civil War.

The defences being constructed around the city were part of the landscape of 'reddish sand', of fir and larch and 'jasmine bushes' that had formed the author Vladimir Nabokov's first ideas of beauty;[12] a countryside inhabited by few people, and people who themselves might have comfortably belonged in another time. Now the air continually rolled with the drums and snapping lashes of distant heavy artillery; yet many of those women and older children on their shifts, their calloused hands and sharply protesting backs gradually adjusting to the demands of heavy spadework, were curiously cheerful about their labours, despite the horrible hazards. 'I and two others were sent to help dig trenches,' recalled Leonard Polyak, at that time a young teenager who had been drafted in to work twelve-hour shifts as an electrical apprentice.[13] This time-out from the electrics plant took them into the heat-hazed August countryside. 'We were taken by train to Oranienbaum and then walked to the village Ust-Ruditsa. We dug deep anti-tank trenches there.' They camped there, continuing their work for a few days. But then came the chime of danger. 'We began seeing soldiers retreating from Estonia,' Polyak recalled. 'They said to us: "Guys, why are you sitting here? Get out, because the Germans are right behind us!"'[14] Polyak did get out, catching one of the very last trains into Leningrad. From that point onwards, there would be no escape.

In the city, there was the heavy press of anxiety, a sense that there was no longer any agency against this enemy, but out in the country, even vulnerable under those wide motionless skies, here was a feeling of concrete achievement, of communal courage and defiance. All knew of the proximity of their enemy; at this stage, the Wehrmacht forces were barely more than thirty-five miles away. But the education system under Stalin had inculcated a sense of history's lessons. Many youths were fully conversant with the 1812 Battle of Borodino, and the way that Napoleon's forces, which had seemed set to dominate the world, were instead consigned to a freezing and lethal retreat.

More than this: under the direction of senior Leningrad official Aleksei Kuznetsov – and with a genuine sense of communal effort – the fortifications built closer to the city were in their own way a terrific achievement. Out of that red earth had been gouged canyons sufficiently deep for any advancing tanks to topple into. In addition to this, there were thousands of new concrete pillboxes, and vast quantities of barbed-wire barricades. This was the work of around half a million Leningraders, many of them quite new to construction. The defences that had been erected further away from the city had – while not quite halting the enemy in its tracks entirely – significantly slowed it. The pilots of the Messerschmitts above, gazing down upon an extraordinary workforce that stretched out in a line many miles in length – were not spraying them with bullets out of idle malice. The contribution that these civilians had been making constituted a deeply unwelcome and unexpected setback. Moreover, it was a sign of organizational ingenuity that the Germans – in all their adherence to the belief that they were dealing with sub-humans – could not quite absorb.

One document issued by the Wehrmacht High Command observed of these defences that the 'Russian' is a 'master of camouflage, entrenchment and defence construction. With unbelievable speed he disappears into the earth, digging himself in with unfailing instinct so as to utilize the terrain to make his fortifications very difficult to discover.'[15]

A Kremlin delegation including Malenkov and led by Molotov himself had been dispatched to Leningrad in late August amid fear back in Moscow that the nation's second city could be lost imminently. Even as the Soviet navy had to abandon its Gulf of Finland outpost in Tallinn and send its warships back to the Kronstadt naval base just outside Leningrad, there was urgent discussion of the chief priority: the evacuation of all industry from the city. There was less urgent discussion about the people; they would have to take their turn behind the machinery. And amid all the arguments, the Germans were severing the lifelines. At the end of August, the railway tracks that snaked out from the city – vital arteries that had to be kept pulsing – were being cut off one by one, seized by the Wehrmacht.

The authorities had at last managed to arrange for some half a million mothers and small children to be conveyed east to safety, deep within Russia: an extraordinary exodus that was carried out at speed. But as the rail and road links were destroyed, some 250,000 of the city's most vulnerable citizens, among them babies, remained trapped. Also trapped, amid all the workers, were huge numbers of refugees from the countryside who had been trying to escape the Nazi onrush into their towns and villages.

Within the ranks of the Red Army stationed nearby there was a generalized sense of confusion: orders for tanks to be positioned in lines facing the oncoming panzers; soldier Semyon Putyakov wrote in a (forbidden) diary that 'things are a total mess . . . we are constantly moved from place to place'.[16] To the south of the city, volunteers from the Leningrad People's Militia Army now occupied the trenches and dugouts constructed by civilians. Despite the impression of movement, their world was becoming tighter and more constricted.

Elsewhere, deep in Ukraine, Army Group Centre was beginning to encircle Kyiv: it was necessary for that city to be captured as a springboard towards Moscow. Army Group South was focusing on plans to attack the Donbas region and Kharkiv, part of the drive towards the oil-rich Caucasus.

And in the early days of September came Army Group North's swoop east along the Gulf of Finland, and also through the lightly forested lands a few miles to the south of Leningrad. That flow of tanks and jeeps and men now enveloped the city of Shlisselburg, just a few miles to the east of Leningrad, and which lay on the shores of Lake Ladoga.

All land routes to Leningrad – road and rail – were now blockaded. The city was surrounded. In Army Group North, there came a dizzying moment when some men, in the gentle hills that lay about thirty miles to the south of Leningrad, were gazing with binoculars upon its gilded skyline, and upon the dense cloud of smog that lay above it. Those soldiers were anticipating the order to take the battle to the Soviet tanks and artillery that stood between them and the prize.

But the velocity of Barbarossa had slowed; even attacked by over three million Wehrmacht soldiers, the Red Army defences had not quite been shattered as anticipated. Plans were in flux. By this stage, Hitler's High Command was dismissing any idea of simply conquering Leningrad and occupying it. At the very beginning of Barbarossa, it had been the intention to seize the city's mighty industrial works, in order to deprive the Red Army of vital materiel. But many components – and workers – had been sent hundreds of miles to plants in the east, far from the Wehrmacht's reach. And, in any event, the main goal was Moscow.

So instead, with logic of pure ice, High Command was reaching for a strategy that had been discussed at a special Berlin conference back in May 1941. This was the policy of killing entire populations through starvation. At that conference – attended by the Reich equivalent of senior civil servants – minutes had been taken. 'The war can only continue to be waged if the entire Wehrmacht is fed from Russia during the third year of the war,' it read.[17] The minutes then plunged into a form of psychotic abstraction. 'As a result, X million people will doubtlessly starve.'[18] The shrugging 'X' indicated a figure yet to be determined.

The idea was now that Soviet Russia – so painfully industrialized over the past few decades – would be deindustrialized once more. It would be returned largely to agriculture. Leningrad's population was surplus to any requirements, therefore the civilians were to be prevented from getting out and foodstuffs were to be prevented from getting in. If they were not killed by starvation, then disease would do the job. Joseph Goebbels, Hitler's director of propaganda, was among those who were quite happy to envisage that gruesome scenario. 'The Führer is not concerned with occupying particular cities,' his diaries at the time revealed. 'He wants to avoid casualties among our soldiers. Therefore he no longer intends to take Petersburg by force of arms but rather to starve it into submission.

'Not much will be left of the place,' he continued. 'No doubt there will be a degree of chaos among its millions of inhabitants – but the Bolsheviks would not have it otherwise.'[19]

Shlisselburg was more than just a point on a supply route; it was also an important source of hydroelectric power. Its capitulation would mean that the starvation of the people of Leningrad would be hastened by protracted hours of freezing darkness during the gathering autumn and winter.

A little later, when Hitler met the German ambassador to Vichy France, he was as plain as Goebbels in his view of the city, and of how it had to be torn down: 'Petersburg – the poisonous nest from which, for so long, Asiatic venom has spewed forth into the Baltic – must vanish from the earth's surface,' he declared. 'The city is already cut off. It only remains for us to bomb and bombard it, destroy its sources of water and power and then deny the population everything it needs to survive.'[20]

11. 'The first herald of the hungry plague'

Time itself was being distorted. It was measured out in a series of slow ticks broadcast to the population of Leningrad via the city's radio station. These rhythmic pulses – the sound of a metronome – issued forth from speakers installed by the state in homes and in factories and on the lamp posts of the city's streets. There were those already in the dim bomb shelters who simply stared up at the speakers installed on shelves, the sonorous ticks seeming to mirror the beating of their heart. And then, without warning or announcement, the ticks would begin to gather pace. Faster and faster the rhythm would go; and heartbeats would hurry to match that pace.

The Leningrad metronome was a form of early-warning system. The ticks indicated that German bombers had been detected in the distance. They also became a form of countdown; as long as the pulse was steady, you had time to stop what you were doing and make your way to your local shelter. The creeping speed of the metronome was to evoke the fast approach of the bombers, and of the short distance they had yet to cover. Then, the sirens would start – wails that must have contracted countless hearts. There would also be a harsh voice, commanding attention, demanding that listeners seek shelter. The moaning sirens were then the final countdown.

The really intensive bombardment of Leningrad began on the night of 8 September 1941. But for days and weeks beforehand, endless false alarms, endless ticks of the metronome, had sent the increasingly weary citizens down to shelters freshly dug out of the earth, or into cellars and basements that had been sparsely furnished with wooden benches. Leningraders had sat staring at those radios, their eyes blank within heavy gas masks, worn in fearful anticipation of poison chemical attacks. The night skies above the city had for some weeks been torn with magnesium-bright flashes, mighty guns firing in defence. The bellowing booms rolled through the streets, echoing off the concentric waterways. Citizens on fire watch, posted on roofs, looked at the not-too-distant horizon and watched the amethyst sky dotted with the red and orange of distant battle. Those trying to sleep had the constant sense of flickering in the dark. The people of Leningrad were obliged to live by night, as well as day, and in this sense, time was also being distended.

The slow, spreading realization that the city was being systematically cut off from the rest of Russia was also warping Leningraders' perception of time. 'I live only in the present minute, not even the hour,' wrote museum academic Georgii Knyazev. 'I don't speak about days any more. Fate has granted another minute – and I am grateful to her. I read, I write, I think . . . And what there will be even a minute later, I try not to think about.'[1]

As an academic, he was also reaching back through the centuries, seeking historical precedents for comfort; there was little to be found. He gazed at a portrait of Archimedes and thought of how he himself faced invasion. 'Enemies have already burst not only into the city, but even into the house where the great philosopher is living,' he wrote. Knyazev recalled the legend: the philosopher pleading not for his own life, but for his mathematical work to be spared from destruction. 'Don't destroy my circles!'[2] Leningrad was facing an implacably barbarous enemy; Knyazev feared for its own intellectual treasure.

This sense of time as a distended perspective was shared by the poet Olga Berggolts, who not long before had met with an artist from her home town of Uglich, and together they had discussed the giddying span of the years. 'He thought about our descendants,' she wrote, 'about the future, about our heirs, who will come here to take all their inheritance.' They spoke of 'the changing face of the Russian land', and they were both thinking not only about 'our stormy times' and 'not only about tomorrow, but about The Great Time, stretching into the far future'.[3] For Berggolts, time stretched out like the illimitable Russian landscape. The literary critic Nikolay Punin, in conversation with a friend, agreed when that friend indicated the streets around and declared of the city: 'This is time. War is space.'[4]

Even the city's public clocks registered the dislocation of time; many had already been stopped by the shock waves of bombing. A clock face built into the facade of a nineteenth-century office building might tell one time; a clock on a market square would tell another.

Elsewhere in the city, the student Natalya Uskova was finding that the loud ticks from the radio were making rest impossible. 'Night,' she wrote. 'The metronome peacefully taps out seconds. It keeps us on alert and anxious all the time. Any second it could stop and the siren will sound.'[5]

And as the gentle land around the city was being torn apart by pitched battles – Wehrmacht artillery aimed towards Leningrad, Red Army guns pointing into those covering woods – so too was Leningrad undergoing its own transformation. The bomb shelters had been constructed with some speed throughout the summer (the same summer that construction of the city's smart new metro system had just started), and though the streets still clattered with trams, pavements in the centre were frequently piled up with sand and timber, all set for the building of further shelters and observation points.

Up until 8 September, a semblance of normality remained when it came to groceries in the city. It was still possible to venture into a cafe and order a bowl of beetroot soup and a 'plate of buttered semolina'.[6] Some restaurants were even offering full menus. Elsewhere, on some of the busier squares, old men sat playing chess or dominoes. The libraries were still open; it was possible to borrow copies of Dickens's *David Copperfield* and the socially concerned writings of Jack London.

But the schools had not reopened for the new autumn term, and the suspension of education was heard by all as a deep-tolling warning bell. The children themselves – when not playing among all the piled-up sandbags along the banks of the Neva and elsewhere – occasionally received more informal tutoring. The Pioneer Palace was still open for the city's young people. This was the first acknowledgement that Leningrad was facing an unusual ordeal.

The freedom to buy groceries was soon replaced with rationing. For older people this was a familiar hardship. They could still recall the torturous restrictions both of the last war and of the civil war that followed it; there had also been the gruelling food shortages of the early 1930s caused by Stalin's demoniac drive to collectivize farms. The rationing this time was not immediately draconian, but the limits placed upon ordinary items such as salt and household matches contributed to a wider and growing sense of unease. Still the far-off guns echoed, and each day Leningraders absorbed what information they could – even the news seemed rationed – from the Leningrad edition of *Pravda*. Each fallen Russian town and village was noted and in a sense crossed off; civilians were constructing their own mental maps of the Wehrmacht ring around the city, and a sense of those deadly forces surging ever closer. Friends calling to each other in the street would announce the names of the latest villages that they heard had fallen.

Yet the season also offered some more natural distractions. Autumn comes early so far north, and by the beginning of September the leaves were 'turning amber yellow, lemon yellow, scarlet'. The weather was 'radiant'.[7] The botanical gardens, as well as the grander Tsarist parks that lay on the city's fringes, attained an atmosphere of prelapsarian innocence; man may be inflicting horrors against man in this vast global war but here among the trees, and near the glittering waters of the Neva, there could be found a sense of life that worked to older, unchanging and unchangeable rhythms. While few had the time for aimless wandering in the glasshouses of the botanical gardens, or around palace grounds, there were many who were able to draw comfort from the idea that these emblems of the city's beauty stood unchanged and unmolested.

Any wider sense of the 'golden' weather bringing the consolation of beauty was soon to dissolve, however, for those early autumn skies were also perfect for German bombers. The metronomes were soon to start ticking even more remorselessly.

In the time since the launch of the invasion, those who governed the city had been scrambling to prepare for an inundation of Nazi troops. Andrei Zhdanov together with Aleksei Kuznetsov and Kliment Voroshilov, were sitting behind taped windows in the Smolny

Institute. They were trying to prepare for a war more total than their leader Stalin seemed willing to contemplate.

When Barbarossa had been launched, sleek Zhdanov had been on holiday in Crimea, and in the aftershock he had shuttled between Leningrad and Moscow, for meetings at the Kremlin attended by Stalin and Lavrentii Beria. Stalin's chief concern was evacuation, with emphasis upon the factories making tanks and aircraft. Under the guidance of Isaac Salzman of the Kirov Plant, that mighty undertaking – all those guarded trains and flights of skilled workers – had proceeded a great deal more smoothly than the faltering attempts to spirit Leningrad's small children out to sanctuaries in the countryside.

There was a point that month when Zhdanov made a key decision independently of his leader in Moscow. He and Voroshilov had seen the reports of how the Wehrmacht forces were sweeping ever closer like a flood tide. It might be a matter of days before the swastika was seen in the streets of Leningrad. The Red Army – fighting Germans and Finns from every direction – seemingly could do little to hold back the advance. Now was the time to arm the workers.

The Leningrad Military Defence Council was brought into being. The idea was a little like the British Home Guard, except this would involve thousands of men and women drawn from the remaining factories. Each factory and plant was to form its own detachment. First, the factories themselves were to be turned into fortresses – festooned with barbed wire, armed guards at gates. But on top of this, the workers were to be fully trained in military drills and taught how to use automatic weapons.

There had been an old Bolshevik distaste for arming the workers: as well as the ideological unsoundness of the idea – this was work for the Red Army, and for the security forces of the NKVD to ensure that that army did not in any way disobey the political diktats of the Kremlin – there was an element of risk, too. By giving lethal weapons to workers, there might be the chance that some of the ideologically unconvinced would turn those weapons against their socialist comrades.

Zhdanov's view appeared to be that the nightmare about to overwhelm the city far outweighed these theoretical drawbacks. As well as the male factory workers, women and male office workers in the city would be given their own weapons training, with the sorts of guns used for hunting in the Karelian forests. (As the war progressed, some 800,000 women from across Russia would join the Red Army.) In addition, the innovation of the Winter War with Finland – the Molotov cocktail – was to be replicated in Leningrad (though naturally under a different name).

The fear in the Smolny Institute was that Leningrad was facing a street-by-street invasion; and that the only way to resist would be by using snipers and other guerilla tactics. In late August, Zhdanov made a radio broadcast; it was heard in every home, on every shop floor, and issued forth from the loudspeakers in all the city's grander streets:

> Comrades, Leningraders, dear friends. The direct threat of attack of German-fascist troops hangs over our native and beloved city. The enemy is trying to break through to Leningrad . . . We will be steadfast to the end! Not sparing lives, we will fight the enemy, we will smash and destroy him . . . Victory will be ours![8]

The aim went beyond simple armament; Zhdanov was fearful of a city-wide panic that could be triggered either by terrible rumours filling the vacuum of solid information or by the authorities vividly spelling out the imminent danger. There were angry telegram exchanges between Moscow and Leningrad; Stalin originally was intensely displeased by the very idea of the Leningrad Military Defence Council. As well as the dilution of ultimate power, there was – it seemed – a sort of reckless independence in the minds of Zhdanov, Kuznetsov and Voroshilov. This was compounded by Voroshilov having given voice to his bitter feelings that the senior commanders of the Red Army were useless and little better than traitors.

The city was ever more firmly encircled; anyone who did manage to slip south past its defenders unchallenged would face either the forces of the Wehrmacht, encamped in the surrounding woods and suburbs, or the bullets of the Luftwaffe burning through the skies above. To the north of the city, looking out into that Karelian forest wilderness, lay the equally unsympathetic forces of the Finnish army, busy fighting their Soviet counterparts. All that remained was the vast expanse of Lake Ladoga.

Just thirty miles outside Leningrad, swastikas were flying. The 41st Panzer Group and the 18th Army were on the brink of capturing and holding the historic and elegant suburb of Krasnoe Selo. In Tsarist times, this had been a rich area of fine summer dachas and exquisite churches, amid woodlands of birch and aspen. The town and the surrounding countryside had remained popular for holidays in Stalinist times too. The sudden presence of German soldiers in the streets and at the railway station was dumbfounding for the locals. Yevgeniya Novozhilova was eight years old when the invaders materialized; she remembered long nights of distant thunderous fire and the sky glowing red.[9] The municipal authorities had tried to secure the local bank and its deposits but they were too late. Families with livestock were immediately forced to surrender pigs and goats to the Wehrmacht. A new mayor was installed; the violence and oppression began at once. There were executions of 'partisans' and 'Bolsheviks' and, of course, Jews. The Einsatzgruppen moved into the local municipal buildings. Those who were put to work by the Wehrmacht – there was a local timber and logging industry that was useful to the Germans – received cabbage soup bulked out a little with flour. The children of the area found that they had new schoolteachers (including some volunteers from Estonia and Lithuania). Education was reduced to the barest basics: many children spent their days foraging for dandelions, nettles and other edible weeds in order to help stave off the fast-spreading hunger. And from just outside the town, the German guns bellowed.

Along the coast a few miles west of Leningrad, the Soviet 8th Army was trapped by the Wehrmacht in a flat region known as the Oranienbaum Pocket, very close to the landscaped splendour of the Peterhof Palace. Here, the Russians were facing oncoming forces with their backs quite literally to the Gulf of Finland. The area – and the bitter, desperate, unceasing fighting – was to attain symbolic weight: the Red Army, although enclosed, at least had the support of the navy in those waters, the area being close to the naval base at Kronstadt.

There was also the fierce artillery power of the Soviet warships *October Revolution* and *Maxim Gorky*. As intractable as von Leeb's Wehrmacht forces were, there was an equally granite determination throughout this region not to let them advance any further: if the Oranienbaum Pocket were to be swallowed up, Leningrad itself would have very little left in the way of defence. The firepower of both the army and the navy – the formidable guns on board those warships pointing inland – was deployed with both consistency and fury.

The wave of death was rolling fast across the Soviet Union; far to the south, Army Group Centre was menacing Kyiv and its surrounding regions, its forces so close that hundreds of thousands of Red Army soldiers would soon find themselves trapped, fighting what Hitler termed 'the biggest battle in the history of the world'. The roaring air would be hazed with particles of dust and blood; among the Soviet forces, almost half a million lives were to be extinguished here under crushing artillery and piercing bullets. It would be necessary for the Nazi forces to secure this region – firmly establishing a bridgehead on the Dnieper river, as well as appropriating agriculture and forced labour – before focusing more fully on the ultimate prize: Moscow. Army Group South was on the point of conquering the industrial Donbas region and the peninsula of Crimea, tactically important for Black Sea access.

The Nazis' murderous intentions were beginning to solidify: if Leningrad could be left to starve – the city turned into a vast, silent necropolis – then von Leeb's Army Group North would be at liberty to spare forces for that final, triumphant advance upon Moscow. Such was the confidence among the Nazis that their press conferences portrayed the entire Soviet system as close to dissolution.

In Leningrad, amid the jagged ill-will and desperation of the political wranglings, the wider truth of the Soviet leadership seemed clearly discernible: Stalin had not fully absorbed what its population was facing and the local authorities – though working hard to turn the entire city into an instrument of total war – were themselves helpless against the Wehrmacht forces.

But the night of 8 September 1941 struck a quite different, resonant note of fear. All had been anticipating the Luftwaffe bombing raids. All had been in those musty basements, sitting on bare benches, some trying to read, as the ticks of the metronome held their funereal rhythm. On the roofs of the grander buildings, under those threatening autumn skies, the volunteer fire-watchers had been bracing themselves for the attack that could not be held back.

The raids had already been stepped up; Leningraders had been fast adjusting to a new world in which their homes – however contingent – might simply be smashed into the ground. In shared communal apartments in the bigger old St Petersburg houses, roof-pulverizing bombs were accompanied by sticks of incendiaries, raining first dust, then fire. Those homes that did not catch fire were sliced open. Apartments nearby were left in chaos; one observer recalled that all her possessions were simply strewn about, as though a child had been playing and had not tidied anything away. In one block, a few streets from where the bombs were falling, the occupant looked on, paralysed with fright, as the door of her apartment shuddered violently, and then slammed open, as though forced by a furious poltergeist. The booms made rational thought impossible.[10]

The fury and the quantity of the bombs that were delivered on the evening of 8 September, however, brought an intimation of calamity that went far beyond the destruction of individual apartment buildings or tenements or factory blocks. The poet Olga Berggolts – who at that stage was very active as the commissar for her residential building – was among those quick to perceive what it was that the Germans had managed to hit.[11]

In the midst of all the confusion among the leadership – Zhdanov and Kuznetsov trying to anticipate the anger of the Kremlin, as well as the remorseless cruelty of their enemy – the Party authorities had made one vast and extraordinary and lethal mistake when it came to the city's supply of non-perishable food. Everything from grain to pasta to sugar to dried meat and dried fish had been stored in enormous quantities on one site: the Badayev warehouses. That night, the warehouses, mainly of timber construction and dating back to the start of the century, were hit.

The fires first licked and then consumed the food – tons of it, across several warehouses, piled to the rafters, now melting, seething, hissing. The meat, the fish, the blackening caramelized sugar. The conflagration had a voracious obscenity as the flames gulped through all the warehouses and the air of the city was filled with the pungent and at first puzzlingly unidentifiable aromas.

'We gathered in the yard and saw a red and crimson glow in the sky,' wrote Zinaida Fedyushina, who was then a schoolgirl. 'This was an amazing sight. It seemed to us that it claimed the entire sky from the Moscow railway station to the Admiralty. Later we learned that it was the glow from a fire – the Germans had bombed the Badayev warehouses storing the food supply for the denizens of the city.'[12]

These, said Olga Berggolts, 'were Leningrad's food reserves, and when they burned, a dense oily cloud rose into the sky and covered the evening sun; an alarming, almost red twilight fell over the city, as during a total solar eclipse – the first herald of the hungry plague'.[13]

Vera Inber had, remarkably, been at the theatre that evening, to see a play entitled *The Flying Bat*.[14] The air-raid alert had come just at the interval; the manager stepped on to the stage and announced the fact calmly. There was not quite time to evacuate the auditorium, and so the audience were asked clearly and slowly to stand, and to line up against the walls, where they might find more protection should the roof come crashing in. Half an hour later, the performance resumed. After this display of cultured defiance, it was time to leave the theatre.

Inber at first did not understand the significance of the 'blue dusk mixed with reddish reflections and scarlet lights'. It was only when she rounded a corner and saw the sky filled with 'mountains of smoke' lit fearsomely 'from below with flames' that she understood. The 'food stores were on fire'.[15] From this point onwards, the city's descent – into hunger, into fear, into a paralysis of nihilistic despair – was fast and steep.

12.   'Wait for the silver night'

The piano notes were elegiac and romantic and insistent. They could be heard echoing off the dusty red walls of the courtyard of a smart apartment block on Marat Street, near the canal. They would stop, then begin again; a melody repeated, a phrase restructured. In any other time, there would have been nothing remarkable about the source of this music, a work in progress. But that piano was playing in the rare moments of silence between air-raid warnings, and the sonic horror of bombs connecting with roofs and roads.

The man at his piano was the composer Dmitri Shostakovich. His flow was continually halted by the sirens that obliged him to run from his flat and down into the block's air-raid shelter. Shostakovich should by rights have already left Leningrad; many of the city's artists – from some members of the Leningrad Philharmonic to a few of its gifted ballerinas – had already been evacuated. But as the bombardment intensified, Shostakovich had remained in his tasteful apartment, working with dizzying speed upon the composition that would commemorate this nightmare.[1]

He was composing his Seventh Symphony. The idea for its theme had germinated just before the shock of Operation Barbarossa; in other words, it had not been conceived as a direct response to the invasion. It might even have been conceived as something subversive, but this new threat had given his work a newer, more urgent emphasis. The first movement – beginning with an uplifting march that slowly, darkly, transformed into a fiercer, more poundingly martial sequence, rising almost to a note of percussive hysteria – was loosely termed 'invasion'.[2] The real music of death – the mocking whistles of falling bombs, the shock waves of detonation – was filling his world.

Shostakovich – with his round, pebble-glass spectacles – had apparently tried to volunteer for service in the Red Army but been turned down on medical grounds. He then offered to become a fireman: a crucial role in the flame-ravaged city. But the authorities – the same Zhdanov and Kuznetsov who had once regarded the composer with cold suspicion – were now most insistent that all their fellow citizens should know of his great composition in progress. Radio Leningrad, when not broadcasting the time-twisting ticks of the metronome, was tasked with the boosting of morale; Shostakovich was summoned to its studio at the House of Radio on Italianskaya Street to announce his plans to the city, telling the audience in his high pitched and urgent voice:

> An hour ago, I finished the score of two movements of a large symphonic composition. If I succeed in carrying it off, if I manage to complete the third and fourth movements, then perhaps I'll be able to call it my Seventh Symphony. Why am I telling you this? So that the radio listeners who are listening to me now will know that life in our city is proceeding normally.[3]

Neither he nor anyone listening could have imagined for one moment that this was life 'proceeding normally'. Just days into the relentless, savage bombing campaign minds were becoming dislocated by the trauma. But it is possible to say and hear something while knowing that the exact opposite is true. In such grim circumstances the defiant declaration was more important than the reality. But Shostakovich also went a little further: there was a piano in the studio and he was able to give those listeners a much-abridged foretaste of the work. Words might have been malleable but in music lay the truth.

And that music – on first hearing, bombastic and unsubtle – was layered with such complexity that perhaps even Shostakovich was not quite the master of it. Both Stalin and Hitler had, for a time, imagined that classical music might be a means of communicating ideological purity, guiding the hearts and souls and minds of listeners in the 'correct' direction, but Shostakovich understood that music was not quite so governable. The later intimations from those who knew him well that the symphony was conceived as a broader piece about oppression suggested that it had started as a response to Stalin's oppression rather than Hitler's.[4] His friends would be invited to his flat for further previews, sometimes decamping to the building's bomb shelter mid-recital until the all-clear permitted its conclusion.

How can any artist be in complete control of what they create in such frightening circumstances? Could Shostakovich himself be sure which side of his bifurcated nature was prevailing as the notes formed in his head? But whatever his intentions – conscious or otherwise – the composition was of huge importance to the regime.

On the same day as Shostakovich's broadcast, his fellow artist, the poet Anna Akhmatova, was also summoned to the House of Radio. Her words were needed to fill the hearts of Leningraders with courage. This was an extraordinary request from a regime that had sought to destroy her. She assented, her speech invoking Alexander Pushkin, Dostoevsky and the vision of Peter the Great. But most particularly she spoke of 'the image of the Leningrad woman standing during an air raid on the roof of a house . . . protecting the city from fire . . . A city that has bred women like these cannot be conquered.'[5]

As it happened, Zhdanov could not allow either Akhmatova or Shostakovich to stay much longer in the city: their lives simply had too much propaganda value to risk. Even with the blockade, it remained possible to fly chosen people out. Again, from Akhmatova's point of view, this was a bewildering moment of vindication. She was sent south to Uzbekistan, and provided with an apartment in Tashkent. Shostakovich and his family were moved first to Moscow, and thence to Samara, a smaller town deeper in the safer southeast. He continued to work on the symphony, though in conditions far removed from the material comforts that he had enjoyed in Leningrad. His Symphony No. 7 would later become an international symbol of Russian defiance; by the time it did so, Leningrad's survivors would be walking the streets of the dead.

In early September 1941, the nights – when not being torn apart by the demonic melody of waves of bombers – were warm and clear, and in different times the nocturnal city, under the fat moon, would have had a luminous quality, the smarter boulevards rich in bright street-lights, the domes and the spires sharp against the stars. But now the dark of the blackout brought only sleeplessness and fear and moments of animal panic during those split seconds when the murk was suddenly illuminated hideously.

The night when the food stores in the Badayev warehouses had been incinerated, and when the acrid smell of burning sugar spread across all the city's islands, was merely the overture to the Luftwaffe's own dark symphony. By day, shells from artillery whistled through the sky, puncturing and destroying masonry before anyone could even register their approach. By night – the city smothered with an eerie silence, and the streets so dim that walkers could not discern pavement from road – the bombers circled the city with apparent impunity, despite the efforts of anti-aircraft gunners and the Soviet air force. These bombing raids – incessant, and focused on residential as well as industrial targets – were changing how Leningraders viewed their own lives.

The extraordinary thing was the speed at which those same citizens appeared to adapt to days and nights dominated by grinding anxiety. After completing overnight fire-watching duties, or looking after restless children in claustrophobic cellars, they then went out to do a day's work. Some even found time to go to concerts (there were still a number of musicians left in the city, and the auditoriums were still open), and indeed to the theatres, where there were still nightly performances. But bomb by bomb, building by building, the city that they loved was being violently dismantled. Homes were being destroyed, families were being displaced, and there was no suggestion of help from anywhere.

'At half-past seven in the evening, when I was having a rest,' wrote the archivist Georgii Knyazev, 'the whole of our building suddenly began to shake. There was an outburst of firing from the anti-aircraft guns and the machine-gun batteries. The first moment was frightful.'[6] To the south of the river, German bombs and incendiaries had cut open an industrial complex, and brought fire into its heart. The inferno was so vast and uncontrollable that it could be seen reflected in the black waters of the Neva.

During those first few nights of bombardment there was a moment of communal horror when German bombs detonated on the city's zoo. 'The elephant perished,' recalled Knyazev. This was the elephant

Betty, who – with her intelligent tricks involving coins and carrots – had been such a firm favourite among Leningraders. 'According to one source of information, it received contusions . . . but according to another, it was injured by shrapnel. It was in great pain and they shot it . . . the unfortunate zoo has suffered all the horrors of a real hell.'[7] Vera Inber noted in addition that people 'say all the monkeys are killed . . . and that a maddened sable is roaming the streets'.[8] The zoo – like the botanical gardens – held a sentimental place in the lives of Leningraders. The destruction of innocent animal lives was felt keenly; so too was the horrible distress suffered by the city's pet dogs during these nights of roaring, blasting violence: the animals trembled and there was nothing that their owners, also trembling, could do to comfort them.

As well as the terror there was a sense of bitter betrayal: the sudden, savage belligerence of an enemy that had until the summer been a notional ally. There was not that great a sense of surprise about Nazism itself: few in Soviet Russia had been under any illusions about the nature of German fascism, or about the homicidal impulses that underlay it. None the less, this was a war that was being waged against civilians. The people of Leningrad had had to adjust with speed to the idea that the enemy did not wish to conquer them; it wished to kill them.

(Curiously, only a matter of weeks beforehand, the Leningrad authorities had been hyper alert to anonymous letter-writers and notice-board correspondents who were welcoming the idea of German rule. Even under the panopticon gaze of Stalin's NKVD, there were a few in Leningrad who so determinedly loathed Communist rule that they thought Hitler would be preferable. In a few people, overheard in unguarded drunken moments, there was another kind of desire articulated: one that was deeply anti-Semitic. There were some workers who declared to their friends that the Nazis would improve Leningrad because they would purge the city of all its Jews. Then the rest of the population would be free. There was that deeply buried seam of anti-Semitism that continued to run through Leningrad society.[9] The proximity of the German forces, on the other hand, and the bombing, served to drive it deeper.)

The news of the burning of the timber-framed Badayev warehouses – and the lingering odour of charred food that hung over the city's streets – had still not quite registered in its enormity. While the destroyed stockpile would have fed the city's population of two million for only a short time anyway – a few weeks at the most with rationing – the mere fact of the carelessness in storing all the food in one place, plus the sense that there was no immediately obvious way to replace it, had still not fully percolated. The continuing bombing through September was much more pressing; it made it impossible for anyone to live in anything other than the present. The idea of preparing for any sort of future was abstract as long as the metronomes ticked, and as long as every single apartment, every single home, could conceivably be smashed to atoms in a blink.

The psychological impact of those first few nights of bombing was profound. 'Our building shuddered all over,' wrote one diarist of a night she had taken shelter with her children in her neighbour's apartment as the Luftwaffe swooped over. 'It seemed as though the very ground was writhing in convulsions. My teeth were chattering with fear, my knees were trembling. I took refuge in a corner, clutching the children to me. They were sobbing with fear.' She and her children survived the night. The next day she 'found some grey hairs'.[10]

But the days for many Leningraders now also involved endless contemplation of death. Residents emerging from bomb shelters and basements would gaze upon houses, now communal apartment blocks, that had been neatly sliced apart – wallpaper, pictures, even sticks of furniture exposed as if the door of a giant doll's house had been opened wide. The suddenly homeless wandered the city in a state of shock, searching for anyone in authority who might direct them to a new roof under which to shelter. Meanwhile, those whose own dwellings had been spared could only sit in fear that their turn would come next.

In the centre of the city there were further torments: those huddling in low-ceilinged brick cellars suddenly saw their shelters as tombs. It was easy to imagine that rubble from the bombed building above would block the single entrance and bury them alive, breathing dust in the darkness with no hope of rescue. But where else could they go when curfew was sounded and the metronome's ticking began to speed up neurotically?

Older citizens, like the wheelchair-bound Knyazev, had reasoned to himself that the bombs were merely the heralds of the Wehrmacht; that soon there would be fighting in the streets. 'The whole city is bristling with bayonets, machine guns, firing points, obstructions,' he wrote. 'In some streets . . . barricades are being erected . . . What are we to be witnesses of? The hardest of days and hours are coming.'[11] His own anxieties led to him trying to envisage all the worst possibilities; the extremities to which he himself might be driven. He imagined his beloved wife dead; he imagined the beauty of the city's architecture – the Hermitage, the Church of the Saviour on Spilled Blood, St Isaac's Cathedral – torn to the ground by vengeful invaders. What then, he wondered, would he do? He contemplated suicide as a solution: 'It would seem that hanging yourself is the best way,' he confided to his diary. 'The noose, pulled tight by the weight of the hanging body, usually lies above the thyroid cartilage and, exerting pressure from front to back and the sides, at the same time as blocking the windpipe, compresses the major blood vessels of the neck and the vagus nerve.'[12]

Pravda was urging resistance with daily pronouncements. 'Fortify all the approaches to Leningrad,' ran one such. 'Transform each outpost, square, street and alley into bastions and fortresses and make them impregnable to the enemy . . . Leningraders have one and the same task to accomplish – to defend the city and annihilate the enemy.'[13]

Perhaps there were some who drew strength from the idea of what would amount to a final confrontation. But, as ever, there was also a suggestion of threat from the authorities: an exhortation against those who shrank back and hid in their fear. 'You won't elude death in this way,' the newspaper pronounced. 'It will come just the same, only it will be a shameful death, to the sounds of the jeers and the taunts of the executioners.'[14]

In mid-September, the weather began to change; the dark evenings grew murkier with heavy cloud and rain began sluicing the streets. This brought a flicker of hope to some of the citizens, who looked at the skies and prayed that it would be impossible for the Luftwaffe bombers to fly, or at least to target their homes with any kind of precision. But still the planes arrived. And the Leningraders were not wrong: while the Luftwaffe's central targets were the factories and the shipyards, residential districts were also in their sights. The idea was to make life unliveable.

Among the early casualties was the eighteenth-century Fontanka Palace – the building that had been converted into communal apartments which were home to literary critic Nikolay Punin and his extended family. He and they were elsewhere in the city that night. 'We put out the lights and stood at the open window,' he wrote. There were 'red rocket flares', a bomber that 'droned with a high pitch'. But then came a different kind of sound: a 'whistle', 'loud and piercing'. Then, a 'terrible crash, thunder'; and the whistling started again. An hour or so afterwards came the thick silence of night. 'The moon shone,' wrote Punin. 'It was quiet in the garden.'[15]

The dawn illuminated the extent to which all their lives had been so determinedly upended. The Fontanka Palace – and the apartments within – had been rendered uninhabitable within a fraction of a second under that moonlit night. The floors were shattered, the 'corners were slanting' and great cracks and fissures now zig-zagged up the walls. But more: all the small domestic tokens of familiar life had been hurled around and destroyed. 'The cupboards lay on the floor and everywhere there were shards of dishes and glass among pieces of the fallen ceiling . . . home has ceased to exist here,' wrote Punin.[16]

There were other tokens of disorientation: from the Academy, Punin observed the Neva filling with 'smaller ships', Russian vessels crowding in from the Gulf of Finland; meanwhile, the German planes were dropping not only bombs but leaflets exhorting the citizens to surrender immediately. The poet Olga Berggolts, just a few streets away in the House of Writers, had also been examining dropped leaflets, some of which bore the enigmatic threat 'wait for the silver night'.[17] There were others marked with a symbol that meant 'bayonet in the ground'. These leaflets were not about surrender, but about stoking fear. In Olga Berggolts's courtyard, it appeared to be working. She heard two older women telling one another that 'he [Hitler] promised gases'.[18]

There was one quiet night – one broadly free of Luftwaffe raids – when she and her writer colleague Nikolay Fomin listened instead to the distant echo of field guns from beyond the boundaries of the city. They stood ready with gas masks, imagining the German forces pulsing forwards, the tanks approaching their building. The building's caretaker, an elderly lady referred to as 'Aunt Masha', appeared and told Berggolts that 'the bottles with gasoline were ready'.[19] Both were perhaps too loyal to Foreign Minister Molotov to give these projectiles the name that the Finns had used. 'A murderous silence reigned in the motionless moonlit city,' she wrote. 'The sounds of the deadly battle going on in the outskirts reached here as a weak, restless, rumble.'[20]

There is a Fabergé egg created in 1901 – fashioned from gold, enamel and seed pearls, and now permanently on show in an art museum in Baltimore – that contains an extraordinary golden miniature palace. This unintentionally kitsch item is a representation of the Great Gatchina Palace, which itself is a highly ornamented structure: an example of the eighteenth-century Russian aristocratic enthusiasm for an idea of Englishness. The real palace, which lies about thirty miles south-west of St Petersburg, was built by the Italian architect Antonio Rinaldi for Count Grigorii Orlov on land that had been presented to Orlov by Catherine the Great; this was apparently in gratitude for his help in the assassination of Tsar Peter III, which had in turn raised her to the Russian throne.

The palace, of pale limestone, was designed in the classical style, but also with a distinct and conscious nod towards an historical English 'hunting castle' or baronial theme (from some angles, the structure looks a little like Blenheim Palace). The scale was certainly comparable: 600 rooms, vast galleries and an elaborate maze of vaulted cellars. The parklands, also English-inspired and created by English gardeners, had features such as 'The Isle of Love' and 'The Labyrinth'. The community of Gatchina had by the start of the twentieth century become known as Russia's best-kept and healthiest town, showcased in international exhibitions for the quality of its education and health services; in addition, the Gatchina Palace itself, continually favoured by a succession of Tsars, blazed early with the innovation of electric light. The 1917 revolution and the subsequent civil war naturally brought violent, tumultuous change even to this small, quiet town, with its onion-domed cathedral and broad boulevard of shops and taverns; and yet something of its old soul remained. The palace, like so many others, was turned into a museum (some of its treasures were carefully preserved as artistic exhibits – others were sold on the international market in order to boost the finances of the early Soviet system). The town was renamed Trotsk in the early 1920s in honour of Leon Trotsky; the cold shadow that fell over his name in the Stalinist era meant that the town had to reverse that decision by 1929.

When von Leeb's Army Group North reached Gatchina, the palace was immediately overrun along with the rest of the town. With the earth-trembling drumbeat of invasion drawing closer throughout that summer, the palace museum's curators – like those at Tsarskoe Selo – had done what they could to evacuate or hide the remaining art and antiquities. But the speed of the advance had been breathtaking – and by the time the Germans arrived, there were statues only half-buried in the parklands. The looting began at once, the pilfered treasures shipped back west (the Fabergé egg was not among them, having somehow ended up in Chicago in the 1930s before being bought for that Baltimore art collection in the 1950s).

And the palace itself was transformed into a swastika-adorned headquarters for Field Marshal von Leeb and his various commanders – plus, naturally, the accompanying Einsatzgruppen and Gestapo. The town was fortified. It attained the feel of a garrison. (It had been so before: in the hours following the Bolshevik revolution in 1917, it had been selected by counter-revolutionaries to house Cossacks: 'The prospect of lodging an entire Cossack division in the Palace was not a happy one for me,' wrote Count Valentin Zubov, who also noted with some wonder how the men in the vast stables settled down for the night using their horses as 'pillows'.)[21] The Nazi appetites both for opulent comfort and a certain level of glittering-chandeliered vulgarity were also to be satisfied here: a base that suggested that they were the new aristocrats. Gatchina, like the elegant Leningrad suburb of Tsarskoe Selo, also to be overrun, contained a population of civilians faced with military occupiers who controlled every aspect of their lives. The cruelty was immediately apparent. 'Germans walked the streets with whips,' recalled resident Grigorii Nikov.[22] The Nazis established brothels in the town's main street for their soldiers: initially inhabited by enslaved sex workers trafficked from Estonia, and then supplemented with local women. The Nazis also gazed upon the cathedral, and upon the semi-hidden tokens of a submerged Russian Orthodox religion – and, in the interests of securing further compliance from disgruntled local Christians, began permitting services once more, which took place in the church's crypt. The priests who were restored to their offices were also used as intermediaries between the Nazi civic authorities and the townsfolk. The people, although not being systematically starved, were entirely dependent upon their new masters for the scant rations they did receive.

Yet in this darkness, there were occasional curious outbreaks of accord: soldiers of the Spanish Blue Division, inspired by Franco, and who had been volunteering alongside the Wehrmacht, were not regarded by Gatchina's people with as much hostility as were the Wehrmacht, and there were odd instances of elderly Russians enjoying Spanish guitar music. In the midst of this occupation, von Leeb and his forces must certainly have imagined themselves to be reasonably secure: not long after the incursion, Gatchina was renamed 'Lindemannstadt', apparently after General Georg Lindemann, commander of the 18th Army, who himself – together with his forces – was redirected further south to become part of the tide pushing towards Moscow.

The plan for Moscow was naturally paramount: until it fell, and the Communist regime collapsed, all of this – occupation, oppression, terror – was essentially irrelevant, lacking wider meaning or purpose. The artillery emplacements a little north of Gatchina, pointing towards Leningrad, were the expression of that nihilism, maintaining regular, throaty roars as they fired shell upon shell, seeking to turn architectural beauty to bloody dust, while in the skies above the Luftwaffe continued its lethal dominance, creating nightly blossoms of fire in a city now tortured by fatigue.

Many Leningraders seemed to be suffering a form of PTSD just nights into the bombing, and understandably so. To have suffered one such raid was one thing; to have the planes return again and again, night after night, made sleep impossible, and pure cold rationality hard to hold on to. There were some who hallucinated air-raid sirens, making them sprint unexpectedly for the shelters. There were others who would suddenly freeze, imagining that they could hear the unearthly whistle of an approaching bomb. Hour after hour of reluctant wakefulness, night into day, day into night, made the borderline between reality and nightmare fluid; there were Leningraders convinced that bombs were being aimed at them individually. Some came to believe on those terrible nights that they would somehow be safer in the open air, as opposed to the dust-choked confines of cellars; that the explosives intended for them would simply hit the buildings instead.

Those Leningraders who had made a closer study of the previous wars and civil war that century understood perfectly what was going on: this was bombing psychosis. Ordinary people were living as though they were soldiers on the front line, subjected to as many as twelve bombing raids a night, the aim of which was to wipe them out. The enforced lack of sleep tore down all the mind's defences. And the Germans were inflicting this suffering with scientific calculation, bombers making their runs at intervals that would first lull civilians into exhausted sleep, then jolt them awake with terror after minutes.

Compounding this intense psychological fatigue was the rhythm of work. Because such vast numbers of men had been corralled into the defensive forces of the Red Army – and because so many of those men, inexperienced with arms, had been bloodily killed in the first few weeks of the invasion – equal numbers of women had to be found to work in the city's mighty factories: the Kirov Plant, the Bolshevik Plant, the Elektrosila and the Lenin Works. While quantities of materiel had been shipped out, the frantic efforts to create more munitions went on. This wasn't just about assembling tanks; it was also about creating landmines, hand grenades and the Katyusha rockets that produced an unearthly and disorientating scream when fired. But there was more to do on top of that: smaller plants that had once produced luxury items such as bottled perfume were also turned over to the war effort: those bottles were now larger and filled with liquids intended to burn. Workshops that had once produced sewing machines and typewriters were now also turned to the production of armaments, while clothing and textile and shoe factories focused their efforts on making uniforms and boots for the swelling numbers of the Red Army.

Mothers who had once been full-time home-makers were now propelled into the factories, their infants cared for in works nurseries. Often, 'work' now no longer simply meant one post, as it had in peace time. People might have as many as four or five jobs, being directed to one workplace and then another as production lines demanded. Women who had never before worked in industry had to learn the intricacies of production lines, and of the assembly of weapons and rockets, very quickly.

Another reason for the shortfall of workers was mass expulsion. Around the beginning of September, just as the city's escape routes were being methodically blocked, there were ironically some three-quarters of a million people from the outskirts of Leningrad and in its surrounding countryside who had been rounded up and deported; these were people of German and Finnish heritage. Both groups had been part of the city's life for centuries. They had been farmers, tutors, skilled craftsmen, merchants. The Nazi invasion meant that not one of them could be allowed to stay anywhere near to the city.

Many such Germans and Finns were loaded onto barges and sent via Lake Ladoga to north-eastern cities such as Archangel or to towns in northern Kazakhstan – as far away from their countrymen as possible, to prevent their joining forces in any kind of way. These evacuations of presumed hostile aliens were markedly more successful than many of the earlier efforts to get children out of Leningrad.

For the teenage Yura Riabinkin, tiredness was blended with intense frustration; the scholar of Tolstoy who had studied the histories of

Russia's past wars was out in the courtyard of his apartment block at midnight, gas mask on, looking up at the sky as 'German planes flew past over the city at lightning speed'.[23] He had a theory: that Hitler's forces had been halted and so, in blind fury, the Führer was seeking to smash the entire city of Leningrad into dust. Writing his diary past midnight, the boy recorded a day as well as a night in which there had been no fewer than eleven air-raid alerts. He catalogued the shattered sites that he had seen: these included pretty houses (now communal flats) in Krasnaya Street in the south of the city – what had once been terraces of amber- and apricot-coloured apartments were now punched through and smouldering. There had also been a hit on Theatre Square – one of those corners of old Leningrad that had remained the centre of the city's artistic pride through Tsars and Commissars alike; it was dominated by the Kirov Theatre, but also an enclave of rather beautiful architecture, grand nineteenth-century houses with facings of russet red and lemon yellow. For all that Leningrad was a modern, brave, industrial powerhouse, its citizens could never resist looking towards the ballet and music conservatoires of that district with the sense that this was where the heart of the city really soared.

A few days later, Riabinkin – who had a chest condition that made him unfit for youth-cadet duty – had signed up as a fire-watcher. His nights now involved crouching in an observation post, or on the upper storeys of schools, his eyes flickering at every flash and boom from nearby anti-aircraft guns. The fires from incendiaries blazed in playgrounds; Riabinkin lurched into action, helping to smother them. He had an acute sense of his own mortality.

There was one night when he and his companion were up on the roof, surveying the darkened city around them. Then, close by, the sudden glare of a searchlight beam reaching into the sky, followed by a hissing noise, 'getting louder and louder'. A falling incendiary bomb: Riabinkin and his companion were barely thinking as they scrambled from the roof and literally jumped through the rooftop door down to the attic below, not touching the steps. Then came a race to the main staircase as the explosions began above. In an instant, 'it became brighter than day'. The roof had taken a direct hit from incendiaries. Riabinkin, bruised, scrambled back up the steps through 'dense, acrid smoke that seeped into our throats'. They used shovels to extinguish the glowing thermite that threatened to spark an inferno. There were mounds of sand and the shovelling was frantic. 'Bright light gave way to deep darkness,' he wrote.[24] Others had joined them on the roof; after the dazzle and the adrenaline of shock, there was now a sense of milling around in silence. The all-clear: and Riabinkin, now back inside his observation post, fell into an instant sleep.

At this early stage of Leningrad's ordeal, there could still be found a sense of unity, and of purpose. In the case of Riabinkin, this also meant that in his nights off duty, he relished his visits to the theatre with friends. Extraordinarily, the theatres at that point were still functioning as though nothing were happening. Several evenings after that bomb crisis on the roof, he went to see a production of a J. B. Priestley play called *Dangerous Corner* – a ripe middle-class melodrama involving the gradual revelations of extra-marital affairs, homosexuality, attempted rape and murder. Fifteen-year-old Riabinkin considered it fine escapism. 'A wonderful stage setting, on the whole an excellent piece,' he wrote, 'but unfortunately rather like a huge vaudeville production.' With that subject matter, it possibly could not have been otherwise. 'But,' Riabinkin concluded, 'I liked it so much that I ranked it alongside *An Ideal Husband*'[25] (an Oscar Wilde play also revolving around dark marital secrets and blackmail).

The artillery shells that materialized from the sky in daylight hours were 'worse than bombing', said Vera Inber. She recalled how these attacks began, and the way that once-familiar roads like Vereyskaya Street were at once rendered unrecognizable. But just a week or so after all the shelling and the bombing had begun, there was an entirely new kind of unease. It came when she answered her telephone. It was a call from the city's exchange.

'A fresh young voice said: "The telephone is disconnected until the end of the war,"' she wrote. 'I tried to raise a protest but knew in my heart it was useless. In a few minutes, the phone clicked and went dead . . . until the end of the war.'[26]

13. 'They do not leave our earth in peace'

The cutting of all the city's telephone lines was a further slip down into the abyss of continuous fear. Those that had had home telephones – the administrators, the officials, the Party operatives, the senior office workers – felt that stomach-lilt of unease. Even in a city of some two million people, it brought the sharp pang of isolation. First, the roads and the railways had been blocked and now the means for crying out to the wider nation for help was also severed. There was another factor that so many people were trying hard not to talk about, yet it was increasingly dominating thoughts right across the city: the ratcheting tightness of rationing.

Even in its very earliest stages, hunger is not just physical; there is a strong psychological element too. The hunger of one who is fasting is tolerable and sometimes can even be satisfying because the faster knows that at the end of a set period, there will be bread, there will be meat. Simply imagining a hot *shaverma* – thin slices of juicy lamb or beef, served with tomatoes, cucumbers and onion, wrapped in freshly baked *lavash* bread – or a simple dish of *vobla*, a salt-dried Caspian roach, traditionally washed down with sharp cold beer to balance the intense saltiness – gives an edge of anticipation that lends shape and purpose to the emptiness. The audible shifts and spasms of an empty stomach are temporary discomforts; it will not be long before that hunger is sated. And so, psychologically, it is possible to continue with other matters – with work, with reading, with listening to music – without the mind jittering with frustration and agitation.

But when the hunger is imposed, when it is inflicted, then even the very first hours of that deprivation set off a form of jangling unease. The body constantly wants more food than it is being given. But there is no more to be obtained. Here is a small portion of black rye bread, no larger than half an envelope. Here is a blob of yellow margarine that may be applied to the bread, but perhaps might not quite cover it. Here is a bowl of soup containing thin strands of cabbage or beetroot. Here is a tiny, round, potato fritter, possibly a little spiced. Perhaps there is a larger oatcake to be had as well.

But all these edibles come sporadically rather than all at once. While taken together they might conceivably have been accounted at least elements of a meal, the delay between such individual snacks simply sets the stomach protesting harder. And in psychological terms, the difficulty is this: these minuscule portions of food – tokens of nourishment – might be available to you today. But what of tomorrow? And what if those who are distributing the food are aiming not to raise hopes? What if you detect in their manner the awful possibility that tomorrow there may even be less?

The futurist Leningrad author Daniil Kharms – formerly habitually dressed as Sherlock Holmes, complete with deerstalker and pipe and now confined to the cruel cell of the Kresty prison psychiatric wing – had captured the terrible rhythms of food deprivation when the city had undergone horrifying shortages during the Stalinist famines of the early 1930s. His poem 'Hunger' outlined a framework that the older Leningraders all remembered.

> This is the onset of hunger:
> you wake up vivacious,
> then weakness sets in,
> then boredom breaks out,
> then strength loss ensues
> to rid you of acumen,
> then calmness advances.
> But then terror takes over.[1]

For the people of Leningrad in September 1941, the new hunger – and the new dread and discomfort that went with it – began with the bombing. It had taken just a few days, between September and October 1941, for citizens to cross that terrible border: on one side, the normal world where supplies of such things as fresh meat and fish and pastry and sweet puddings were taken for granted – and the other, where suddenly everyone was intensely preoccupied with rationing, and where suddenly even humdrum items such as dried spiced pork or boiled sweets were unthinkable and unattainable.

By early October, this new world of persistent, low-level hunger was in its own way somehow beginning to diminish the impact of constantly fired artillery shells and night-time bombing. Food – both the lack of it and fantasies of mad abundance – was beginning to dominate both thought and conversation. In one musty brick bomb shelter, during the course of a midnight raid under an iron night of frost, citizens sat captivated as two bakers recounted a trip to Paris many years back to take part in a competition to which one had contributed a sculpture fashioned entirely from chocolate.[2] There was something almost pornographic about the relish with which this story was both told and received.

Everyone had ration cards. The rations were calibrated according to occupation. The staple of black bread was key. On 1 October 1941, the daily amounts were 800 grams for front-line soldiers, 600 grams for soldiers in rear units and workers on intensive assembly lines and 400 grams for other workers. All other Leningraders – from the mothers to the students, the nurses to the librarians – had to make to do with 200 grams each.[3] This would amount to a small slice or a block about the size of a cigarette packet.

Extremely limited supplies of foodstuffs could still come in by plane and air-drop, but they comprised the smallest fraction of what was necessary. In any case, the Luftwaffe pilots were the masters of the Leningrad skies, and transport planes were liable to be shot down before they got through. In the earliest days of rationing it was still possible to obtain small amounts of such items as vermicelli, and there was tremendous excitement in one suburb when a consignment of cabbages was delivered to what had been a restaurant and was now a form of public canteen. Perhaps they were not entirely fresh but, for whatever reason, they were distributed to local residents on a first-come, first-served basis. 'The next day we ate cabbage till it was coming out of our ears,' recorded one diarist.[4]

There were also canteens attached to factories and other firms in the city that were still serving dishes such as beetroot soup and beans in pork fat, although again the amounts per person were very strictly rationed. Some who had anticipated with dread the short-ages to come had stockpiled small quantities of lentils, of pasta, of spiced sausage in their homes. There were those who still had a little sequestered chocolate. Perhaps these stocks offered a temporary period of psychological relief, but even to look at a small jar of len-tils knowing it would never be replenished once empty could not possibly lift the spirits for long. 'There is a steady flow of saliva,' recalled one diarist.[5]

The ingenious trading began quickly; for example, beer (also severely rationed) might be exchanged with alcohol-dependent drinkers for a few oatcakes. Other delicacies seemed rarer than amber, spawning sudden violent pangs of nostalgia for items such as mustard. Meanwhile, even in the earliest stages of famine, salt became a universal craving. Workers in canteens facing hot bowls of sparse cabbage soup yearned for salt to make it savoury, and also to give it some illusion of body. The academic Georgii Knyazev was very keenly aware of those who were (deservedly) receiving more food than him; how could an archivist ask for more than a worker smelting the steel for the weapons that would save his life? But as he catalogued the allowances that he and his wife were entitled to, that sense of undiminished hunger was magnified. In addition to the 200 grams of bread, they could – for a few days in that sharpening cold October – also get 100 grams of meat, 100 grams of 'fish prod-ucts', 100 grams of vegetable oil, 200 grams of cereal and 50 grams of sugar.[6] This was about twelve teaspoons' worth. In the absence of salt or other condiments, the raw energy of the sugar was valuable. But again, there was also that lurking fear that – with the Nazi blockade in place – even this sweet slender lifeline would soon vanish.

Olga Berggolts had received a message from her Aunt Varya, sum-moning her to see her grandmother, who lived in a suburb to the south-east of the city. The reason was that her grandmother wanted to 'say goodbye'.[7] Berggolts was confused at first: why was her frail grandmother, who was largely housebound, being evacuated? Then she understood Aunt Varya's words, though their meaning had not quite penetrated, so fixated was Berggolts's mind upon her civic role. 'Today we've got an emergency meeting of political organizers at the

Regional Committee,' she told her aunt, not quite able to conceive that the death of her grandmother might be more important.

But then, as though a switch had been flicked, reality rushed in on her. She hastened to catch a tram (the service was patchier but the city at that stage was still endeavouring to run them as normally as possible), and as it wove its way through the industrial quarters of the city the sky above 'rumbled and rolled'. Berggolts, lost in her thoughts, did not realize that she was being shouted at by the conductor. They were near the end of the line and an artillery attack had begun. The shells were falling through the clouds. There was a 'prolonged howl, a shell flying very low overhead',[8] and then, moments later, the bass boom of a vast explosion. Out in that thin, exposed, semi-rural suburb was her grandmother's house. Would it still be standing by the time she got there?

To her relief, she found it untouched – the house, she observed, was light, partly because of those 'silver, mortally rumbling clouds':

> The only thing that was dark was the tremendous icon of St Nicolas the Wonderworker in the corner, which had scared us as children and with which my 'iconoclasm' had started before joining the Komsomol. A red lamp burned in front of Nicolas the Wonderworker, and so the brown haughty stern face of the old man with a mitre . . . seemed more implacable and deathly . . . At that moment, a strong explosion shook our house and the red lamp in front of the impassive face of the saint swayed from side to side.[9]

This was, in one sense, what Stalin's League of the Militant Godless had sought so hard to quash in earlier years. This was the religion that they could not tolerate. But it was deep in the bones. Olga Berggolts herself – despite her pride in her own strict rationality – did not feel remotely inclined to condemn it. She saw the authenticity. She saw that it was an integral part of her grandmother's nature, and of her life. With the screaming of the shells heard close by and overhead, the room was slightly removed from time. Her grandmother was 'lying on pillows, a white shawl tied around her, peasant fashion', wrote Berggolts. 'Her face had become very small and wrinkled, her eyes sunk very deep, but they looked out of their hollows with wisdom and enlightenment.' Berggolts studied the hands of her grandmother, with all their 'nodules and calluses', and reflected upon the harshness of the life that she had lived. 'This is how she dies; slowly, solemnly,' wrote Berggolts. 'How she says goodbye, gives her blessing . . . This is her last labour in life. Not death – the last act. She dies in the Russian way, or rather departs – devoutly, understanding all.'[10]

In the midst of bombardment, and at a time of growing hunger, there was an almost merciful tranquillity about this death, too. Here was an eighty-seven-year-old woman, with children, grandchildren, a woman who had lived – and grieved – through Tsarist reform and tyranny, through the peasants leaving the land and coming to the growing cities, through the coming of the wonders of electricity, and of the vast human experiment of revolution. All this: and still she was watched over by the large eyes and the stern face of St Nicolas the Wonderworker. The cold days of darkness that stretched ahead for all Leningraders would see a resurfacing of icons, and of people turning to the closed Orthodox churches both for food and also for some form of spiritual comfort or even explanation. Even true believers in the faith of socialism required other consolation.

In one hospital, soldiers brought back from the front line and almost delirious from their wounds spoke to visitors. One soldier invoked tanks repeatedly: that was all that was needed, he said over and over. 'Darling tanks.'[11] Another soldier was fixated upon trenches. It was seemingly all that he could think of. He said: 'They do not leave our earth in peace.'[12]

As well as the slow creep of hunger, the bombing campaign was removing another foundation stone of human well-being: a sense of home. When the German bombs dissected the houses and apartment buildings, it wasn't simply that they were made instantly uninhabitable, or that private lives had been exposed to the cold open air. It was all those tiny tokens of the life before: everything from toys to lamps to pillows to old books to slippers and favourite coats to handmade quilts. The loss of a secure roof – and the tramping through the city towards the homes of relatives or friends in the hope they could offer accommodation – was compounded by the gnawing sense of old photographs and letters from loved ones that would never be seen again. The bombs were hitting the foundations of identity, while the developing hunger was beginning to corrode the notion of perfect free will. How could one be free when all one could think – and dream – about was food?

The survival of the heavy physical infrastructure of the city – of its factories, of the warships berthed in the Neva – was a source of fear, an electric current of anxiety that ran through the Kremlin. In the early days of the bombardment – and with the dawning sense that the city was essentially enclosed by the enemy – there was drastic movement. Marshal Voroshilov, who had been so essential a part of the city's governance in times of peace, and yet in the space of just a few days had seemingly failed in his duty to protect it, was dramatically stripped of command.

The moment had come with a plane flying in from Moscow. It bore the formidable figure of Army General Georgii Zhukov. It was he who personally handed Voroshilov the letter from Stalin that told him he was immediately dismissed. Later, the journalist Alexander Werth recalled being told that, while 'there was complete chaos at the front, Voroshilov, believing that everything was lost, went into the front line, in the hope of being killed by the Germans'.[13] In the end, he returned to Moscow. And Zhukov saw immediately the nightmare that the city faced.

First, the *opolchenie* – that is, the workers who had volunteered (or had been conscripted) for military service – were completely, horribly, out of their depth when facing the bullets and the artillery of the enemy directly. They did not have the experience to handle their weapons; they did not have the agility in terms of speed and movement. There had been next to no training and the arms that they had been provided with were barely adequate. It was the oldest story of war: spurred and fired by giddying patriotism and adrenaline, these thousands of men (and there were women too in those forces) imagined that their enemy would simply fall before them. Instead, amid plains of birch and pine, across prospects of lakes and in leaf-crunching woods, they were being cut to pieces in their thousands by fiery ammunition. The wounded soldier who had whispered that the earth was being disturbed would himself have seen many dismembered bodies.

The second cause for official dread was the paucity of the city's surviving air defences, trying hopelessly to defend the night skies against the lethal incursions of the Luftwaffe. Zhukov perceived immediately that Leningrad needed scores more fighters and bombers. That the rest of the country was also in such need would not have been lost on him. The Wehrmacht, further south, had been blazing through Ukraine: Kyiv, Odesa and the Crimean peninsula were themselves on the edge of conquest. It had to be assumed that Leningrad was in similar danger. How then might the Nazis at least be denied the city's industrial riches?

Those plants that had not been evacuated, or had only been partially emptied, would have made enticing prizes. The Izhorsk and Kirov factories were still working at an intense pace making ammunition and artillery, as well as parts for tanks and planes. There were factories in the south of Leningrad that were acutely vulnerable not just to the enemy's fire, but also to incursion: the Wehrmacht's forces were only a few miles away. As far as possible, there was internal evacuation: workers were moved to factories at the far northern edge of the city. The plants in the south, although still functioning (no capacity could be lost) were carefully threaded with high explosives. The intention was that, should they be overrun, the factories would be blown sky high. The director of the Kirov Plant, Isaac Salzman, wrote a letter (co-signed by the chairman of the trade union committee) to the Leningrad edition of *Pravda*. Its headline was stark: 'We Will Die, But We Will Not Surrender Leningrad'.[14]

The city may not have been ready to yield, but the splendours of another of its grand suburbs had already fallen. Nazis were teeming through the streets of the town of Pushkin – just twenty-five miles south of Leningrad. The proximity was such that the spires of Leningrad could be seen. The German army was a day's march away. Pushkin was best known as the location of the extraordinary

Catherine Palace, one of the greatest of Russia's cultural treasures. The town had previously been called Tsarskoe Selo – The Tsar's Village. Following the Bolshevik revolution, it became Detskoe Selo – the Children's Village. Pushkin had been educated there, and it was Stalin's latter enthusiasm for the national poet, on the 100th anniversary of his death, that had led to the town being renamed again. The astonishing eighteenth-century structure of the Catherine Palace, constructed for the empress and hugely expanded over the coming decades, with its columned baroque exterior of sky-blue and gold and white, continued to dazzle under the Communists. Its interior – the Portrait Hall, the Light Gallery, the vast ballroom, all mirrors and gold – had also been cared for. Also within these seemingly infinite chambers were the Chinese Room – a rich confection of elaborately lacquered panels and porcelain – and the Amber Room. As Operation Barbarossa had begun, the art historians and administrators who took care of the palace's treasures had to work fast and frantically to conceal what they could: from paintings to antique embroideries, silken furniture to golden sculptures. In contrast to the Hermitage, where precautionary packing had been taking place for months, the Catherine Palace was more vulnerable, possibly because the Nazi occupation of the village had simply not been foreseen.

Treasure was stuffed away into arched brick cellars; as much antique furniture as possible was crated and transported back to Leningrad. But in the case of the palace's greatest jewel and ornament, there was a sense of helpless paralysis. The Amber Room – originally fashioned in 1701 using slabs of the Baltic Sea's most sought-after material – was made up of a series of exquisite panels. A Danish amber craftsman called Gottfried Wolfram had been commissioned to work with a sculptor called Andreas Schlüter. This great chamber of amber – the gemstone ornamented with gold leaf and mirrors – had originally been constructed in Germany for the Berlin Palace. But early in the eighteenth century, it was presented to Tsar Peter. The panels were dismantled and transported to St Petersburg and a chamber within the new Catherine Palace was nominated. Over the course of nearly two centuries – until the revolution – the room had been a source of private wonder for gilded aristocrats. Designed in such a way that,

when lit with candles, the amber had its own interior glow, it mesmerized many; further garlanding the chamber were statues of angels
and gold-leaf detailing studded with jewels. The effect on dark nights
was unearthly. It was a source of intense aesthetic fascination: even
Hitler, who appeared to have little interest in the baroque architecture
of the city that he sought to destroy, knew of the Amber Room.

And so in October 1941 the Nazi looting team – men who had
robbed art from Viennese Jews, from grand homes in Poland, from
salons in France – moved into the Catherine Palace and began dis-
mantling those panels of amber. For the first time since 1716, they
were packed up; the chamber was left naked. They were destined for
Königsberg Castle. The Nazi intention was that the chamber should
be rebuilt there, and opened up to the German people. As the tide
of war turned, that vulgar triumphalism would turn to panic and
the custodians of Königsberg would once more take down the large
heavy panels and pack them in crates. What would happen next – the
Allied bombardment of Königsberg, the flames spreading through
the city and the apparent disappearance of the Amber Room – would
become a mystery that remains unsolved to this day. Was 'the eighth
wonder of the world', as it was once termed, engulfed in the fire? Or
was it spirited away? If so, to where? (Amber Room documentaries,
outlining theories involving disused railway tunnels in Poland, are a
thriving sub-genre of reality TV even today.)

The broader point was that the violation of St Petersburg's history
could not have been more direct or more violent. Not even Stalin's
eager iconoclasts had ever been so careless of aesthetic heritage. Cultural looting, naturally, was a feature of war, and had been since the
days of the Roman empire. But the Nazi regime elevated it almost
to pathology. The sack of the Catherine Palace by the Nazis was
brutal in its symbolism. There was the utmost contempt from the
invaders for those whom they were invading. A short walk north
lay the smaller, though no less beautiful, eighteenth-century Alexander Palace (and small is relative – it was still slightly larger than,
for example, Buckingham Palace). Originally built as a retreat, it
had served that purpose into the twentieth century with the last of
the Romanovs. In 1917, as the Provisional Government had taken

control, Nicholas II, his wife Alexandra and their children were relocated to the Alexander Palace, where for a time they remained
under house arrest. After the family had been moved out later in 1917,
prior to their grim final hours the following year in Yekaterinburg,
the palace – like the Catherine Palace – had been the responsibility of
the new Bolshevik state. It had been decided to turn it to fresh use as
a museum for the public.

But its marbled comforts, its sculptures and richly detailed porcelain, could not be completely dismissed as a place for people to live as
well: one of the wings was turned into a rest home for retired NKVD
staff: a fine reward for careers of terror. Another wing, more whole-
somely, was dedicated as an orphanage for 'Young Communards',[15]
presumably with all the breakable antiquities safely stowed in other
parts of the house. The invading Germans also had this palace firmly
within view: not just for looting (as with the Catherine Palace, the
museum staff had tried as far as possible to remove art, but so short of
time, they could only hide a great deal of it in the palace's basements,
and around the parkland) but also as the backdrop for their military
triumph.

The Alexander Palace was to be overrun by the Wehrmacht's
Army Group North. They could never resist defilement: the landscaped gardens that fronted the palace were designated as a graveyard
for fallen SS officers and its basements, thoroughly stripped of any
objects of value that had been concealed, were converted to cells for
imprisonment and torture. All this just twenty or thirty miles from a
remaining, unevacuated population of one and a half million whom
those Army Group North commanders were set upon exterminating.

This sense of horror naturally extended to the small population
of Pushkin itself; as at other small communities, the Wehrmacht
had arrived not merely with a contingent of Nazi Party art looters
but also with the SS. They made their murderous intentions clear
immediately. Most of the Jewish residents of the town, about 300
people, were ordered to congregate in the landscaped park near the
Alexander Palace. Families – mothers with small children – were
watched by their Gentile neighbours as they walked along the roads.
In some accounts, they began singing old songs; this might have been

to persuade the younger children that this was just an outing to the park on an autumn day. The leaves on the trees were blazing like amber. Once they were all assembled, the nightmare began.

Some were murdered with bullets. Others – as later excavations uncovering the bodies found – had had their skulls stoved in with rifle butts. This was not the only killing ground. There was a square in front of the Catherine Palace, and it was here that another fifty or so Jews were brought together. They were shot, and when they fell to the ground the Einsatzgruppen relieved the corpses of their valuables. All in all, around 500 bodies were buried in a mass grave near the folly known as the White Tower.[16]

The town's other residents would be forced to live under this brutal regime as the merciless siege of Leningrad continued. News of the acquisition of the palaces had certainly spread among the industrial populations of Leningrad. And with it came that pressing and maddening sense of the enemy's proximity: tauntingly close. It would have been the equivalent of, say, the Nazis invading Britain and looking out over London from the vantage point of Windsor Castle.

Yet there was still strength at that moment, among soldiers and citizens alike. Factory manager Irina Zelenskaya wrote that 'curiosity about tomorrow is one of the stimuli sustaining me to live'.[17] In the days to come, that sense of 'curiosity' would, with growing hunger, become slowly dulled in many, like a guttering oil flame. Even before the really serious starvation set in, Leningraders would begin to notice other changes and transformations within themselves.

14. 'The terrible wonders we saw that night'

There was something strange about Ira Riabinkina's skin. During the daylight hours, the little girl would get odd 'blue blotches' under her eyes. On top of this, if she ran around with other children, she would very quickly get a 'stitch in her side'.[1] Elsewhere, older people noticed changes in their own colouring. Some detected a yellowish tinge to their faces. And there were teenagers who were suddenly finding physical exertion difficult; the effort to climb many flights of stairs was leaving them breathless and slightly hunched over, as if they had aged decades during the course of the ascent. One diarist noted that that autumn was marked with 'shortages' as opposed to outright famine. In the House of Scholars, it was still possible for elderly writers to drop in and receive a bowl of hot soup made chiefly with oats. For the very small children, there remained a few sweets to be cut up and shared. But as the cold steel sky settled over Leningrad, and the first few flakes of the winter's snow began to fall, it was hard to maintain any kind of fighting spirit.

The bombers were still roaring overhead at night; and the literary critic Nikolay Punin had taken to using the bomb shelter beneath the vast splendour of the Hermitage Museum, near the cellared art and sculptures that there had been no time to remove. At that stage his sleep – like the sleep of countless Leningraders – was torn and fluttering. His own local shelter was little more than a trench to the rear of his apartment building. The advantage of the cellars of the Hermitage was that the bombing was almost inaudible. If there was an explosion nearby, then the floor would shake, but even the anti-aircraft guns were heavily muffled. 'There I can catch a bit of sleep, for some reason more secure that there's no danger,' Punin wrote in his diary, 'although no one knows whether the Rastrelli arches [those of the eighteenth-century architect] will hold.'[2]

He and others had also noted the changing composition of the

streets: the unheralded fact that Leningrad's population had recently
been supplemented with Red Army deserters, taking their chances
against a scavenging existence and the prowling threat of the NKVD
(if caught, deserters would be summarily shot). These were soldiers
who had been facing the Wehrmacht on the front line. Given the
paucity of their training, their grim levels of inexperience, it may
be assumed that many of these soldiers were traumatized, fleeing in
a form of mentally abstracted state. Their comrades on the front line
were learning with the most terrible speed about pain and squalor
and fear.

Even those who had been drafted into the Red Army before the
Nazi invasion – and who had picked up some skills and an idea of
what to expect – were still facing extraordinary challenges. Yakov
Pikus had been promoted to sergeant just weeks earlier. Red Army
training was not only about technology: it was about the physical
limits of discomfort.

'It's interesting how they trained us physically,' he remembered.
'In the [winter] mornings it was mandatory for us to perform morning calisthenics, undressed down to our waist.'[3] This was out in the
freezing countryside, amid the piercing northern winds. 'We had
these mugs with us . . . back then there was no toothpaste, just little
boxes filled with tooth powder,' he continued. 'After morning exercises, and still shirtless, we had to go brush our teeth. Of course, we
needed water. So we would break ice, collect some water, and use the
powder.' But they were still half-naked and exposed. 'We didn't want
to do it, but the junior commanders stood there watching.' If anyone
gave in to the cold, 'he would have to go peel potatoes at night. We
were young – we did what we were told. Naturally, people started
getting sick. You could not stay in the barracks, because the constant
coughing was unbearable. Some became so sick that they were dismissed from the ranks after this conditioning.'[4]

But this form of training was, it transpired, also vital: victory
would go to those who could withstand the lethal winter weather.
By the autumn of 1941, Pikus and his comrades were out in the open
frosty landscapes just a few miles from Leningrad, manning anti-
aircraft artillery and anti-tank guns. There was already a critical

shortage of ammunition. The artillery worked perfectly well, but – rather like the food – there was a diminishing amount of materiel to feed it with, as Pikus recalled:

> The Germans wanted to starve Leningrad to death, and to some extent they succeeded. And it so happened that at that time we had nothing to shoot with. Our anti-aircraft artillery was on hunger rations: we only got three shells per cannon. And a barrage with three shells . . . better to do nothing at all. It was useless; there was no way to do a barrage.[5]

The rations of ammunition were one thing; the food rations were another. Apart from the carefully calculated oblongs of bread, there was rarely a great deal more than watery soup. They were facing forces who – by comparison – were living like gourmands. Wehrmacht ration packs were rich in sausage meat and tuna as well as bread and grains. In the battle zones that ringed the city, the German soldiers would sometimes cook in the open; the smell of sizzling meat added another layer of torture for the few Leningrad citizens who – on those autumn nights – desperately ventured forth from the streets into the wooded countryside in the hope of scavenging vegetables from the earth. The hazards of artillery strikes, or of searing sniper bullets, were deemed risks worth taking. From a short distance away, German soldiers would look on as Leningraders emerged from trees and started scrabbling at the soil of fields in the hope of finding any kind of vegetables. The orders issued to those soldiers were harsh: any civilians within bullet range should be shot without hesitation. There was, in those early days of the siege, a concern on the German lines that there would be mass breakouts from the city as the hunger sharpened: that hordes of civilians would be attempting to escape. They had to be stopped because they had already been condemned.

Yet there were also concerns about what the indiscriminate killing of unarmed women and children might do to the morale of the young Wehrmacht soldiers, for many of whom this was their first experience of war. There were suggestions that if such killings were wholly necessary, then they should be conducted discreetly. And even then, the strict lineaments of borders written on paper were slowly dissolved by the instinctive impulsions of human nature. The Leningrad hordes were not materializing. But individuals were.

By that darkening autumn, some Leningrad women were offering to the Germans transactions that barely needed any form of spoken language: sex in return for food. Sometimes the young German soldiers honoured their side of the bargain, handing over bread and spiced sausage for these women to take back to their families. Other times the post-coital reward would be no more than a small piece of bread, the soldier keeping the rest of his ration for himself.

The temporary command of General Zhukov over the Leningrad defence forces had dramatically increased an already serious rate of bloody injury and death among the Red Army troops. Zhukov himself was impervious to losses; as he would have seen it, this was about the greater defence of the Motherland, against which the killing of individual soldiers was of no account. But even as Zhukov would soon be pulled away from Leningrad to face the wider Wehrmacht threat to Moscow and to the rest of Russia, the campaign to protect Leningrad would fall back into the hands of city overlord Andrei Zhdanov. Zhdanov was a drunken politician, not a military strategist; and the blood-letting continued in profusion.

To the senior commanders of the Red Army, there was still no reason to suppose that the German goal was anything other than invasion, and it was their job to ensure that the forces of the Wehrmacht could not get through to the streets of Leningrad. They could not at that stage know that Field Marshal von Leeb's intention was more terrible – a ring of unyielding iron around the city until each and every one of its inhabitants was an emaciated corpse.

For von Leeb himself, the sudden chill and dark of autumn had brought small flickers of doubt. It had become clear in those twilit days that the various changes of plan for Barbarossa had also, ironically, had a corrosive effect upon the condition of the Wehrmacht in Army Group North, not for lack of sustenance, but of morale. They were now overstretched, in terms of equipment, in terms of supplies, but also in terms of sheer tiredness. These fresh untested young soldiers had been burning with intensity through the summer and the early autumn. But now, on these plains of the north, they were facing a new kind of conflict some distance removed from the adrenaline-inducing rush of conquest.

The Red Army understood the frantic need to keep even just one breach in that Leningrad barrier open: the thinnest of umbilical cords to the outside world. There was a site around thirty miles east of the city that lay on the banks of the wide, fast flowing Neva, just a little south of the vast Lake Ladoga. It was a bridgehead, a spit of scrubby soil, about three miles in length and a mile in width. If any sort of overland supply line into Leningrad were to be maintained, then this particular narrow stretch, which came to be known as Nevsky Pyatachok (*pyatachok* being a small five-kopeck coin – the name was a reference to the smallness of this patch of land), was going to have to be held by Red Army troops. So theorized General Zhukov, at least. War is filled with fixed ideas, and it is upon these that thousands of lives come to be held in the balance. The Nevsky bridgehead would in the months to come prove to be a terrible killing field, but in a wider conflict where so many small patches of grassland across Russia became suffused with blood, its name would come to have scant resonance outside of the memories of Leningraders themselves (and the history-conscious Leningrad-born Vladimir Putin, who visited a monument there). German troops had positioned themselves on that Nevsky spit by September, and it was late in that month that the grim Russian effort to recapture and hold it began.

The operation required Red Army troops to cross that wide rushing river. Several units were dispatched to its flat shore – trailing with them quantities of ammunition, grenades and guns. They arrived to discover only a very few boats to assist their crossing. The rest they would have to somehow improvise. So it was that large numbers of men – with all that equipment – stepped into swaying makeshift vessels that had been lashed together. This chaotic beginning was only the start of a terrible series of battles that would cost the lives of many thousands of men. On that first night in September the Red Army forces began their crossing under what they hoped would be the cover of darkness across the river. The night would not hide them; out on those wide glittering waters, they became easy targets for German gunfire as bright flares of orange and red shot into the sky and threw a terrible lurid light upon the black waters beneath. The air was illuminated with the bright red trails of shells fired at helpless flesh.

Countless craft were sunk; countless men drowned, their breath disappearing in the shockingly cold water of the Neva. Yet more vessels followed, precarious with vast loads of ammunition and too many for the German forces to shoot them all out of the water. Finally, the assault on the German positions on the Nevsky bridgehead began. But the Wehrmacht forces – a tentacle that had wrapped its way around the south of Leningrad and up its eastern side – were implacable. More and more Red Army soldiers – hundreds, then thousands – were sent to make the crossing by any means they could contrive. A minuscule bridgehead was established by the Soviets; the Wehrmacht were determined to erase it.

The men who based themselves in wooden huts on this grassy riverland were subjected to levels of bombardment that left more than a few of them deranged; the sensory and emotional overload of the artillery shells, the lightning-flash explosions, the screams of the wounded and the dismembered, the unending cacophony became a new kind of hell.

Abram Sapozhnikov had been fighting relentlessly since that fateful day in June. By the time he was called upon to make the crossing to the Nevsky bridgehead, he was already deaf in one ear: the result of incessant bombardment.

> I got to a destroyed paper mill in Nevskaya Dubrovka. There, the chief of staff of the 86th Division met me and said, 'You are taking command of a platoon.' He gave me a list – the entire platoon consisted of Uzbeks, and Tajiks . . . There were only three Russians in it who knew the language; the rest did not understand the Russian language. I had to accept and proceed. I immediately received orders for the platoon to set up and maintain communication lines between the 330th Regiment, positioned on Nevsky Pyatachok, and the command of the 86th Division on the right bank.

The terrible wonders we saw that night, the goings-on, only God knows. I remember the Neva was alight with parachute flares. The Germans fired machine guns from the right and left flanks, and shelled us repeatedly. Battalion after battalion arrived at the crossing: first went the infantry and sappers; signalmen were told to wait for orders. None came that night. We witnessed frightful things. Before our eyes a shell would hit a boat, it would rise up in the air and all those voices would cry out, 'Help!' But what could we do, we were up next.[6]

Having made shore on the other side, the horrors began multiplying. Sapozhnikov and his men found themselves running through a narrow ravine which was filled with the dead and the nearly dead: 'living meat', as he put it. The soil was sandy but this was still a primitive form of trench warfare: the Red Army dug into theirs and their Wehrmacht opponents a short distance away huddled similarly. For Sapozhnikov and his men – mingling with all ranks, and a dazzling range of Soviet nationalities – there would not be one moment of safety for the next few weeks as they endured bombs and bullets. One night he ventured forth, checking telephone wire connections. The air spat with gunfire; men a short distance away fell and Sapozhnikov felt his 'hair moving'.[7] Heart palpitating, he found cover, and then very carefully started to remove his cap. He was convinced as he did so that part of his skull and his brain would come away with it. He gingerly touched his head. It was 'intact'. The Wehrmacht sniper's bullet had scorched through his cap with millimetres of clearance.

Field Marshal von Leeb and his lieutenants, having relied upon threadbare and frequently inaccurate intelligence, had been working upon the assumption that the Red Army forces, weak to begin with, would become weaker still under continual assault. And yet the reverse seemed to be true: no matter how many hundreds, how many thousands of Red Army soldiers were slaughtered or taken prisoner, more materialized from those flat eastern horizons, and in ever greater numbers. The Wehrmacht had taken great care to destroy and pulverize the airfields, yet their own Luftwaffe were being challenged in the skies by Soviet fighters, and their soldiers below were frequently targets. What before had been an ineluctable and deadly advance from the Germans to the north was starting to feel more like a cold stasis. The change in the weather compounded this feeling.

In the lands around Leningrad, the deep autumn would bring not only the first flakes of snow, but also prodigious rainfall of biblical force. In the green countryside to the south and the east of Leningrad, the immediate effect was to turn roads of dust into sucking primeval swamps. Tanks and other vehicles became steadily trickier to manoeuvre. More than this: the driving cold and the inescapable damp were exposing deficiencies in Wehrmacht uniforms.

To the south, there was still movement: Ukraine was conquered. And the advance to Moscow continued. But in the north, von Leeb's multitudes of men lacked the comfort of momentum. At this point they were simply mass executioners and nothing else. On their route through to Leningrad, Army Group North's SS units had taken special care – amid the village fires and the widespread looting of food – to home in on asylums and specialist hospitals: and they had been punctilious about seeking out and identifying mentally and physically disabled people and murdering them. This was not a secret that was kept from the delicate ears of Army Group North higher commands. Everyone from von Leeb downwards knew why they were there. They were the exterminators.

While the forces of the Red Army had stabilized, and while it seemed to the eyes of German soldiers that they were continually and miraculously regenerating, the best that they could offer in those colder days was paralysis in thick mires. The propaganda arm of Army Group North produced thousands of leaflets, with a distinctively anti-Semitic slant, which the Luftwaffe dropped on the heads of both the Red Army troops and the citizens of Leningrad, emerging from their shelters after more shelling:

To All Men and Women Citizens of the Soviet Union, and to the Honest Commanders and Soldiers of the Red Army. The victorious German army will cast off the chains of the yoke of the Communist and the Yid . . . Your happiness and life are in your hands . . . Don't believe the lying words of Communist/Yid propaganda . . . Abandon your defence and take up arms against your Communist and Yid oppressors. Go over to the side of Germany. This way you will hasten your liberation and put an end to your people's pointless bloodshed.[8]

As well as the venom of the Jew-hatred, the particular cruelty of these leaflets was the grotesque promise that Red Army soldiers who surrendered would be welcomed and 'treated well', as another leaflet proclaimed. They also promised cigarettes and also tempted with 'nourishment'.[9] The reality that faced any and every Soviet prisoner of war was intentionally a slow and terrible death: over the coming months, an almost unimaginable three million men would be held in pens under pitiless open skies, and among those who did not succumb to starvation or to disease were those who would have their hearts finally stopped by the savage cold. The leaflets dropped on civilians were aimed partly at women, exhorting them to write to their menfolk on the front and beg them to lay down their arms, adding that their own ruler was cruel and capricious and that many of their fellow civilians had suffered in Stalin's 'torture chambers'. There was another exhortation on those leaflets: a plea not to blow up Leningrad's industrial plants. The leaflets reasoned that, when the Germans took control, everyone would want to see their modern civilized world rebuilt. Again, the distance between this and the reality is breathtaking. To the Nazis, Leningrad was already a city of the dead.

To accuse Leningraders of fatalism would be quite wrong: they were by no means passive in their acceptance and understanding of the grim ordeal that was only just beginning. But the suffering they had endured before was framed within the steel-grey familiarity of Soviet power, and the way that it was exerted; this time the malevolence was without voice, and beyond appeal or reason. The pendulum of Leningraders' psychology began to swing between bitter determination and rising fear.

In families, the arguments over those ever-thinner rations had already started: siblings convinced that brothers and sisters had managed to secure secret extra helpings. Relatives and close friends began eyeing each other with hostile suspicion. They could feel these transformations taking effect within themselves, and they were perfectly aware of what was happening: the paranoia of hunger. But as much as their rational minds coolly appraised these symptoms, darker emotions could not be kept in check.

And with the heart-racing ill-will came the start of the dreams. Fifteen-year-old Yura Riabinkin found himself suffering visions of 'bread with butter and sausage';[10] as the hungry nights stretched out, even the dreams became rationed: the sausages disappeared and all he could dream of was bread. 'I might take up philosophy one of these days,' he confided to his diary, after having envisaged the city being hit with chemical weapons, and all remaining particles of food being contaminated. 'There is a folk riddle that asks: "What is the shortest thing in the world?" And the answer goes "Human life".'[11] Riabinkin tried hard to find intellectual stimulus, in part to fire a sense that there was still a future, in part to find some respite from the unrelenting depression of life at home. His days were spent not poring over books but rather standing in queues on behalf of his mother, who was working despite her own intensifying weakness. The queues at bakeries and grocers were long and unmoving, people standing for hours in the increasingly icy winds cutting through from Lake Ladoga and the north. And here there were instances of sour, sudden, unstoppable paranoid rage: civilians convinced that bakers were hiding loaves from them in the backs of their shops – and shopkeepers having to barricade themselves in for fear of riots starting over these non-existent hidden supplies.

There were moments of indignity that had a certain mad ingenuity about them as well, though. The inferno that had melted the Badayev warehouses, and all those succulent stocks of dried meat and sugar, had continued to burn for several nights. The smoking, seething ruins were gutted and skeletal, but there were Leningraders who set out for them armed with shovels, hoping to capture the caramelized sugar that had seeped into the earth. Here was a mad and desperate form of alchemy: seeking to summon the ghost of sweetness from the soil. They mixed the earth with boiling water, stirred and distilled it, boiled it again – and then declared that the brown product that they were sipping was indeed marvellously sweet.

Set against this grimness were manifestations of the city's artistic exceptionalism. Extraordinarily, despite the ceaseless bombing, the thin rations and the cold, there were still concerts being performed at the Leningrad Philharmonic Hall. '[Aleksandr] Kamensky played Tchaikovsky's Piano Concerto and gave the "Prater Valse" as an encore,' wrote Vera Inber. 'Already the concert hall has lost its festive look,' she had to admit. 'It isn't heated and I had to keep on my coat.'[12] Encouragingly, though, there 'were a lot of soldiers in the audience'. There were still a few cinemas open too: another means by which family members might at least for an hour or two be transported away from their hunger, and from each other's corrosive tempers.

Nikolay Punin had been observing the coming of the snow; how in the daytime it had started to settle. 'The snow is so beautiful, this day is so beautiful in its fragility,' he wrote. He confessed to his diary a development that the authorities would not have cared for in any of their civilians. 'Today I have been praying all morning,' he wrote. 'I am not speaking, I am praying silently, in my heart. And it is just as silent as the snow.'[13] It would not be long before the shuttered churches of Leningrad were to start receiving visits from numbers of others who yearned themselves to commune with authorities higher than those at the Smolny Institute.

The senior academic Georgii Knyazev was by contrast frightened and bewildered by the sinister transformations of his work colleagues. By this stage, they had all moved into the one small office, working around a pot-bellied stove (that iron pot belly also distinctly underfed – there was a growing shortage of fuel, and tiny lumps of glowing coal were scarcely sufficient). 'The protection of the archives troubles me greatly,' he wrote. 'Today I did the rounds of the entire storage area and issued a whole series of instructions.'[14] This was not labour for its own sake: these archives were, to him, the beating heart of Leningrad. His colleagues could no longer share his passion:

Little by little, my colleagues are giving in. One of them, who looks gloomy enough anyway, is lashing out at everyone with a sick bad temper . . . Another has become completely glassy-eyed, and a third has retreated into a profound silence. One woman . . . gazes around with unseeing eyes. Whatever she is thinking as she lives through what is happening, she hides inside herself . . . And I have suddenly become fed up, alone in this roomful of people who are somehow ebbing away inside themselves.[15]

The transformations were physical too: as well as a yellowing of complexion, legs sometimes seemed to both swell and harden, making walking painful. In a few of the city's less fortunate residents – jobless even in times of peace and often alcohol-dependent – some of the changes were equally frightening; their faces were not merely start-ing to darken but to blacken in patches. In communal apartments and bomb shelters alike, Leningraders were spending their evenings in deeper and more intense silences, punctuated by the shivering shock waves of distant explosions. Their bodies and their minds were mutating.

In the first few days of November, the bread ration was cut once more. In addition, the city's power supplies, in that worsening snow and lengthening dark, were faltering and increasingly uncertain under German bombardment. The shocking thing in the winter days to come was in part how unshocking so many Leningraders found their first sight of death. Even the children adjusted with the most terrible speed to the fact of corpses lying in public areas. As the relentless cold moved in, and as the hours of light diminished day by day, the city's uncanny duality would very soon turn into something else: streets haunted by somnambulists who were moving beyond the ordinary realm of sleeping and walking; people so close to the edge of death that it seemed to others miraculous that the life-fire still flickered within them.

15. Primeval

Borders were not simply lines on maps: they were about identity; they were about beliefs; they were even about philosophy. The Wehrmacht soldiers encamped in the lands that ringed Leningrad, or walking through the streets of small villages and towns near its outskirts, were some thousand miles away from the border of their homeland. Their commanders were convinced that this distance would come to seem as nothing: that the people who dwelled in these forests and plains would be forced to learn and understand and accept that the borders had dissolved, and that their lives and their thoughts would henceforth be guided by the Nazi sensibility. In the Wehrmacht-occupied town of Gatchina, efforts were made via public pronouncements to tell the citizens that this was not a war on the Russian people; they were instead being 'liberated from Bolshevism'.[1] These public pronouncements would also focus on the need to destroy Jewish influence. The propaganda that Wehrmacht soldiers had been force fed had initially focused on the inferiority of the Slavic people. But here, under the sullen autumn skies and amid watchful, silent civilians, how many of those young Germans seriously imagined that soon this would be their unchallenged domain? Real conquest meant the penetration of not merely geographical but also personal borders: reaching inside, remoulding identities and politics and beliefs, so that the conquered people were transformed. But the Nazis only truly understood persuasion through terror; they continued to walk the streets with whips.

Away from the small communities that compassed Leningrad – and to which many German soldiers held close for the comforts on offer – the ancient landscape was starting to make a nonsense of their modernity. Field Marshal von Leeb's Army Group North – and its advanced tanks and weaponry – had spent the summer blazing its way through the forests and along the tracks of eastern Europe using technologically honed firepower that could not be halted. But the relentlessly wet autumn – the rainfall in Leningrad Oblast, the *rasputitsa* sweeping in over Lake Ladoga, and which was consistently heavy at that time of year – turned soil to tyre-sucking sump. Even the most impressive vehicles were struggling in the taiga miles to the south of Leningrad – woodlands with rudimentary roads, dense prospects of alder and aspen and lakes and spongy peat bogs. The Wehrmacht soldiers who were dug in closer to the city – such as Wilhelm Lübbecke, based with his men in the village of Uritsk (now Ligovo), from which, from the 'top of a tall building',[2] it was possible to see not only the spires of Leningrad, but also some of the Soviet navy's great battleships at anchor on the Neva – were beginning to tire. For the infantry, the adrenaline of the speedy advance was giving way to the discomforts of living in bunkers dug amid cold, wet woodlands. As Lübbecke recalled:

In building our rear bunkers [they] followed a standard method of construction. After digging out waist-deep holes between 1 to 5 square metres in size, they erected log walls and heaped part of the just excavated soil against them. Following the placement of heavy timber beams or tree trunks to serve as a roof, they then covered the top of the bunker with the remaining soil. Despite offering little protection in the event of a direct hit by the Red Army's heavy artillery, the bunkers offered us a measure of warmth from the freezing temperatures outside.

At Uritsk, my assignment as the F.O. required me to spend perhaps three-quarters of my time in one of the various bunkers located along the front or even out ahead of our infantry's frontline. In contrast with the rear bunkers, the frontline bunker was little more than a covered ditch with a slot for observation.[3]

This was a regression in time: bringing the subterranean life of the First World War to the forests. The use of horses – necessary for dragging artillery and equipment and supplies along marshy roads – brought a flavour of earlier centuries. Added to this in a general sense throughout the region was an increased pressure on these soldiers from their own SS watchers: 'It became standard policy to terrorize the troops from evading a likely death at the front,' wrote historian

18. In the Russian Orthodox faith, icons of the saints were believed to be literal windows through which Heaven could be seen. Older Leningraders cherished icons depicting St Nicolas the Wonderworker.

19. As the League of the Militant Godless sought to extinguish faith in the city in the 1930s, the leader Stalin himself became a form of secular faith icon: his image, and his unreadable smile, inescapable across Leningrad.

20. Even through the darkest days of both siege and purges, Petersburg comedian Arkady Raikin (*pictured right*) prompted deep laughter. He satirized officialdom but was loved by the people and the authorities alike. His work is still adored now.

21. Before the revolution, the Stray Dog Cabaret was where the city's finest poets gave recitals in the early years of the century; by the time of the starvation siege, the café long gone, their work being broadcast on public loudspeakers throughout the city to boost morale.

22. The Nazi invasion of Russia – Operation Barbarossa – was launched on 22 June 1941 and was greeted both with horror and incredulous shock. Death on an unimaginable scale swept across eastern Europe.

23. Leningrad citizens were swift to volunteer for a range of defensive work, including being bussed out to the country to dig anti-tank trenches under Luftwaffe gunfire.

24. Internationally renowned Leningrad composer Dmitri Shostakovich volunteered as a firefighter in late summer 1941 He would later be evacuated; but he was already composing a symphony dedicated to the city's struggles.

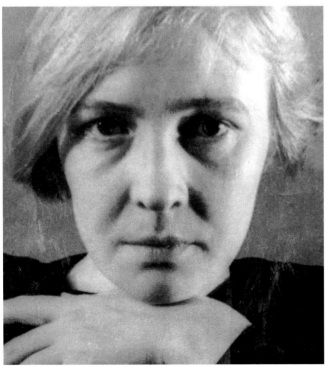

25. Poet Olga Berggolts was a Party commissar and a dedicated Bolshevik, and the passion of her verse was filled with love for this revolutionary world. But she and her family were to suffer terribly in the siege.

26. Fifteen-year-old Yura Riabinkin was a devoted chess-playing Young Pioneer – the Soviet youth organization shown in this promotional painting from 1937, here guiding tourists.

27. The city was encircled by the Wehrmacht; what began was a campaign of bombing and shelling that threatened to take the city apart stone by stone.

28. As the remorseless bombardment continued, defences became elaborate: factory roofs were painted grass green or fitted with camouflage netting. There grew superstitions about which sides of certain streets were more dangerous in terms of attracting explosives.

29. The city's teenagers were thrown into fire-watching duties in autumn 1941, often having to hurl themselves into bombed attics to try to extinguish incandescent incendiaries.

30. The daily ration of black bread for many individuals steadily shrank as winter approached; soon it would be little larger than a cigarette carton.

31. The city's bakeries had to start finding new ingredients for their bread, including edible cellulose and cattle-feed. All knew the intense digestive discomfort that would follow – but it gave the temporary illusion of fullness.

32. Continual bombardment crippled the city's power and water supplies as the harshest winter in years descended. Homes were left in darkness; and water had to be drawn from freezing rivers and street stand pipes.

33. Many Leningraders became refugees in their own city in 1942: communal apartments made uninhabitable by bombing, the snow swirling in through unrepaired windows.

34. Daily hunger weakened the old and the young alike by December 1941; numbers of the dead through starvation multiplied daily, to the extent that the gravediggers could not keep up. Mass graves and mass cremations awaited.

Omer Bartov, 'by promising them certain execution if they were caught.'[4]

With this came the suggestion of another form of regression: that of a degeneration of human nature. The Wehrmacht forces holding the rear areas of Army Group North – those huddled communities in Lithuania and Estonia – were blended with Einsatzgruppen and Sonderkommando death squads. In the Lithuanian town of Kaunas, there was a gaunt fortress dating from the Tsarist era. One day in October 1941, some 9,200 local Jewish people were marched there. In the fortress's interior courtyard, Soviet prisoners of war had been directed to dig out deep pits. The assembled Jews, forced to move through dark stone corridors and tunnels, and being violently stripped of any valuables along the way, now found themselves out under the sky, surrounded by stone walls. They were ordered to descend into the pits naked and lie on the freshly dug earth. Outside, the engines of noisy tractors were turned on to muffle the echoing noise of the machine guns and the cries of the dying as the killing began.[5] This was just one of many such episodes of mass murder throughout the Baltic states in that autumn of 1941 in which thousands of Jews and Roma died.

The infantry and artillery troops of the Wehrmacht at the Leningrad front may have been unaware of the exact horrors that were being perpetrated in the lands that they had marched through, but they must surely have understood, through all the efforts from the authorities to coarsen their own attitudes, the essential nature of the war that they were bringing down upon helpless civilians. The punishments meted out by their own superiors – major derelictions answered with swift execution – were in part calculated to blunt their sensitivity to suffering. These German soldiers were also being told how the demonic Red Army tortured and mutilated their prisoners, their own mental landscapes and imaginations now bordered with extreme violence on both sides. In a world of horror, either they would inflict the suffering, or the suffering would be inflicted upon them.

And while, in those woods and pastures and wetlands that formed the once-fruitful countryside around Leningrad, there might have been stasis, the deep deafening pulse of the guns continued. The bombardment of the city was unabated, even as the Red Army and the mighty gunships of the Baltic Fleet attempted to extinguish it. The artillery pieces just outside Leningrad, and aiming at its heart, were huge, some shells weighing 44 kilograms. These lethal projectiles could fly up to eight miles. They were deployed in the daylight hours: an initial bombardment followed by several hours of non-stop firing, all the way through the morning and the afternoon. Proximity to the city meant proximity to the vast Soviet warships positioned by the granite banks of the Neva, their own huge guns pointing back at the enemy in those wooded suburbs. The Soviet battleship *Oktyabrskaya Revolyutsiya* (*October Revolution*) and the floating battery *Marat* maintained their own fierce fire, but nothing could dislodge the Wehrmacht. Equally, though, even if Nazi High Command had been so minded, the Wehrmacht still was not in a position to enter the city: it did not have the capabilities to deal with the intensity of street-by-street fighting. Another difficulty von Leeb faced at that point was that many of the fresher German troops arriving at the front were young and wholly inexperienced in battle: they were certainly not prepared to face a resistance as inexorable as the Red Army would offer.

To the south, Army Group Centre was renewing its push towards Moscow – 'Operation Typhoon' – partly with the help of resources from Army Group North. A few weeks previously, Hitler himself had flown to Smolensk to confer with von Leeb about the overstretched position of Army Group North and how it might be relieved. Von Leeb was to be granted more soldiers from the Blue Division of Spanish volunteers. There was a new plan too: striking much further east of Leningrad. Much of the land they would have to cross in the process was little better than a quagmire, and slow tanks and vehicles and horse-drawn wagons would face ceaseless attacks from Red Army defenders, but the sharpening air and the falling temperatures had brought von Leeb to the view that the hard Russian winter might in one crucial way prove an advantage: tanks and artillery could be moved with greater ease along forest roads made solid by ice and snow. And so it was that a target came into view.

The aim was a town some 120 miles east of Leningrad called Tikh-vin. The objectives were threefold: to provide a northern flank for the forces advancing towards Moscow, to forge a link with the Finnish army north on the Karelian Isthmus, and to choke the last of Leningrad's most slender supply routes. Tikhvin itself was, and is, a site of some extraordinary religious architecture: the sixteenth-century Monastery of the Dormition, dazzlingly facaded in white, pale pink, orange and green, with exuberant onion domes and spires of blue; the Tikhvinsky monastery, which until recent years had boasted an array of different-sized bells so that a rich range of notes could ring out as if from Heaven. The Dormition monastery had – until the League of the Militant Godless reached it – contained an exquisitely beautiful golden icon depicting Mary and Jesus. The legend ran that in the fourteenth century, awe-struck locals had watched as it some-how simply floated down from the sky. There were later legends that the icon had been fashioned in Antioch by none other than the apostle Luke. It was displayed on the inside door of the monastery and Orthodox believers took comfort from another legend: that the Tikhvin Icon had the divine power to protect Russia from murder-ous invaders.[6]

The Stalinists had removed it at some point in the 1930s; though even the most godless of the Militant Godless did not quite dare destroy it. Instead, the Tikhvin Icon was placed in a local museum, to be seen by the eyes of both the idly curious and the devout.

The town had lain on a bustling trading route since the fourteenth century; by 1941, it also lay upon an important junction for rail and road from deeper east in Russia. It was an artery for Leningrad; even with the city surrounded, there were limited supplies coming into Tikhvin via rail, and then being shipped across Lake Ladoga, despite the Luftwaffe pilots' best efforts.

The region was also rich in bauxite, which was vital in the production of aluminium. The conquest of the town would add to the pressure on Moscow.

That assault – the Wehrmacht pushing forward through the useable roads, and their assault craft gliding across the wide, lapping Volkhov river – began on 16 October 1941. In the morning, the sky was crystalline;

but there were ice crystals beginning to form on tree branches and, later in the day, the snow began to fall. The Red Army defenders had not been anticipating any such enemy action; numbers were slender because greater forces had been deployed a little further north at Lake Ladoga to help the efforts there to protect any possible shipments. But as the Wehrmacht armour and vehicles began to materialize on the roads just a few miles from Tikhvin, the ferocity of the resistance was intense. First, there was fire from above: the Soviet air force swooping in. And the Red Army mustered men and tanks, moving them through a cloying landscape to try to beat back the invaders.

Then the icy weather that had been so keenly anticipated by von Leeb suddenly relented; there was a thaw, and the endless downpours resumed. The effect upon both the Wehrmacht and the Red Army around Tikhvin was to drag them yet further back in time. It was necessary in some places to abandon tanks to the glutinous bogs; equipment and weaponry had to be carried by bearers, as though at Agincourt. In one instance, a Soviet T-34 tank not only became trapped in grey mud, but under that monsoon-like onslaught sank into the ground up to its turret. And at each tiny village that lay between them and Tikhvin, the Wehrmacht forces faced fierce counterattacks: single-storey wooden houses and associated barns contained troops who unleashed hails of bullets and mortars upon the Germans as they advanced slowly through the torrent. In many cases, the efforts were vainglorious: huge numbers of Soviet prisoners were taken (thence to face the strong possibility of death by starvation or exposure). But an invading army that had understood itself as capable of securing lightning-fast victories was having to adjust to this frightening regression to almost primeval conditions.

Even the Führer felt a tremor of unease about the Tikhvin operation.[7] Von Leeb was flown back to the Wolf's Lair for a special conference. Hitler was anxious – especially in view of the needs of Army Group Centre as it came tantalizingly close to Moscow – that valuable armour and equipment was being driven towards a region that might prove a terrible trap.[8] But von Leeb was equally anxious about the prospect of the Wehrmacht being pushed backwards, away from the town; as well as granting the Red Army the luxury of a victory, it would also keep alive the possibility of salvation for the people of Leningrad. Tikhvin had been selected as a target primarily because it would hasten mass starvation in the city, which would in turn place lethal pressure upon Stalin. Von Leeb, as much as his Führer, was now fixated upon the absolute necessity of ending millions of civilian lives, extinguishing the breath of an entire city. The destruction of Leningrad would surely hasten Stalin's own end: Moscow could be seized, the Bolshevik heart cut out, and the Nazi victory be made secure. Moreover, von Leeb was maintaining his faith in winter: while the Tikhvin push was currently a swampy nightmare, the ice would return, the swamps would freeze and then the tanks would roll freely once more. On hearing this, Hitler's own doubts and anxieties dissipated; von Leeb had renewed his sense of purpose.

Such plans were easy for generals to formulate in warm rooms; for the Wehrmacht and for the Red Army reserve forces – many of whom had themselves been based in or around Leningrad and transported further east to meet this slow incursion – this cold land of bogs and rivulets, of thin trees and uneven forest floors, where shelter was scarce and scanty supplies of food had to be brought in either on foot or dropped haphazardly from military planes above, was in some senses prehistoric. Both sides faced the grimmest penalty for desertion – under the all-seeing eyes of the SS and the NKVD alike – and yet on both sides, in the woodlands around Tikhvin, increasing numbers of men slipped away from their regiments out of terrible desperation. Their chances of survival, let alone of thriving and building new lives, were impossibly low; moreover, the cold returned and now with a ferocity that could incapacitate armies as well as individuals. No lone man – insufficiently uniformed or fed – could hope to withstand the sudden temperature drops and blizzards.

This was especially true of those soldiers who had been transported from Leningrad. They had already had to endure weeks of progressive malnourishment. The onset of the more piercing cold additionally made the German forces sharply aware of their own deficiencies in terms of both nutrition and clothing.

★

And so the tiny railway town of Tikhvin, previously only ever noted for the divine luminescence of that golden icon, became a curious and vital landmark in the wider struggle for survival: a fulcrum upon which the future of both Leningrad and the wider Soviet system seemed to pivot. The Wehrmacht commanders understood that, unlike many of the smaller communities close to Leningrad, Tikhvin – even though conquered – would not be permanently subdued, and could certainly not be turned into a garrison: the counter-attacking Red Army forces were too fierce, too relentless.

These efforts were being led by a Soviet military commander – broad-chested, square-headed, but with a curiously soft gaze – called Kirill Meretskov. Just weeks earlier, he had been lying – pulsing with pain, his ribs shattered by the blows of a torturer – in one of the dark concrete cells of the Lubyanka prison in Moscow.[9] The man who was now in charge of the 4th Army had been subjected to the psychotic violence and paranoia of Stalinism. Commander of the Soviet General Staff from 1940 to 1941, and created a Hero of the Soviet Union after his efforts in the Winter War with Finland, Meretskov had – just days after the Nazi invasion in 1941 – been arrested by the NKVD. The fires of the purges, which had largely died out by 1939, had been reignited by war, and by the way that Stalin and the entire military establishment had been thrown off balance. Meretskov had been beaten with rubber truncheons in an attempt to make him confess to treason and espionage. There was no evidence; Meretskov – like so many thousands of others – was wholly innocent. Ironically, as well as the infliction of pain, there had been calculated starvation: the unchanging Russian penal manoeuvre.

As anyone would, Meretskov gave way after some intensive days with one of the NKVD's chief torturers. He confessed, and a list of names of military 'conspirators' – eagerly sought after by secret police chief Lavrentii Beria – was compiled. Their deaths swiftly followed, yet Meretskov himself was freed, and soon reinstated to full commanding status within the Red Army. The circumstances of his original arrest, the reasons for his physical ordeal and finally the rationale concerning his release, were secret, and the files were later destroyed.[10] So it would seem that neither Meretskov nor his comrades could have had any understanding of why he had been arrested (or, indeed, released), save that perhaps the Soviet Union could not now afford to waste any more military experience. He was brought before Stalin in full uniform. Friends were shocked by his appearance: once healthy and ruddy, he was a haggard ghost. Now trusted with the military defence of Leningrad, Meretskov was in command of the Tikhvin counter-attack and the efforts to save the city from annihilation.

His own internal landscape, the borders of his own philosophy, remained little changed despite his Lubyanka ordeal. The arbitrary cruelties of the Soviet regime might still at least be placed in the context of striving towards a better, purer society; the opposing forces of Nazism, by contrast, offered nothing but squalor and death. In other words, Meretskov's ideological conviction had not been dented, nor any of his military fervour cooled.

Tikhvin fell to the Nazis on 8 November 1941; the tanks that had been mired in pools had made it through. In the course of the battles to save it, some 20,000 Soviet prisoners had been taken. More than this, ninety-six tanks and eighty-six artillery pieces had been captured. The railway junction was now at the mercy of the destructive forces of the Wehrmacht; the consequences of this would be that even the most meagre supplies of grain and dried meat would have to be diverted a further hundred miles to the north-east before they might be transported across the rapidly freezing Lake Ladoga. This was the moment of Leningrad's utter isolation in the darkening days.

But in audaciously pushing the borders of the battle that much further east, von Leeb had simultaneously exposed his own forces to a taste of the suffering that they were inflicting upon others. When the frost hardened, the Wehrmacht, so far as it could, 'clung to towns and villages' for respite; there was otherwise little to protect them in those log-lined dugouts from the raw Arctic winds and the fast-thickening snow.[11] And for his own part, Kirill Meretskov began to work with some speed in the effort to crush them. While lack of experience was equally rife on both sides, Russia had its deep hinterlands from which huge numbers of young men were being drawn. Meretskov soon had three armoured divisions as well as thirty infantry divisions under his overall command as the Volkhov Front (as it was known) became one of the main fault-lines of the conflict. Also nearby were two cavalry divisions; just a year or so earlier, there might have been those in western Europe who would have regarded such things as an amusingly romantic and hopeless throwback to the eighteenth-century battlefield. Yet under those winter skies of iron, and amid those ever-darkening forests, suddenly such forces could seem fleet and nimble and supremely adaptable when compared with growling tanks halted in smothering bayous of mud. In the coming weeks, the efforts of the Red Army (troops eventually being brought in by the train-load), combined with the Soviet air force, would make Tikhvin, briefly, an unexpected nerve centre of the war.

As Red Army soldier Yakov Pikus was later to recall:

> I had frostbite. You know what kind of uniforms we had? Puttees, boots, and footwraps, that's all. But it was minus 35°C! So if you are lying in the snow . . . It's not like we were going into attack from a five-star hotel. We had nothing. At best, we had dugouts and trenches; but most of the time during the offensive there was no time to dig one out and we did everything outside. It was hellish. It was so cold, and on top of that, we were underfed. If we were full, I don't think it would have been as bad. I think about 90 per cent of the entire army was frostbitten.[12]

Quite apart from the primitive conditions that the opposing forces faced, there was something immeasurably old and terrible about the nature of Army Group North's intentions: if it had been the case that they were trying to invade and dominate Leningrad – appropriating its beauty and its industry for Germany – there would still be no justification, but there would at least still be the pulse and breath of humanity. But Wilhelm Ritter von Leeb – confident in the wishes of his Führer – had absolutely no flutters of doubt about this ancient impulse to mass murder. The scale of the plan was what made this kind of warfare new, but the psychotic compulsion was the most terrible of the primeval instincts.

Psychosis was to breed psychosis: a counter-attack by the Red Army in a tiny village near Tikhvin saw savage revenge being inflicted upon a clutch of cornered German soldiers; they were later found on a frozen lake, impaled upon the ice, bayonets thrust through their shattered chests, transfixing their corpses. Were any of these German forces reading – as some Leningraders and a few Red Army soldiers were – Tolstoy's *War and Peace*, and his account of the moment in 1812 when Napoleon, having marched his Grande Armée across eastern Europe, into Russia and into the nightmare bloodshed at Borodino, starts to feel the first intimation of unease about this vast landscape and about its people?

> When he listened to reports that the Russians still stood their ground . . . a terrible feeling, like one experienced in dreams, seized him . . . Yes, it was as a dream, when a man sees a villain coming at him, and in his dream, the man swings and hits with terrible force, which he knows should destroy him, and [yet] he feels his arm fall . . . as limp as a rag . . .[13]

Meanwhile, in Leningrad, dreams and waking reality were starting to fuse and intertwine, the dizziness and fever of hunger filling even night's deep sleep with the horrors of the day. And even when awake, some people were walking along riverbanks without seeing the real world before them, instead staring at visions, and at different worlds.

16. Trances and Fevers

In her youth, the poet Anna Akhmatova had been a sleepwalker. The image recurred through her verse. 'I know only one city in the world, and I can find my way round it in my sleep,'[1] she wrote of St Petersburg. Other writers also associated the city with somnambulism: its people impelled through its streets as though in haunted dreams. For some, it was poetry itself that created the power of a trance. Akhmatova's friend Lidiya Chukovskaya recalled how – in the Stalinist days of terror when Anna Akhmatova could not publish or even write down her verse, but had to intone it, like an ancient shaman – she was so transfixed by what she had heard that she had no knowledge of how she had got home through the city streets that night. 'I had been sleepwalking. Poems had guided me, instead of the moon, and the world had been absent.'[2] As autumn deepened into winter in Leningrad, the growing hunger, the snow and the prospect of the long darkness were beginning to induce trances and dream states.

An architect called Esfir Levina – perpetually giddy with emptiness, and facing the grim daily prospect of long bakery queues for a nugget or medallion of what was now no longer even bread, but an alchemical concoction of oilseed and bran – tried to make the interminable walks through deep snow tolerable by conjuring daydreams of a walking companion. She and her imaginary friend would discuss Leningrad houses and commercial buildings in that unlit twilight dusk, the fat flakes of snow falling silently. There was one day – as she and her ethereal companion were drifting along – that Levina was close to the brink of walking into another world. 'I walked slowly,' she told the apparition in her diary, 'and felt that you were walking next to me. I wanted to lean on your arm and say that I am very tired, that sometimes it is hard for me to write composed letters. Then I came to. I was alone on a deserted street.'[3] Esfir Levina had in fact stopped moving altogether; she had lost consciousness. Her imaginary dialogue had kept her from the brink. Already there were others – older, frailer – who had come to a halt in those streets of snow, slumped a little, sank further: and then were taken by the creep of hypothermia.

There had been little let-up in the bombing, but it was the hunger that now threatened with terrible finality every single civilian in Leningrad. The bread ration had been cut even further by the end of November. Even those on heavy production lines – and soldiers in those increasingly frozen forests, where the temperatures were now falling to minus 20°C – were receiving tiny quantities of carbohydrates. Mikhail Pelevin was a fifteen-year-old machine operator working at the Kulakov factory. He was intensely aware of the privilege that this brought: access to the works canteen. He knew of a number of other teenagers who yearned for positions at the same factory. Here was why: a ration coupon in the canteen could buy you 'three bowls of hot yeast soup and a bottle of soya milk'.[4] Real milk had become an unattainable luxury: the dairy farmlands to the west had long since been seized. The Soviet authorities – and their scientists – were scrabbling to find ways to synthesize calcium and protein. Elsewhere, at the Kirov Plant, regular meals were still on offer in the canteen, but the sparse ingredients required slightly more imagination to trick the body into accepting that it had been nourished. There, the soup consisted of soybean powder, vegetable oil and ersatz flour. The soy gave an illusion of body, and savoury taste. There were accompanying flat-cakes composed partly of sawdust. The chief aim was for the workers to believe that they were full.

The city's electricity supplies were stuttering; hydroelectric plants had been either damaged by bombs or deliberately sabotaged by the Germans. In the city's communal apartments and tenement buildings, this meant all light and power could disappear without warning, leaving residents in the pale snowy dark. It also meant that the factories were disrupted; it was not long into that deepening winter that production lines frequently ground to a frozen halt, and those multitudes of workers who before the war had been subjected to the most severe punishments for simply being twenty minutes late now found themselves wandering out of the factory gates in the early afternoon, leaving the darkened mass of buildings behind them as they set off in partial fugue states not knowing even how they would be able to boil water for tea.

And for the full-time mothers, the children, the elderly – people who did not have the comforts of warm production lines, with heated recreation areas and the promise of hot yeast soup – the days when the sun barely rose became a new exercise in both physical and mental endurance.

For Yura Riabinkin – who had by now turned sixteen – the hunger and the cold were desperate, but so too was the transformation of his little family. The long evenings, swaddled in layers of clothing, with his mother and his little sister Ira, in a small communal apartment frequently lit only with candles, were bringing them all to the edge of endurance. The crushing depression, the thick silence, the inability even to read in that guttering half-light, turned them all into snarling enemies. Yura's sister would become hysterical with rage if she suspected that either her brother or her mother had taken a larger share of whatever rationed scrap they had received. But Yura's mother was subject to these rages too, which would be turned upon her son. She was out working all day, and had to take Ira with her since all schools were closed. It was Yura's job to queue at the bakery and any other grocery store that might just have unexpected supplies. The boy was diligent: he would be up at 4.30 a.m. and along to the bakery – only to find that the queue was already snaking down the street. And there they would all remain for hours in that unceasing snowfall. Sometimes there would be a bonus: tiny quantities of horsemeat, a handful of cereal. On the days that there was not, Yura's mother blamed her son with the most terrible scorn.

'I am sitting here crying,' he wrote. 'I'm only sixteen years old, you know.'[5]

On top of that, he was ill: a lung condition was fast becoming pleurisy. But every morning, down into that snow-piled street he would trudge in his thinly lined boots, passing houses and tenement blocks half demolished by the bombing that had never stopped. He would make his way to the shops of the main market, Sennaya Square, which had been so central in the more morbid passages of

Dostoevsky's fiction: the old hay market, scarred by drunkenness and cruelty. Now in the early winter of 1941, starvation was giving the wide historic square a new and even more terrible aspect. In the early hours of the morning, in that silent cold, the sky blank with snow, and the roofs and domes and turrets white, the queues would form, silent, desperately tired, fingers and toes either numb or pulsing with the pain of frostbite. Hours would pass in a mass trance; often there would be a suggestion, a rumour, that weird telepathic impulse that occurs in crowds: there was food. Real food. Meat. Grains. A location would be mentioned, and then the queue would swiftly, liquidly dissolve into a mass of desperate fighting, crying anarchy. Riabinkin was there one dawn when the crowd rumour turned out, extraordinarily, to be correct. The sixteen-year-old was able to elbow his way to the front and in some triumph procure '190 grams of butter' and '500 grams of sausage made from horsemeat and soya'.[6]

But at the root of it all – even on the occasion when he managed to get hold of four litres of beer, an excellent bargaining commodity, of which he couldn't resist knocking back 'half a litre' himself – was a dreadful sense of humiliation, as well as physical anguish. He wanted desperately to read great literature, to learn calculus, to advance every corner of his learning, to lose himself in pursuit of knowledge and aesthetic beauty. Yet for the main part, his life was confined to long weary queues and then evenings of piercingly cold candlelit torture – the flickering light playing on dark wallpaper and dulled eyes – with a family who had been too long without any sign of affection or love. 'I haven't heard a calm word from Mother for a long time. Whatever topic she touches on in conversation leads to shouting, swearing, hysterics.' But food was the source of their all-encompassing misery: 'When Mother shares something out, Ira and I watch like hawks, to make sure she does it accurately.' Poignantly, he confessed to his diary: 'It's a bit embarrassing to write such things down.'[7]

Leonard Polyak, a year or two older, was in the more fortunate – a term very relative in such circumstances – position of being an electrician's apprentice. This meant that he had constant access to a large factory: it brought the consolations of not only regular hot soup but also escape from the ever colder conditions of home. None the less, death was steadily slouching towards his family. He and his parents and siblings had had a lucky escape back in September: during shelling, the windows of their apartment had been blown out, but the apartment building itself stood steady, although there was no replacement window glass to be found. 'Our factory was located at the convergence of the Fontanka and Neva rivers near the residential buildings on Repin Square,' Polyak recalled.[8] This was near the Admiralty Shipyards, a district of rivers, canals and docks crisscrossed with stone bridges dating back to Peter the Great.

As the siege had taken grip, Polyak and his young colleagues would arrive at the works each day, prepared for twelve-hour shifts, and would note how the rations were diminishing. 'The rations were getting smaller and smaller. Soon there were bread shortages and real hunger began; people started dying,' Polyak recalled. 'My mother and I only survived because we continued to work. The biggest casualties were among people who lost their energy, lay down, and couldn't get up again.'[9]

By late November into early December, the population was suffering what would prove to be the most severe winter in decades. (The city was rarely a mild prospect throughout that season, but temperatures would rarely be expected to drop below minus 15°C.) Even if there had not been war, even if there had been a peacetime abundance of food and fuel, those dark months would have been an ordeal for most ordinary Leningrad families. Now the Arctic plunge itself seemed like an act of war, compounded by a growing shortage of fuel to burn, and spluttering, flickering supplies of electricity that would cut off in the early afternoon and stay off all night. Strength was required to fight the frozen dark, but human agency was being eroded by the gnawing emptiness of hunger.

Polyak recalled how much the family owed to their grandmother:

[She] had an iron will. She would wake us up in the morning and send us off to work, despite the fact that the house was freezing – we had no water or electricity – and buckets of water would freeze in the apartment.

The living conditions and hygiene were terrible. We had no place to wash ourselves. We had to go to the Fontanka river in order to fetch water. There were steps that led down to the water, but the stairs iced over because of spilled water and the climb became torturous. What saved us was that we had some firewood in the cellar of our shed. We always had a stock of firewood because my father supplied firewood to the city. This saved us.

Our home became a communal apartment. Our relatives came to stay with us. Unfortunately, three of them died right in our home. They were already in very bad shape when they arrived, and they died at our house. My mother and I had to take their bodies out. In Leningrad's Oktyabrsky District, where we lived, there was a cul-de-sac that they started using as a collection point for corpses. All the dead were taken there. This was near Dekabristov Street, formerly known as Ofitserskaya Street. That is where we took our relatives.[10]

The start of that December had brought another unforeseen crisis to the centre of the city: the disposal of the dead. Hospital mortuaries and cemetery morgues were already seeing corpses stacked 'like logs'.[11] The backlog was developing far faster than the city's gravediggers could deal with: the graveyard earth was iron-hard under the Arctic frost and these men like everyone else had been living for weeks on rations that had depleted their muscles of the power required to dig through it. It was in those early days of December – the plump snowflakes floating and filling the air, settling in mounds on wide and increasingly unrecognizable streets, that the first of the bodies on sleds were seen. The elderly – and tiny children too – were dying fast, in the communal apartment buildings. Their grieving families would swaddle them in white sheets and place the bodies on sleds which would then be pulled along the silent streets to grim collection points.

Many died anonymously and unmourned. A 'top secret' audit commissioned by the city's authorities into the state of Leningrad's morgues in those first few days of December 1941 uncovered a chilling new reality. At the Vesely Poselok Cemetery, for instance, there were 'thirty-five unburied corpses, of which thirty-two corpses are unidentified. All thirty-five corpses have been lying on racks in the morgue for 6–7 days. Burial has been delayed due to a lack of manpower: there are no gravediggers.'[12] Meanwhile, at the Serafimovskoe Cemetery, 'seventy corpses left by relatives have been lying in coffins at the cemetery since 1 Dec. 1941 . . . Burial has been delayed due to a shortage of gravediggers, of whom there are only four.'[13] At the Bogoslovskoe Cemetery, the disposition of the dead was even starker: 'in the snow of the cemetery lie five corpses left by relatives'.[14] The extreme cold slowed the process of decomposition. Along with the endless snow, this meant that many corpses throughout the city did not even make it to the cemeteries, packed in ice under snowdrifts or lying forgotten in the frosted, darkened corners of communal apartments with shattered windows open to the frozen air, their grim, gradual decay unnoticed until the spring, when the full obscenity of the Leningrad necropolis would become plain.

In the meantime, as the stiff cadavers lay brittle and drawn, there would be another reason for not drawing attention to their deaths: their ration cards. Even in the midst of their loved one's grief, an unreported deceased might still bring extra bread – and even rare luxuries such as dried peas – into the home. In the darker days to come, there would be a few who in the extremity of desperation would find other ways of repurposing the dead, the ice and the hunger eventually numbing any taboo thoughts. And beyond this, it would start to produce a hitherto inconceivable hardening of the soul. Each successive day would bring an erosion of old kindness, and a new emphasis on the plain facts of physicality: pain, fever and terrible gastric complaints.

Cold was a dangerous enemy even for the young and the fit. For Yelizaveta Zinger, who was fifteen years old when the dead weight of the blockade set in, it was a struggle to find a key to endurance as the snow hit. In the days before the war, she and her seven siblings, some belonging to the Komsomol, enjoyed a hugely active life in the city. Zinger herself – the youngest – was highly adept at rounders. It was after she had finished a game, sweating profusely, that she met the young man who would later become her husband. By that time, she was working at a 'semi-conductor manufacturing laboratory' in the city. Her husband-to-be, Leonard, was an artist working as a builder. His ambition was to study fine art. The war roughly pulled the young sweethearts apart, Leonard drawn into the army, Yelizaveta staying in Leningrad. They would not meet again for many years. By that early December, Zinger's sisters were all called away, working in hospitals and elsewhere; her brothers were serving at the front. She was left in the apartment with her mother:

> People were dying quickly. Houses stood empty. We were lucky because we had an iron stove. We fired this stove with wood. It was warm in our house. And those who did not have a furnace installed potbelly stoves. It did not help much, and people would freeze and die. I also slept in a winter coat and felt boots. Mother also covered me with a blanket. We were starving.
>
> Those who worked at a plant were given 150 grams [of bread]. 250 grams and nothing else for two people – that was tough. We didn't do anything. We just sat and talked. We waited until we went to bed, and in the morning, I would get up and go to the bakery. The bakery was next to our house. It was useful. It was forty degrees below zero – very cold. I would put on a coat, my mother wrapped me in a bed throw, a nice woollen blanket. And felt boots, of course. My legs were wrapped in newspapers. I put on my brother's huge boots and went to the store. There would be six people in the store. I would be the first. Very few people could make it. The rest were either dead or about to die. That's how it was.
>
> I would bring these 250 grams of bread . . . I would cut it exactly in half. I made sure of it. On the radio they told us not to eat all the bread at once. But how could you not? Of course, we ate it right away. And there was nothing more for us to do. We would go to bed again just to get up early in the morning and go to the bakery again.
>
> Some people had supplies: biscuits, sweets. Unfortunately, we only had coffee. We tried to make pancakes from that coffee. That didn't work out, everything was ruined and we couldn't eat these pancakes.[15]

As experimentation with food synthesis went, that was relatively benign. There were those elsewhere in the city who were starting to consider whether materials such as wood, leather and the glue used by carpenters could be eaten. Here was a further instance of deepening duality: the rational mind understood with diamond clarity that these food substitutes were worse than useless, but the stomach was – all too briefly – none the less happy to be fooled, sending signals to that same rational mind of temporary satisfaction.

Since the autumn the city's authorities had been hunting for new additives that would give the impression of bulking bread out. First, they turned to residual supplies of oats. These had been intended for horse feed. Instead they were remilled and then mixed with dough. When these supplies dwindled, there was another sharp idea: Leningrad's breweries had stocks of malt and barley, which again could be utilized as part of the dough mixture. For Leningraders, this not only gave the bread a heavy moist texture, but also a distinctive and unpleasant taste. By the deep autumn, they were beyond the dainty concerns of their tastebuds. Malt and barley at least had a little nutritional value. But then these supplies started to dwindle as well.

The city's scientists, at work in hospital laboratories, were applying themselves to creating alternatives with some urgency, not least because they had their own families – and their own stomachs – to think of. Bread could only be supplied to all citizens if a new filler product to bulk it out was developed. The idea, promoted heavily by Andrei Zhdanov, was 'edible cellulose'.[16] Was it at all possible to extract such a substance from wood or cotton? There was a technique called hydrolysis that used water to break down such substances into their chemical constituents. Soon the scientists were reporting that it was indeed possible to process cellulose, giving it a form where it might be added to the bread mixture, chewed and swallowed without harming the person who was eating it. There was one overriding problem: while this edible cellulose certainly did give stomachs the impression that they had been filled, it had zero nutritional value and could not be digested. The resulting bread would provide a fleeting sense of satiation, but the bulk of it would pass unchanged through the digestive tract, causing pangs of abdominal pain along the way. Leningraders all knew that almost half of their daily bread ration was part of an experiment: yet what choice did they have? Around that time, there was also an acceleration of the use of cottonseed oilcake – a substance looking a little like loft insulation, derived from cotton seeds, which, unrefined, are poisonous to humans and animals alike. Its chief use in more normal times was to make cattle feed. Now cottonseed oilcake – an idea apparently suggested by Leningrad dock workers who saw a derivative of it being used as fuel for ships' engines – was redeveloped for human consumption.

Yet here too was an instance of the intelligence of the city; and of Leningraders' relationship with Andrei Zhdanov and the Party superiors who were trying to hold this civic realm together. Even before the cottonseed oilcake was added to the bread, it had become the subject of gossip and speculation in those freezing bread queues. 'A rumour has spread,' ran an official note, 'that . . . the adult population of Leningrad will be issued oilcake instead of bread, and children biscuits.'[17] In those same queues, there was fervid speculation that this meant that the last of the city's stores of food were almost exhausted, and that there was no prospect of the Wehrmacht's iron stranglehold being broken. The result, according to the official note? 'Huge lines have formed at food stores and bread bakeries. People are beginning to gather at three or four o'clock in the morning and they stand there all day in anticipation of some kind of food.'[18] Given that the temperature was well below zero, and never climbed above it, the act of simply standing in an icy wind that was scouring faces red was by itself an almost suicidal act of endurance. But those who were labouring at the still-functioning factories – who did not have anything like the time to spend in such queues – were themselves becoming feverish with anxiety about the immediate future. There were mothers who were working at the Red Banner Factory No. 29 and the Rubber Footwear Plant who were telling one another that, while they expected to 'suffer through', there would be 'nothing to feed their children'.[19]

For some of the older workers who had lived through the hunger of 1919–20, the privations resulting from civil war, there was a crucial psychological difference this time. Back then, hunger could be borne because it was in part for a noble and proper cause: the defeat of the counter-revolutionaries, and the flourishing of a true, equal, communist society (and, of course, they were rather younger then).

The hardship was grim but thanks to the historical inevitability of socialism, it would be overcome. But in December 1941 there was little hope of any kind of victory. The confidence was gone. 'We are simply starving to death,' stated one worker at a quilted-jacket production line, 'and the idea that victory will be ours – that's nothing more than a fairy tale.'[20] The further diminution of the daily bread ration a few days earlier had instilled a deathly pessimism in many. At one workers' meeting at the Red Banner Factory, some were brave enough to declare that the authorities and the military had been too slow in trying to break the German encirclement; that the workers could now hardly 'put one foot in front of another' and that death would claim them before the blockade could be breached.[21]

These workers at least had some fleeting comforts, even as they staggered giddily on their production lines. First there were 'red corners' – communal areas that they could rest in during break periods, sitting with colleagues around a glowing stove and drinking 'tea rum' (mainly tea, but occasionally enhanced). This – although many would not have cared to admit it – would also provide vital psychological respite from the heavy depression of home life.

In the midst of all of this, the German shelling continued; efforts to camouflage factories with netting and blended paint were of limited use. Leningraders at work producing military supplies might without warning be torn apart in a split second of sunburst light. Those workers who survived their shifts might, after a slow walk past blackened, smouldering shell targets, arrive home to find their families – grandparents, young children – lying motionless under blankets, staring, neither talking nor moving, but simply watching the dark.

Many of these families had kept pets: small dogs, caged birds, cats. By those first few days of December, in a winter that seemed as though the light would never return to the earth, the more active family members started appraising those beloved animals in quite a different way.

17.   The Fear of Mirrors

'When hunger began and, as is said, people began to eat cats,' recalled Leningrader Nina Pekina, 'it never entered our heads that one *could* eat cat'.[1] Questions of morality suggest an innate quality of humanity; of all the species on earth, only humans appear to have the capacity to choose between good and evil. Yet philosophers will argue that such choice is illusory; what we imagine are rational decisions are simply animal impulses that we seek to explain by turning them into coherent stories. Similarly, an old argument might also have run that humans – as opposed to animals – have an innate sense of disgust. That there are degrees of behaviour that cannot be imagined simply because the physical impulse to be sick would make them impossible. Yet the multiple atrocities of war – not merely those of the Nazis, but stretching back through the centuries – would by that token have been inconceivable. To kill a defenceless man or woman in cold blood; to raise the gun or the knife to a total stranger and to end their lives in welters of blood – the instinct for disgust seems starkly absent on these occasions. And on another level – the most basic, desperate need for food – what once seemed apparently instinctive responses of revulsion somehow started dissolving with the most terrible speed.

In some ways, it is easy to follow the progression. When you see a bull in a field, or pigs scampering around in the mud, you don't automatically envisage a plate of succulent beef, or crisp rashers of bacon. You know perfectly well where the delicious meat comes from, but you are so separated from the means of its delivery – the slaughterhouse blades, the slippery abattoir floors – that the connection between the living animals before you and the food that they become can still remain abstract. They are farm animals; this is what they are for. When that focus is changed, however, and fixed within a domestic environment, then suddenly the imagination is filled unpleasantly.

By December 1941, with the temperature now sometimes falling to minus 25°C, and with supplies of grain and pulses so sparse that, for some, the tiny wedges of bread were all the solid sustenance there was, there were a few Leningraders whose eyes moved in the direction of the darker corners of courtyards and tenement back alleys, scanning the white snow and the streaks of mud near drains that themselves were now frozen solid, alert to the slightest hint of scurrying. There were people forced – to their own astonishment – to consider catching, killing and then eating rats.

In some cases, such desperation was born of misfortune. Leningrader Yevgeniya Manonian recalled the plight of a near neighbour, a man who had spent his working life on the railways. Somehow, when out in that snowy darkness, tramping through the slippery streets, this railwayman had managed to lose his family's ration cards. This was effectively a death sentence. The authorities were implacable: no cards, no food; there was little enough even for those who had them. Something then switched within the stricken man: a new way of looking at what had once been a familiar world. He would have to catch rats. There was nothing else to be done. Their blood was hot, they had flesh: therefore they could be eaten.

And so, by night – and presumably well away from streets in which he might be recognized – the railway worker padded through the snow, amid the gaunt, unlit tenement blocks, moving through this city of winter shadows. It was not recorded how he managed to catch the creatures, which themselves must have been on the edge of exhaustion if their cunning failed them that far, but for fifteen successive nights until he was issued with fresh ration cards he took rats home. He skinned and boned them, and then he and his wife would fry the meat. Revulsion was an impossible luxury. Instead here was the infinitely comforting taste and feel of sinewy flesh. The railway worker had committed no crime; the horror simply involved the consumption of filthy scavengers.[2] But once that border had been crossed, how many more could be breached?

The next level – one involving questions of morality and ethics rather than simple, plain disgust – was the killing of domestic pets. Leningraders were as affectionate about their animals as everyone else, and in that deathly winter the bonds grew tighter. On evenings when residents in frosted apartments – their every breath clouded and lingering in the air – had to take to their beds, wrapped and swaddled as much as they could be, their pets would sometimes join them, dogs and cats alike, sharing that primeval instinct for mutual warmth, huddling down with their owners, bringing comfort with their own body heat and their own jittery pulses. But Leningraders who did not own pets themselves now found themselves gazing upon these animals – as increasingly emaciated as their owners – and seeing only food.

'Horses, dogs and cats are disappearing from the streets,' wrote one diarist.[3] Another – a young boy called Valerii Sukhov – marked the occasion in that early December when his family at last crossed the line. 'Yesterday we caught and killed the cat,' he wrote. 'Today we ate it grilled. Very tasty.'[4] Elsewhere in the city, Varvara Vraskaya learned of a mother who had killed the family cat secretly, butchered it, and used it to make soup. But she knew very well that, no matter how hungry, her daughter would be too horrified to consume it. So the mother lied, telling her daughter that she had prepared 'rabbit soup'.[5] Another child recalled the molten hatred she felt for her stepfather when she came to suspect that he had killed her beloved Irish setter and then eaten it. Diarist Olga Matyushina, meanwhile, was neighbour to an old lady who had a pet cat upon whom she doted. The old lady was called Tatyana, the cat Murzik. Tatyana was repeatedly told by other neighbours that she ought to use the cat for food, and was always horrified by the very suggestion. But as the cold and the hunger crept in further, Tatyana at last gave way to terrible temptation. She too used the flesh to make soup. She was found dead in her apartment a few days later, her wasted body lying near that pot of cat soup, which had gone entirely untasted. To the end, having summoned the will to kill her beloved pet, she just could not bear to cross that final bridge.[6]

Those who were nearer to the evergreen forests began foraging: everything from frozen, trailing weeds to pine needles and pine cones. There were other, odder ideas that caught on with startling speed: the boiling of cow and horse skin, to make aspic, which would then be combined with a lump of wood glue and some leather in one big pot. The smell was indescribable and the taste was repugnant, but this extraordinary combination at least gave the stomach the illusion of having been filled. The glutinous mixture had to be seasoned with vinegar and salt, which were themselves in limited supply. Something similar was also made using carpenters' glue, the idea being that anything containing any form of organic component could somehow, with imagination, be repurposed as food. The principle of boiling leather belts to extract a broth that could simulate nutrition was then expanded a little further as the supply of belts began to dwindle: shoes (those of the dead with no further need for them), and leather briefcases and suitcases.

Sofiya Mirskaya, who at that stage was just ten years old, and sharing an apartment with her mother (her father was a doctor who was frequently sent to the front), recalled the time:

> To try to survive, people boiled belts. They got a kind of glue out of the belts. People somehow rallied together. We bonded on the hall where we lived. Once, we were invited to a feast. The food turned out to be a kind of aspic, a jelly made from belts. There was also something called *duranda* that we ate. It was made from seed hulls left over after oil was pressed. The seed leftovers were pressed into very hard cakes. It wasn't sold in stores. I don't know where people got it. But we got it and grated it and made it into a flour. Then we made pancakes from it and ate them.[7]

(Images of the starving eating leather were present in the work of seventeenth-century poet John Donne, who would later be celebrated by the Leningrad-born poet Joseph Brodsky. In Elegy II: 'The Comparison', Donne refers to the deadly French siege of Sancerre, part of the persecution of the Huguenots: 'Or like the scum which, by need's lawless law/ Enforced, Sanserra's starvèd men did draw/ From parboiled shoes and boots and all the rest/ Which were with any sovereign fatness blessed.')[8]

Other communal apartment residents were alerted to another possible food substitute when they observed, late at night and in the dark, rats scuttling about in uninhabited rooms that had been damaged in blasts. There was something in the walls that seemed to be drawing the creatures in: it was the wallpaper paste, which then had been frequently a mulch of flour and water and glue. Word spread through the streets: if wallpaper paste was good enough for the rats, then might it help to fill men too? There was, incidentally, a rise in the rat population because so many of the city's cats had been caught, killed, cooked and eaten. The rats had no predators other than man himself – and even by this stage, only a few Leningraders had set out with the express intention of hunting and consuming them. One resident was shuffling along an empty frozen street of tall nineteenth-century houses and apartments when he was stopped in his tracks by a swirling dark mass, moving across the white snow like some kind of weird grey amoeba: it was a vast swarm of rats, packed close in to one another, flowing like a murmuration of starlings. Thankfully they were not running in his direction.

Another intense psychological – as well as physical – difficulty was mothers having to explain to their small children why tiny rations of bread had to be cut into three portions to be consumed throughout the day. Then, on those rare random days when their ration cards and the grocery stores yielded a small potato, or some lentils or oats or dried peas, those mothers also had to explain why they could not have more. One child was taught how to tell the time by his constant anguished inquiries about when he might have something else to eat: his mother, holding back tears, telling him to look at the clock, and wait for when the big hand was on twelve and the little hand was on three.[9] There were infants who – by some ancient foraging instinct – were scrabbling with tiny fingers in the gaps between floorboards for individual grains of rice or millet that might have been dropped. Mothers tried to distract their children with the most colourful fairy stories, but the children would counter with stories of their own, about giant pots filled with potatoes and how they could eat every single one of those hot potatoes and carry on eating all day and all night.[10] How could any mother condemn this when the dreams of adults were suffused endlessly with fat pastries and vast slabs of meat? When hunger would allow them to sleep, such dreams were cruel, but the painful insomnia was worse. One woman, picking up a tip from *War and Peace*, would try to lull herself to sleep by counting to 1,000. But as she slid into the twilight of unconsciousness, suddenly there would be terrible visions of lamb and beef. Others were tormented by the imp of the perverse: in their determination not to think about food at all, their minds were wrenched and they started dreaming up fantasy menus (with the most modest of ingredients, including hot, freshly baked crusty bread and rich stews with red meat and pearl barley).

Then there was the anguish that parents felt for infants too young for explanations or soothing expressions of hope. A terrible side effect of starvation was that it made lactation difficult. Some mothers stopped expressing milk altogether. One, driven to an extremity of desperation, drove a blade into her arm and let her baby suck blood from the wound.[11]

Amid the grim temptations of cats and rats, many knew that even this was not the final degradation: that there was one food source remaining that no one ever dared speak of and yet was beginning to surface in the most desperate minds.

It might seem inconceivable that in such circumstances people were still anxious to hear music, or even to see plays, yet in those first few days of December the city's Philharmonic Hall was still offering (pared-down) performances – and Arkadii Raykin's Leningrad Theatre of Miniatures was still – just – staging dramas. There was a recital of Beethoven's Fifth Symphony and Tchaikovsky's 1812 Overture. The latter was a strikingly optimistic choice: the rousing theme that had been written to commemorate the triumph of Russia over Napoleon's invading forces. Such a piece would require a full orchestra at its most vital. The fact that any musicians at all in Leningrad could play at that moment was in itself a feat of strength. The Philharmonic Hall was profoundly cold, the musicians part-wrapped in quilted jackets and sheepskin (their arms kept free), and it was noted that the drummer, by repeatedly striking blows, had the best deal in terms of keeping himself warm.[12]

There were actors from the Leningrad Theatre of Miniatures who had actually decided to make the basement of the Philharmonic Hall their home: the theatre was nearby and they were too fatigued with hunger to think about making any longer journeys. Somehow, like the musicians, a few of them managed to keep going, and they were much valued not just by Leningrad civilians, but by many Red Army soldiers too.[13] The actors were only getting the now-standard

125 grams of bread a day, and sometimes possibly a little extra soup, or slivers of meat. But they felt, as the actress Yevgeniya Mezheritskaya said, that the theatre 'had become an island of joy in a sea of grief'.[14] They also persisted through outbreaks of shelling: in a performance of one comic play, involving drunks, the audience were required to troop in and out of the auditorium on several occasions as the boom of explosions grew nearer. It always seemed to happen as the actor Nikolay Rudashevsky came to the line: 'Who the hell stamped on my foot?' When at last the performance was resumed once more, one audience member cried out: 'Let's just skip that line!'[15]

The theatre was an incongruous and fierce pulse of life in a city that had elsewhere given way to a haunted silence. And its founding principle of satire was present even in its off-duty staff. There was a bookkeeper at the theatre who noted sourly – and lethally loudly – that while the citizens starved, Leningrad's overlord Andrei Zhdanov started each day 'being served cocoa in bed'.[16] Such outbreaks of dissent, even in this time of emergency, were still being collected by NKVD informants and being reported back: Zhdanov himself saw the memo about the cocoa and 'underlined . . . these references to himself'.[17] But the anger wasn't directed against him alone: there was a widespread (and justified) suspicion that senior Party officials – those with apartments in the exclusive Leningrad City Council First Residential House – were ensuring that they themselves were well fed. 'I myself saw them bringing the bread to Smolny [Institute],' one reported complaint went. 'They're probably sitting there stuffed . . . Our rulers, of course, are full. They get not only bread, but lunch and dinner. So they don't care about us, about starving people.'[18]

The accusations of injustice were levelled more widely too (and again, justifiably). For in a food chain that was itself so fragile – military drops via aeroplane, late-autumn shipments of flour brought in via Lake Ladoga before it froze over, and thence distributed to warehouses, then cafeterias and bakeries – it was inevitable that some would seek to siphon off what they could from it. Such was the extremity of that winter that the law-abiding could contemplate becoming criminals for the sake of some flour, or a little sugar or soya. Those working in the bakeries: how superhuman would they have had to have been not to swallow furtively some of their own products fresh from the oven? Those working in the warehouses among so many sacks of grain: how could they envisage the need of hundreds and thousands of people when they themselves were simply pilfering relatively tiny amounts of what would look to them like an abundance?

There were outbreaks of more calculated crime as well: there were associates in the food stores, sometimes led by managers, who organized the black-market sale of stolen wheat and soya products. Occasionally gangs formed in cafeterias too, carefully conspiring to misappropriate foodstuffs, and to conceal their crimes through altered paperwork and false accounting. In most cases where the crime was detected, the penalty was as severe as it could be: death. Yet at a point when Leningraders were starting to die in such vast numbers, the penalty seemed less of a deterrent.

And even when no crime could be proved, there remained the suspicion of it in hungry minds. 'What a merry life!' said Ksenya Matus of bakery workers, after she had spent an entire day waiting in a ration line. 'Bastards! How far is it still possible to drive such miserable, helpless people? If they were to be left just one day without eating, if they were to endure but one-hundredth of the lot that we've endured . . .'[19] Elsewhere, Irina Zelenskaya recorded that 'on the way to the consumer, an awful lot sticks to the hands of the cafeteria, the storehouse and other workers despite all sorts of workers' inspections. If it were not for that, everything would be good.'[20] And yet it would not. Although the rations were diminishing, Andrei Zhdanov and his deputies held back from making any public proclamations about even more dramatic shortfalls caused by enemy action rather than crime: it was not considered wise to let Leningraders know that the truth of the famine was even worse than their own individual suffering would suggest.

Leningraders were noting the sharper physical transformations in everyone from the youngest to the oldest, and in men and women alike. The term applied in Leningrad's hospitals was 'dystrophy'. In short, these were the physical marks and tokens of weeks and months without proper food. As well as the more horribly familiar signs – chiefly, the ever-swelling, distended bellies and the corresponding withering of legs and arms – there were symptoms that were uncanny. It was noted in some young children of both sexes that starvation produced startling amounts of facial hair. (This was the result of wild hormone imbalances in growing bodies that caused hair roots to multiply.) What made this doubly unsettling for those who saw them was that the deprivation of nourishment had also produced arthritic-style side effects in their limbs and spines, so that there were some small children walking around like miniature elderly adults: stooped and slow and hirsute. Time had accelerated hideously for them, their bodies now apparently carrying the weight of decades. Conversely, time seemed to have come to a juddering halt for huge numbers of older children for whom extreme, savage hunger had halted the onset of puberty.

It was a theatre director called Aleksandr Dymov who noted this disjuncture of time and physicality in adults too. It was not simply that starvation brought on an early old age in physical terms: it also affected the brain, in such a way that one's identity also somehow became elderly. 'Old age is the fatigue of well-worn components that are involved in the working of the human body,' he wrote, 'an exhaustion of man's inner resources. Your blood no longer keeps you warm, your legs refuse to obey you, your back grows stiff, your brain grows feeble and your memory fades.'[21]

But these transformations could also bring moments of terror. Many Leningraders grew afraid to glance at themselves in mirrors. One diarist wanted to cover up a large apartment mirror but was reluctant to do so since this was usually done only in the room of one who was about to die. Another diarist, a Party worker called Aleksandr Buyanov, succumbed to terrible curiosity one day in that half-darkness and looked at himself in the glass. He recoiled with fright: what he saw threw him 'into a fit of madness'.[22] For a few Leningraders there was a recollection of the unsettling Gogol story 'The Nose' – rooted firmly in an old and familiar St Petersburg – and the horror that a reflection can bring. 'Kovalyov stretched and asked for the small mirror standing on the table. He wanted to look at the pimple which had, the evening before, appeared on his nose. But to his extreme amazement he saw that he had, in place of his nose, a perfectly smooth surface.'[23] For many Leningraders, their mirrored reflections now resembled unnerving strangers; it wasn't just the skeletal gauntness – large eyes in shrunken faces – it was also the facial growths and discolouration. In some, hunger had dramatically darkened the skin; in others, the skin yellowed or in some cases acquired a pale mint tinge. In addition to this were swollen limbs: Leningraders would find with painful bewilderment that their boots were increasingly difficult to pull on.

There was another unexpectedly cruel side effect: a weirdly sharpened sense of smell. Even in that numbingly cold northern air, Leningraders were increasingly aware of all the piercing odours of the city: the noisome drains, the tang of woodsmoke. But there was one respect in which this heightened power actually became a form of torture: and that was when Leningraders were either in their local groceries and bakeries, there to collect their meagre rations, or within the still-functioning canteens of factories. It was not that there was much food for them to smell, but even a few uncooked peas and lentils were now exuding aromas as strong as incense. Naturally the vile adulterated bread, with all its oilcake and shavings, could be fully inhaled as well. The cruelty was that this only made digestive systems protest harder, as though the body's internal workings were crying out in rage that they were being denied. People tried to find means of somehow distracting their stomachs, as though those organs had wills of their own. Some would crouch with legs held up against the abdomen, offering some form of embrace.

The transformations of temperaments became worse: loving families – mothers, children, grandparents – now staring at one another with a hatred that could not be contained. The accusations and counter-accusations: the souring suspicions that tiny quantities of food – a hoarded sliver of chocolate here, a tiny strip of ham there – had been stolen and eaten. There were mothers looking at their small children with fury and there were older children looking at parents and beginning to wonder – to their burning shame – when they might at last die so that the children could be free of them. The horror was that every Leningrader knew what was happening to them; they understood – at the most basic level of reason – that the violence of their emotions was a result of their brains being starved. But understanding the source of these frightening feelings could not smother them: in those communal apartments, with families living in close proximity, there could be no attempt to hide the shouting, the vicious accusations.

And now, in that blizzard-blown December, those arguments would echo from the cracked windows of once-elegant houses, out along canalside streets, white and grey with snow and ice: sporadic signs of life behind dead walls that would then become mute once more. For another element that many Leningraders now began to find acutely odd was the new silence of their once noisy and always active city. It was not just a matter of the absence of tram bells (there were now tram cars motionless in the middle of some streets, as though abandoned where they were – without reliable electricity, regular services had ground to a halt). And it was not just the diminished distant background noise of the vast factory and machine plants, and the Neva dockyards, where again animation seemed to have been suspended. It was also the fact that in those streets – still filled with dark figures, but moving very slowly on the crisp glittering snow – all the old hubbub of urban humanity had vanished. There was nothing. The city's bells had been removed long ago by a Stalinist regime that resented their message of a life beyond. But there were Leningraders who found the total silence extraordinarily oppressive. The city, with its unfamiliar bombed-out perspectives, and darkened windows staring like blank eyes, had acquired a nightmarish quality. Because of the extreme cold, any errand – to queue for a ration or search for firewood – became an expedition. But even the most ordinary journey could sometimes result in strange and disturbing experiences. 'It was hard for me to walk,' recalled Yelizaveta Zinger, at that time a teenager working as a nurse at one of the city's hospitals. 'I dressed warmly and walked very slowly. A man appeared next to me. He was also wrapped up. I didn't see where he came from. I was walking in the middle of the road; he came up and walked next to me. I noticed how he turned yellow. He fell and died.'[24] Under royal blue December skies, the sight of death became less and less remarkable, and less and less shocking. Electrical apprentice Leonard Polyak remembered how he would arrive at the factory each morning and how, upon reaching his work station, it would not be unusual to find the worker from the previous shift now sitting sightlessly, having died unwitnessed during the night.[25] Each day, in some part of the factory, bodies would be removed. They would have to be stacked up with the others outside the overflowing mortuaries. There was no longer any wood to construct coffins. It was all needed to warm the living.

That sense of enforced inactivity in the deadly cold, and the lack of any means of fetching wood, preyed on many, including ten-year-old Sofiya Mirskaya:

> There was no public transportation. The winter was terribly cold that year. The tram cars stood, dead in the snow. You could move only under your own power, and you didn't have the strength to do it. Our apartment had two rooms and a kitchen. The kitchen was very small and didn't have a window. My mother said we would burn everything except the piano in order not to die of the cold. We closed off both rooms and lived in the little kitchen. We had a gas stove and a little wood stove. That wood stove saved us from the cold. There was no heat, either. We started burning everything. We burned the curtain rods, the chair, the furniture. Finally, we burned the books. We burned up the encyclopedia. The encyclopedia had covers made of papier-mâché. They burned wonderfully and we were glad of the heat.[26]

Others galloped their way through fuel supplies rather quicker, all their furniture long ago consumed in desperate blazes. Doors were considered: but how might the pernicious frost be kept out when apartments lay wide open? And because of the city's intermittent power supplies, there was yet one more trial that made the lives of the citizens that much more primitive: the failure of Leningrad's water supplies. Running water could no longer be guaranteed.

Anna Novikova, who had also been drafted as a nurse, recalled the grim circumstances in the dormitories in a building that had once been a school, and near where German shells had ripped through streets, leaving shattered apartments but also mangled, torn corpses. 'There was no food, no water, no sewerage,' Novikova remembered. 'There was nothing. To make tea, we melted snow. Sometimes we'd melt the snow and discover there was blood in it.'[27]

And the lack of sewerage – at first the disruption in the water supply had been sporadic, but it soon became more widespread – now reduced many Leningraders to a point that pre-dated the Middle Ages; for at least in a village there were latrines. In the middle of a large, ruined, silent city, where the temperatures were sometimes dropping to minus 40°C as the night set in, how and where could these once-dignified citizens relieve themselves? No running water, plus the problem of frozen pipes, made vast numbers of indoor lavatories inoperable. To use slop buckets? But where could they do so that would be even remotely hygienic? And on top of that, how could they expose themselves outdoors without their bodies becoming numbed and then damaged by that intense and terrible frost? In communal buildings, people started to find first corners and then darkened stairwells in ruined and abandoned apartments. In the midst of this helplessness – distress and humiliation heaped upon suffering digestive systems trying to process so many indigestible ingredients – there was also a wider understanding that the collapse in hygiene brought with it another lethal threat: epidemics of cholera and other illnesses. Yet who was going to clean up? Who possessed the strength required to go down to the frozen canals and rivers to fetch and carry water along icy pavements, and to keep that water from freezing over? It was certainly beyond most older people, and the mothers with children too. The clothes they wore day after day remained upon them at night, supplemented by layers of blankets and the cast-offs of the dead. In this sense, another of the city's transformations began: women dressed in men's clothes, men in women's. Gender began to disappear; many were now simply bodies, with swollen bellies and limbs hard and pulsating with pain and with facial skin so tightened and shrunk that eyes bulged.

Some were lucky enough to have fractionally more access to supplies of food and also to sources of warmth. As well as the few factories that were still functioning, others that had ceased production remained open, partly for the sake of their workers: a sanctuary during the day where they might be able to stand relatively close to a pot-bellied stove and share with colleagues the atrocious weight of the ordeal that they were all going through. On the intellectual side of the city, institutions such as the House of Writers were still open. Here, poets and other academics might find it was still possible to at least have a few sips of hot yeast soup, even if it was served in gut-tering candlelight in a room so cold that rime glittered on the walls.

Then there were the city's hospitals. While their nurses and doc-tors were seeing the extremes of suffering – from maimed soldiers brought in from the nearby front line to the heartbreaking sight of small children, mute with distress, bellies swollen as if close to bursting – there was also at least light and warmth. For the wounded soldiers, too, the rations were slightly better, and this had the psycho-logical effect of making the food crisis seem a little less precipitous.

Bertha Gutkina, aged seventeen, had volunteered for nursing duties:

> Of course, somewhat better food was brought in for them. Plus, they would give us girls, the ones who took good care of them, a piece of bread or a bit of sugar. I remember this Polish boy . . . he had lost both his hands. He had fled from Warsaw and ended up on that [Red Army] front. From our hospital, he was sent on to Siberia. He kept thanking me. He couldn't write. I wrote for him when it was neces-sary. It's terrible to think about that time.[28]

Yet there was a paradox about the hospitals of Leningrad: in a city where all were suffering, and where all were ill, those who were being treated were now privileged. Little children brought here and fed small cups of jelly and soya milk had a better chance of survival than many of those lying listlessly under blankets in shadowed homes, surrounded by toys that could no longer stir them. Similarly, elderly patients were now nursed by staff who had the energy to check on their needs, and indeed to check their pulses to see whether they were still alive. This was a luxury not extended to the increasing numbers of old ladies and gentlemen out in those streets of dim apartment blocks, and on the banks of solid canals and freezing rivers, who had stopped briefly under that swirling snow and then simply and slowly collapsed into that blank whiteness, at last succumbing to the dreams that had been pressing in on them.

How the hospitals kept going was perhaps a mark not so much of competent civic organization but more of Leningraders pulling together: from the doctors – themselves frequently faint and dizzy through hunger, even as they performed life-saving operations – and the teenage nurses who had never previously imagined themselves caring for seriously wounded soldiers, there was an uncompromising sense of priorities. Moreover, the constant activity and workload – though intensely fatiguing – did give them all one invaluable bonus: a sense of purpose.

For some, the question of how to face death – how even to salvage some kind of meaning from death – was intensely pressing. The art historian Nikolay Punin felt close to capitulation. And in that moment of ultimate crisis, an old sense of religious certainty suddenly flowered in its full colour. 'For a long time I have wanted to write *De profundis*,' he wrote on 13 December 1941. 'Tonight, starving, I thought about this topic. *De profundis clamavi*: Lord, save us . . . We are perishing. But His Greatness is as implacable as the Soviet power is unbending.' The death of individuals here and there, he thought, was not important to the regime as long as it had 150 million of them. By contrast, 'His Greatness, resting in the heavens, does not value earthly life as we do.'[29]

Punin was convinced that the tokens of death were upon him. 'I am writing with a cold, numb hand. Some ten days ago, in the morning, I felt a coldness in my body; it wasn't that my body was cold, because it was still warm in the room. It was the first touch of death. We are living in the frozen and starving city, ourselves abandoned and starving. I can't recall the snows ever falling in such abundance.' (This was not an illusion: the city was at that grim moment in history also being hit with the most severe winter that it had suffered for decades.) 'The whole city is completely covered in snowdrifts like a shroud,' he continued. 'It is pure, because the factories aren't operating, and it is rare that smoke rises from the chimneys over the houses . . . the city is buried like the provinces, white and crackling.'[30]

In that weird and paradoxical beauty – a silent city thick with pristine snow under winter skies of amethyst – Punin saw the end of the world:

They carry the bodies in plain caskets on sleighs and bury them in mass graves. The courtyards of the hospitals are heaped with bodies, and there is no one to bury them. It has been over a week since there was an air raid, but there are gaping holes in every building on every street – a reminder of the most terrible events. For a long time there hung an arm up to the elbow, attached by someone to the fence of the garden of one of the destroyed buildings.

And yet such was the metamorphosis of the city's people that all the passers-by seemed inured to this and other bloody horrors. 'Dark crowds of people walk past with faces swollen and earth-like,' Punin wrote. 'They simply suffer.'[31]

In a sense, Punin was an innocent: he imagined that he had seen the lowest depths to which the people of a city could be forced. He had been horrified by the image of the sliced-off arm, hanging there for so long on that fence – a symbol of stark obscenity. Yet he had not envisaged a possibility that was even worse: that of the arm being removed by those who had found another use for it. In the days to come, other citizens would start to find that the most horrifying rumours – tales of figures seen taking fresh bodies from the piles near cemeteries – had more than a kernel of truth. The city's authorities too would be scrambling to address outbreaks of the most nightmarish taboo.

For Punin, additionally, there was one possible lifeline available only to the city's most vulnerable residents: an assurance by authorities that evacuations were planned, and would be executed as soon as possible. As a thread of hope, it was undeniably slender, but it was there. None the less, on that evening near midwinter, he was becoming increasingly convinced that thread had snapped:

At night I feel the loneliness most of all and the senselessness of petitions and prayers, and sometimes I cry quietly. I think each of us quietly cries if only once every twenty-four hours; some at night, like me, others, perhaps, during the day. And there is no salvation. And one can't even be imagined, unless you give in to daydreams. 'We turned our backs on Him,' I think, 'and He on us.' And I know that this means to give in to dreams. '*Miserere*,' I mumble, and add – there it is: '*Dies irae*'. Lord save us.[32]

18.   This is My Blood

The cold was now so fierce that it froze time to a standstill. The hands on the faces of bedside clocks in the city's apartments became locked with ice and frost. But time was suspended in a deeper sense for so many too: some elderly people could now barely leave their swaddled beds. And on midwinter days when the sun barely rose, and the thick snow continued to fall, and the shadows crept stealthily around the room, they were removed from the ordinary stream of time. They lay in states of such physical depletion that all they could do was stare. Seconds, minutes, hours gelled and lost any meaning. In the world outside the city, there was movement and fire, night and day. Within the city, on those noiseless streets, and in apartments where frost lay hard upon interior walls, there was no longer even the ticking of clocks. Those who lay in their freezing beds were sometimes beyond even asking for help. They no longer had the will to do so. 'Time is empty, but not free,' observed Lidiya Ginzburg in her diary.[1] But there was more: those who could go to factories and work, power cuts and bombing raids permitting, still lived their days as a continual passing of minutes and hours. Those who were now too atrophied to walk even down stairs, let alone streets, now found that time had disappeared. The hours – day and night – had neither purchase nor meaning. The only real measure for their lives now were ever slower and more irregular heartbeats.

The condition of 'dystrophy', as opposed to plain malnutrition and starvation, was classified as a unique illness. Even at the start of the blockade, conditions were regarded as being harder than the hunger that had afflicted the city during the civil war of 1919–21. Then, it had been possible to bring an occasional edge of revolutionary romanticism to the hunger. This time it was different. The physical symptoms tended to come in three stages. First there was the wheezy tiredness, combined with weight loss, giddiness and incessant, ever sharper stomach pangs. This was the stage at which teenagers such as Yura Riabinkin found to their bewilderment that even to climb a flight of stairs was hard work.

The second stage – the stage that was currently filling so many of the city's hospital wards – was more acute pain, more dramatic weight loss (cheekbones sharpening, visible ribs) combined with erratic fluctuations in body temperature, occasional swellings (bellies, legs) and discolouration of the skin. The swelling was sometimes the cause of psychological confusion: how could it be that they were gaining weight? But they weren't: this symptom (oedema) would occur when the body could no longer process waste fluid, so it would build up around the tissues instead. In addition, gums would recede and bleed; and around the abdomen and in the limbs would arise a sensation described as 'the ants' – muscular quivers that felt like insects moving beneath the flesh. Even in these cases there was still a chance that the dystrophy might be reversed: the cure was nothing more complex than three vitamin-filled meals a day. Even in hospital, though, this was more of an aspiration than a reality.

The third and final stage was understood by all Leningraders as heralding an unstoppable descent to the grave. It began when the body had consumed all its own fat and was now gnawing at muscle. On top of this, organs such as the liver were now only flickeringly functioning. Dysentery would develop. The sufferer had no appetite: even if food had miraculously appeared, it would be too late. All they could do was lie down, immobilized, incapable of little more than staring at the shadows of winter twilight on the ceiling. The listlessness and apathy of the second stage gave way to an almost undead condition, with the added cruelty that – even with slowed and confused mental processes – the sufferer still knew perfectly well what was happening.[2]

One extra layer of suffering lay in the spiritual side of the condition. Even those who helplessly succumbed to accumulating days and weeks of hunger might hold on to a hope that as their limbs weakened, their minds and their souls would somehow remain bright, enabling them to find ways to fight the dissolution. That the loss of physical ability might be balanced by a determined rise in mental strength. Of course, this could not be: brains were as starved as any of the body's other organs. But there was a sense here of the Stakhanovite ideal: just as one man was burnished into legend with impossible feats of productivity, then surely Leningraders – whose own spirits had been forged in some extraordinarily testing fires – would rise to resist the fascist intention to kill them.* And the steeliness had its own cruelty. Those racked with joint and muscle pain, almost unable to move, were deemed by the better-nourished to be 'losing heart': told that they would have a chance of survival if they willed it, but that they had allowed that will to be extinguished.

In times of the direst crisis, outbreaks of Darwinism were perhaps as inevitable as death itself; to healthier Leningraders, the worst afflicted were the very image of that which they most feared. Even doctors shuddered as they examined starved patients. 'Their skulls break through,' noted Mariya Konopleva, an art specialist turned volunteer clinical nursing administrator who had accompanied a medic on his rounds in the hospital. '[There is] an outline of a skull under skin the colour of wood, dirty wood.'[3] She also noted that the doctor stated that many patients were starting to show more clearly their 'affinity with the monkey'. 'It is terrible to see these "monkey-like" symptoms on the faces of young people, obviously doomed, as well as older people,'[4] Konopleva noted. This was Darwinism taken to a stark degree: sufferers were seen as no longer belonging to the same species as the still-healthy.

On the other side of the coin were dying Leningraders who saw their approaching end as a strangely human liberation. As Lidiya Ginzburg observed: 'Dystrophy gave a man a protective indifference, under cover of which he could die relieved . . . death without resistance. Death without surprise . . . Death leaving no trace of life.'[5] The mortal shackles being shucked were not just those of the icy blockade itself, but of a life where the mind and the will were continually

* Aleksei Stakhanov was a miner in the Donbas who in 1935 mined fourteen times the size of his daily target quota for several days and was instantly made a media folk hero. From that point, any Soviet worker who went beyond what the state asked was lauded as 'Stakhanovite', though the original achievement might well have owed more to technology than to brawn.

policed. As with the excessive drinking habits of some Leningraders, there was an element here of defying a system that required the sacrifice of the will for the greater good of all. In death, the will was free.

In this midwinter of hunger, the embrace of holy love was desperately sought by some. The churches were not wholly darkened. Five places of worship in Leningrad had been permitted to restart services without fear of reprisal. Partly this had been allowed by the authorities not just to boost morale but also to forestall Nazi promises of religious freedom under fascism. The Orthodox Metropolitan Aleksii of Leningrad conducted services every Sunday in St Nicholas's Cathedral. The Church could not offer food to supplicants. It could not even offer the wine and the bread of communion. But it could offer the faith that another life lay beyond this mortal hell.

That there were any priests or nuns left in Leningrad was itself remarkable. During the years of Stalin's Terror, those who had served the churches had been exterminated in large numbers (the metropolitans – equivalent to bishops – in the chief cities of Moscow and Leningrad had been spared), and by the time in the late 1930s that the authorities had relaxed their stance a little, the Russian Orthodox Church was almost moribund. Because the religious schools and seminaries had been shut down, there were no youthful priests or clerics or nuns. The few who had survived were older. When Operation Barbarossa had begun, Metropolitan Aleksii was swift to position the Orthodox Church and its followers as fundraisers both for the war effort and for the Soviet Red Cross. Here was a body determined to speak with the same voice as the secular authorities. 'War is a holy cause, however,' Aleksii had proclaimed, 'for whosoever undertakes it out of necessity, in defence of the truth, and accepting his wounds and sufferings, and laying down his life for the people of his blood, for his homeland, he follows in the wake of the martyrs to an imperishable and eternal crown.'[6]

Blood sacrifice for blood kindred; the words were aimed partly at those Leningrad citizens who had been drawn from the smaller towns and villages and rural districts in previous years: it was in the hearts of those with countryside roots – with the strong remembrance of local priests, of church bells, and of all those moments in the life of a family sanctified by the Orthodox faith – that faith had been hardest to extinguish. 'Therefore the Church blesses these deeds,' declared Aleksii, 'and everything each Russian person does for the defence of his Motherland.'[7]

These were fine words for the Red Army: but by the twilight of midwinter, the great cathedral – an exterior of golden cupolas, pillars of white, walls of pale blue – could offer little to the thickly wrapped figures who in their terminal desperation imagined that some crumbs might be found there. By this stage it was increasingly difficult to tell women from men. Greatcoats and boots had been acquired from the dead. Hats were pulled down over heads; midriffs and legs were puffed out with many layers. St Nicholas's was among the few cathedrals that had not been seriously molested, although its more precious treasures had been expropriated long ago. Even its candles were now in seriously short supply: they were needed elsewhere. Without electricity, the interior, which once burned with gold, was cold and dark. Each Sunday there was a service, presided over by Aleksii or one of his clerics, breath hanging in the air like still clouds. Orthodox services are much longer and more concentrated than those in Catholic or Anglican churches. Sacred texts are intoned and chanted. Among the supplicants who moved towards the cathedral like uncertain automata through the snow were some who had not tasted the bread and wine of communion for years. But the blood and the body were now acquiring a new and more terrible reality: the focus not of faith but of salivating need. In residential streets not far from the cathedral, on black nights that froze like iron, there were those who were preparing to cross one of the most fundamental ethical lines.

Those long streets of tall houses, the wide avenues that had once twinkled bright with shop fronts and cafes, played host now to severe tests of morality. It was increasingly common for elderly people to falter, and for desperate people to steal their ration cards while feigning help. This was neither ordinary human greed, nor ordinary human wickedness. Those who stole felt intense guilt but rationalized that the fainting elderly had very little chance of survival anyway. Starvation brought the slow dissolution of identity: people became criminalized almost instinctively. Yelena Kochina had watched in her apartment as her husband Kima had whittled the end of a walking stick until the point was arrow sharp. His scheme was simple: he had identified a bakery, more dimly lit than some of the other neighbourhood stores, from which it would be easy to steal bread. A simple act: create some distraction, poke the sharpened cane into a loaf, pick it up and make a quiet escape. Any considerations that this would be in effect stealing someone's rations – their chance of survival – barely surfaced.

Kima defended the immorality of his thefts with the argument that the bakery staff were essentially doing the same. Bakery workers showed few signs of dystrophy – they did not have blackened faces, they did not stoop – and his wife had her own suspicions confirmed when she handed over her ration card and was given a piece of bread that was substantially lighter than it should have been. She went back to demand the missing portion and it was given to her without a word.[8]

Inevitably, convincingly forged ration cards were also in circulation. Again, on the scale of human wickedness, this had to be balanced against the horrifying need of many refugees, trapped in the city, who had somehow been omitted from the bureaucracy of life and who could only possibly survive via criminal lifelines. Counterfeit ration cards worked best in the shops that were teeming with desperate Leningraders who had been queuing for hours. In the confusion and the semi-darkness, hard-pressed counter staff could not double-check every card put in front of them.

Criminality grew, and outbreaks of violent theft became more frequent. There would also be more corruption in the supply chains, from the crews of planes that delivered supplies (over the course of that winter, some 6,000 tons of foodstuffs were flown in – a bare fraction of what was needed, but the blazing gunfire from the Luftwaffe made even that amount an extraordinary success), to the staff in factory cafeterias and city bakeries who processed them. Temptation was both inevitable and tragic. The city authorities would know about it, as would the wider citizenry. But even with families drawing ever-increasing numbers of corpse sleds through those residential streets there somehow remained a ghost of civic cohesion. Some younger people, like Tatyana Goncharenko, retained their faith in the world that the Bolsheviks had shaped, convinced that no matter what else happened, socialism was the moral ideal to which all must adhere. Socialism was itself the purpose of life; she and her generation were not there to be served by the state but rather to put themselves at the service of all the people. This was what made their lives better and more valuable than those of the demonic fascists. This was why – even when individuals died – the light of their society would never be extinguished. 'We believed,' said Goncharenko simply.[9]

Bolstering this faith were the likes of Vera Inber and Olga Berggolts, who had been trying to spread comfort and solace through poetry: Leningrad was possibly the only city in the world whose citizens, facing extraordinary human catastrophe, were encouraged to draw spiritual strength from the verse that was declaimed from the loudspeakers that had been set up in all its residential districts. Their keenest admirer was a fellow poet/warrior called Nikolay Tikhonov. Born in St Petersburg in 1896, he had seen action during the First World War, and had also taken up arms in the Civil War and, latterly, in the bitter Winter War with Finland. Now a striking figure dressed occasionally in a blend of urbane shirt and fur-lined animal skins, Tikhonov was a man whose faith lay wholly in literature:

> During nine hundred days of the Siege, Leningrad remained not only a city of armed struggle but also a city of militant poetry – in the broad sense of the word. Ice, fire and cold, gloom and bitterness could not deny its unique spiritualized poetry that had been given to it for centuries and continued to inspire its poets, artists and musicians.[10]

He added that 'an emotional, encouraging poem was sometimes more important than a story or a leaflet'. But his language occasionally gave involuntary nods to religion. He said of Olga Berggolts's relationship with her many radio listeners that she became 'a sister in anger and sadness'.[11]

But in this most fundamentally literate of cities – where books were prized as a distinct element of one's identity – some found a new way to try to feed themselves. Just before the war – and a little after it started – Leningrad's publishing houses were responding to fresh enthusiasm for classical Russian works. They produced huge print runs of the works of Pushkin. Also greatly in demand was *War and Peace*. As we shall see, some used this epic work as an alternative to the Bible: within could be found the secrets of fortitude and of moral strength that could carry people through times of the greatest emergency and distress.

Tolstoy's masterpiece, with its extraordinarily detailed and textured battle scenes, its profound insight into the psychology of human conflict and crisis, was also found by some to be a para-religious survival text. 'Tolstoy had said the last word about courage, about people doing their bit in a people's war,' observed Lidiya Ginzburg. 'And no one doubted the adequacy of Tolstoy's response to life. The reader would say to himself: "Right – now I've got the proper feeling about this. So then, this is how it should be." '[12]

Back in the summer days of 1941, some 100,000 fresh (if abridged) copies of Tolstoy's masterpiece had been either sold or distributed to libraries (of which the city was intensely proud). The length of the work made multiple volumes necessary. Now, in apartments heavy with the scent of kerosene (fuel for cooking and lighting), desperation drove even the most devout bibliophiles to deconstruct these precious volumes. The binding – like carpenter's glue, or wallpaper paste – could be boiled and used in soup. The heavy papier mâché covers would work as satisfactory – if all too fleeting – fuel to keep stoves warm. And the pages themselves – all the printed words – were also torn out, scrunched up and used as food. 'At home, we started eating our books,' recalled Tamara Zaitseva. 'Mother soaked the pages in water, and we swallowed the liquid.'[13]

Leningraders moving through the darkest valley of desperation were now considering the foulest means of survival. The depravity began with the black markets, operating furtively, transactions made in shadowed courtyards. Families were ready to part with gold and silver heirlooms for the sake of contraband food. By that December, there were sellers who were offering meat. Many buyers were too hungry to question its provenance. 'We would go to the black market,' recalled soldier Samuil Hedekel. 'One time, we bought meat. It had fat sewn on to it with thread. When we brought it back, we were told that it was human meat.'[14]

The horror was instant, but somehow there was little element of surprise. Sennaya Square, the city's old hay market, was where many such secret bargains were made: a golden fob watch proffered, or an old silver bracelet, and sometimes in return there would be red meat, which they were assured was dog or cat or even horse. In the physical pain of starvation, the rational mind might be seduced into believing anything. In December 1941, however, there were forty-three arrests for 'people eating' and the word passed through the streets and through the tenement and apartment blocks at speed, for they simply confirmed what many had been quietly suspecting.[15] The majority of those arrested were women: refugee mothers who had brought their children to the city in search of sanctuary where none was to be found. They were not monsters but parents who were willing to contemplate the most hideous acts simply to keep their suffering off-spring alive.

There was a demand; and it was being met. The numbers of arrests would continue to rise during the coming weeks. The city's cemeteries and morgues still had bodies stacked like logs; and in the persistent freezing air they were perfectly preserved. Corpses did not even need to be robbed from the grave. They were simply carried back to bombed-out apartments or garden sheds, where they might be butchered accordingly to be passed off as something else. Legs and buttocks, where the meat was more plentiful were hacked off first. Leningrader Dmitri Likhachev first heard rumours, then had them confirmed. He himself had been fortunate enough to not even contemplate such consumption, but he could not bring himself to summon even atavistic disgust for the mothers who did. 'When your child is dying and you know that only meat will save it,' he wrote, 'you'll cut some off a corpse.'[16]

The nauseating rumours steadily became ever more terrible fact: one Leningrader making his way along a street saw the body of a woman lying face down in the snow. A leg had been removed, as though the corpse had been attacked in the tundra by wolves. Again, there was an absence of surprise. This was the world that they were

being forced to live in. Equally, though, there was an unacknowl-
edged shift in how people understood human nature. Cannibalism
was one of those primitive barbarities ascribed either to the enemy
(and the Nazis were frequently accused), or to primeval societies.
The sense that it could be happening not only in their own city but
also even in their own apartment block brought a sense not so much
of revulsion as a shudder of the uncanny. A desperate mother, on
the brink of hallucination, trying to feed a child was one thing, but
what of those men still strong enough to handle knives and hack-
saws who were able to butcher fellow humans without going mad
themselves?

Some tried to swat away the rumours with alternative explanations of why limbless bodies were found half covered with snow.
Perhaps they had been caught up in shelling – a horrific way to die
but at least the victims of impersonal explosives rather than of a man
looming over them. 'A normal cultured person would never have
any compelling conditions to decide to touch human meat,' recorded
diarist Dmitrii Kargin.[17] For him, the grotesqueness was difficult to
credit. Yet he also knew fundamentally that the rumours were true.
So who then were these defilers who moved unseen among the larger
populace? 'It is necessary to consider participants in cannibalism
more likely not normal people,' Kargin continued, 'but those who
are losing their minds or who have gone completely mad.'[18]

As with the counterfeit ration cards, it became apparent even from
the first arrests that cannibalism occurred most frequently among
the trapped refugees of the city: those who had fallen through every
kind of civic safety net. Yet there were others too. The feared security services of the NKVD formed a special unit to investigate cases
where there appeared to be a more organized element. It was claimed
by an army food-supply officer, for instance, that there was a ring
of medical workers who were consuming body parts from corpses.
There were those drafted to work in oversupplied cemeteries who
reported bodies being spirited away. There were hospital workers
investigated, one such who not only assiduously removed the gold
fillings from the mouths of the dead, but also took home the bodies
of children, which he would then cook and feed to his family (even

the NKVD worked on the assumption that this worker's children had no idea of what it was that they were eating).

There was an official document prepared in Leningrad and sent on to NKVD chief Lavrentii Beria (himself no stranger to the depths of human depravity). In it were listed case studies – people who were actually apprehended – taken from that deathly midwinter: here was a worker at the Karl Marx factory and his son, also employed there, sharing their communal apartment with two women. The men murdered the women and then partially ate one of them. There was a shipbuilding engineer who presented himself at the morgue of the Bogoslovskoe Cemetery: his story was that he lived at a workers' dormitory and he was in search of a woman who had gone missing from that same residential building. He was certain that she was dead, and he wished to identify her body and give her a proper funeral. These were days in which so many bodies stacked so high – withered, discoloured – were quite without any kind of identity. The dead lay in blank anonymity. The man claimed to have found the remains of the woman, and the bewildered cemetery workers relinquished the body to his care. The man took the body to his apartment (the workers' dormitory was a fiction) and there he removed the heart and the liver and consumed them.[19]

Similar necrotic opportunism was present in the case of a milling-machine operator at the Bolshevik Plant: suspicious colleagues broke open his locker to find the remains of a human leg, carefully wrapped in cloth. Aware that his crime had been revealed, the worker confessed and pointed his supervisors to an area in the factory grounds near some fencing where he had concealed two more legs in a sack. These he had obtained from unburied bodies at the Serafimovskoe Cemetery.[20]

But there were even darker instances too in which it seemed that the hunger and the siege had completely unmoored the sanity of the sufferers. There was a plumber at a packing plant who murdered his wife and then told his son and nephews that the meat he was giving them had come from the body of a dog. In a shadowed corner near an apartment block was found a bag containing not only bones but also the remnants of a cooked human head. There was also a case of a mother – the wife of a soldier – who had suffocated her eighteen-month-old daughter and then fed her to her three older children.[21] It was not long before similarly dark stories were spreading: mothers turning upon their own loved ones.

This was the turn of the screw: gothic rumours that made even hospitals sites of anxious wariness. Nurses were quietly telling patients never to leave their children unattended in the clinics lest they be snatched away for food. For the authorities, and the investigating NKVD, there were other questions too: what was to be done with those who confessed to cannibalism? What if the 'cannibals' concerned were helpless refugees without ration cards, who had foraged for grave meat as they once might have foraged for vegetables? And then, what of those who removed parts from unidentified bodies, souls who had already died? Lieutenant Colonel Dr David Verkhovsky was in charge of the Military-Sanitary Administration of the Leningrad Front. On his team were several psychiatrists. Unlike the vengeful and violent NKVD, a body such as this was genuinely interested in gauging the mental health of those who had plunged so far into depravity. But there was another edge to this too: the individuals who confessed also had to be assessed in terms of the threat they posed in the future to wider society. The emphasis was not on compassion but on protection of the social structure: would these people in future years be 'socially dangerous'?[22]

The crime of eating human flesh was also in a sense divided: a sharp distinction was drawn between those who had fallen upon dead bodies in desperation and those who had deliberately killed in order to procure the meat. When murder had preceded the cannibalism, things were more straightforward – there was no pitying psychological analysis: in these instances, the firing squad awaited. There were also cases of the blackest of black marketeering: dealers in human flesh who passed it off as animal meat. The 300 or so who were caught also paid with their lives. But in the majority of other cases the authorities seemed to appreciate that the motive had been sheer desperation rather than malice, and confined their punishment to detention rather than death. Nearly 2,000 people were to be imprisoned for the crime of cannibalism. A more pressing concern to the Soviet authorities then – and in the future too – would be the erasure of all traces of such events. The horror was one thing, but the shaming shadow cast over this most civilized and literate of cities was utterly intolerable.

Even those guilty of far less terrible transgressions could suffer agonies of conscience. For teenager Yura Riabinkin, whose most serious misdemeanours involved tiny quantities of dried apricots and some chocolate powder – the remorse and shame were almost as intense as the hunger itself. He was a Pioneer, a young socialist; his sense of self was founded upon an idea of honour and honesty. Throughout that December, the endless queuing for food, the scrabbling for any kind of rations – a bit of pasta here, some curious fruit soup there – had been his sole responsibility. After a pre-dawn expedition which could last hours, he would sit in the communal flat – the family's old political map of Europe still hanging on the wall – and watch the hands on the clock. Eleven o'clock in the morning was a grim marker: from there, the remaining hours of the day stretched out limitlessly.

He recalled one day when his will had buckled and he had swapped a tiny portion of rationed sweets for 'sweetened cocoa'. The reason? He calculated that his little sister Ira would not enjoy it, and so perhaps increase her older brother's share. But in the course of his journey home his will was further bent out of shape: driven mad with temptation, he crammed half the cocoa powder ration into his mouth. It had taken just a moment, a lightning bolt of impulse. Worse, the offence was compounded when he lied to his mother, claiming that three packets of cocoa had been stolen from him in the street, snatched from his hands. He watched his mother sinking down into helpless tears at the loss of the sweetness; and the remorse surged within him like nausea. The psychological repercussions were hideous. 'I have lost my integrity, lost my belief in it,' he wrote. 'I have reached the end of the road . . . I have slid down into that abyss called depravity . . . I am an unworthy son to my mother and an unworthy brother to my sister.'[23] He thought about his mother 'in her summer shoes' in that lethally freezing weather, and all the efforts she was making with the local authorities to secure evacuation. The teenager no longer considered that he had any right to be saved.

'I am a ruined person,' he wrote. 'Life is over for me. The prospect that lies ahead for me is not life.' The idea of suicide had, for some days, been flitting through his diary entries. Now the idea began to take on a new and more terrible form. 'I would like two things to happen immediately,' he wrote. 'For myself to die, here and now; and for Mother to read through this diary. May she curse me as a filthy, unfeeling and hypocritical creature . . . I have sunk too low. Too low.'[24]

Yet the exact opposite was true. By acknowledging his sin, even if only to his diary, Riabinkin was affirming his own deep humanity. Had he or his family been among those who held vestigial faith in the old Orthodox religion, there might have been some relief in confession. Perhaps it would have made no difference. The diary was the confessional booth and the boy had understood about the absolute necessity of facing wrongdoing (no matter how intensely forgivable anyone else might have found it in the circumstances). It was truly remarkable in the midst of city-wide cold-eyed survivalism that such finely tuned sensitivity – in all the torment that it brought – had not been extinguished.

There were instances elsewhere too – not of the fires of guilt, but of weirdly impulsive acts of generosity, sometimes directed towards strangers. Near the Fontanka embankment in the silent indigo twilight, a passing woman saw that a man had sunk into the snow. She had a tiny quantity of sugar wrapped up in her pocket; she stooped and fed some to the man.[25] Such a gesture could not be justified in terms of logic: if this man was really at the threshold of death, the sugar might have revived him temporarily (as glucose did with the patients in hospital) but perhaps only prolonged his life by a matter of hours. Yet the sacrifice was as impulsive as its opposite: theft. There were deep instincts that were not animalistic.

And perhaps the most human quality of all was imagination; and specifically, the kind of imagination that could keep the sensation of hope alive. In all the grinding miseries of Yura Riabinkin's household – himself, his mother and his sister – there was the idea of evacuation. Word of it had continually spread, through his mother's workplace and through her repeated expeditions to the offices of local Party officials. She was assured – as were many other small young families – that their names were on the list, and that the day would surely come when their embarkation to safety could begin. Round that pot-bellied stove in the communal apartment, itself fed fitfully with wood rations that seemed all too finite, escape from Leningrad was projected on to the imaginations of the Riabinkin family like some extraordinary film. The fact that each day brought more disappointment – his mother returning home with no further news – did not seem to matter. The idea remained alive (even as Yura, in his agonies of remorse, considered that his own life was not worthy of such flight). The teenager himself had noticed in mid-December – in the deepest pits of his misery – news of the military developments outside the city. The German blockade remained implacable and tight, but in villages and towns some distance to the east a revivified Red Army was now starting to inflict suffering on their tormentors. Riabinkin heard on the news mention of a town called Tikhvin, which some weeks earlier had been taken by the Wehrmacht but which was now in the sights of the Soviets. The name Tikhvin caught in his mind: a sense – if only small – of some significance.

The significance was this: the Red Army was indeed poised to retake that railway junction, and that town with its beautiful old monastery. The counter-attack would be launched by the 4th Army and the 54th Army. Under intense blizzards, and in freezing temperatures inimical to life, the Red Army advances through the forests would be slow and painful and bloody; Meretskov's armies would first seize the railway line and then the town, and among the many who would be cut to pieces by bullets and shells were the men of the Spanish Blue Division, the same soldiers who had charmed Gatchina's old folk with their guitars. By the darkness of that midwinter, and 500 miles further south, equally implacable Red Army counter-thrusts and defence would ensure that the Nazi push to Moscow would be halted within twelve miles of the city. These developments – these humiliating halts and withdrawals – would somehow only serve to increase the German appetite for destruction: reason had long since given way to automaton violence.

19.   The Children Who Could Not Grieve

There were days when the winter shores of Lake Ladoga would glow with unearthly colour: a pale amber sun barely rising above the horizon, the shoreline beech, willow and spruce trees, on low hillocks, topped with snow, bathed in a tangerine light, casting shadows of pink and mauve. On other days, the ice blocks that had formed like huge concrete slabs near the shore could range from pure white to steel blue to a deeper green, under snow-laden skies of iron. The lands that overlooked the waters were rich in pagan beliefs – the curious behaviour of the lake's water level, rising and falling, was attributed to supernatural agency – but the region from the nineteenth century onwards was also popular with visitors, and was deemed especially attractive throughout the White Nights. The lake itself spans about 150 miles north to south and fifty miles west to east, and even in the modern age there were sailors who were wary of it. Throughout the years, countless ships had sunk amid unexpectedly violent waves and currents. The geology of the lake was difficult to fathom: wind might generate waves in the north that would increase with power the further south they got. But there was also unpredictable churn that could batter both sides of a vessel simultaneously, inflicting terrible damage on hulls. 'The lake is stormy and filled with stones,' wrote one Russian scientist attempting to research the problem.[1] Insurance companies would be wary of any ship intending to traverse the lake: storms that even the most experienced sailors could not foresee would have the power to batter ships so hard that all their hatches would burst open. In addition to this, that rising and falling water level could also bring submerged rocks and other hazards closer to the surface.

In the winter, the sailings would stop as the vast ice blocks accumulated, grinding against one another, creaking and shrieking in that northern darkness. In the unusually cold winter of 1941–2, the last sailing – carrying a cargo of flour – was on 29 November. That ship had only just managed to avoid the ever-closing ice-floes. It seemed for a while that the impossibility of sailing might comprehensively doom the city. Throughout the autumn, shipping had been pushing hard, facing consistent attack from the Luftwaffe: cargo boats laden with oats, with biscuits, with flour, had been sunk. The jeopardy had been intense and yet some supplies had got through. Without the cargo boats, what were the Leningrad authorities to do?

In fact, they had been looking with some keenness at that thickening ice. A week beforehand, they had tried an experimental short journey across it to a town called Kobona on a spur of land some twenty miles across the lake. The shore on this part of the lake is U-shaped, and at the bottom of that U is the town of Shlisselburg, which had been captured by the Nazis. This Ladoga experiment bypassed them: using 350 horses, drawing sleds, they made the journey across the ice and came back laden with sacks of flour.

The further drop in temperatures had raised a more serious proposition: the use of motorized vehicles. Confident that the ice could now bear the weight, some sixty trucks were sent across the route that had been taken by the horses. They too came back from Kobona, and this time with tons of flour. The process was not easy: driving on ice had its own unique difficulties, not only of grip, but also of navigation, especially on days when the snow fell and the eye could not perceive the difference between the ice and the sky. None the less, here was a possibility of breaking the blockade.

Zhdanov and his colleagues in the Smolny Institute sent encrypted communications to Moscow, requesting permission to establish a fully working road on the ice. Stalin by this stage was aware of the starvation, and of the growing number of deaths. Some of his subordinates in the Kremlin were immediately enthusiastic about the idea, telling Zhdanov that, via this new 'road', hundreds of tons of flour and grain – and, crucially, ammunition – could be dispatched to Leningrad every single day. Stalin himself was said to have been less enthusiastic, even though he gave his assent. 'I warn you that this entire business affords little hope and is not of serious significance to the Leningrad Front,' he wrote on the memo that gave the go-ahead for the road.[2]

His pessimism was, in a way, easy to understand. While the

Soviet Union had made vast advances in terms of industry and technology – from hydroelectricity to giant dams to entire rivers being rerouted – now was a time of want, and of shortage. Those vast German armies were still, unbelievably, menacing Moscow, and while the factories in the east were churning out materiel at almost preternatural speed, it was a struggle to keep up with desperate demand. Could sufficient trucks be spared? Was there even enough flour and other foodstuffs? Just months before, people across Russia were being inspired in this war by the screening of Sergei Eisenstein's *Alexander Nevsky*, the grand centrepiece of which was that epic thirteenth-century battle on the ice with the Teutonic Knights. Was the prospect of a Ladoga ice road too reminiscent of a pre-industrial past? Perhaps, too, there lay in the Soviet leader's heart a leaden sense that Leningrad was already dead: that there was little use in making great efforts to save a city the pulse of which was already flickering. Certainly in the years to come there would be a growing sense that Stalin had abandoned Leningrad to its fate, whether from anger or malice or simple crushing despair none could say. By contrast, Zhdanov and Kuznetsov were energized with the possibilities.

But a little like the naval convoys navigating the fury-flecked depths of the Atlantic and the North Sea, so daily lines of trucks travelling rather further than the experiments – not to Kobona, but to more easterly destinations along the shore of Lake Ladoga, where more regular supplies might be guaranteed – would also be facing unique and terrible jeopardy. It would have been understood to all that once regular journeys across the ice began, so the Luftwaffe in the thick skies above would attack them. Here was a range of extraordinary obstacles to face: how best could drivers navigate the trackless, featureless ice, and what could they do once the inevitable bombs started falling, shattering and melting that ice around them?

This was a fraught exercise in logistics, but very much in keeping with the relentless modernization of the USSR. Where once that surface would have carried sleds and skaters, how could it be determined that the ice would reach down to a depth that would allow heavy motorized vehicles to move across it? In the latter part of November, a small team of hydrographers set themselves up along the shore: they had to make holes in the ice to probe the depth; and they also had to move out steadily further and further from the shore to continue this work. It was precarious: there were places where the ice was still only around ten centimetres thick. In addition to this, the weather was grim. Unlike the forested inland, where a form of shelter was conceivable, the wide open expanse of the lake was exposed to the full strength of bitter Arctic winds whose relentless nature made it difficult even to stand upright. Lieutenant General Zakhar Kondratiev was in charge of that Red Army Road Transport Unit. 'The snowy dust was blinding their eyes,' he said of the technicians. 'The stormy wind was burning their faces and it was sweeping people off their feet. The reconnaissance men, increasingly far from the shore, made test holes as they went, measured the thickness of the ice and set landmarks.'[3] At this stage, they had to make do with sleds and horses: it was impossible to know if there was any stability. But with painful progress, they made their slow way across. 'Danger lurked at every step,' recalled Kondratiev. 'The ice was cracking menacingly.'[4] But after some days' work, the team had succeeded in pushing out to a remarkable distance, and this time with vehicles: some thirty miles from the shoreline, the route very carefully flagged (on that grey ice, and in those storms, the fear of becoming lost must have been intense). 'At the 56th kilometre from the shore, the wind increased to a gale,' said Kondratiev. 'A snowstorm then began.' There were also sudden outbreaks of breathless tension. 'The ice became thinner, sagged more noticeably, and the first cracks appeared.'[5]

Here was a dreadful prospect: water suddenly gurgling from a fissure, spreading fast across the surface. 'The soldiers strapped themselves together with ropes. They went in a row, keeping intervals. Everyone kept a close eye on his comrade and, in case of trouble, was ready to rush to the rescue immediately.'[6] In addition to this, though, was the hazard posed by German lookouts, and artillery fired from a distance. Explosions blew terrible holes in the ice: soldiers plunged into unthinkably cold water, and when hauled out again by those nearby were dead from hypothermia within minutes. In the horizonless blizzard, navigation to the far shore of that U shape of land was harrowing; yet a day later, the pioneer expedition made it. A route had been picked out; what was now needed was the human support and infrastructure to make it viable for hundreds, for thousands of vehicles.

The first full test trip spanning some forty miles across the lake, shore to shore, was made with horses, just to be certain that the hydrographers had not miscalculated the thickness of the ice. It was successful, and the transport units on either side swiftly made ready to carry out tests with laden vehicles. This required even more in the way of steady nerves: the prospect of being tipped into that dagger-cold darkness preyed on many minds. Lieutenant General Feofan Lagunov was driving one of the first trucks carefully leaving the secure shore-line. The surface, he remembered, 'was sagging. Under the wheels, now and then, cracks scattered in different directions. A characteristic sound resembling the sound of tearing rubber could be heard.'[7]

The very idea of being on that ice clearly made the instincts scream. There was little choice but to push forward. 'Through the ice, as transparent as glass, we could see the dark depths of the bottom and the air bubbles escaping from the wheels,' continued Lagunov. 'The [vehicle] had to be driven with great care. As soon as I took my foot off the pedal or slowed down a little, the rear wheels would start to skid.'[8]

But the links were established, and now a remarkable improvised infrastructure could be put in place. On both shorelines of that frozen blankness, Kondratiev recalled, 'the woodlands were humming with a multitude of voices', and in the echoing cold, there was the rasp of saws and the 'clatter' of axes. New temporary warehouses were being built from timber on both sides of the lake, and new roads were being marked out and laid from the western shore into the city. Naturally there was constant attention from the Luftwaffe in the skies above, Soviet fighters doing what they could to defend those below.

But what of the ice road itself? At a time of near constant, freezing snow, how would it be possible for any route to remain visible? This, it was felt by the authorities, was a job for women. Some 300 'White Angels' were recruited and sent to set up base by those wooded shores. Among them were some already experienced traffic controllers. They would be sent out on to the ice in shifts, taken by truck, dotted along the route. They were dressed in white (hence the nickname) and they would be equipped with powerful flashlights (despite the visibility to enemy planes – that much couldn't be helped) and large red flags. It would be impossible for them to be out in that raw and featureless ice for prolonged periods, so a series of huts and igloos equipped with small stoves (carefully positioned above the surface of the ice) was swiftly built. These would provide constant hot drinks, and the nourishment of hot soup. For of all the roles to be taken in that terrible winter, this was among the most uniquely vulnerable, requiring not only sturdy physical fortitude, but also nerves like taut cabling.

These huts along the route would also contain portable coverings that could be laid over any dangerous-looking cracks in the ice as well as emergency supplies of medicine and some radio equipment. All this would be intensely necessary because, across a distance of some twenty miles on the ice, with lines of trucks a constantly available target to bombers, and with the journey across the lake having to be made at very careful speeds estimated to take about an hour and a half, there had to be preparation for the most dire circumstances.

'It was forty degrees below zero in December and January and February,' recalled Dora Fagina, who was among the new platoon of traffic controllers. She and her colleagues had been genuinely inspired by the speed of the logistics, and by the courage too. 'Smart people – heroes – thought that it was possible to get connected with the Earth [the land outside the city] by way of lovely Lake Ladoga,' she said. 'And they made it happen. I consider them heroes because that was very difficult . . . There was no track! They had to make a road that a truck could drive over.'[9]

The line across the frozen lake ran roughly parallel to the German positions some ten miles south along that shore. The Wehrmacht knew instantly and precisely what was happening. They made it their business to try to stop it. But almost as soon as the route opened, it was not being used only for the transportation of foodstuffs and weaponry. There were women and children making the journey from Leningrad too. The evacuations, so comprehensively muddled and aborted, had begun again, although on a cautious scale to begin with. Those rickety trucks that had held grain and spiced meat were to be packed with mothers and frequently tiny children, enduring as best they could the cold as the vehicles processed through the blasting wind across the ice.

'The road was being shot at,' recalled Dora Fagina. 'The roads had to be changed. I worked as a traffic controller for three months. Well, how could I help? Children and their mothers were leaving the city. Of course, it was very hard because the only thing I could give them was a glass of hot water because we had tents and wood stoves.'[10]

Those temporary stations on the ice would prove over the coming weeks to be shrines offering extraordinary sanctuary and comfort. Fagina continued:

> The road was fired on, yes. We would try to leave at night in order to avoid being caught in that. Of course, we were fired on. And the shell craters that would appear . . . sometimes vehicles would get stuck in them, and there were times when they fell all the way through. I saw that. People died. The drivers were heroes, too. Volunteers were taken from the Leningrad Front. They would drive.[11]

In the weeks to come, the evacuations would step up; great numbers of young families would be sent across the ice. Convoys would also be necessary. If it was down to lone, individual trucks, even the most assiduous White Angels might not have been able to prevent accidental twitches of steering wheels which would end up with the vehicle marginally changing direction and eventually heading further and further away from the shorelines and into the centre of one of the largest freshwater lakes in the world.

And as much as it was vital to bring food in, the ice road – or Road of Life, as it was swiftly dubbed – was also seen by the authorities as the only possible way to take large numbers of children and women out of Leningrad to safety.

The Germans were still encamped around the city, and Field Marshal von Leeb's conquests reached some 120 miles east of Leningrad and south-east of Lake Ladoga. In addition to this, the Luftwaffe – although having been distracted by more fiery battles to the south – was still a menacing presence in the skies. But the Road of Life was an idea that represented more than desperation. It also suggested a high level of faith: not in God, or in the powers of nature, but rather in the endurance of perfectly ordinary individuals.

There was another flicker of light: amid the spruce and alder and mossy terrain that formed the landscape near Tikhvin – ground that in its icy solidity trapped some German vehicles that had been wedged in frozen streams – the Wehrmacht forces were beginning to feel the bite of winter almost as much as those whom they were besieging. Partly because of supply-line difficulties and partly the result of an age-old arrogance about the certainty of victory in Russia, many German troops did not have adequate winter clothing. Neither did their Soviet counterparts at first, but while they were waiting for the factories in the east to create and distribute supplies of fur-lined boots, gloves, hats and quilted jackets, they were more adaptable, having faced this climate year after year in peace as well as war. Amid the slender trees in the landscape around Tikhvin, Red Army troops were stuffing paper into boots; straw was bulking out tunics. The Wehrmacht, by contrast, had boots that leaked; and that moisture would bring frostbite roaring in. In such conditions, with a newly assertive Red Army putting the Wehrmacht forces around Tikhvin on the defensive, frostbite was a serious concern. The skin around the toes and fingers would begin to blister, and amid the pain, the flesh would then start to blacken. With no treatment, the tissue beneath the top layers of skin would also begin to freeze, resulting in further agonizing ulceration. If left for long – and in that exceptional winter, there was not much time to reverse it – fingers and toes would be transformed into a state of blackened mummification. Soon after, there would be instances of 'auto-amputation'; that is, the affected parts simply snapping off.

This, plus exposure and hypothermia, left an ill-covered army in no state to fight back, and it would later be asserted by General Erhard Raus, a panzer commander who had been in that frozen landscape, that the weather was a curiously unanticipated but lethal enemy. 'Lacking winter clothing and adequate shelter, the Germans suffered more casualties from cold than enemy fire,' he recalled.[12]

But the battle for Tikhvin was for many a kind of psychological switching point. Until then, the Germans, although static, were still undefeatable. The Wehrmacht's Army Group Centre had been pushing and pushing closer to Moscow; even though its progress had slowed in the autumn, there had been a nightmare inexorability that made Stalin demand to be told the complete truth about the situation by Zhukov, 'like a Communist'.[13] By mid-November, the Wehrmacht had advanced to within a mere twenty-two miles of Moscow: a day's walk, in other words. The pincer movement that was creeping around the city meant that Wehrmacht commanders in Krasnaya Polyana to the north had edged a little closer still: just eighteen miles away. It was said that through their field glasses they could make out Moscow's domes. There were tank divisions pushing through the landscape to the south too. Despite an autumn of sluicing rain, and of tracks turned into sloshing marshes, they had made it this close.

Yet the grip of winter had the power to turn armies into statues. Not only was the Wehrmacht paralysed, the failure of the supply lines meant that for over 100,000 soldiers, frostbite would bring not only severe pain and reduced dexterity but ultimately mutilation too as extremities simply died.

And against them that December, General Zhukov and his Red Army raised an array of forces that must have looked to some Wehrmacht soldiers as if they had been scooped from different centuries. Advancing towards them – from the centre and from the north – were not merely divisions of the effective T-34 tanks, together with properly equipped infantry – but also Cossack cavalry regiments, striking on horseback. In addition, there were Red Army troops dazzling in white – the proper camouflage for the taiga. Equipment and men had been drafted from the east, where it appeared that Japan presented no further threat to Russian borders. There was one other element that helped the Soviet pushback: the skies above were so lethally cold that the Luftwaffe was unable to launch concentrated attacks – there was insufficient de-icing fluid.

Against the size and the symbolism of Moscow holding back Hitler – who ordered Army Group Centre into defensive positions by mid-December – developments to the north in the little town of Tikhvin may have assumed marginal significance. But the way that the news of the Wehrmacht being pushed back there was received in Leningrad showed that people understood. The blockade was by no means over; the bitter struggle would go on. But a door had been prised open. With Tikhvin came the restoration of the railway lines that ran east from Leningrad, towards all the Russian towns and cities with plentiful supplies. A link could be forged from Tikhvin, via Lake Ladoga to the north, thence across the ice, and thence into Leningrad. This would be another and better escape route for all those desperate mothers and children: to get them transported across the lake and safely aboard trains that would carry them hundreds of miles east to safety.

'Tikhvin has been recaptured,' wrote Yura Riabinkin, 'as has Yelets . . . in the Moscow direction our troops are beginning to drive the Germans out of the areas that they had occupied'.[14] But what were the prospects for evacuation? The teenager's mother had been making daily visits to the Smolny Institute to check where her family stood in terms of being spirited out. There was the prospect of being allotted spaces on a Ministry of Construction lorry. But by the beginning of January, Riabinkin could not envisage himself leaving. He looked at the remaining blank pages left in his notebook and wrote that perhaps the diary itself was measuring out the amount of time he had left. He observed in himself the symptoms of morbidity: the gross swelling caused by fluid retention. 'I have become waterlogged, each cell of my tissues contains more water than it should,' he wrote.[15] Meanwhile his mother's thighs had swelled and hardened to a new degree.

Christmas Day had brought for some Leningraders a moment of dizzy secular exultation: a noticeably increased bread ration – the first dividend of the Road of Life. It was not much in itself but the fact of it opened up possibilities that no imagination had in the last few weeks been capable of entertaining. There were scraps of dried meat; the occasional apricot. Yet for thousands upon thousands of people, the slide into the abyss had been too vertiginous. There would be no escape. Yura Riabinkin – now past his suicidal remorse over the pilfered handful of cocoa powder – had settled into a new phase of illness. Almost unable – and certainly unwilling – to move, he now gazed around the family's apartment and was overcome with the memories of life. 'There used to be a sofa standing there, a dresser, chairs, an unfinished meal on the table, books on the *étagère* [an open bookshelf], and I would be stretched out on the sofa reading *Les Trois Mousquetaires* while enjoying a snack of white bread, butter and cheese or else munching chocolate.'

The literature-loving teenager thought of Pushkin, and quoted him, writing, 'I was "always satisfied with myself, my dinner and my wife" – well, I didn't have that last commodity,' he added, 'but to make up for it, there were games, books, magazines, chess, the cinema . . .'[16]

The confirmation came at last: the Riabinkins were to join the evacuation across the Road of Life. Yura's mother – herself almost unable to move – found a new fiery energy directed at her bloated son. It was possibly the desperation of love, but to Yura's ears it sounded like hard anger. 'Nowadays she often hits me, swears at me, shouts at me,' he wrote. 'She gets wild nervous attacks, she can't bear my worthless appearance.' She accused her son of pretending to be 'ill and feeble'. 'But I truly am not faking my weakness,' he wrote. 'Oh, Lord, what is happening to me?'[17]

The day came: a few belongings in a bag that could be placed on a sled and dragged to the muster point in the city centre where the three of them would climb aboard a truck with other young families in similar circumstances. Except that when it was time to leave, Yura could not. He was sixteen years old and he needed a stick. But now he could not find it. As his mother and his sister made ready in that apartment, Yura tried to stand, but he could not remain steady on his feet. He sank back on to his bed. It is impossible to know what his mother and his sister were thinking as they gazed upon him; or indeed what – if anything – he said to them.

They were forced to go without him. The mother was herself barely able to manage stairs. She and the little girl – with their bag of necessaries – left that dark, cold apartment, shuffled out into the snowy street and made their way to that truck. How often did the mother look back? How often did she think, in the course of that walk, that she would instead turn round, climb those stairs, embrace her son and somehow get him out too?

Perhaps there was too little time. Perhaps the teenager had assured them that he would be perfectly all right, and that he would fend for himself. Perhaps the prospect of the journey ahead held its own fears and distress. But the mother and Ira were presently on that truck, being driven north out of the city, out into the sharp-tasting landscape of fir and larch, and out towards the vast frozen lake. Then, as the vehicle, its lights on, got into position behind the trucks and cars and buses in front – a careful and tightly packed convoy, each guiding the one behind – they looked out over that silver blankness.

It cannot be known whether Yura Riabinkin ever really managed to rise or walk again, or whether he found some discarded crumbs to keep him going for a little while. In his final diary entry he had written: 'Only God, if such exists, can give us deliverance. Let Him save us now, then never ever will I have to lie to my mother again, never will I have to soil my honest name, it will become sacred to me again.'[18] Even a boy with the most complete new Soviet education could not resist at least imagining that there was a God. And imagining that with deliverance would come redemption.

It cannot be known if Yura even had the strength to light a gas lamp or candle as the short winter day ended and night once more closed in. And it cannot be known precisely when the boy died. But it does seem certain that he died alone.

And as his mother and little sister held on inside that freezing, unheated truck, through the deepening twilight, the beams of the headlights growing stronger, they had no idea of what would become of him or themselves. The truck made it across the ice (in this, unlike so many others, they were fortunate). But at the first staging station, as they were being transferred from truck to train, the physical effort – and perhaps the intense distress of separation – proved too much for the mother. She died; quickly it seemed. And the little girl was left an orphan: one more out of almost uncountable thousands.

Many, many years later, researchers were able to track Ira (now Irina) down. She had been fostered within the system and now had a family of her own. Irina's belief – her own personal faith – was that her older brother had lived. That he had managed to survive but somehow was never quite able to find her. It is possible to see how even this belief – distressing as it was – was better than the prospect of a boy left to face death all on his own.

★

The darker fact is that, were it not for these diaries, Yura's death would have never been registered or acknowledged by anyone else. How could it have been? His passing was but one among so many, unnoticed and unmarked; in all those tenements, how many babies, how many young children, died on the same day as Yura? The numbers cannot be known. How many mothers faced the unfathomable pain of gazing on their bodies? And how many would never be remembered or commemorated in any way, consigned to the cold blankness of unmarked mass graves? The keeping of diaries was a practice that had been encouraged by the authorities; these testimonies might instruct future generations about the fortitude and strength of socialism when faced with the death-hold of fascism. As it was to turn out – with anonymous mass graves proliferating around the city – these scraps of pages, from Riabinkin and others, were literary gravestones, the only things marking their existence.

But in the feverish struggle for survival, there was no room for the luxury of loving remembrance. And for the Leningraders preparing themselves for the freezing ordeal of evacuation, salvation was still far away. The Road of Life itself – the very idea of it alive with danger – brought anguish to so many: a last thread of hope that was frequently snapped for families just as escape seemed possible. Even without the constant threat of incandescent artillery shells puncturing the ice, the sheer stresses placed upon those uncertain surfaces – the daily lines of trucks, moving in either direction – created cracks which soon became fissures. In the first two weeks of the operation alone, 157 trucks suddenly pitched headlong into holes that materialized seemingly from nowhere. Even with the doors kept open, the shock and then the stabbing cold of the water meant escape for the drivers was often extremely difficult: where to get any kind of hand-hold when you have been plunged into that deep blue depth? To have an expectation of survival in those circumstances, you would have to hope that the accident occurred not far from one of the traffic controllers' huts or tents.

On top of this was the prospect that awaited evacuees: mothers, already weakened by months of hunger, were required to sit with their children in unheated trucks, the wind slicing across the lake sharpened further by the velocity of the vehicle. Some of the trucks were open; women would hold on as best they could to wriggling, distressed infants. Medical worker Olga Melnikova, stationed on the ice along with the controllers, witnessed some excruciating scenes. 'These people looked horrific,' she said. 'Their children were so tiny, so wizened – we called them "the aged little people".' And sometimes, she said, in the urgency to convey as many people as possible, some of these mothers were on 'the open sides of trucks', clinging on precariously with limbs numbed. 'Just imagine what happened when the trucks hit a bump,' Melnikova said. 'The mothers, jolted by the sudden impact, could not keep hold of their children. Their precious bundles flew out of their hands and down on to the ice. The drivers would not stop – but the poor little children were killed on impact anyway. We would find clusters of corpses out on the open lake.'[19] The tiny babies could never be identified.

Equally, those on the trucks had to find a way of repressing their panic when shells exploded ahead or behind them. One Russian family that I know remains haunted to this day by the story of Larissa, a young girl – an orphan – who was being driven across the ice with many other orphans. She was already in distress: she had been separated from her best friend, who was in one of several trucks behind. After the loss of her parents and family in such terrible circumstances, she had clung to her friend as one fixed point of stability and love. Now Larissa watched with disbelief as the trucks behind were shelled. In an instant, they were destroyed; and the fragments surrounded a dark hole that had been punched in the ice. There was no possibility of turning back; rather, instead, there was acceleration. The life of Larissa's friend had been extinguished in a heartbeat, and there could be no chance to mourn.

Yet amid these nightmarish experiences, the evacuations continued; day by day, skeletal, staring figures shuttled out of the city, and thence into these columns of vehicles for that ninety-minute ice-crossing. Those who made it entered what must have seemed a form of paradise. In Kobona and other towns on the opposite shore there were supplies of hot strong tea, and chocolate. There were signs proclaiming a 'welcome' to the 'dystrophics'.[20] Care had to be taken too:

after periods of starvation, overeating could be extremely dangerous, resulting in agonizing and occasionally fatal digestive revolt (the
system unused and unable to cope). For the tiny children, there were
supplies of warmed milk and rusks before they were packed on to
their onward journeys.

There was something else they met with too, after those weeks
of darkness: simple, unaffected and unstressed kindness. It was not
that Leningraders lacked either compassion or heart, but the hunger
produced a certain emotional hardness, a calcification that could not
have been helped. Children and mothers alike, being ushered on to
trains and, on reaching their destination, being guided into hostels
and other sanctuaries, were once again gazing at people who were
healthy: smiles, sparkling eyes, round faces, colour. By contrast,
those who ministered to the mothers and children recoiled, at least
internally. They were looking at the living dead. 'Everyone is blue-
black, bloodless,'[21] observed one helper of the people disembarking
from the trucks. For some, the journey had come just that shade too
late. On the long train journeys to the cities in the east, many evacuees simply died. The trains were too crowded to allow their corpses
to be carried among the tightly packed living; and so they had to
be given rudimentary trackside burials, deep beneath the ever-falling
snow.

The numbers of evacuees continued to rise: after weeks of twilight
paralysis, the Leningrad civic authorities now seemed to have recovered that instinct for order. Hundreds of evacuees became thousands,
and during the weeks to come, while the ice held, they would in
turn become hundreds of thousands. The bravery of the drivers had
to hold as firm as the ice; overnight, the temperatures would plunge
once more and the surface ice of Ladoga would refreeze, a new con-
figuration of crystals. With each new day, the trucks embarking even
before the sun had risen, the ice would take the weight of countless
tyres and vehicles, and little by little, its surface would yield and melt.
It was a slow process, but as the days progressed into afternoons, what
once was pristine ice became slushy. Tyres would now be hissing
through moisture, pushing gelid water to either side of the rudimentary track. Looking on, utterly open to the cruel winter skies and to

the constant possibility of bombardment, were those extraordinarily brave traffic controllers, armed only with flags to guide drivers whose snow-dazzled vision was leading them off course.

But the operation encapsulated a sense of reviving purpose. There was one other reason for this too: the supplies of not only bread but also items such as cured meat that were making their way into the city were now to be shared among fewer people. The evacuations in the end succeeded in removing some half a million of the most vulnerable people out of Leningrad. This meant half a million fewer mouths to feed. But there was of course another reason why rations could now once more be increased: the city's death toll. As we shall see a little later, the full accounting of the dead was shortly to come, and the numbers would be so huge as to be beyond grasping in any ordinary way but to which the processions of figures drawing behind them sleds bearing bodies wrapped in winding sheets – so common now as to be wholly unremarkable – bore testimony.

So too did the vast numbers of orphans who had to be housed and cared for before they could be evacuated. Here were children who in some cases simply could not mourn or grieve: the depth of their trauma was such that sometimes they were wholly unresponsive. Meanwhile, for the adults who were trying to look after them – either having been alerted by neighbours or simply having found them wandering the streets or standing vigil over the bodies of their dead parents – the emotional toll was also intense. History teacher Aleksandra Mironova had decided to take a job in one of the city's orphanages when the city's schools closed, and it was to here that some of her own former pupils came. But there were also grim discoveries. In one apartment, there were two little girls who were too weak to walk; they were shuffling around, searching for crumbs on the floor, while seated in an armchair above them was the corpse of their mother. There was an uncle, Mironova discovered, but he had more interest in the family heirlooms than he did in the two girls, whom he was happy to abandon to fate. In another apartment there was a little boy lying in bed beside his mother's body. He was distressed beyond rationality. When it was gently explained to him that he should go with the grown-ups to a new home, he became hysterical about leaving his mother, shouting: 'Mama, what did they do to you? Mama, what are you doing to me?'[22]

In one of St Petersburg's museums of history is the notebook of a twelve-year-old girl called Tanya Savicheva. One by one she lost each member of her family that inexorable December: she solemnly noted each death as it occurred. Grandma, uncle, then mother . . . 'Everyone died,' she wrote. 'Only Tanya is left.'[23] She too was found by a specialist team of carers, and though she was eventually taken to a new sanctuary away from the city, she did not survive for long.

Distress caused the most intense psychological repercussions that manifested in curious ways. One little orphan would not acknowledge the deaths of his mother and father. Rather, he was fixated on quite another memory: recently, his father had managed to obtain (or steal) a tiny quantity of jam. The boy, according to the orphanage worker, 'did not feel the losses [of his parents] but his recollections about the compote were radiant.' This was in an earlier and perhaps rather less enlightened era of child psychology. The boy's determination to fix on something other than abysmal horror might have been a sign of strength. Elsewhere, there was a little girl who likewise had been coaxed from the family apartment and its dead inhabitants. She knew she had lost everyone; but the one thing that made her visibly upset was the apparent wilting of her house plant. She was observed holding it, willing it back to life, as though it had been as central to her life as her family.[24]

By the height of the horror, the city had eighty-five orphanages, and many were barely able to cope. The staff and the children alike suffered the same skeletal rations; and there were instances of adults unable to resist the temptation to steal from the children's share. There were also intense difficulties caused by sporadic water and power supplies. Very often, small children were made simply to lie in the dark, upon filthy beds. A few fought like fury. Others were too weak to move. They could not even be coaxed into playing games. All they could do was gaze at the walls. On top of this the adults – even those with the very best intentions – could not know how to offer proper help and comfort to children who had watched their parents die in grotesque ways. Many other children were placed in homes because their fathers were in the army and their mothers – required to work multiple shifts in different factories – could no longer cope. There were children whose mothers had had breakdowns; this had resulted in little girls and boys being accused by their maddened parents of having stolen food from them. Such children were regarded as being under direct threat and were removed from their parents for their own safety. There was a view among some Leningraders that the State might be in a better position to give succour to the little ones. It was not.

Now they faced the prospect of crossing Lake Ladoga, and of having new lives shaped for them in unoccupied regions of Russia where food and light were still plentiful. These children would still be institutionalized (and there were occasional stories of little girls and boys who – when seeing any soldier – would instantly imagine that it was their father, and run and cling to the man). And in the years to come, there would be different challenges that would accompany the efforts to return them to their home city.

But for the children – and for Leningrad's adults – this chink in the deadly blockade was the start of a remarkable mass psychological phase. After months of the most desolate isolation – a starving, silent city seemingly forgotten and abandoned in the cruel tumult of war – Leningraders would start to sense that they were no longer alone, and that there were distant strangers who were fighting for their salvation. The Ladoga Road of Life provided more than food and rescue: it repaired the agonizing rupture with the rest of the nation. The siege would continue, scything through life; but the confinement was no longer solitary. Arrested time would be restored to its proper rhythms. Even when the months of January and February brought the eventual deaths of hundreds of thousands who had been in decline for months, and when the streets themselves would be littered with thousands of purple-faced corpses, frozen in the snow, something new would enter the souls of those who still lived.

20. Scythians So Embellished With Nature's Pride

The image of flooding was pervasive in the city. It was partly to do with the way that from certain prospects, the streets appeared to be floating on the many waterways – the canals, the Neva, the Fontanka. The miracle of St Petersburg that Peter the Great had conjured might also vanish like an illusion beneath the roiling waters of an angry sea. There was some basis in fact for the metaphor of this city that issued a constant challenge to nature. There was the constant threat of rising waters: storms out in the Baltic Sea could lead to surges in the Gulf of Finland which would then lead those cold grey tides to seep and lap and rise against the embankments before gushing over them and into the streets. It had happened – most famously and most hauntingly – in November 1824, when the waters rose so high – some four metres or so – that it appeared that the city had sunk. The currents were fierce; many who plunged into them were drowned. Countless animals, horses, dogs, died too. The classical facades of the grandest structures were lapped with Baltic waves. 'Till drowned Petropolis now stood/ Like Triton, waist-deep midst the flood'[1] as Pushkin later wrote in his famous poem 'The Bronze Horseman'. Aside from the grim aesthetic spectacle, the flood also made plain the city's intense duality: the way that the highest society commingled with the poorest, forced to live in darkness and squalor. It was that squalor – the rudimentary cesspits, the basement warrens that formed dwellings – which came to haunt the city in the aftermath: as the waters receded, so vicious disease took hold as the city was ravaged by a terrible cholera epidemic.

By the early weeks of 1942, some five months into the blockade, a different sort of flood threatened the city: one of death itself. There were so many people whose bodies had been tortured too far. They had already begun their journey to the grave, beyond saving even if help had been available. In those early weeks of the year Leningrad was drowning in a tsunami of mortality. Ironically, the prospect of life and renewal was being mooted at the exact point when death came to claim over 20,000 people a day. 'All the worst is behind us,' proclaimed Pyotr Popkov, the local Party Secretary, answering to Andrei Zhdanov. He was speaking on 13 January. 'Ahead of us lies the liberation of Leningrad and the deliverance of the Leningraders from death by starvation.'[2] In the strictest terms, he was telling the truth: the Road of Life was bringing trickles of fresh sustenance and removing the city's most vulnerable from danger. Most of those remaining were essential to the defence industries. But the city was still in the abyss of dark and cold; power was never certain and even those fractionally larger rations now shared among fewer hungry people only stimulated appetites into yearning for the return of everyday cooked meals. 'People are living on their last hopes,' wrote the wheelchair-bound academic Georgii Knyazev. 'Those who weaken just go on dying.' At the university, he noted, 'research fellows are dying one after the other'. An elderly colleague of his called Lavrov 'crossed the dreadful line at the beginning of January. Having grown weak, he lay helplessly moribund.' In addition, he wrote of his friend Svikul, 'whose fifteen-year-old son Vova, an unassuming lad, has just died'. Knyazev and his wife started discussing their own 'life-forces'. 'What border have we reached?' he wrote. 'Where is the line – that dreadful line – which, once crossed, a person can never step back over?'[3]

The numbers of the dead were, to those who lived, unfathomable. They were pulled along icebound streets, and at some crematoriums lines of bereaved family members waited, hoping that their loved ones might receive a dignified farewell. But the multitude of corpses made this a practical impossibility for most (though not everyone: Vera Inber attended the funeral of Professor A. A. Likhachev, an academic. 'The body, without a coffin . . . was lying in the Conference Hall on an oval table placed on a piece of plywood,' she wrote. There were obsequies – Inber's partner intoned the Latin *Sursum corda*, a eucharistic prayer meaning 'Lift up your hearts'. Even if the faith itself was smothered, the aesthetics of it were still considered pleasing.[4] But for the more ordinary citizens, the mass graves were being dug: and the dead had to be disposed of fast.).

Where once the spectacle had been silent, there was now a terrible sense of the dead on the move: an obscene transportation which was the opposite of the Road of Life. Yelena Averianova-Fyodorova was one who travelled it:

> We took my grandmother to the cemetery on a sledge. And now we were behind someone else – in an endless chain of dead people, mostly without coffins. But that's not the only thing. It's all right if people are taking their own relatives, but what's much worse is that whole lorries are going past laden with bodies, undressed, unshod bodies, all lying anyhow and in different bits of clothes ... While we were there, six lorries and three horse-drawn carts full of bodies arrived. It was horrible to see! And how many more there were that had been brought there earlier but hadn't been buried![5]

At least those corpses had made it that far. In the centre of the city, half covered with snow, were bodies that had gradually been reduced to fragments. At the Piskaryovskoy Cemetery workers summoned enough strength to dig one vast mass grave: so vast that it could absorb the bodies of some 40,000 people. In addition to this, one of the city's brick factories was transformed into an industrial-scale crematorium. The authorities were considerate towards those who would be carrying out the mass burnings. As well as making sure that they had plenty of 'rubber boots', 'canvas mitts' and 'waterproof aprons', these women and men would also be granted improved rations and 100 grams of vodka daily.[6] In the circumstances, on frequently near-empty stomachs, this may have been a sufficient quantity – around half a pint. Certainly it should have been sufficient to numb sensitivity as the work of burning corpses continued round the clock.

And in the wider sphere, there was no sense that the scale of such mass losses had dimmed individual grief; it had not. The pain for all family members, losing their loved ones in succession, was blade keen. But the wider health concerns were understood as well.

While the winter frosts lay upon the city, decomposition was slowed, but soon the thaw would come, and with it might come illness and infection on a biblical scale. The fear was that the corpses would carry the plague. But there was another potential source of disease too, this one already present: in the stages just before death, huge numbers of victims began to suffer what was described as 'starvation dysentery'. Their fatal weakness was compounded with acutely distressing filth, violent and wholly uncontrollable. Apartments were made fetid; with no running water, and only the prospect of buckets lowered into ice-holes to provide it, the chances for the victims and their families to achieve any humane level of hygiene were remote. Very often family members – similarly afflicted – would not even have had the strength to take slop buckets beyond communal stairwells. The city's innocent snow cover went some way towards disguising the disgustingly putrid state of the streets, hiding all the sewage that the frozen, halted water supplies could not take away. The warmth of spring would change that situation quite dramatically.

Despite the slight improvement in rations, many thousands more continued to cross over the line that Georgii Knyazev had speculated on. Among them was the futurist poet and children's author Daniil Kharms, imprisoned near the start of the siege for his declarations that the city would fall and his refusal to accept any kind of military role. His strategy as soon as he had been arrested was to feign insanity – he was, like Hamlet, but mad north-northwest. He convinced his NKVD captors and the judge, and when he was remanded to Leningrad's Kresty prison he was placed in a special psychiatric wing. This in itself was unusual. Throughout the later part of 1941, a large number of the city's prisoners had been marched out of the gates, issued with military uniforms and sent to the front line as newly minted infantrymen who were expected to face the full wrath of Wehrmacht fire. Many of those held in Kresty – a grim redbrick structure, noted for its cruciform blocks that enabled guards to look down the corridors in all four directions from a central point – were political prisoners rather than more conventional criminals. This jail had once held Leon Trotsky; it was where Lev Gumilev was forced to share a cell with a continually changing roster of prisoners while his mother Anna Akhmatova pined outside the prison's vast gate. In this institution, members of the toppled provisional government, apart from Kerensky, had been incarcerated for a time. To Leningraders, the sight of the prison was not precisely a deterrent, because it was understood that any unexpected denunciation or accusation could land you in there (a sibling having had an unauthorized conversation with an American visitor, for instance), and that nothing could be done about it. None the less, it was a constant reminder of the state's absolute power over all mortal souls.

A marked feature of Russian prison and Gulag life, both through Tsarist and Bolshevik years, had been the granting and withholding of food as a means of asserting physical and mental control over the prisoners, and also as a means of psychological torture. As the siege of Leningrad tightened, however, it became impossible to distinguish between the treatment of prisoners and the treatment of civilians. Innocent and guilty, those who were free and those who were convicted, became as one: the walls of Leningrad's prisons might as well have been torn down for all the relief that the inmates would find were they at liberty – the city itself had become one vast, terrible prison. And as civilians had no agency in the quantity of bread that was earmarked for them, so Leningrad's prisoners were reliant upon guards who were as hungry as themselves.

There were accounts of desperate attacks: prisoners launching themselves at one another, in fights for food and, in some circumstances, in struggles not to *become* food. We don't know exactly how Daniil Kharms faced his final day. He had been gaunt enough when he was arrested, as is evident from his mug shots – his eyes wide, pale and piercing.[7] He died at the beginning of February 1942. In a twist of wholly unnecessary cruelty that not even hunger had been able to extinguish, the prison authorities told his widow that he had been transferred to another prison at Novosibirsk, a city deep in the eastern primeval forests of Siberia. (Kharms received posthumous artistic rehabilitation following the death of Stalin, but has once more become a forbidden voice in Putin's Russia. Early in 2024, a schoolteacher in St Petersburg claimed that she had been fired because she devoted a class to the anti-Stalinist anti-war work of Kharms. Sensitivity to the subversive power of literature remains a hallmark of that totalitarian society.)

Kharms had represented an ungovernable poetic spirit in the city. And there were huge numbers of book-loving Leningraders for whom literature itself proved the most powerful psychological lifeline; the city's libraries had always been distinctly, proudly well stocked. And the National Library – which had not only housed rare original manuscripts but also provided reading rooms and lending services – had somehow, throughout that deathly winter, kept the doors open to readers. Before Operation Barbarossa, up to a thousand librarians had worked there full time. Many had been drawn into the military, and into the icy Karelian forests; many others had simply died. By the early months of 1942, there were only some 200 employees left. The most valuable collections, ranging from Voltaire to the handwritten pages of Catherine the Great, had been spirited to safety further east, rather like the treasures of the Hermitage. Yet the library's grand reading rooms had managed to continue functioning during the early months of the siege. The librarians were there not only for the public, but for the military and the civic authorities too. Sometimes Andrei Zhdanov would request classical or even technical texts. There were apparently other times when he asked for escapist fiction, leaving it to the librarians to judge which works might best help relieve the anxiety of his vacant hours. Librarian Yekaterina Suslova recalled the curious atmosphere of the institution – and the presence of its users – at that time:

> The lonely, sick workers are lying ill in the rooms of the archive. Small groups of soldiers are continuously present . . . In pitch darkness, on one of those days when there isn't even enough kerosene to light a lantern – and you can't enter a depository with an oil lamp, it's against the rules – the archivist . . . enters the depository.[8]

The stacks were a darkened maze; but as though blind, she had memorized each shelf, each subject. And in maintaining this secular sacredness, the librarians could find in each grim new day at least a glimmer of interest that lay beyond the narrow confines of their own lives: to seek dialogue with the books that they were commissioned to hunt out. Equally, for those who made a habit of attending the library, there was an element of nourishment in the very journey itself: a self-imposed task, to read Diderot, to consult Hobbes, to absorb Petrarch, or even St Petersburg's more contemporary poets. Unlike in domestic settings, where family books had been consigned to stoves for human warmth, or stripped and picked apart in desperation as a food source, books here were sacrosanct.

By the last weeks of 1941, the reading facilities had been moved by necessity into the building's cellars: readers could request the great classics, while also using the library both as a shelter and as a form of spiritual refuge. But eventually the facility succumbed to the harshness of the blockade: the interrupted water supplies made it impossible to stay open.

Even that extremity proved to be only a short pause for the readers who were yearning for the reminders of humanity that the books gave them. The volumes destined for lending to soldiers were a blend of exciting escapism and solid practicality: textbooks on camouflage through history, or road construction in cold climates. The other point was that books of any stripe were also a form of dialogue: so very important in a city of silence, where the vast numbers of the dead removed the hubbub of voices.

The extent of Leningraders' regard for literature also became apparent when specialized teams from the library were authorized to enter the apartments of the dead. In a socialist society, where material gain was shunned, it was still considered acceptable to own huge numbers of books. There were expert collectors whose antique volumes were sometimes of enormous value. In those communal apartments in large nineteenth-century houses, where the fittings such as chandeliers or large mirrors were now chipped and mottled and neglected, it was not unusual to find bookcases filled with well-preserved splendour, even rare first editions from the likes of Turgenev or Dostoevsky. Leningrad book expert Fyodor Shilov was fascinated by the psychology of the city's many bibliophiles. In one desolate apartment – empty save for the lavish bookshelves – Shilov speculated on what literature had meant to the former owner:

> The books are all on the history of Russia, focusing especially on the history of the Church and the schism. The owner passed away from emaciation and not only had not sold his books, he kept on buying more until the last minute, getting carried away with his purchases because they were cheap; food is expensive, but books are going for a song . . . What was the deceased trying to accomplish?[9]

Another writer, Vitalii Bianki, also noted a resurgence of biblio-mania in the city. The book trade – through either libraries or swapping or by purchase – was curiously recovering its vitality. 'Most of what is being bought up is exciting "pulp" stuff, adventure novels,' he observed. 'And old classics. Anything that describes a life not like the present one. Collectors and lovers of rare books continue their maniacal and, of course, quite fruitful, chase after valuable, now dis-counted, items.'[10] Even Georgii Knyazev, though fretting over the intense thinness of his wife, now managed to find a place near the hot stove to devote an entire morning to reading the poetry of Baudelaire.

The dead were mourned in numbers unfathomably great. Every house, every apartment block, contained its own individual agonies. The poet Olga Berggolts's second husband, Nikolay Molchanov, had passed over that death line imagined elsewhere by Georgii Knyazev. His body had been hollowed out. Berggolts's poem '29 January 1942' was dedicated to his memory. Elsewhere, a young Leningrad diarist was negotiating a snowy street when she saw an uncommon varia-tion on what had become a heartbreakingly common sight: a woman was dragging a sled up the street bearing a corpse, but rather than simply being wrapped in old cloth or a blanket, it was swaddled in a rich pale-blue velvet-like material. There had been an effort here to mark death with dignity and love, in the full knowledge that the body itself would be destined for a mass pit, lying promiscuously among many others in the same trench. The sensuous and colourful material was a final statement that this life – whoever's life it was – had mattered. But the spectacle had also stuck out because, as much as one loved one's own family, it was difficult and rare to feel pangs of pity for strangers. The sheer number of deaths had somehow made that impossible.

All Leningraders knew that many thousands of people must have perished. Some diarists dared to imagine that it might even be hun-dreds of thousands. They were correct; though the siege was to continue for another two years, it was during that winter that the vast majority of the Wehrmacht's victims were claimed. There are estimates that some 800,000 died between October 1941 and March

1942. In a city with a fast-declining population, would there come a day when the dead would outnumber the living? In February 1942, the snow was still falling and the temperature – having risen very slightly – suddenly dropped again to as low as minus 30°C. There were corpses lying in frozen puddles on bombed wasteland, part-submerged in blue ice. It would not be long before the ice would melt. There were corpses lying under undisturbed bedclothes, in apartments with broken windows where snow had swept in and dusted beds and floors with a thin layer of frozen white. It would not be long before snow turned to water. There were corpses in the darkness of bombed tenements' stairwells; no one in the course of that deathly winter had had the strength to drag the bodies of strangers to those queues at the cemeteries. 'The deceased were light and seemed like little children . . . and they didn't bend, because they were frozen,' observed Nikolay Punin. 'They lay everywhere, especially in the morning. Probably people brought them out from their apartments at night, and put them wherever possible.'[11]

In this sense, the unusually harsh winter, and the medieval siege, had made the dead of Leningrad resemble the petrified citizens of Pompeii, suspended in that moment of their final pain. But the return of life to the earth would bring their swift decomposition. There had to be a plan. What is more, that plan had to be carried out by a greatly depleted population: the success of those Ladoga evacuations had further emptied the city's dwellings. With so many of the men drafted into the Red Army, the city's women already had to work in the factories, cook and distribute the food, tend the sick and look after the orphaned young. Now they were going to have to face the sickening task of not merely body clearing but also the cleansing of apartments and buildings and courtyards that had become blotted and piled with frozen faeces.

Already, outbreaks of typhus were starting to spread through those dark communal apartments. All this had been part of the Nazi calculations: those who were not slain by bombs or shells or hunger would instead succumb to disease. The application was modern but the principle was age-old. The traumatic outbreaks of 'starvation dysentery' continued; only the pervasively sharp, cold air prevented some districts of the city from smelling unbearably foul. But this was also about the final stripping away of the last shreds of human dignity; death was not clean, but besmirched and vile and odorous.

Despite renewed bouts of shelling, Leningrad's water supply was restored. Citizens now had access to what seemed like the most extraordinary luxury: water that ran from taps rather than having to be fetched in large pails from miserable holes in the ice. And this in turn made it possible to face the unholy obscenity of the frozen bodies and of the frozen waste. Residents formed groups, and the commissars of the streets and the neighbourhoods began to organize trucks, so that the waste might be shovelled up and transported to the city's edges, and so that the corpses might be taken to freshly dug mass graves. With some wonder, even among themselves, the women of Leningrad, block by block, street by street, squared up to the work that they knew they would have to undertake themselves. Many were trembling, though through physical weakness rather than apprehension. Sofiya Mirskaya remembered that 'everyone who was able to went outside. They used crowbars to break off the ice with the human waste frozen into it.'[12]

'We were all surrounded by these huge, frozen piles of waste,' remembered Yelena Martilla. 'Whole buildings were enclosed by dirty snow mounds, some reaching as high as the second storey. And now, anyone who was able to walk or even crawl got outside and began working, using sledges, barrels, bits of wood and whatever else came to hand.' The orders to work had been edicts; yet the labour had a form of transfiguring effect too. Paradoxically, it brought a fleeting sense of liberation. 'We had declared war on dirt,' recalled Martilla, 'and through this declaration, the isolated and the inactive regained a sense of purpose.'[13]

The task was not only disgusting but also hazardous owing to the incessant shelling. Being outside could bring death without warning. But the need to cleanse streets and blocks and apartments was itself a means of survival; there was an instinctive understanding that to be clean was to be more fully alive.

Sofiya Ostrovskaya was one who articulated this new sense to herself in February 1942, as the hillocks of frosted human ordure were heaped up on spades by gangs of women, some of whom were sharing rare cigarettes. She herself was giddy with happiness: the water that had been turned back on had started running freely in her apartment too. She wrote in her journal, addressing an imaginary audience:

> You, all manner of Europeans, can you really understand this fully, you who have not known the hunger and the collapse of 1919–20, you who do not apprehend with your petit bourgeois five senses what the Russian citizen endures having entered for the second time 1919 in 1942? Yes, yes, dearest Europe, you do not know that among us there is developing – or perhaps has already developed – a sixth sense.[14]

This was a sixth sense for staying alive; there was something curious in the address of this triumphalism to 'Europeans' as opposed to 'Germans', who had after all inflicted this horror upon them. She was also careful not to invoke the hunger of the early 1930s, which had been visited upon the city by Stalin's actions. None the less, here was a striking and sour and defiant pride. 'We are very poor, very dirty and very ignorant,' Ostrovskaya continued. 'We are clumsy. We are rude and cruel. But we are Scythians; we are Scythians, bearers of a new sixth sense.'[15]

The Scythians were the nomadic people of the steppes who had flourished centuries before the coming of Christ. They raided and conquered, they had compassed epic landscapes on horseback, and even though they were eventually subsumed into other tribes and civilizations, the term 'Scythian' remained a by-word for centuries, denoting a certain ferocious barbarian nobility. The great Timur, or Tamburlaine, had been celebrated by the Elizabethan playwright Christopher Marlowe as having originated as a 'Scythian shepherd'. If Sofiya Ostrovskaya was addressing the Wehrmacht, and the people of Germany, then she had a warning for them. 'You are older than us, you are much, oh so much, smarter,' she wrote. 'In us, however, still lives an ancient human being, one wise in instinct and *living* then by his sixth sense . . . Just think about that, dear Europeans. Are you not frightened of us?'[16]

21. 'The air was ripped like silk'

Mass murder had become a tedious chore. Those who were com-
pelled to commit it could not even rise to the stature of monsters. In
1942, the German soldiers billeted in shivering villages not far from
Leningrad might well have agreed with Stalin, who was said to have
averred that 'one death is a tragedy, a million deaths is a statistic'.
Through the winter, they had gazed at the spires of Leningrad in the
distance. Their field guns had fired shells beyond number, smashing
the city of the starving stone by stone. Yet many of these men were
numbed to the effects of their fire, and some had passed beyond even
that state. There were some Wehrmacht soldiers who were bored.

To find the deliberate extermination of hundreds of thousands of
people wearying might seem beyond comprehension: immorality on
a new scale. Yet the killers could not see the people that they were
murdering. And the incessant propaganda of the Nazi Party insisted
that these Soviets were brutish, animalistic. That their deaths did not
count in quite the same way. The destruction that the Germans were
carrying out was mechanized and remote; they could not see the swollen bellies, the withered limbs. And in a strange way, the Wehrmacht
men were as much in purgatory as many of their victims: motionless in a savage winter amid eye-throbbing snow, deep-frozen mires
and lakes, with no sense of impulsion. The exciting momentum of
the summer – those hundreds of miles of effortless conquest – had
given way to a weird, uneasy stasis, in the midst of weather that these
city-born men had never before known. In this curious period where
their entire world seemed frozen into immobility, boredom was
not so much an expression of boundless cruelty as simply their own
imaginations becoming atrophied. How many could truly understand
exactly what it was they were doing in these crunching forests?

There were some who went rogue simply in order to restore some
kind of emotion – fear, excitement – to their lives. Wilhelm Lübbecke,

who was based in a small village just a few miles from the outer ring of Leningrad's suburbs, recalled how one of his men devised his own individual missions:

> Soon after Christmas, Schütte began to complain to me that he was bored with the monotony of his routine with the gun crew. One subfreezing night, he decided to take action and snuck alone across the snow-covered No Man's Land that separated us from the enemy. Armed only with his MP-40 submachine gun and a satchel containing a kilo of dynamite, Schütte slipped past the Soviet sentries and crept up to a Red Army bunker. As he heaved the satchel inside, he shouted to the doomed Russians, 'Here's your bread!' Fighting his own war, he pulled off this crazy feat at least a couple of times. On the second occasion, I even heard the sound of the dynamite's explosion.[1]

It might have been imagined that the authorities would have disapproved of such freelance actions. Far from it. 'What had begun as an unauthorized action soon won the approval of our superiors,' wrote Lübbecke. 'On my and their recommendation, Schütte was later awarded one of Germany's highest military decorations, the Gold Cross.'[2]

There were other hazards too that winter that kept the blood of the Germans coursing fast. One was the intense skill of Soviet snipers. Lübbecke found that even as he was starting to acclimatize to the enduring dark, the ever-present danger from these marksmen kept him alert. 'As the snow grew to a foot in depth, it became much easier to travel by ski than on foot when I crossed the couple of hundred yards between the forward and rear bunkers,' he recalled in his memoirs of the winter landscape that had become his world. 'More importantly, skis allowed me to move much more swiftly across the open area that was exposed to the fire of Russian snipers.'[3] Sharpshooters had been posted in large numbers among the multistorey buildings at the edge of Leningrad's suburbs, approximately a mile away from the front line at Uritsk. This situation reflected the Red Army's effort throughout the war to field larger numbers of betterequipped, well-trained snipers than the Wehrmacht.

It also afforded him and his men an opportunity to pay tribute to their ever more determined enemy:

Our snipers considered the Soviet scoped rifles superior and preferred to use captured Russian weapons rather than the equivalent German rifle. When I once had the opportunity to test one, its precision amazed me. The accuracy of sniper fire meant that the number of killed relative to wounded was much higher than with other weapons. Our helmets protected us pretty well from glancing bullets or shrapnel, but if a bullet hit one squarely it would easily penetrate the steel. Being six feet tall, I soon learned to keep my head down and travel quickly through any area where I might be vulnerable. While snipers posed a great threat to us, most of our casualties at Uritsk resulted from the enemy's regular artillery barrages. The Red Army's artillery was highly accurate and equal to its German counterpart in capability.[4]

And this was one of the few reliefs from what Lübbecke described as 'the tedium of war'. Other diversions had their value. 'Gambling seemed foolish to me,' he wrote, 'but I frequently joined the other men in my bunker at night when they played a "thinking" card game called Skat at night.' That, plus drinking and smoking, also helped to divert attention away from a maddening and chronic complaint: the itching caused by lice.

Our basic uniform was completely inadequate in the subfreezing conditions we confronted at Uritsk. Once the quartermaster finally distributed our thickly padded white uniforms a couple of months into the winter of 1941–1942, they only proved to be barely sufficient to keep us warm in the harsh Russian climate. With only two uniforms, we laundered our clothes whenever our situation at the front made it possible. Wearing the same clothes and underwear for two or three weeks without changing, soldiers were almost always covered by itchy bites from the ubiquitous body lice, even in the cold of winter. You could feel them and see them crawling around on you. We would strip off our shirts to kill them, but could never rid ourselves of all of them.[5]

And so such concerns – from the constant torment of bodily infestation, to the awareness that one's head might be within a marksman's sights, to the sense that soon the Red Army would be prepared to launch vicious counter-attacks, and the fact that the hundreds of thousands of civilians they were besieging were miles away and out of sight – meant that the lives and the deaths of those civilians were almost impossibly abstract.

Those who sought to defend the city were finding their own ways to combat the torture of the lice. Red Army soldier Henrikh Dudnik was to recall years later a certain weird pride that he and his men managed to avoid ending up like their German enemies, their bodies swarming and teeming with parasites. There had been a point in the early months of 1942 when he and his unit suddenly came into close combat with a party of German soldiers in a dugout amid some birch woods. Dudnik's unit prevailed and were able to take prisoners. Dudnik recoiled. 'They were covered with lice,' he recalled.

The Red Army, he said, had its own methods of dealing with this battlefield torture:

> I would take a bucket of gasoline and soak my clothes in it. The clothes became clean, but had a yellowish hue. Back then we were outfitted with T-26 tanks, which had gasoline engines that were taken from aircraft. So we would use the aircraft fuel for laundry. There was no real need to wash it because you could just dip it in, put it on a tree, and then put it on in half an hour. This is how we avoided lice.[6]

There was no way of avoiding fear or pain, though. The Germans, if ill clothed, at least were well fed. Breakfast, for Dudnik and his men, largely revolved around 'crackers'. Later in the day – if the unit was lucky – there would be hot porridge. The miserable truth for huge numbers of soldiers in the Red Army amid those snowy woods was that they were consistently racked with hunger. There was never enough to eat. There were times when enemy fire might result not just in human death but also – if the men were fortunate – in horses being torn to pieces. The deafening echo of an explosion; a dismembered horse, with hunks of flesh hanging on the branches of a tree: such an event was to be celebrated. On those occasions when Germans were captured, there was also food to be found: carried in small bags on their belts. Here were fantasias of tinned goods: sardines and herring. There would also be sausage and bread. For Red Army soldiers, it was not merely the paucity of food that was torturous but also its grim monotony. So the delivery of horse flesh or garlic sausage danced on flattened tastebuds. In common with the citizens of Leningrad, these soldiers would gradually find the supply lines improving as the German military stranglehold was eased just a little.

One thing that Red Army troops never went short on was vodka. The official daily ration that Henrikh Dudnik and his men were given was 100 grams, sometimes more when casualties were high and the dead men's vodka ration was redistributed. Early in the war, when production lines in the east were working frantically to manufacture fresh weaponry, advancing into battle – crouched with four other men inside a tank – required fresh levels of faith and courage every single day. Which was worse – to be one of the infantry, riding outside the tank, open to every searing bullet, or to be crammed within that tight metal interior, aware that at any moment could come a supernova flash of light, followed by flame and black smoke and the prospect of being burned alive like a medieval martyr? 'How can I put it?' recalled Dudnik years later. 'You are in a tank driving toward the battlefield. It is unpleasant. You fear getting hit any second. With heavy tanks, the armour was a bit thicker, but it could still be pierced with thermite shells.'[7]

There came a point in early 1942 when Dudnik was convinced that death would have its day: 'The tank was pierced and a shell fragment hit me . . . I was even on fire, I still have a mark on my arm,' he recalled. 'My leg was hit so badly that it hung on by a thread. This was all near Leningrad.'[8] His comrades managed to fight through the flames: Dudnik was in no position to rescue himself. The others pulled him out, his leg dangling uselessly beneath him. They also managed to get him to some field medics; and from there he was transferred to hospital, where he spent six weeks. That was by no means the end of his war; he was back on the front line later in the year. But whereas the Wehrmacht troops, paralysed in those snowdrift-piled villages, were now in the position of waiting uneasily, the Red Army – drawing in troops from the far east of Russia, and from the southern Soviet republics of Kazakhstan and Uzbekistan – was now beginning to find fresh power, even amid the welter of bloody deaths and injuries. (The sheer number of conscripts, across the Red Army as a whole throughout the Great Patriotic War, is still quite impossible to comprehend other than as abstract images: some thirty-four million men in total. The losses were too huge for the mind to truly compute: nearly six and a half million killed in action, half a million cut down by disease and a further four and a half million missing or taken prisoner. The numbers on the Northern Front represented only a fraction of that total – but they were still dizzying.) The psychology of driving a hated invader out is markedly different from that of an army that can no longer quite see or even envisage its ultimate purpose.

All the while, the disintegrating lives of the people had been captured on film. Since the start of Operation Barbarossa back in June 1941, some twenty-two of Leningrad's cinematographers had – with the full assent of the city authorities – spent their days capturing the faces and the streets. They had boarded the trams and moved among the workers in the dockyards and the factories; they had been the companions of fire-watchers on roofs and captured moments when civilians in attics managed to grab hold of sparking, fizzing incendiaries and plunge them into sand-buckets. They had been swift to arrive at the zoo when a Luftwaffe bomb killed Betty the elephant. These cameramen had also been recording the first intimations of that terrible hunger: the coming of the snows, the immobilized buses and trams and then the bodies drawn along on sleds. Their gleaming lenses had been focused on bakery queues, and on the uniform black-coated lines, heads and bodies swaddled. Their cameras did not flinch from death. Their commission had been to capture all that happened: a very literal outbreak of Soviet realism. In the manner of Eisenstein, and his principles of montage, the task of this film team was to piece together an indelible visual record of Leningrad's war, including the evacuations across Lake Ladoga and their remarkable footage of the Red Army – white-clad, on skis, riding horses and driving tanks – processing through the weird beauty of those pine-forest battlefields.

Many of the images are unlikely ever to be widely seen. As the film – originally titled *The Defence of Leningrad* – was being edited for public exhibition in the spring of 1942, Zhdanov and his deputies viewed the initial rough cut and were horrified by how much suffering and hunger were depicted; how many images of grim food queues. Not all of the more harrowing images were disallowed, and death was acknowledged, but there had to be a narrative frame of movement, of progress, of defiance. The film that emerged – retitled *Leningrad in Combat* – remains an extraordinary exercise in the cinematic appropriation of events, and of time itself.[9]

The first cut had opened with a triumphal shot of the Bronze Horseman, suggesting the city's long pre-Communist history and hinting at a future in which such monuments would remain eternal. Zhdanov was having none of it, and so the re-edited film instead opened on the city's statue of Lenin. Shot from below, the great revolutionary, himself – like his embalmed corpse in Moscow – suspended in one moment of time – held the screen like a Colossus, gesturing out across the wide River Neva, and the prospect of canals, bridges and the busy naval dockyards.

The film's opening titles – with stirring string and brass music – were a precise echo of the aesthetics of the American film industry; the Russians might have laid claim to the form before Hollywood. And that melodically pleasing score continued as the film-makers laid out their reel of memories. Starting on 22 June 1941 – a montage of city loudspeakers, and of Leningraders gathered in the sunshine to listen to them – here was their experience rendered for them (and the world) to watch. As well as the incendiaries, and the shots of bomb damage, the winter footage told in part the story that Leningraders associated with themselves: men and women of all ages gathering in the public libraries, candles flickering everywhere, as they reached for books and sat reading. There was also a short sequence of a pianist – again, working by candlelight – setting his score up in his apartment and starting to play. This was the indomitable spirit of the cultured Leningraders, the film was saying. Yet there were also sharp, brief moments – acknowledgements – of horror: a body slumped in the snowy doorway of an apartment block and several passers-by stopping to see whether the figure was alive or dead. (The shot was not held long enough to provide an answer.) There were also scenes of cloth-wrapped corpses being drawn along the street. In one shot, the deceased had been afforded the very rare luxury of a real wooden coffin.

But this was supposed to be a film about spirit and inspiration: there was interesting footage of the supplies that had been brought in by plane, the aircraft manoeuvring on icy runways, the food being unloaded, then the planes turning round and taking off again. And certainly, the footage from the Road of Life − naturally, no trucks seen disappearing into the lethal waters − has its own kind of poetry: a large pair of vehicles in the forefront, acting as ploughs, so the night's snow is parted like the Red Sea, leaving just the clean ice below; then the vehicles follow. Despite the stirring music, and the reassuring voiceover, the cinematographers also captured the unsettlingly lifeless landscape: the vast heavy skies, the front lights of the vehicles trying to penetrate the steel-grey murk.

There was an emphasis on the military: artfully composed sequences of white-clad skiers speeding bravely towards German lines; forest-obscured artillery guns, the barrels rising out of snow-packed clearings, firing their shells towards the enemy. Leningrad had always been defended, the film suggested. The citizens need never have had any fear.

Brilliantly, there is also footage of Andrei Zhdanov himself, notably chubby and beaming, within the panelled offices of the Smolny Institute, surrounded by colleagues and greeting heroic soldiers who are being awarded medals. One has his hand vigorously pumped, but Zhdanov is overflowing with happiness: he then grabs the man in a full embrace and kisses him on the lips. The kiss is held for a few seconds. This is counterpoised with the city's clean-up, which the cameras contrive to make uplifting rather than squalid: streets filled with teams of people, using pneumatic drills to burrow into stubborn ice, shovelling pristine white snow (containing ordure) into open trucks which then move swiftly away. In a rare moment of unintended comedy, there is a shot of a watercolourist who has set up his easel in the street to capture the spectacle of the clean-up, as though this itself was a moment of purity to be commemorated.

How did this seem to the Leningraders who were trooping back into the city's reopened twenty-eight cinemas? The thaw is coming to the city, says the film, and with it the rising sap of renewal. A young woman – again, clearly chosen for her healthy appearance – is captured chatting flirtatiously with a young soldier. There may have been cynical Leningraders in the audience who wondered if she might have been one of the 'blockade wives' who stayed fed by dint of their sexual generosity. There are tank traps, barrage balloons and cheerful troops in trenches rolling themselves cigarettes. It seems curious now that this was a film about a siege that was still very much holding the city in its grip; yet the final shots show the statue of Lenin superimposed over naval yards and factories teeming with life and fully operational once more.

Those naval yards and factories were still targets; women and men were being killed on assembly lines. The German shelling was remorseless; death was random and instant. Even far from the city's most vulnerable targets, a sense of constant threat was palpable. 'I am distressed and very much afraid,' wrote the poet Vera Inber – strikingly, since she had herself spent time with the Red Army close to the front lines. 'I write about it without false shame. I am afraid.'[10] The talk among her friends was that the Germans were 'very close to the city'; somehow that menacing proximity felt all the sharper in the thaws of spring. Part of this might have been due to the clearer skies: after the thick swirls of snow that had filled the air, the advent of cold, fresh sunshine not only illuminated a city that partly lay in bisected ruins but also magnified the glory of the surviving Peter and Paul fortress, with its defiant spires, and the baroque wonders of St Isaac's Cathedral and the Hermitage – there was still so much left that the enemy had not managed to pulverize.

Neither was there a sense that that murderous presence was in any way being pushed back. And with the spring the shelling was accompanied by renewed assaults from bombers; the Luftwaffe had been freed from the near immobility of its frozen winter paralysis. The shock of their return was registered with bitterness as well as fear. The cruelty of it was that the gradual increase in rations – the intense sensual pleasure of hot broth, with vegetables and meat – had revivified a general appetite for life. Yet the news was of ever more death. 'Suddenly the air about the Neva was ripped, like silk,'

Georgii Knyazev wrote. 'And immediately a rumbling noise started up somewhere. Ahead of me the passers-by had already flattened themselves on the snow. All of this was stupefyingly sudden.' On another morning, another barrage: 'A shell whistling over my head, a second, a third . . . and bang! Bang! Bang!'[11] He survived: the shells had landed elsewhere; but across the city people had their skin shredded by shattered glass and others lost their hearing in those tremendous shock waves.

Leonard Polyak, the teenage electrician, had already witnessed so much death at his own factory: workers who had collapsed, emaciated and empty. The renewed aerial onslaught required a fresh nimbleness. 'Our factory was ten kilometres from the front line,' Polyak remembered. 'The front was three kilometres away from the Kirov Plant, and we were a bit farther away. There was a huge ship, the cruiser *Kirov*, next to our factory's wall. The Germans could see it very well.' The tempting targets were one thing, but the Germans had vantage points too, confirmed Polyak:

> There is an area called Duderhof, south of Leningrad. There is a place there called Voronya Hill, where we used to ski before the war. The hill was captured by the Germans and they could see the entire city from there. Our factory was an excellent target and it was shelled all the time. I found myself in a number of very difficult situations, and it was a miracle that I survived. Here is how we protected ourselves. Next to our [work] station, there was a tall boiler that had been removed from a steamship. It was two metres tall and very sturdy. We set up a space inside it and hid there during the attacks. It was safe.[12]

Yet the entropic effects of that winter were now starting to catch up with the young man; though Polyak had avoided scurvy (unlike many others), the steadily reduced rations had progressively weakened him, day by day, slowly and insidiously so that each degree of change was hardly noticeable. It was in the spring of 1942, as he was walking to the factory, that his body, without warning, gave way. 'In late March I collapsed from exhaustion on my way to work,' he recalled. 'I was picked up and taken to a nearby school that had been turned into a hospital. I do not remember being taken there. I came to. They nursed me back to health a little. I was in the hospital until mid-April. I have a document saying that it was second-degree dystrophy.'[13]

His survival was doubly fortunate. There was a hideous paradox that became apparent among the city's heavy industry workers in the spring of that year. Even though they had had marginally better rations, and closer access to heat and warmth and light and companionship, the mortality rates for these men and women suddenly started to climb precipitously. The attrition of strength was one thing, but also that spring the authorities – with the approval of the Kremlin – had started to step up military production once more. In the biggest of these factories, there were new and fresh and urgent demands being made upon the most high-skilled and experienced of the workers: longer hours, greater exertion. The moral pressure was enormous: the defence of the city rested upon their thin shoulders. But like Leonard Polyak, they had been silently wasting; for many, the new efforts were to prove fatal. In March and April 1942 deaths of factory and defence plant workers climbed to a terrible peak higher than that of the previous winter.

Elsewhere, while the evacuations were still in progress, there were fresh hazards to be faced by Leningraders. German bombs were dangerous enough, but the prospect of crossing twenty miles across the thinning ice of a thawing lake was perhaps even more so. Yelizaveta Zinger was a young girl when her family finally found their names on evacuation notices in the early spring, when the snow still lay upon the city but the branches of the trees were dewed with drips. First, they had to make their way to the Finland railway station, essentials carried behind them on sleds. They and other families then boarded a train that would take them close to the edge of Lake Ladoga. Yelizaveta was possibly too young to feel much foreboding at the prospect of what was to come, nor would the girl have heard any of the horror stories about the children and the mothers and the drivers who had fallen victim to German bombs hitting the ice. By March 1942 the bed of Lake Ladoga was punctuated with such trucks, the bodies still inside. A little later, with the ice ever more brittle, there would be one terrible day when some eighty trucks would disappear into the depths.

Yelizaveta made herself busy as her family prepared to be loaded into the back of a truck, looking out across that limitless expanse of ice. 'My sister did everything, while I looked after her son,' she later remembered. It was time to make the journey. 'There was ice on Lake Ladoga, but it was thin.'[14] On the train she had seen older evacuees succumbing at last to the winter starvation; even with the prospect of hope held out, they could not summon the strength for the journey to come. The girl was acutely aware of these deaths, and so perhaps this was what enabled her to face the truck with such equanimity. 'When we were transported across Ladoga, the driver took us across the lake, he knew a narrow path along which he could drive his three-ton truck,' she recalled. 'I told myself that this guy was a hero, this driver was a hero.' He was, as indeed were the White Angels – those women with ruby-red flags who helped to guide them. And on the other side of the lake lay the beginning of a new life. 'He brought us out, helped us to reach some church. It was heated, there was a stove. Of course, we rushed in to get warm.'[15] And from there – meeting with kindness and food and even the sound of laughter (many evacuees recalled how disorientating the noise was after months of grim silence) – began a route that would take her, her family, and so many others, to towns and cities thousands of miles to the south-east, to the warmth and the red sands of Uzbekistan.

It was too soon to smell the Leningrad lilac, one of the city's most emblematic blooms. Yet among those citizens who were now looking with fresh wonder at their slowly increasing rations, with the onset of thaw came a new and lively sense of Leningrad's natural life. There were also fresh moments of dazzling auditory wonder as in the Bolshoi and Nevsky prospekts an impossibly light, musical tinkling was to be heard: the bells of trams.

'The rails appeared from underneath the yard-deep snow, and the first tram went along them accompanied with the applause of thousands of people,' wrote the author Nikolay Tikhonov, with perhaps a shade of sugary exaggeration. 'It was not a swallow but a tram that brought the spring to Leningrad in 1942. The common hardships of the blockade knit the people closer together, and everybody in the first tram cars tried to be kind and considerate.'[16] The larger point was that vehicles that had remained motionless in the snow, without power or the human will to drive them, were now gradually being restored. The rumble along the rails was one thing, but the rough melody of the bells made hearts jump: they sounded like life.

22. Lilac

'In the Russian woman resides our only great hope, one of the pledges of our revival,' wrote the nineteenth-century novelist Fyodor Dostoevsky. In his great St Petersburg novel *Crime and Punishment*, published in 1866, the nihilist axe-murderer Raskolnikov can only find true salvation through Sonya, who – through her own sufferings as a Petersburg sex worker, a 'certified woman of the streets', as her own father describes her – is also emblematic of a certain idea of the strength of Russian womanhood. It is not enough for Raskolnikov to break down and confess his modernist evil; she, in her love for him, must help him bear the weight of it, and share with him the hard and stony road to redemption.[1] This idea of the Russian woman as the vessel of suffering – the one who endures – but also the figure who is most in touch with the soil and with the soul – was woven through Russian fiction. Tolstoy's idealized peasant women – radiating health, walking barefoot, wearing red neckerchiefs – were figures of strength, of immense sexual power, and ultimately the foundations of Russian character itself. When, in *War and Peace*, the worldly St Petersburg- and Moscow-haunting urban sophisticate Natasha starts dancing to the balalaika, as if entranced, it is as though the ancient truth of the Russian spirit is suddenly being communicated through her body.[2] In Leningrad in the spring and summer of 1942, the extraordinary strength and fortitude of the city's women – the women who had endured suffering and the deaths of their families, who had pulled bodies through the snow, who had cleared the homes and the streets of the dead and of their filth – was now subconsciously being linked by many with ideas of fertility and growth and regeneration.

'I would like to write verses and poems in praise of woman,' wrote Georgii Knyazev, 'as wife and companion. In praise of the wives who struggled and survived . . . Perhaps a future poet . . . will compose verses or a poem in praise of a wife who bore all burdens wholeheartedly and selflessly and supported her husband with all her might . . . the fact that I am alive I owe entirely to my wife.'³ Yet this was also an old, almost pre-Soviet way of thinking: in this new realm, women and men were equal. And the academic Knyazev had rather underplayed the essential structural centrality of women to the city throughout its ordeal: not merely helpmeets dedicated to the care of their husbands, but the engines of civic life itself. It was the women who populated the factories and the hospitals, and who laboured at multiple jobs to keep the semblance of civilization alive. But, perhaps in keeping with the characters created by those great nineteenth-century Russian novelists, it was also women who were beholding the city's parks and the gardens, gazing at the thawed, snow-cleared soil, observing the first blades of grass pushing through and under-standing the underlying pulse of life that could be harnessed in order better to defy their enemy.

It would not be long before the artists were capturing that quintes-sential Russian wartime image: women with headscarves, working the rich dark soil. But the fields being ploughed were the gardens and the parks and the public landscapes of Leningrad, the most striking of which, captured in a watercolour later reprinted on postcards sold throughout the Soviet Union, was that of furrowed earth in the pre-cincts before the proud domes of St Isaac's Cathedral: two Leningrad women tending the seeds, sowing for a more certain future.

Here was the archetype of Mother Russia: not merely signalling defiance to the enemy but also asserting a claim over a greater span of time than their German torturers could imagine. The agriculture in front of the cathedral was also captured in widely circulated pho-tographs: women in headscarves with large watering cans (and those watering cans had been made on special production lines – thousands of them); images that had a resonance that stretched back over one hundred years and, ironically, rather further back than the Stalinist industrialization of the collective farms. In this way, that constant pervasive fear in the city – the crawling sense that the Germans remained coiled around Leningrad like some gigantic venomous ser-pent, striking frequently and viciously – was in part allayed by this novel form of toil. But it was more than that too: from the little gardens and plots of land on Vasilyevsky Island to the larger parks (in part inhabited by anti-aircraft guns) that lay in the city's suburbs, here was purpose that was not merely defensive or reactive: it was instead productive. In this way, tiredness could be overcome: the sowing of all these seeds – the root vegetables, the green salad vegetables – was in itself fruitful.

The work took place under exposed skies: the ignorant malevolence of loosely targeted artillery, the shells that would not be seen before they pulverized the flesh. Explosions continued to tear the open ground apart. German firepower had also shattered the greenhouses of the city's botanical gardens throughout that cruel winter; even without these gaping sharded holes, the buildings would have been impossibly difficult to heat. Some of the rare plants had been evacuated to the city's hospitals. But now, out in the fitfully warming sun, this was labour that gave Leningraders something to look forward to: not merely an insurance against future hunger but also, more humanly, the intense sensual pleasure of tasting fresh food. In narrower strips near the Neva embankment, other seeds were sown: those of the brightest, most colourful flowers. These were not intended as food: rather, the Leningraders knew that after that monochrome winter of death, the eye would revel and delight in bright oranges, magentas, incarnadine reds. The music of birds was an accompaniment: both startling and giddyingly delightful.

The women of the city had for some time also been at the forefront of the most direct form of life preservation: blood donation. Since the beginning of Operation Barbarossa and through to the deepening autumn of hunger, the city's medical facilities had been asking for volunteers and many had gladly come forward: first, because there were husbands and brothers out on those front lines who might be in need of blood when wounded; second, because as the rations started becoming more slender, there was the incentive of additional biscuits or pieces of chocolate in order to aid recovery.

And those delivering the blood supplies were frequently themselves young women: the teenagers who had been signed up for nursing and ambulance-driving duties at the city's hospitals, who had observed the myriad incarnations of death and suffering that the hunger and

35. When death came in frozen apartments, all grieving families could do in many cases was load the corpses on to sleds and drag them to certain streets designated by the authorities for collection.

36. The final terrible stage of starvation: walkers who would collapse slowly into the snow, in trances of lethal apathy as death crept over in January 1942. Many bodies remained frozen in the streets.

37. Wood for coffins was a vanishingly rare luxury (it was needed for fuel); the bodies of infants were swaddled and consigned with all the others into mass graves.

38. The terrifying journey across the iced-over waters of Lake Ladoga: many lost their lives in the depths – but the 'Road of Life' opened up a supply line and ended the city's fearful isolation.

39. As deaths ran into the hundreds of thousands, the survivors faced the prospect of a spring thaw unfreezing the accumulated filth, bringing plague: a desperate city-wide clean-up ensued.

40. Leningrad's factories had long needed the heavy labour of women; not just because of the siege and the war, but also because of the Stalinist purges some years beforehand.

41. The ultimate display of artistic defiance: Shostakovich's Seventh Symphony (Leningrad) received its 1942 premiere in the besieged city, the performance relayed out on speakers so encamped Wehrmacht soldiers outside the city could hear.

42. Before the war, agricultural workers forced into the city had brought with them cultivation skills; by the summer of 1942 these were deployed in all of the city's green spaces.

43. The labour of women was foundational to the besieged city; not least in the mighty armament factories that were supplying the newly resurgent Red Army.

44. General Leonid Govorov (*left*) was an artillery expert who brought lateral thinking inspiration to the fight against the Wehrmacht; he had also retained his Orthodox faith, even as the authorities sought to smother the Church.

45. The fighting around Leningrad was continually brutal and bloody for months on end in 1942 and 1943; both sides struggling amid forests and swamps, mosquito heat and lethal cold. Every push by the Red Army would be countered by a Wehrmacht that dug in with venomous strength.

46. There were times in the nearby woodlands and marshes in 1942-3 that – when not covered with snow – trench mazes became tank-trapping bogs.

47. January 1944, and General Govorov's artillery, in combination with the weight of the Red Army, finally drove the Wehrmacht back: the siege was broken, and the exultation was intense.

48. The speed at which civic life was restored was startling; but the pulsing pain of grief – from innumerable little orphans onwards – was still too great to absorb.

49. In January 1944, with the Wehrmacht beaten back and the siege lifted, Red Army cavalry surveyed the (landmined) ruins of the once imposing Peterhof Palace.

50. Those Leningraders who had been evacuated returned in 1944 to a city described by poet Anna Akhmatova as a 'terrible ghost'.

51. The fireworks – golden, red and green – and vast naval lights that marked the end of the siege in January 1944 looked to the thousands of onlookers at the river banks like miracles; the city had been in darkness since 1941.

52. By the 1960s, youth culture had entered even Leningrad. But pop music was policed, and gatherings of young people had little chance for subversion.

53. It was into this gaunt, torn city that Vladimir Putin was born in 1952. His parents had lost their first child to starvation during the siege. A shadow remains on the city today.

54. The cemeteries were filled with unmarked mass graves; the identities of so many dead were obliterated. But the city came to be filled with passionate, heartfelt memorials.

the cold had brought. Anna Novikova – one such teenager – had been through those months and was herself reeling from a continual lack of sleep. What sustained her were her friendships with the other young women who had similarly been called up for these strenuous duties.

'There were loads of wounded coming from the front,' she recalled years later. 'They were a terrible sight: dirty wounds . . . It was horrible.' That said, she was consistently impressed with the stoicism of these men. 'The patients were so good,' she remembered. 'They didn't grimace, didn't even ask for much. They only said, "Dear nurse, could I get something to drink?" or "Dear nurse, it hurts a lot over here." ' In a time of privation – and this extended to a number of medical supplies too – sometimes the only care that could be given was psychological. 'What could we do?' said Anna Novikova. 'We touched the spots where the pain was, and it seemed to ease the pain a bit.'[4]

As with the city outside, there was no way that the ravages of hunger could be held back: they spread like a plague. Anna Novikova recalled how 'dystrophy began spreading within the hospital. Not only the patients, but also the staff started getting sick.' Many were instructed to gather essential belongings, and to join the families who were embarking across the ice of the Road of Life. Anna Novikova was not among them. 'But nevertheless, we were young,' she recalled. 'We believed that everything would be OK.' This was even the case when the monstrous tide of deaths came not in the winter but cruelly in the first weeks of the spring of 1942. As well as all those dying in the factories, there were huge numbers of soldiers – either also weakened or wounded – who were not going to survive. 'When I recall now how the wounded died . . . they were rolled up in rags and stacked,' said Anna Novikova. 'A car would come, and they were loaded in the car like firewood, and the car transported these dead soldiers to the Bogoslovskoe or Piskaryovskoye Cemetery. It was a horrible sight.'[5]

She was also part of the general drive to keep the city's levels of donated blood high: so vital to so many of those men on her wards. 'I was given another responsibility: I had to go pick up donated blood,' she said. 'The Blood Transfusion Institute was on 2nd Sovetskaya

Street. It was twelve kilometres [seven and a half miles] from our hospital. So I would walk one way, get the blood, but then had no strength left for the walk back.'[6]

In that spring of 1942 blockade life was transforming into something quite new. The city's wellspring of creativity started coursing once more. The much-loved comedian Arkadii Raykin – who had been touring the country's front lines, bringing appreciated and uninhibited laughter to troops who otherwise had only 100 grams of vodka to look forward to each day – was granted an honour by Leningrad that brought him back to the city: he was given control of the Leningrad Theatre of Miniatures, the music-hall-type venue through which comic criticism of the regime and its stereotypes had somehow evaded punishment by the authorities. Moreover, this feat of survival had extended to the grimmest days of the siege, as some of its hungry actors insisted on continuing to appear on the stage through the winter. By January 1942, in the depths of the frost and with the ovens of the bakeries cooling in the power outages, only then were its doors shut and the performances cancelled. The advent of light, the renewed hum of power and the fresh regularity of supplies across Lake Ladoga once more changed the situation. It would soon be time for the theatre to begin regular, full-scale performances again. It was by no means alone.

Zhdanov and his Party deputies were also thinking about high culture, and about the importance of the city reasserting its sense of self. To this end, on 1 March 1942 a decree was issued recalling the artists of the Kirov Theatre. They had not gone far; most were still at home on paid leave, struggling like everyone else to find warmth and sustenance. Many had performed in concerts for troops: sailors at Kronstadt who became tearful at any chorus of rising voices in harmony, a glint of beauty in an ugly, grey and bloody world. The baritone Ivan Nechaev had performed regularly with a company called the Ensemble of the Red Banner of the Baltic Sea Fleet.[7] This became a weekly fixture: a live concert given for soldiers, and in part by soldiers, that was also broadcast on the radio. Nechaev would conduct, and every week he would tell the troops, active and wounded, to send in their special requests. These would be sifted and selected and passed back to Nechaev by the city's Radio Committee. The bulk of those writing wanted to hear old Russian folk songs. In this, their tastes were close to that of their supreme leader, but that was not the reason for their impulsion: those old songs were the songs of the generations, and of the dead. Their performance was intensely moving and transfiguring for many, playing upon the most sensitive chords of the heart. To this end, Nechaev himself also became the conduit for the most piercing memories; years later, Leningraders would remember both the music and the sound of his voice as one of the period's rare comforts.

Also remarkable was an even more venerable Kirov company tenor called Pavel Andreyev, who had the distinction of entertaining troops in both world wars. Andreyev's operatic speciality was the larger Russian roles – Prince Igor, Boris Godunov. Perhaps his battle-weary audiences were susceptible to sentimentality, but he was famed for being able to reduce vast crowds of men to tears. When the blockade of Leningrad began in earnest, he was one of the cultural treasures that the authorities sought to protect through evacuation, but Andreyev was having none of it. He and his wife Lyubov Andreyeva-Delmas insisted that they were staying. 'All the performers must not leave the city,' he said. 'Who will entertain the fighters in their brief hours of leisure and inspire them to feats of arms? If I have to, then I have enough courage and strength to take up a rifle.'[8]

And in Leningrad, no matter how much ordnance was being launched at the city, its palaces of rich culture had to open once more. There were opera singers with the Kirov Theatre like Sofiya Preobrazhenskaya; and ballet dancers such as Yevgeniya Gempel and Tatyana Shmyrova, thin and unrehearsed, yet ready to stand before the lights once more.

And as well as the Kirov Theatre, there was also the Musical Comedy company, based at the Pushkin Theatre, which staged the lighter, happier operas. There are photographs from that time of tickets being sold in the streets outside, and they conjure a sense that the city was also reaffirming its own exceptional heritage. The musicians were recalled – at least, those who had survived. Again, remarkably, numbers of them had managed to continue deep into the midwinter, until the point when the entire city had come juddering to a halt. But they too were deemed essential by the city authorities. The Leningrad Philharmonic was proof not only of life and soul – its fresh concerts not just for those in the auditorium but also relayed via radio to listeners across the city – they were also there to deliver a signal to the Wehrmacht soldiers so immovably encamped around the city's suburbs: the music was there to perplex and to confound. These armies had come to exterminate: and yet from the spires and the speakers of Leningrad issued forth the sweetest classical Russian music; the most aesthetically extraordinary defiance of death.

Among all these performers was Nadezhda Velter, an opera singer who in early April sang the title role in *The Maid of Orléans* at the Kirov Theatre; the performance had been broadcast live on the city's radio stations. She recalled the unavoidable poignancy of this return. Her husband Georgii Tsorn was a set designer for the theatre, and after the show she asked him how he thought her voice, and the voices of her fellow company members, had held up. 'I wasn't really listening,' he told her. 'I couldn't take my eyes off your terribly thin faces.'[9]

A ballet performance at the Philharmonic Hall at the beginning of April also cruelly underlined the suffering of the past few months: it had hardly been possible for even the most experienced dancers to maintain anything like the muscle tone that they required. Ballerina and dance teacher Vera Kostrovitskaya recalled with a little incredulity how she and her fellow dancers were pressured into rehearsing standard choreography from *Swan Lake* – a piece to be largely staged for the apparatchiks of the Smolny Institute – and also how the lack of food made them less than steady; there were also the 'blue marks' of scurvy on the dancers' legs. And – as seemed the case across a number of the city's endeavours – it was men who were more debilitated than women. She also recalled how a young male dancer called Petia Korsakov had had extra make-up applied to give the illusion that he was 'living'. Under duress, he performed two dances; backstage, some of the ballerinas tried to help him out with scraps of bread and oil and kasha (buckwheat). 'On stage I led him by the arms as he "danced",'[10] recalled Kostrovitskaya. Off-stage, he fell into a semi-collapse and vomited the kasha. A little after this, continual chronic illness forced him to his bed; and a little later than that, the young man died.

By the spring of 1942, the women of Leningrad were also being asked to volunteer for military service with the Red Army. By this stage, those women were already absolutely central to the city's ever more active armament manufacture: on the production lines for land-mines, 77 per cent of the workers were women; for tank production, 64 per cent were women; in general terms, women made up some 75 per cent of all Leningrad's heavy-industry workforce.

An account of one production line, by Nikolay Tikhonov – in propaganda terms, the literary equivalent of the film *Leningrad in Combat* – was no less fascinating in its granular detail:

> The [enemy] planes are being watched . . . from the grounds of a big factory, where women who have taken the place of the men are working in the enormous workshops. They work intently and in silence. It is not easy for them to do work which requires great physical strength, skill and endurance, but they are persevering and accurate. A woman with blue spectacles over her eyes is turning a shell on a lathe. Her whole body is strained, but you can see by her confident, powerful movements that she is no longer a novice. Showers of big, white sparks play on her hands in their thick gauntlets . . . From time to time she wipes the sweat from her face and listens to the thunder of our guns. Their roar stimulates her tremendously.[11]

There is something oddly touching about the sheer universality of such propaganda: Tikhonov might just as well have been writing of female munitions workers in Derby or Birmingham. He continued:

> A few miles away from them their menfolk are standing in the trenches with their rifles in their hands. They write back short let-ters and notes, which are brought to the factory, and the women take them with their silvery hands. These women were not factory

workers in peace-time. They include young girls who have come straight from school and quite elderly women, but they are now all one fighting family.[12]

Yet syrupy though Tikhonov's account was, it was most certainly the case that Leningrad's women were leaning ever harder into the conflict, rather more pressingly than his own male eyes could see. In the spring, through the Komsomol, more was being asked of them: to take up arms, to train to fight. The immediate cause would have been piercingly apparent to all who had menfolk fighting in the Red Army: the losses had been shocking and prodigious, and throughout Russia women were very much needed to take on a huge variety of military roles. So it was that the training began: they were to be everything from radio operators to drivers to signalling couriers. But there were heavier tasks as well: large numbers would be needed for anti-aircraft duties. There would also, in time, be special women's rifle brigades and regiments, and there were already women fighter pilots, dubbed the 'night witches'. As the war progressed, the Red Army across the Soviet Union would come to take on some 500,000 women, most in rear service units, but a great many out fighting on or near the front. There were women snipers, spoken of with some awe not merely for their cool heads but also for their lethal accuracy. Although Stalinist Russia was a patriarchal society, there seemed little surprise at the ruthless determination and brilliance of some of these women recruits.

The women of Leningrad showed no lack of enthusiasm for volunteering; the only difficulty was that many of them lacked the robustness of women drawn from other parts of the Soviet Union, unoccupied and with full access to fresh food. None the less, the children of the city looked on with some admiration as Komsomol members registered their new recruits, and platoons of women marched down wide avenues on their way to training sessions, wearing raincoats and carrying their newly issued rifles. Their new responsibilities brought a real sense of satisfaction to a great many women: fresh from the better conditions and rations of the mighty industrial production lines, here were opportunities for ever more diverse rations and also a genuine sense of pride after that harrowing winter. Here too was not merely fresh purpose but also the chance to engage in a deeply moral battle for the future of their families, their city and their nation. 'Glory to our servicewomen!' ran the slogan on a stirring mass-produced Leningrad propaganda postcard:[13] in this instance, the servicewoman was depicted by the artist carrying a medical bag, while standing alongside tanks and male troops with guns. But from the start, Leningrad's women were acquiring a much broader range of military training. In the Dzerzhinsky district – a central working-class area later to be the childhood home of Vladimir Putin – female recruits, dressed in freshly received quilted jackets, were being taught to use machine guns.

Here was also an encapsulation – in a modern sense – of the Tolstoyan vision of the strength of Russian women. Leningrad's munitions workers were the descendants of those indomitable peasant folk. A great many Leningraders had passed through some form of barrier; having lived through the hell of ice and darkness, and having emerged into the light, it seemed as though the more ordinary fears had been cauterized. The German artillery shells continued to fall, and Leningrad women continued to work.

But more than this: that city-wide sense of the distortion of time – the metronome ticks, the silence of the starving winter darkness where minutes and hours froze into one motionless mass – was starting to dissolve. With the coming of the sun – and the lifelines of supplies, and the sweet melodies performed in the theatres and concert halls – days were once more imbued with meaning, with purpose and a palpable sense of momentum. 'The lime trees along the Botanical Gardens by the Nevka river have already begun to bloom,' wrote Vera Inber. She observed how, in a little wooden house 'on the other side of the Karpovka, a gramophone was playing captured German records and young militia girls listened to the music, hanging out of the windows.'[14] There was something giddyingly insouciant about this image of youth. News was broadcast on the public loudspeakers: there was 'a treaty of friendship with Great Britain', as Inber noted excitedly 'the journey of Molotov to London [and the Allied] decision to open a Second Front'. She was premature about a second front: despite Stalin's agitated entreaties to Churchill and Roosevelt, the Allies were still in no position to land in Europe, thus relieving some of the crushing weight from Russian shoulders. Yet each day's military developments – those public broadcasts giving updates on every inch of land where the Red Army had gained advantage – were part of a general restoration of keen, vital activity. Time speeded up once more: just as the trams once more speeded down those wide boulevards.

This restoration extended to the way that food once more divided the day into recognizable meals. Breakfast, lunch, dinner: tables set, porridge bubbling and gulping, pans sizzling. 'Nowadays people experienced hunger less often but were constantly striving to prevent it,' observed Lidiya Ginzburg, 'for the very reason that they experienced it less often.'[15] As with the memory of pain, the exact sensation could not be recalled but the desire to prevent it recurring was intense. As time reverted to its normal course, so the immediate smothering of hunger pangs – and the forgotten luxury of smooth digestion – gradually became normalized once more.

Everyone knew that the ordeal was far from over; the talk in ration queues and in factory canteens was all about the daily military developments further afield, from Sevastopol to Moscow. As well as the reawakening of the lime trees, the seeded flowerbeds now burst forth in scarlets and indigos. There was once more the suggestion of lilac: a delight to all those whose olfactory senses had until recently known only human decay. And from this point, even amid continuing casualties, the people of Leningrad started to acquire a fresh incarnation.

23. 'Listen, comrades!'

'We are separated from Russia, ideologically and racially, by a deep abyss,' declared General Georg von Küchler. 'Russia is, if only by the mass of her territory, an Asian state.'[1] One of the logical weaknesses of abhorrent prejudice is that it works upon the assumption that everyone in the persecuted enemy group thinks the same way. But that was very much not the case in Leningrad. These words had been uttered by the sixty-year-old who had succeeded Field Marshal von Leeb, taking control of the Wehrmacht's Army Group North at the start of 1942. Like his predecessor, he had no aversion to the idea or the practice of mass murder. He had fought on the Somme during the First World War. A Prussian Junker, he had, in the wake of Germany's defeat, joined the Freikorps: an enthusiastically psychopathic right-wing paramilitary group. His participation consisted of fighting (or frequently murdering) communists in Poland. Come the Second World War, he was commanding brilliantly successful regiments powering through Belgium and France. And although there were some suggestions that he was fastidious about his troops not being associated with civilian atrocities – causing tensions with the SS – von Küchler was enthusiastic about his Führer, and about his wider aims. Von Küchler's deep racism went beyond evocations of 'Asia'. And it was the war in the east that liberated and gave full expression to this murderous hatred. In the earlier stages of Operation Barbarossa, across the Baltic states, and into Russia, he had overseen not only episodes of anti-Semitic savagery, but also the murder of the mentally disabled.

There are the sorts of generals who hold a respect and even admiration for their adversaries, and then there are those who simply wish to see them all exterminated. The sense of life as being something simply to be extinguished utterly is passed on down through the ranks, as it was to von Küchler's men: the exhortations about the inhumanity of the Soviet commissars dinned into them even as their own supply lines thinned in that lethal winter. Von Küchler's zeal for wiping out the enemy matched that of Hitler. The general took his new command with a boiling energy, and in the first weeks of 1942, his forces faced a fresh and serious counter-offensive from the Red Army: the Volkhov and Leningrad fronts combining in forested territory some fifty-five miles south of Leningrad to try to break the German hold on the city. The hope was that by deploying a scissor movement slicing through one strategic section of the Wehrmacht, very close to the main Leningrad to Moscow railway line, they might prise wider the route through which food, ammunition and more men might be funnelled. The prospect, at the start of that year, was arduous: uneven forests and bare plains enveloped with snow, with temperatures inhumanly low. Moreover, the terrain was such that the usually effective Red Army tanks had no chance of getting through. This meant instead that the rolling series of attacks would have to be carried out by infantry, with artillery awkwardly manoeuvred through this grim wet landscape, and launching fire at men who would be well aware of their slow approach. This was some distance from the cheerful propaganda of the films that would be shown to Leningraders: instead, the four-month-long Battle of Lyuban (the town and its surrounding territory some fifty-five miles south-east of Leningrad, south of Lake Ladoga) would prove a blood-soaked humiliation for the Soviets.

The horses struggled in the cold, sucking soil. The Germans were dug in, with good cover and defensive positions, amid gentle hills overlooking fields of dark earth, and were difficult to hit with any efficacy. Nor could the slow-moving Soviets offer any degree of surprise. In addition to this many of them were in poor condition: the scant rations had left them weak and there were outbreaks of scurvy. They were also filthy, and continually cold. There was little opportunity for washing, nor could the cold be alleviated with the saunas that many were used to. Supply lines were erratic: fresh materiel arrived fitfully. The idea had been for the Soviet armies to encircle the German soldiers; instead, they themselves became the prey among those trees as the Wehrmacht struck back, in an operation that von Küchler's commanders dubbed 'Wild Beast'. The Red Army soldiers also faced menace from their own side: NKVD agents were embedded to ensure that any man who tried to escape an attack, or evade fire, would himself face the bullets of those behind him. And so, as each day brought fresh death, the men hit by German ordnance that brought orange flame to pine treetops – instant countless burned cinders, themselves projectiles, burrowing through flesh – the battle blazed on.

In this corner of the bitter struggle for Russia there was, for both the Red Army and the commanders who plotted to outmanoeuvre the defending Germans, the prospect of despair: no matter how many attempts were made to smash through the enemy lines, they seemed unbreachable. The Soviet soldiers serving in this territory were perfectly well aware of the horror that the Leningraders had been living through: although every letter sent from the city was strictly censored by an entire department of apparatchiks, it was still well understood that the Lake Ladoga lifeline – trucks on ice, soon to be succeeded by regular shipping amid the thaws of spring – was intensely vulnerable. After several excruciating months had passed, with both sides locked in a ghastly death-grip amid those woods, and with Soviet deaths climbing to over 95,000 men, von Küchler's Wehrmacht forces prevailed. The Red Army's General Andrei Vlasov was captured.★

The losses on both sides at the Battle of Lyuban were shocking but they still brought von Küchler no closer to the streets of the city that he was under orders to destroy. In the freezing landscapes to the east and to the north, the Red Army's own defences were stubborn and

---

★ From this point, his own career became byzantine in its complex layers of treachery. This Russian Orthodox seminary student turned lifelong soldier had risen through the Red Army before the war, being sent as a military adviser to Chinese revolutionary nationalist Chiang Kai-shek. Then, as Germany invaded Russia, he had fought in the battle for Moscow, and had been highly decorated. Now, in the hands of the Germans, he decided that he would join them. It was suggested that vicious encounters with the NKVD had made him a fervent anti-Stalinist. And for a time, there was an idea that General Vlasov would form a military squad that would aim to destabilize Stalin and his regime.

ineluctable. Those Russian soldiers were ever mindful of their other foes: the Finnish soldiers to the north, on the Karelian Isthmus. They were also well aware of the power of propaganda, played out for an international audience, for by the spring and the summer of 1942 rumours were being whispered around Leningrad that Churchill and the British might soon be in a position to aid them further. There seemed to be little ideological recoil from any sort of communist–capitalist alliance; many were still reading the works of Sir Walter Scott and Charles Dickens. No matter that the British establishment had sought to help defeat the Bolsheviks in the post-revolution civil war; there none the less remained a cultural understanding. If the British could see how bravely the Red Army was fighting their mutual fascist foe, then they would surely redouble their efforts to open a second front in Europe. To this end, a series of front-line dispatches were being prepared – in part for the people of Leningrad, but also in part for a sympathetic British and American public. Nikolay Tikhonov was posted among the troops into the deceptively peaceful and beautiful forests of Karelia:

> This is the land of pine-trees and water. The lakes entice you to plunge into their shining waters. All is dead-still in the thickets, the marshes are quiet, and only the frogs croak their endless song in the evenings. There is no sign of a human being anywhere. Here and there ruined houses lift up the remains of their charred walls, and lines of barbed wire stick out of the ground. The men have dug themselves in deep in the earth.[2]

Here was a killing ground of stealth, as he observed:

> You can watch a moss-covered tree-stump for hours. It is motionless. Anyway, how can a stump move? Yet it does sometimes just barely stir, for in fact it is not a stump, but a sniper. The mosquitoes dance around him, the birds sing in the bushes, and somewhere a cuckoo – a real grey bird – utters its twofold call. Suddenly a single shot cracks. The echo rumbles over the waste land, and all is quiet once more. There is one soldier less on the Finnish side; the sniper has wiped out that Finn.

He takes out his score-card and adds another stroke to the long column already there. The tree stump changes its position imperceptibly and the sniper is already watching and waiting again. Another shot, and another enemy the less. A volley comes from the enemy's side, but it finds no target, it is too late. There is nobody there now.

Gone are the days when the Finns strutted about upright, or worked in the forward positions. Now they crouch as they run along the trenches and dig themselves in as deeply as possible. Sometimes they call out: 'Russ, Russ, give us some bread! Give us some bread!'[3]

There was some truth in this taunt: some Finn soldiers had indeed been assiduous about mocking the horrific starvation of Leningraders. For that, grim vengeance had been served.

Yet there was another sense in which the Finns were not deserving of complete contempt: the Germans had tried to persuade their military commanders, headed by Mannerheim, to join with them in striking the final blow to Leningrad. But Mannerheim would not assent. The Finnish army would continue to fight for what it regarded as its territory, and it would continue to block supplies, sometimes even attacking the vehicles and vessels crossing Lake Ladoga; but they would not make that definitive killing push.

Meanwhile, despite the horrible losses of the Battle of Lyuban, the Soviet forces in the region were beginning to regroup and rethink. This fresh approach was epitomized by the new commander placed in charge of the Volkhov and Leningrad fronts: General Leonid Govorov, a stolidly handsome forty-four-year-old with an intriguing hinterland, a mind that was given to outbreaks of independence and a unique insight into the particular military knot that Leningrad was trying to unpick. Govorov had spent part of his youth in St Petersburg (in its Petrograd incarnation), studying and working in engineering at the Polytechnic Institute. At the tail end of the First World War he was drafted into an artillery unit: but then came the fires of the Russian revolution. With the bullets of civil war now filling the air, Govorov was conscripted not into the Red Army, but into the Whites, who were fighting the Bolsheviks. The bloody brutality of that conflict in some ways exceeded that of the Great War – the cruelties inflicted upon civilians meant that, for them, the war had not come to an end at all – and something within Govorov snapped quite early on. By November 1919 he had deserted the White forces. First, he fought with some partisans at Tomsk, deep in Russia; then he formally joined the Red Army.

That civil war took him to Crimea and Odesa; it saw him caught up in sieges. But it also saw Govorov – an assiduous and attentive learner – acquiring expertise in artillery. After the war, as Bolshevik society was consolidated, he continued his military career in Odesa, and married Lidiya Izdebska.[4] According to their son Sergei, speaking many years later, part of Govorov's initial allure for Lidiya was his special 'red revolutionary trousers', which he 'flaunted'.[5] The speciality of artillery led Govorov to a military academy, and thence to Kyiv military district, where he studied further. The darkness of Stalin's purges closed in around him – Govorov's transgressions nameless – and it was only the testimonies of admiring superiors that saved him from near-random execution, being shot in the back of the neck. What made this slightly curious – given that so many other tens of thousands of victims were also wholly blameless – was the stark fact of Govorov's spell fighting for the vicious perceived fascists of the White Army. That alone would have been more than sufficient for a death sentence in those weird, febrile, paranoid days. (Many years later, Govorov's grandson Aleksei had his own theory about why Govorov had been spared when so many other loyal military figures were murdered: 'Stalin appreciated his professional qualities, as well as the fact that Leonid Aleksandrovich and his wife were very modest people,' he said. 'Grandfather did not like any gatherings and parties, he did not get involved in politics. He was immersed in professional matters and completely devoted to his work . . . This must have protected him from repressions and saved his life.')[6]

Then had come service in the Winter War with Finland in 1939–40: all those initial defeats on those silent, snowy paths and then – with the help of his artillery expertise – the push to blaze through the Mannerheim Line. The German invasion had taken Govorov to the defence of Moscow, once more taking command of the artillery effort to repel the Wehrmacht. And in the spring of 1942, he was the man regarded by Stalin as holding the means to cut through that German knot. The Wehrmacht had been attacking Leningrad mainly by means of artillery, those illimitable shells turning brick into searing powder. Perhaps the means to counter them would also lie with artillery, and its brilliant tactical use.

There is a striking photograph of Govorov and Leningrad overlord Andrei Zhdanov deep in conference in December 1942: Govorov intense and Zhdanov looking quite remarkably rounded in the circumstances. This was not yet a time for optimism: in the south, the Wehrmacht forces, having left Ukraine slick with blood, were besieging Sevastopol. Moscow was still, at a distance, menaced. But the advent of commanders like Govorov also suggested that there was an intractable youth and energy on the Soviet side; that this war, which had been about defence and endurance, was now on the brink of taking on a different character. Young Ukrainian soldier Anatoly Kibrik, who himself was drafted to the Leningrad front in 1942, recalled being very impressed because Govorov seemed like something of a new breed of officer. 'Colonel-General Govorov had just been appointed commander of the front,' recalled Kibrik. 'He was a former officer of the Russian General Staff, slender and fit. He was very different from the bandit-generals. I remember now how he said: "Sonnies, take care of yourselves." We had never been talked to like that.'[7]

Yet here was a commander who also seemed to have a charmed relationship with his lethal leader: on one occasion, Govorov was summoned to Stalin's office and asked what he needed to smash the German positions around Leningrad. Govorov immediately requested more tanks. Stalin replied that he had no more tanks to give him – except one. With that, he pointed to a novelty inkwell on his desk shaped like a tank. With wry humour, Govorov thanked the leader, leaned forward and pocketed it. He was said to have kept it as a souvenir.

Even as the depleted city of Leningrad started slowly to find a semblance of simple physical comfort – warming sunshine, running water, light to read by – the horror remained with all the citizens: it was there in the still-blank eyes of the innumerable orphans who had not been evacuated. And General Govorov was now having to think about a German army that appeared to have every natural advantage. As his colleague Major General Grigorii Kulik was to write a year later:

> During the long months of the siege [the Wehrmacht] created a strongly fortified area with a ramified system of permanent ferro-concrete defences and a great number of anti-tank and anti-infantry obstacles. Moreover, the German fortifications were based on exceedingly advantageous natural obstacles on the left bank of the Neva, i.e., in the sector where our troops broke through. Here the Germans had before them an entirely open expanse of water up to eight hundred yards in width. Even when frozen the river was an exceedingly strong barrier, as there were no means of taking cover on the ice. The whole of it was under observation and covered by fire from the steep bank the enemy occupied. The height of the bank in the sector of the break-through is from fifteen to thirty-six feet, and the Germans had strengthened this natural barrier with a network of barbed-wire entanglements reaching right out on to the ice, and with mine-fields, etc. Right along the bank of the Neva were two and three lines of trenches, linked together with communication passages with firing points, strong points and block-houses with loopholes. On every mile of the front the enemy had up to twenty-two firing points, which covered the river with dense fire at many levels.[8]

But the roar of renewed industry, the steadily improving food supplies, the schools reopening for the children who remained and the efflorescence of theatre and cinema, unimpeded by the almost constant shelling from those German positions miles away, was turning the mood of Leningrad: bitter defiance was on the brink of something rather more ferocious. General Govorov's encounter with Stalin would have intrigued many Leningraders if they could have heard it at the time. There was evidence in the city of increasing scepticism towards the ruling class; evidence that was being monitored very closely by Andrei Zhdanov and the officers of the NKVD.

'Down with the Stalinist regime. Too much blood has been shed. Three and a half million people are perishing and there is no end in sight. The time has come to help the Hitlerite army. Down with Stalin's reign. It can only lead to the people's ruin.'[9] At the bottom of this handwritten note was an exhortation to anyone reading it to make five copies and pass them on to friends and associates and colleagues with the same instructions. Other sorts of chain letters had been relatively common in Leningrad since the start of the war, mainly those invoking either superstition or God, and their purpose had been to confer a sort of charmed protection upon whoever passed them on. This particular chain letter was on a different and more openly treasonous level, and as such the authorities took it seriously: Comrade Zhdanov was informed. In this instance, the chain was traced back to a nurse and a building manager. But there had been chain letters and leaflets in factories too. Just because it was now possible once more for people to sit outside in the sun, to walk by the river, to enjoy films – simple pleasures made unthinkably sweet by the ordeal they had just endured – did not mean that all the people had forgiven the authorities for failing to protect them.

There had been vivid outbreaks of anti-Semitism, also in the form of anonymous leaflets: vicious wishes that the invaders might come for Jewish neighbours. There were also those among the workers who made public their complete lack of faith in the Red Army. One man was noted as remarking: 'The only reason the Germans aren't bombing is because they're hoping to take Leningrad without having to do that.'[10] Contrary thinking also came in another form that neither the city authorities nor Stalin himself appeared able to quell: the impulse towards religion. The chief archimandrite of Leningrad, Metropolitan Aleksii, remained very visible: in services at St Nicholas's Cathedral, he carried an icon. Several Red Army soldiers appeared frequently at Leningrad services, the most prominent and visible of whom was none other than General Leonid Govorov. There was no possibility that he or his men could be denied their spiritual sustenance. Even more strikingly, when it came to the very gradual improvement of rations, the handful of churches in Leningrad that had been allowed to continue with Orthodox services were now also allocated flour and wine: it was once more possible for worshippers to take communion. Elsewhere in the city, the one remaining functioning synagogue was similarly welcoming Jewish worshippers. Faith by itself could not be counted as dissidence, despite what Leningrad's League of the Militant Godless wished all its citizens to understand. Moreover, the Russian Orthodox Church had done a very great deal of work to raise money for the Red Army; in Leningrad alone, millions of roubles had been collected. The Church was soon able to dedicate a tank, among its other financial achievements.

What the rational atheists were never able to fathom was how Leningrad's believers simply could not help their faith; that it was as natural to some people as breathing. There were a few Leningraders who had written anonymous chain-letter jeremiads about how the city had suffered so atrociously because Stalin had not let the churches prosper. But in the circumstances of that apocalyptic calamity, the structured faith of Russian Orthodoxy did not threaten counter-revolution. Conversely, unquenched anger and nihilist depression might. Turning to God was one thing; threatening to turn to the Nazis was another.

Despair in war is not unusual, but in a city that had seen death on such an obscene scale, it was surprising that open outbreaks of dissidence were still so muted. How could any civilians be expected to look to their leadership for believable reassurance when their families had suffered so hideously and so lingeringly? Leningraders had been shown hell. Nor were they out of it. Their homes were still being hit; their enemies were still just as close. But for the Leningrad authorities, with the city still blockaded, there was a genuine sense of threat in the chain-letter notes of dissent, with their exhortations to follow Hitler; and the NKVD was as ruthless as it had been in the 1930s in rounding up and removing those deemed to be anti-Soviet.

That paranoia was all-enveloping: it extended to a violinist who, that summer, would be central to the city's sense of spiritual regeneration. Karl Eliasberg was now the director of the Leningrad Radio Committee Orchestra: a crucial role, all the more so ever since Party commissar Andrei Zhdanov had decreed that music was to return to these haunted streets. He was a conductor too: very 'thin and imperious'[11] as he raised his baton to the orchestra that had been summoned to play for the city in the Philharmonic Hall in the springtime. No matter how distinguished and dignified his public appearances in black tailcoat, Eliasberg was under secret investigation by the NKVD. His transgression? Expressing the view that Britain had been to blame for Germany attacking Russia in the first place. In the midst of the general enthusiasm for the British, and for Churchill, Eliasberg took the opposing view that the machinations of the British government had led to the destruction of the Molotov–Ribbentrop Pact. Just two years earlier, there would have been nothing controversial about his distrust of Britain: in fact, it would have been very much approved. His crime was not to alter his thinking in line with the sinuous reversals of the Bolshevik regime.

None the less, in the sunshine of 1942, Eliasberg — one of the musicians who had not been evacuated from Leningrad east to Siberia or south to Kazakhstan — was paradoxically safe. He was needed. Zhdanov understood about soft power, and he wished to use a display of artistic virtuosity to demonstrate to allies and enemies alike that Leningrad was indomitable. His plan revolved around the symphony recently completed by a composer whose own relationship with Stalin was fraught: Dmitri Shostakovich.

Ever since his own evacuation from the city in the autumn of 1941, a little before the wave of mass deaths hit, Shostakovich had been moving around the country, working as he went. He and his family were allocated a home in the town of Samara. Despite the sense of the Nazi invasion paralysing the entire country, life here beside the enormously wide River Volga and amid the rich, limitless vistas had been able to proceed almost as normal. None the less, Shostakovich had been operating under the most extraordinary artistic pressure. That Stalin was such a severe judge of music — and had such a strong distaste for anything that suggested European modernism — was one thing. But the Seventh Symphony was to be a monument to a war that was still being fought. It had to pay tribute to the proud people of Shostakovich's home city. It had to express heroism and horror. It is perhaps for this reason that the symphony — when listened to now — sounds a little like a slightly repetitive film score: across all four of its movements it has a metallic, featureless quality, brass and woodwind reiterating mechanical phrases. Clearly such a work – which would be intended for the world's ears – could hardly convey twinkling exultation. But by comparison to, for example, Gustav Holst's 'Mars, the Bringer of War' from *The Planets* suite, in all its martial drama, Shostakovich's work – even rising to its more passionate passages – rarely seemed to leave the same level of musical colour. Yet the aim here was not attractive tunes but something else: almost like a coded message in music. Its real meaning might have been a signal from Russia and its people to listeners in the West that they were not alien; that their music was universal and that their struggle was universal too.

Shostakovich had put the final touches to the piece just as 1941 was ending. Friends gathered at his home in Samara to listen to the score played on the piano; vodka was drunk. 'To the historic confrontation now taking place between reason and obscurantism, culture and barbarity, light and darkness,' the composer declared, 'I dedicate my Seventh Symphony to our struggle against fascism, to our coming victory and to my native city of Leningrad.'[12]

Those who knew him well and loved him had been aware that there were layers within that symphony of ambiguity; that the terrors summoned in the earlier movements might also have been inspired by Stalin himself. Unlike many of his musical compatriots, Shostakovich had elected to remain in Russia, despite the fact that the regime held his artistic destiny in its hands. What happened now in 1942 was a startling reverse: suddenly the regime needed Shostakovich and his talent with an urgency that made him – for the moment – untouchable.

Senior Kremlin figures understood the impact that Symphony No. 7, soon nicknamed the Leningrad Symphony, could have, and the political traction that it could exert upon allies. There was a clamour to have it performed. Many members of the former Leningrad Philharmonic were not easily summoned: evacuation had scattered them thousands of miles deep within Russia's interior. But Moscow's Bolshoi Orchestra was available for a first performance in March 1942: this was relayed via radio to America and Britain. The score was committed to miniaturized microfiche form and sent from Moscow – via

Tehran – across the Mediterranean and the Atlantic to America, where it was placed in the hands of Italian conductor Arturo Toscanini, who was to prepare Shostakovich's work for US audiences. Thus the music acquired its own life: a symphony dedicated to suffering, but also to prevailing strength and courage. The idea was that the music would come to symbolize the powerful, pure hearts of the Soviet people. And this in turn would have the effect in the West of transforming the image of Bolshevik revolutionaries – and of Stalin's regime – into something courageous and morally uplifting: forgotten would be the grubby accommodations of the pact with the Nazis.

This, though, was only the start of the use of Shostakovich's epic work: its full impact – and the transformation of mass death into radiant art – would be achieved only when the Leningrad Symphony was performed in the besieged city itself. This was where the politically suspect Karl Eliasberg was key: Andrei Zhdanov required him to pull together an orchestra that could do proper, heartfelt justice to this work for the city's summer premiere. Eliasberg was reportedly thunderstruck when he saw the scale of what he was being asked to do. Work began at once.

But who to work with? Eliasberg had a list of the musicians who had stayed in Leningrad and worked with the Radio Committee Orchestra. Many of them were dead. The score contained large numbers of parts for strings, for brass, for woodwind. The simple task of tracking down survivors who might yet have the strength to play itself took on an epic quality. There was a twenty-four-year-old oboe player called Edith Matus who had made it through the winter; her instrument, however, was in poor condition and she herself suffered one particular side effect of months of hunger: her fingers were permanently cold and numb, as though they were still exposed to the ice. The starvation had affected her circulation; and this in turn made it awkward for her to handle the instrument. None the less, when she had heard the announcement over the city's radio that musicians were required, she immediately rushed to help: as in other areas of life, this new sense of purpose gave zest and sustenance all of its own.

Other musicians were sought, and news of more deaths came. Eliasberg realized that there were only about fifteen members left of what had been a full working orchestra. Thinking of the concerts that had been arranged for the Red Army and the navy, he was struck with inspiration and he went to Zhdanov with his request. He knew that there were excellent military bands – and excellent musicians – in the armies based around the city. The request immediately went out to General Govorov: who could be spared? As it transpired, there was a wealth of talent to draw upon. While Govorov himself was fully focused on devising military plans, he also understood very well what the symphony would mean for the city and for the war.

And so it was that orchestral musicians were drawn from within various ranks of the Red Army. Rehearsals throughout that spring were fraught. If the NKVD agents might have doubted the ideological soundness of Eliasberg, they must surely have admired his flinty single-mindedness when it came to ensuring that the city's premiere of the symphony would be perfect. Rehearsals took up half a day, every day (apart from Sundays). There were some enfeebled players in the brass section who would come close to fainting with the exertion of blowing; they would be told to go over the same passage, again and again, until they had it exactly right, and at the required strength. What appeared to drive Eliasberg was not so much a sense of fealty to the regime, or a sense of the propaganda urgency: it was a genuine commitment to the art. He too was hungry and he too had suffered. But for the city's greatest composer to have handed him this work of art must have given his life a sense of transcendent purpose: just as the Orthodox believers were once more able to take the bread and wine, so Eliasberg's faith in art might restore a sense of some meaning, and of greater time, beyond the stench and the squalor of death.

And the performance that the orchestra was to give in Leningrad's Philharmonic Hall on 9 August 1942 would have all sorts of echoes and resonances of the military campaigns being fought outside. So much so that General Govorov launched his own startling initiative the night before: guided by his expertise in artillery, he directed an attack on the nearby German lines that was intended not to destroy them (they were harder to dislodge than that) but to put their own artillery out of action long enough to ensure that Shostakovich's work would not be interrupted or silenced by their own fire. To this end, his idea was remarkably effective. The poet Olga Berggolts was among the new aristocrats in the audience: the Party officials (led by rubicund Zhdanov); high-ranking military. But there were a number of ordinary citizens there too, who had made efforts to raid long-disregarded wardrobes to bring out suits and frocks. One young audience member was eighteen-year-old Olga Kvade, who recalled that the 'chandeliers were sparkling. It was such a strange feeling. On the one hand it couldn't be possible – the blockade, burials, death, starvation, and the Philharmonic Hall – it was just so incredible.'[13] The keynote throughout was pride.

As well as the musicians assembling on the stage, there were microphones too: it was vital that this concert would be relayed live, not just to the people of Leningrad, but to towns and cities and lands beyond. For the radio broadcast Eliasberg had pre-recorded a special introduction:

Comrades, a great occurrence in the cultural history of our city is about to take place. In a few minutes, you will hear for the first time the Seventh Symphony of Dmitri Shostakovich, our outstanding fellow citizen. He wrote this great composition in the city during the days when the enemy was, insanely, trying to enter Leningrad. When the fascist swine were bombing and shelling all Europe, and Europe believed the days of Leningrad were over. But this performance is witness to our spirit, courage and readiness to fight. Listen, comrades![14]

'The white-pillared Philharmonic Hall was brilliantly lit,' wrote an exultant Olga Berggolts, 'and all its festive yet solemn appearance was in keeping with the excited, expectant mood of the Leningrad people.' There was a moment of absolute silence, and then the music began. And all the people of Leningrad, whether in the hall or listening to the music on the radio, knew that it was about themselves. They knew that the enemy was still too close to the city, preparing to take it by storm, and that he would try to overwhelm Leningrad with new trials. But the terrible year of siege had neither weakened their resolve nor frightened them, but tempered their will, fusing it in fire and cooling it in ice. The symphony restored to Leningraders the dignity of their aesthetic identity; and this reaffirmation was broadcast to a wider world. 'It was demonstrated by the genial music that was born in that city and was vigorously and freely played there in spite of all the difficulties. This was a victory indeed, and a pledge of the decisive victory to come,' wrote Berggolts.[15]

'Genial' was a curious term for music that seemed to be composed of grey steel. But its true impact was immediately apparent. From within the hall there came a 'storm of applause'. But the music was heard not only among the Allies that night but also by some of the very German Wehrmacht aggressors who were encamped around the edges of the city, and who had picked it up on their receivers. A few years later, Eliasberg was approached by some tourists from communist East Germany; as younger men, they had been on the fringes of Leningrad that night, they told him. They said that they had listened to the symphony, and that at that particular moment in time, in 1942, they too were hungry and frightened, and had seen a number of their comrades killed. They related how the performance that night helped them understand how the people of the city had withstood the siege; and also how it was clear that they were indomitable.[16] There had, apparently, been tears shed. Eliasberg was moved, but sentimental hindsight was easy. However striking the idea of a weeping Wehrmacht, the cold fact remained that their job in 1942 had not changed: the orders were still annihilation.

And the future of the city, and the survival of its people, lay within the power of one particular Soviet general. Govorov had been patiently planning, and in the wake of the extraordinary publicity for Shostakovich and his work, and the plight of the city, he was preparing to turn the Nazi fire back upon the Wehrmacht.

24.   The Fuse of Vengeance

There was now a moment when the tides were changing, and it was surely a moment that many of the troops would have been able to sense. It had come in the days after that extraordinary Shostakovich performance. On the far outskirts of the city there was the flash and glint of field glasses in the sharp northern summer sun: still the eyes of von Küchler and other top German commanders were fixed on Leningrad's undemolished roofs, and on its factories as well. How was it possible that, after almost a year of siege, they remained so tantalizingly close and yet did not belong to the Wehrmacht? The wine was drawn, and so surely must be drunk. But then this was just one spur of a titanic struggle, from Sevastopol to Stalingrad to the rivers and forests near Moscow. Von Küchler had no doubts of the battle to come: the crashing wave of German power that would inundate Leningrad and lead to the final liquidation of its starved population. If some German soldiers had been haunted by Shostakovich's Leningrad Symphony, the sentiment had not extended upwards. Just days after that concert, in late August of 1942, the Germans were contemplating a fresh and definitive assault.

So too was General Govorov, who could see the danger quite plainly, and who was equally steadfast in his belief that the city could not be defended simply by sending masses of infantry moving towards those heavily fortified German encampments around the city. He knew instead that he had to think laterally; to carry out an action so unanticipated that German High Command would be thrown off balance and make a tactically erroneous response. This manoeuvre would still require courage, great numbers of troops and resolute purpose, but if successful would be immensely gratifying and morale-boosting. And so it was, in that late August, that Govorov was ready to demonstrate the depth and range of his acumen.

In the vast ring of German arms and positions that embraced the wider land around the city up to Shlisselburg and the shores of Lake Ladoga, there were some, just a little to the south of that lakeside town, that were vulnerable. Govorov's plan was to send in Red Army troops via the lake and attack the Germans using a pincer movement. The timing was crucial because the Wehrmacht aggressors were about to receive a devastating boost to their weaponry: the massive artillery that had been used in the triumphant conquest of Sevastopol was now being transported up from the south. The sheer weight and volume of such firepower might reduce entire districts of Leningrad to dust.

Govorov's Red Army forces made their attack on the German troops to the east of Shlisselburg, the aim being to hem them in and then to finish them off. In theory, such enterprises seem straightforward, yet the reality of this war for all its combatants was still one of pain and shock and demands to push forward when every instinct and fibre begged them to turn and flee. In later years, soldier Abram Sapozhnikov allowed himself the luxury of being laconic when looking back on his own struggles through a sucking, swampy landscape of deltas and rivulets and clumps of trees. But he still conveyed the dizzying sense of impulsion that propelled him through bloody injury and near death and the sight of his mutilated friends. 'A blast wave knocked me down, and my overcoat looked like a sieve,' he recalled of one such encounter:

> I had four shell fragments stuck in me but they were easily removed. Once, at night, we were sitting in the dugout together with messengers, platoon commanders, infantrymen – there were twelve of us, joking, laughing . . . Suddenly, around 1 a.m., I get this urge to check on our telephone operator, lest he fall asleep. So, I walked out, went down the trench, turned the corner . . . A long-range projectile buzzed over my head and hit the dugout directly. Eleven people . . . hands, legs, everything is turned upside down. I alone remained alive. We survived a lot on Nevsky Pyatachok. There was not a single minute without shelling or gunfire. How I survived, I cannot fathom.[1]

There was another stirring in that changing tide, the invisible current of fortune: General Govorov, although tough and unrelenting in his personal manner, understood that he was not simply moving units around on a map, but dealing with men who loved and laughed and wanted to live. Though those men could not have known it, Govorov was adept at protecting them from the grimmer demands of his own superior, General Georgii Zhukov. Zhukov had his own extraordinary strengths, but his willingness to rely on sheer colossal weight of numbers, to send thousands of soldiers into scenarios where the majority would be torn to bloody shreds, was unyielding. Zhukov's own inclination at that moment of crisis in the late summer of 1942, when vast guns were being emplaced around Leningrad to physically reduce it to red dust, was to send huge waves of men in to attack the German lines directly. Govorov resisted; his method was more lateral, more cunning and would suggest to the enemy a more unnerving grasp of misdirection as strategy.

Govorov's intention was to employ his technical expertise in the use of artillery both to decimate and to shock the enemy into making mistakes. Thus it was that, just as von Küchler was about to order that renewed and more terrible assault on Leningraders, Govorov's bifurcated forces brought blossoms of terrible fire to German encampments south of Lake Ladoga. The onslaught was so ferocious that even the Wehrmacht commanders seemed at a loss. The sky whooshed and howled as thousands upon thousands of shells and rockets poured down upon Wehrmacht positions. For the men in those fortified camps, the air itself seemed composed of fire. Conscious thought would not have been possible; only the scream of animal instinct. For Govorov was deploying a new kind of weapon designed to elicit pure terror: the Katyusha rocket. These projectiles – inexpensive to make and thus ideal for firing in vast, disorientating quantities – produced an unearthly wailing noise as they tore towards the earth. With hundreds and thousands fired without pause for over two hours, there would have been many under the blinding onslaught who lost all power of reason. Following this apocalyptic prelude, the Red Army forces began closing the pincer, making the German corridor narrower and narrower.

The aim was ultimately for the two arms to meet at the Sinyavino Heights, which lay near the lake just twenty miles to the east of

Leningrad; the term 'heights' suggests mountains, but this was really an area of gentle hills. None the less, such inclines – and the military encampments upon them – dominated the landscape around. Take the heights and there would be a significant advance towards breaking the blockade.

But even as tides turn, it takes time before the reversal becomes apparent, and the Germans – after that initial shock – regrouped and fought back. Deep woods of pine trees crackled with flame and filled the air with orange embers. The Luftwaffe was still fighting in the skies above with energy and fury. The Soviet air-force pilots, by contrast, were as tired and fundamentally weakened as their comrades on the ground. In one terrible day of the battle, some forty-two of their fighter planes were shot down. This gave a boost to the Wehrmacht forces below, who were beginning to fire back with redoubled force at the advancing Volkhov Front.

Autumn came fast to the region in 1942, as it usually did. As the air grew colder once more there was stalemate: great lines of armies facing each other across rich, moist peatlands, and half hidden among dense trees. Advances would be made, checked and pushed back. And in the midst of this seemingly unending struggle, a constant stream of prisoners were being taken. The Wehrmacht and the SS had long sailed from the shores of morality, and of battlefield ethics. As noted, throughout eastern Europe, Red Army prisoners – thousands, then hundreds of thousands, then unthinkable millions – were held captive not in barracks or prisons, but in vast pens on flat steppes under the wide open skies. Aside from the sadism, and the easy disregard for life, there was possibly also a suggestion of fear from their German captors: an acknowledgement both of the strength of an enemy that had been considered weak and brutish and stupid, and of its seemingly limitless number.

Around Leningrad, huge numbers of Wehrmacht prisoners were taken by the Red Army. Soon they would be marched through the streets of the city, these well-fed German soldiers looking at the hollow faces of adults and children alike. In time, the Soviet plans for German prisoners would also be brutal and unyielding, if lacking the instinctive psychosis of the Nazis. These men – and eventually many thousands more in both eastern Europe and in Germany itself – would be made to recompense the Soviet people. Wehrmacht prisoners would become slaves serving the Soviet Union. In the harshest conditions, they would be put to work as forced labour in mines and on building sites. A great many would not be returned to Germany until five or ten years later, broken and empty and haunted. A great many would not return at all.

Govorov's lateral assault had saved the city; it made those besieging Wehrmacht forces pause their artillery fire and go to the defence of their comrades. The plan to level Leningrad was at least temporarily halted. There had been that invisible turn in the tide. No one on either side could know it for sure, but as the battle for the city now moved further from it, into that flat riverine landscape, there were other tidal changes, subtle, but sure, in other parts of Russia – notably in and around Stalingrad (about 1,000 miles south-east of Leningrad, and a little to the east of Crimea), itself at the very limits of endurance and atrocity. Suddenly, the Wehrmacht was finding itself hurriedly having to redeploy forces around the country to counter these developments.

The air in Leningrad still crackled with tension, but unlike the previous year, when the rations had started disappearing from view, here was an urban harvest: authorities exulted in photographs of schoolchildren holding gigantic cabbages that had been cultivated in front of St Isaac's Cathedral. The Road of Life – and Lake Ladoga – had provided another form of security; cables laid on the bed of the lake and running to the city ensured a steady supply of electricity. There was light. There was water. There was fuel. Food was still limited, and monotonous too: broths augmented with a little pearl barley, porridge, vitamin C rather miraculously derived from pine cones. But there was also soya milk, and the sight of fresh vegetables – all those vivid greens and the orange of carrots – were giving a mass psychological boost. And the regeneration of the theatres and the cinemas made a huge difference to workers who – unlike the previous winter – were no longer obliged to spend silent, paranoid evenings in flickering candlelight. Now there was the unthinkable colour and splendour of opera and ballet: a fresh staging of Pushkin's *Eugene Onegin* with lavish set designs and a cast in full period costumes. At a performance of Bizet's *Carmen*, some of the singers were surprised to see, through the spotlights, little moving blobs of white cloth all over the auditorium; these were the handkerchiefs the audience were using to dry their weeping eyes. The tears weren't so much for the tragic heroine but for the mere fact that the opera was being staged at all.[2] The ballet *Gayane* was also performed. The dancers for this production, having received more regular meals, were now in better shape. More than this: as ballerina Tatyana Vecheslova recalled, the ballet master had held back a special treat for a few of them. 'It was a bottle of red wine that had been mysteriously preserved,' she said. 'At the time, it was an unthinkable rarity.'[3]

These blossoms of life crowded out remembrance. The countless legions of the dead still went unmourned in the sense of city-wide commemoration: it was still too soon. And with shell barrages constant, there were yet more deaths to face. But at least now it was possible for old men and women to sit by pot-bellied stoves and smoke cigarettes and feel, if only fleetingly, something akin to contentment. After those months of horror, there could be no conceivable greater luxury than ease of mind, and the ability to sleep as though there was a life to look forward to the next day.

Interviewed in 1943 for Tikhonov's propaganda piece, Major General Kulik observed (not inaccurately):

In comparing the battles which took place on the outskirts of Leningrad in the autumn and winter of 1941, in the summer and autumn of 1942 and at the beginning of the present year, we realize what great strides our commanders have made in the art of warfare. In the battles on the Neva the gunners gave a good account of themselves. Their assault on the enemy's fortifications was exceptionally powerful and precise. A devastating whirlwind of explosions raged in the front area and in the depth of the enemy's defences, annihilating the Germans' man-power, firing points, batteries, observation posts, trenches and dug-outs. Many German units, especially those that were in the front area, were utterly destroyed.[4]

But all the brave words could not quite camouflage the horrible losses: the Volkhov and Leningrad fronts were hit badly by Wehrmacht retaliation that autumn of 1942. The hospitals were filled with men either punctured or burned or missing limbs. True, there was the relatively recent innovation of penicillin, and it had been possible to get some into the Leningrad region, but although supply lines were an inestimable improvement on the months before, those wards still saw scenes of horror, observed by the young Leningrad nurses who had been co-opted from their quieter educations. Anna Novikova considered herself inured to some of the more terrible sights, but the pressure was still intense:

> So those [soldiers] who had gangrene received penicillin shots. But for wound treatment, it was mostly iodine and hydrogen peroxide. We didn't have bandages at all, there was nothing coming in. So we started washing the bandages in carbolic. They were horrible, but we soaked them in carbolic, rinsed them, and then used them again. What could we do?

There were also terrible instances where chloroform and painkillers had run perilously low. So those men who had been shot and who still carried the bullets within them were presented with a stark choice by Novikova and the doctors. 'We made agreements with the patients,' she remembered. ' "Will you endure this? You need this to survive. If you can handle this, we will get the bullet out. If you can't, we can't be responsible." '[5]

Amid all the crying wounded and the silent dead in those watery wooded marshes, the Wehrmacht under von Küchler had made a stout and fearsome defence in the wake of General Govorov's initiative. Day by day the skies and the ground began to grow icy once more. But there was a difference now: this was a Wehrmacht that was paralysed. There were desperate exhortations from Nazi High Command to neutralize Leningrad definitively, but now, as winter stalked close once more, the two opposing forces were deadlocked.

Among the Red Army troops were some who would have read the specially printed excerpts from Tolstoy's *War and Peace*. As the

shades of autumn crept over, and as the shelling and the fire on both
sides continued day after shortening day, there were some who were
beginning to think in terms of the Battle of Borodino in 1812, when
Russian soldiers faced Napoleon's invading forces. They did not
stop those forces getting through to Moscow, but Borodino was
the terrible blood-drenched point at which Napoleon's army faced
an opponent as grimly unyielding as itself. 'But though by the end
of the battle the men felt all the horror of their actions,' wrote
Tolstoy of that battlefield, 'though they would have been glad to
stop, some incomprehensible, mysterious power still went on governing them, and the artillery men, sweaty, covered with powder
and blood . . . though stumbling and gasping from fatigue, kept
bringing charges, loaded, aimed . . .'[6]

And on those plains, did the Wehrmacht commanding officers,
like Napoleon's forces, experience 'that dreamlike feeling that the terrible swing of the arm fell strengthless', and know that their 'moral
strength' was 'exhausted'? Were they, as in Tolstoy's account of the
French invasion, 'like an enraged beast mortally wounded as it charges',
knowing it is doomed but unable to stop?[7] The Red Army troops who
had read the excerpts – many of which dwelled upon the philosophy
of war – would use them as a frame for their own understanding and
hopes. Perhaps the Wehrmacht officers too had read Tolstoy's passages
on the unseeable anarchy of the battlefield:

> A commander in chief is never in those conditions of the *beginning*
> of some event, in which we always consider events. A commander in
> chief always finds himself in the middle of a shifting series of events
> and in such a way that he is never able at any moment to ponder
> all the meaning of the ongoing event. Imperceptibly, moment by
> moment, an event is carved into its meaning, and at every moment of
> this consistent, ceaseless carving of the event, a commander in chief
> finds himself in the centre of a most complex play of intrigues, cares,
> dependency, power, projects, advice, threats, deception.[8]

As Govorov's Red Army forces, encamped upon that crystalliz-
ing winter earth, readied themselves for the definitive battle for the
Sinyavino Heights, the Wehrmacht's Army Group North now had to

split its strength, sending reinforcements further south to Stalingrad, where the Red Army was not merely pushing back but beginning to overcome and liquidate the German invaders. The beast was bleeding. It had thrown so much of its weight into this vast land, destroyed so many millions of lives, and the Russians, after months of retreat and recoil, were now more than simply a barrier. Now they were moving to destroy their destroyer.

There is an extraordinary photograph of the young Wehrmacht officer Wilhelm Lübbecke and his men in a dugout in the Demyansk region at Christmas 1942. In this cramped space, the soldiers, sitting together, have managed to procure bottles of alcohol. More: they have extemporized a Christmas tree – a small affair – for which they have also managed to contrive decorations.[9] Did any of them seriously imagine that the land they had been attempting to conquer would accept them? Yet Lübbecke's own account of that winter – written many years later – illustrated the fears that continued to motivate himself and his comrades. In this instance, his company had just successfully killed a number of Red Army soldiers in their own dugout:

> Around this time, the Red Army had begun to deploy loudspeakers on the frontlines to spout propaganda and threats delivered in perfect German. Perhaps a week after my successful elimination of the bunker, a soldier from one of the regular infantry companies asked me if I had heard the Russians calling out my name over the loudspeakers. Replying that I had not, he informed me that these broadcasts were threatening me personally, announcing, 'Lübbecke, when we catch you, we'll cut off your nuts!' Apparently, a captured German soldier had identified my role in destroying their bunker.
>
> From experience, I regarded this warning very seriously. In at least one recent instance, the Russians had castrated a sergeant and a corporal captured from one of our regiment's infantry companies. We discovered them the next day, dead from loss of blood. Such brutality reinforced our determination to avoid being taken prisoner by the Red Army at all costs, even if we had to take our own lives to escape that fate. This mentality was totally different than the mindset

we possessed during the French campaign. If surrounded by French troops, I would have surrendered with confidence that I would be treated humanely.[10]

At that point, he appeared blithely unaware of how captured Red Army troops had been treated by the Germans: mass murders as though they were simply so much surplus humanity. His war – and that of his fellows – was to continue for many long painful months yet. But for the besieged people of Leningrad, that opposing momentum was fast gathering pace.

The planning for Operation Iskra (*iskra* means 'spark') was intense; the aim was to finally open up a land corridor between Leningrad and towns to the east wide enough to allow through the quantities of both food and hardware that Leningrad needed to thrive. After the failures of the autumn – and in particular the failure to trap and wipe out the German forces south of Lake Ladoga – a new and more innovative approach was rehearsed in that snowy midwinter darkness. Under skies of indigo and in land of ghostly white, the camouflaged skiers – white-garbed – whispered across the snow at speed. Another mistake was rectified; this time vast numbers of Red Air Force fighters were being assembled in the north, determined to deny the Luftwaffe air superiority. By now, there were also better conditions for the soldiers: fresh quantities of winter clothing, fresh supplies of hot food, judicious rations of vodka. They were still under the steel surveillance of the NKVD; any suggestion of a soldier displaying reluctance or backing away was swiftly dealt with by a bullet. But many of the soldiers had a new sense of confidence; a sixth sense that the momentum of the war had changed. The wider world had also played a part, with excited speculation that the next moves of President Roosevelt and Prime Minister Churchill would concern not just the conclusion of the war but also the world that was to come afterwards. But on top of this, a fuse of vengeance had been lit; in this sense, Wilhelm Lübbecke had been right.

The cold, though harsh, was not as bad as the previous year, but it did cause a slight delay in the plan: the attack finally came in the first few days of the new year. On 12 January 1943, the battle was launched. One soldier, eighteen-year-old Moisei Malkis, Odesa-born, and working with a regimental intelligence platoon, recalled many years later both the terror and the splendour of the hours that followed:

> The breach of the blockade . . . it was the greatest thing that I was destined to do. The breach of the Leningrad siege began on 12 January 1943. I remember that morning was foggy. Then artillery shelling started and it lasted for about two hours. I hadn't seen anything like that before. After the shelling of the opposite shore – Shlisselburg and the Germans' front line – green rockets lit up and we began moving on Neva's ice toward Shlisselburg. My comrades, one in the front and one in the back, were carrying those narrow ladders. I ran carrying Degtyaryov's handheld machine gun. It was very heavy . . . I was running on the Neva River toward Shlisselburg. Right after our artillery bombardment, our troops started firing Katyushas. When we began the offensive, the Germans opened heavy fire: the entire shore of Shlisselburg was covered with trenches, with barbed wire in front. They opened fire and I saw so many soldiers fall on the Neva: some were killed, some were injured.[11]

The Wehrmacht had soaked the steep banks of the Neva with water at night as a defensive measure, since they would freeze solid and become extraordinarily difficult to scale, especially under fire. But Malkis and his comrades had been rehearsing for such an eventuality; as well as being experts in negotiating snow, they also learned how to move swiftly on ice:

> Together with my shock crew, we got there and started using those narrow ladders to climb up. Besides that we hurled those grapnels. Those are a kind of anchor that they usually have on ships. So we hurled those hooks up and used the ropes to climb up. We managed to reach the front line. We cut the barbed wire and began the attack. Germans started shooting and were jumping out of their trenches. We even had to engage in hand-to-hand combat, physical fighting. Germans couldn't handle it and started retreating. My platoon – the regiment reconnaissance platoon – together with the others received an order to storm the Preobrazhensky Hill in Shlisselburg. This was the key to taking over the city. We took the hill by storm, and then

the Germans began retreating. We got on that hill, and then took part in the next attack. The Germans left Shlisselburg. They stopped 6 kilometres away from our front defence line. I'll remember that attack for the rest of my life because of how bloody it was. We lost a lot of people, but we still took Shlisselburg.[12]

This fight was not yet over, as Malkis recalled:

After that, the soldiers of the Volkhov Front were marching to meet us. During the attack of 13–17 January, there was combat and we joined up with the troops that were approaching from the opposite side, from the Volkhov direction. We took over some workers' villages. By the fifth workers' village, the Leningrad Front and the Volkhov Front met. We were happy, gave each other hugs, and threw our hats in the air.[13]

It was a moment of exultation; they understood what they had achieved. The Wehrmacht's deathly grip on Leningrad was being prised loose. The veins and the arteries and the heart of the city could begin to pulse and beat as they had done before the war. After so much blood, there was release. The shadow had not yet been dispersed; the Wehrmacht were still very much there in the countryside. But it would now be possible to re-establish road and main railway links, and each of these arteries would pump fresher blood in.

And for young intelligence officer Malkis, there could be no relenting (even though he and his comrades revelled in the discovery of a German food store – here was butter, an unthinkable delicacy, and bread, and in great quantities too). There was still more fire to face: the Germans were fighting back with venom and some desperation, given their own fears of the Red Army's brutality:

We moved forward towards Sinyavino peat bogs. The Sinyavino field . . . There we carried out night reconnaissance by fire. Here is what that means. We initiated an advance and the Germans opened fire at us. Meanwhile our commanders were in the trenches, noting where Germans were shooting from, recording their firing position coordinates to take them out later. We cut wire fences again and advanced to the neutral line, and at that moment the Germans opened hurricane-like mortar fire. They used six-barrel mortars, the Nebel-werfers. Every bomb whistled with its own particular howl. It was a horrific scene. I was wounded in that battle. A head injury, right here, in the jaw.

'A Kazakh saved me,' he continued. 'His last name was Garifu-lin. He got me out of there. My entire body was covered in blood. He pulled me out of the battlefield [and] brought me to the hollow where the battalion first-aid post was located.' And he knew what he and all those Red Army comrades had achieved. 'We breached the Leningrad Siege! We finally were able to breach the blockade!' said Malkis. 'Connection was established via Ladoga, and then through the railroad, which was near the front – Leningrad was now con-nected to the mainland!'[14]

25.   Golden Stars Streamed Downwards

'It was odd to be here again,' wrote British newspaper correspondent Alexander Werth in 1943.[1] He had been born and brought up in St Petersburg, and now, in defiance of the continuing German blockade, he had been granted a visit to the city by the Soviet authorities. Apart from the survival of the 'yellow stucco' of the 'Imperial Senate', the 'little humped granite bridges' across the 'Venetian' canals, the great dome of St Isaac's Cathedral and the Admiralty with the 'tall needle spire which Pushkin watched from his window on those brief summer nights', Werth was suddenly anxious to see what had become of his old childhood home. 'When we turned into the Mokhovaya, I saw the tall bay-windows of number twenty-nine . . . and the top one of those bay-windows had been my own room.'[2]

Werth was seized with rich memories:

> It came back very vividly – the nickel bed in the corner nearest the door, and the open fireplace . . . and the two large cupboards full of Russian, English, French and German books . . . The best things in the room were a big Persian rug my father had brought back from the Caucasus, and the all-round view from the three windows around the desk – I watched from here the rioting and shooting going on during the February Revolution with excited crowds running this way and that and one day smashing up a police station just a little down the street.[3]

What could possibly have survived in that former family home? What did he imagine that he would find? The apartment stairs, once bright with 'white imitation marble walls', were now painted 'dirty brown'. 'The hall was dark and empty' and the doors to all those old rooms of memory were padlocked. There didn't appear to be anyone there; even in this sub-divided communal home, there was no trace of human presence – just a very old-looking note proclaiming: 'Ira, I'll be back next week.'[4] The note itself seemed to carry a hint of unease. 'Why this deadly stillness' in an apartment that had now become 'a dirty slum'? Perhaps the full weight of the ordeal that Leningrad had been through had not quite percolated through to England; surely it was obvious to Werth's Soviet escorts that all within this apartment had been among that backlog of hundreds of thousands of corpses to be burned. The thought occurred to Werth at the end of this visit: 'There was a smell of death about the house.' But that was not what he was in Leningrad to see. Instead he was guided towards a group of children outside who were singing, and happily boasting about how their soldier fathers had been awarded the Order of the Red Star. 'This was Leningrad. And it was alive, as alive as the shrill joyful voices of these children,' he wrote. His old home had been St Petersburg; it had transformed into Petrograd; but now both those cities had vanished, as Werth saw it, and 'Leningrad had become the only reality.'[5]

This was reportage aimed at a British audience, an attempt to boost enthusiasm for what Werth – and large numbers of writers on the left – regarded as a much truer and more worthwhile alliance than any other. Was this not the city that was shaking off recent trauma by staging theatrical musical comedy routines featuring that recent London musical hit 'The Lambeth Walk'? (The very idea of this – a middle-class composer's cartoonish idea of how London's cockneys enjoy themselves, staged by working-class Leningraders as grand and authentic entertainment – is still quite startling.) But in other ways, the transformation of the city after that wilderness of winter night was striking: the rich lilac blossoms made reality once more. But the other development – as ordinary food such as salted fish and fried eggs began to return to Leningraders' plates – was that of a growing sense of exceptionalism. The term *blokadniki* – those who had endured the blockade – was a badge not so much of suffering victimhood as of pride.

It had been on 19 January 1943 that the official pronouncement had echoed through the city's public speakers: 'Special announcement: The Blockade has been broken. Leningrad is free!' There were children who had sat up that night, listened to the thunderous boom of artillery, and understood that it was being fired not at them, but rather at the Germans. And on the night of the announcement, no one slept. Though there was snow on the ground, there were some who gathered outdoors under the moon without overcoats – they had left their apartments in fugue states of disbelief and ecstasy. 'Who could be asleep at such a time?' declared one worker. Olga Berggolts, mindful of her duties as a public poet, intoned her own views to Leningraders via the radio: 'In January last year we were burying our comrades in the frozen earth . . . naked and in common graves. Instead of a farewell address, we gave them an oath: "The Blockade will be broken, we shall win." '[6] Soldiers, too, were jubilant: one relayed his joy that despite receiving an 'enemy bullet in the head', and with the blood streaming down his face, he had still played a full part in destroying 'the cursed reptiles'.[7]

Just a few days later and the news would come through that the German forces besieging Stalingrad had been wiped out. The invisible tides of war had decisively turned – it was reported with glee that among those taken prisoner had been one 'General Field Marshal [Paulus] and 24 Generals' among some 90,000 others.

This was not to say that death was done with the city: Germans were still encamped not too many miles away and Leningrad was still being shelled relentlessly. Food and armaments were getting through on that widened road-and-rail corridor, but to the west and the south of the city the Wehrmacht were harder to dislodge. There was no possibility of relaxation, but that did not mean that the coming spring was not being relished. The harshness was underpinned by a deeper layer of steel. 'Professor Abramson, a very gifted surgeon, and lecturer at our institute, was killed yesterday by a shell,' reported Vera Inber. 'Half his head was torn off. Marietta saw him yesterday, in his coffin. The head was hidden by a gauze bandage, the empty space being filled with cotton wool.'[8] In addition to this, vast numbers of apartments in the city had been gouged and sliced by German artillery: windows burst inward, roofs punched through. But even more terrible were the bloody injuries: a teenage boy, caught in the debris of shelling, whose feet had been mashed into pulp and whose bleeding was copious. He was heard to cry: 'What a waste! I am so young and what have they done to me! It's a waste!'[9] It was not only homes and factories: the projectiles were landing in and around the grounds of hospitals too. The city remained vividly on edge.

Curiously, the Germans were also persisting in showering the city with propaganda leaflets, as though somehow, after all the blood and the death, these would incline the Leningraders to welcome the invaders in. One such leaflet told of how the Russian Orthodox priests would once more press their religion on the masses under the Soviets; the Germans clearly could not imagine that a certain number of Leningraders would have been perfectly pleased if they had done so.

When the Luftwaffe struck the city, the procedures were still straightforward and the air-raid sirens and shelters were still there. Against the shelling, however, no warning could be given; the choice for Leningraders was either to stay in shelters the entire time (which, of course, would hardly have been permitted by the authorities or the NKVD) or to take their chances in the streets outside as if playing some outsize form of Russian roulette.

And so the chances were taken; nothing would forestall the determined efforts at regeneration. Soon into that spring, the city staged an Olympiad of Children's Art. This took place in the halls of the Pioneer Palace where not so long ago Yura Riabinkin had played chess with his friends. After months of dilapidation, the building had been restored to something like its old brightness. And the aim of the Olympiad was clear: all those Leningraders who had seen the blank gazes of haunted orphaned children in the previous months were to have their hearts lifted by their indomitable recovery. There was singing, musical recitations, dance performances. Younger children staged their own puppet theatre. There were exhibitions of their drawings and of their clay modelling. It was the displays of traditional Russian dances that made the deepest impression on spectators who knew that, just a few months previously, the city's children could hardly move through the weakness of hunger. The spring of 1943 saw a rapid thaw – snow swiftly giving way to gurgling currents – and though apartments and houses and factories still 'swayed' as the shells materialized as if out of nowhere, there was a sense that Leningraders had indeed been transformed by their mass ordeals. The change could be heard in the eager declamations of theatrical lines and even in the incongruous notes of Hawaiian guitars that could occasionally be heard echoing through the Philharmonic.

This sense of renewal was even more pronounced in the mighty industrial citadel of the Kirov Plant. Chief Engineer N. D. Puzyrev remarked that 'now I look back on it, I already find it hard to imagine or describe how people lived during those days'.[10] That year brought in natural wonders: women being presented with red roses; huge crops of blackcurrants, redcurrants and raspberries. Scientific reason told Leningraders that these were to be appreciated for their vitamin C (rather more appealing than pine cones). But it was their sheer sensuous delight – the rich juicy burst of flavour – that left some people transfixed, not just by that moment of pleasure, but all the pleasure that they had missed.

The news was continually about epic battles in other parts of Russia: the extraordinary ferocity of the tank engagement at Kursk, the largest the world had ever seen, and the resulting crushing of the Germans there. The momentum of the fresh tide was sensed. On sunny Sunday afternoons, the wide crossroads of Nevsky Prospekt were milling with people, as they had done before the war. 'In the past it used to be one of the main centres of prostitution,' noted Alexander Werth, hurriedly clarifying that it was nothing of the sort now.[11] None the less, the busy commingling of 'soldiers and girls' suggested that the young people were in search of what might be termed romantic opportunity. Leningrad – Petrograd – St Petersburg – had never been a city that was reticent about sex. An older actress said approvingly of her younger co-stars that, after the months of starvation, they were 'nice and plump again'.[12] The city's mayor, Pyotr Popkov, was keen to emphasize in an interview that even the city's factories were being turned to more tender purposes. Leningrad was an important manufacturing centre for 'consumer's goods' as he put it, and among the buttons and combs and hosiery and shaving brushes, they were also very busy making 'eau de cologne' for the troops, and 'perfumery for the army girls'. These were important because these young people were themselves 'starting to produce babies'. They were notably 'strong and healthy babies too. Very good quality babies.'[13] Elsewhere, there had been exhortations to the city's young women to get back into the habit of wearing make-up and lipstick. There was a particular shop 'near the old Catholic church' specializing in cosmetics, with two young women behind the glass counter. 'Leningrad had something that Moscow didn't have,' wrote Alexander Werth. 'A shop where scent was sold freely to anyone. The scent was in dainty little bottles with golden labels, and was called "Boyevye Podrugi" . . . It does not mean "Soldier's Sweetheart" though that is, perhaps, the person for whom it is primarily intended; it means literally "Women Comrades in Battle" or perhaps "Girlfriends in Arms" though that sounds a little ambiguous.'[14]

Yet recovery for younger teenagers and children had not been so simple. Despite the optimistic visions of propaganda writers, this was still a city of orphans: children growing into adolescence who had seen and experienced the most terrible things. In the delta of the Neva river a little to the north of the city centre lie the three Kamenny Islands; and on the largest of these was (and is) another of those grand architectural throwbacks to the Tsarist era that the new generation of Communists could not quite bear to do without. Amid tall birch trees, there is a cluster of eighteenth- and nineteenth-century grand dachas – some that might even be described as mini-palaces – dating back to the time when St Petersburg's aristocrats felt the desire to retreat to a less public realm. In the years just before the revolution, the wider public had found their way there, and in the White Nights this became a favoured spot for young courting couples. As well as the lovely paths through the woods, the waters around had offered the possibilities of messing about in boats. By 1943, some of these grand houses on the island had been reconfigured as retreats and rest homes for the city's teenagers, especially for those who had been drawn from their schools aged thirteen or fourteen to go and work in the Kirov or Obukhov factories on the armaments production lines. The palisaded splendour of the houses had been remarkably undisturbed by the war; lustrous chandeliers still hung, exquisite vases remained on pedestals, large mirrors reflected surviving marble statues of various Greek gods. Upstairs chambers had been converted into dormitories, segregating the girls and the boys. Nearby villas had also been converted for the same purpose. And the intention was that the children would be brought here for holidays of two or three weeks, or even a month.

The daily routines were light: up at eight, a few minutes of 'physical exercises' and then a range of activities. There was football, volleyball, art and card games. There were excursions and a well-stocked library. This was an extension of the principle of the Pioneer Palace, but the emphasis now was on regeneration. Food was absolutely central. There was kasha, and hot rice pudding. There was meat, there was fish, there were blocks of cheese and plentiful bread and jam. In addition, each adolescent received a bar of chocolate each day: English chocolate was for some reason especially prized and savoured. These young people frequently had no older relatives in their lives; all had perished. And working on the assembly lines, they were only too well aware of just how fragile their own lives were: the noises of the shells – the 'sizzle' that filled the air when one landed close – filled their imaginations. The Soviet instinct was that these older children would find succour and warmth and recovery while in the arms of the state; a pre-Soviet instinct, also present, knew very well that the dreadful deaths and absence of parents and loved ones would continue to cast shadows on their lives. The authorities – and the twenty-something-year-old commissars who supervised the occupants of these respite homes on Kamenny Island (the easternmost of the three bridge-linked islands, which shared its name) – did not lack for compassion towards their charges. There were instances when distressed younger residents ran up to female commissars shouting 'Mama! Mama!' and holding them tight. This was not delusion but reflex: as if, in their suffering, they had stopped growing. The supervisors sincerely wished to help heal them, and to create hope for the future. But the war was still being fought, and their city was still being hit.

In Leningrad's restored classrooms, still younger children had returned with some energy to the fascinations of stories and of maths, of biology and science. Their young imaginations were filled with fantasies of military vengeance: of how the Germans would be made to pay a terrible price for their crimes. Many had siblings who were fighting at the front, and writing home (a concept that itself was frequently only just stabilizing, as larger families and social networks established themselves in undamaged communal apartments or tenement blocks). And those letters, filled as they were with fiery rhetorical intentions, further inflamed the children. In addition to this, ever larger numbers of German prisoners of war were being marched through the city; to see the hated enemy up close, brought down and with hunted faces, was a source of enduring fascination to them.

Leningraders were correct to detect a certain frenzied and nihilistic quality to the shelling that continued through the late summer and autumn of 1943. And there was more of it in that period than at any other point: in September 1943, some 11,500 shells were launched at the city. Certain streets – even certain sides of streets – acquired superstitious reputations for attracting more explosives than most. And no one could ever get used to the split-second carnage: tram stops on busy avenues, crowded with waiting passengers, instantly becoming slicks of blood and body parts. 'K. saw a torn-off arm with a cigarette in the fingers, still smoking,' ran one report.[15] Mutilated corpses lay among spilt shopping bags. The only sense in which the city had adapted to these daily outbreaks of mass murder was the speed with which the scenes were cleaned up: firemen would arrive not only to douse any flames but also to hose down the pavements so that the blood was sluiced away. 'The fascist beast doesn't have any hope of victory,' declared one factory worker. 'He senses that he is living his last days before Leningrad, and that's why he's shelling the city.'[16] Others were quoted by reporters, saying: 'I want more quickly to wipe these vermin from the face of the earth,' and, 'We will never forget the bloody evil deeds and murders of the hated enemy.'[17]

The Wehrmacht had reached that stage of war where destruction formed its own kind of gravitational field: they had to fire more and more shells because the idea of death was all that they had left. Each and every one of those soldiers knew what was happening: the way that the German forces had been overwhelmed at Stalingrad, at Kharkiv, and in a hundred other towns and villages. They also knew that Soviet vengeance would not stop at Russia's borders. Yet to the north of the city, on the Karelian Isthmus, was an even more curious form of war: that of silence and stasis. Here the Red Army was acting as a 'covering force'; two armies, Red and Finn, in that dappled green landscape, not firing, not advancing, not retreating. The mossy ground had been transformed for war: trenches gouged out to topple tanks, circular camouflaged firing posts and subterranean dwellings. The silence of the forests was broken by the firing of a token howitzer in the direction of the invisible Finnish enemy just a mile or so away; that enemy then sent an equally tokenistic response a few minutes later. The fight with the Finns was one that had been started four years previously. The tenacity of that distrust and hatred – even if the two sides did not actively launch large offensives – was still strong.

Even as the German shells whistled and sizzled, there was thought not just about Leningrad's haunted children but also the city's wider population, and how they might cope with the future. For the purposes of propaganda, Professor Moshansky of the Leningrad Health Department was confidently asserting that 'there were no cases of insanity or other nervous diseases due to bombing and shelling'.[18] The mayor of the city, Pyotr Popkov, was happy to attribute this to the beneficence of the Communist spirit:

> Remember that no town has to work as Leningrad has been, and is, working. Everybody feels that he is part of the show, and that every hour of work he puts in is part of the defence of Leningrad. The impulse to work, therefore, is very great . . . The people of Leningrad have become like a large family, united by common hardships and their common effort.[19]

It is possible, psychologically, that there was something in this. But Popkov was not quite correct to say that the city's hardships were shared by all. There were many Leningraders, in their dealings with the Smolny Institute, who remembered how some of it had smelled powerfully like grand 'dining rooms' during the worst weeks and months of the hunger, and many others who had heard the spreading rumours of the hot meals, and of the plates left half-eaten, and of the meat and the rice then thrown away.

And presiding over the city still was Andrei Zhdanov, still as plump and portly and fogged with alcohol as he had been at the start of the city's crisis. But the propagandists were beginning to suggest that, unlike the mayor, a rather more elevated future lay in store for Zhdanov; that his war conduct, and his skill and expertise in keeping Leningrad alive, meant that he might in time be considered a 'successor'. Within the city, it was close to blasphemy to speculate on the evil day when the Soviet Union would have to forge a future without Stalin. None the less, it was no secret that Zhdanov was a favourite of the leader.

The year was ending with the Germans to the south of the country in crippled retreat (even as the shelling of Leningrad persisted right up until 29 December). The tide had become a riptide, Russia's would-be conquerors being swept helplessly back, from Novgorod, from Uritsk. The Battle of Kiev in the last weeks of 1943 left so much of that city as a pitted smouldering shell: a surprise assault from the Red Army, cutting the supply links of the Wehrmacht's Army Group Centre, then being countered with an equally vicious response from back-up panzer groups, tanks and infantry slowed to the speed of a nightmare in sucking mud. But the end of the year, and the start of 1944, saw those German forces too being smashed and overwhelmed by vast Red Army numbers.

In Leningrad, the early days of the new year – fir trees in some apartments decorated with tinsel – found the nights disturbed by what sounded like continuous thunder: this was the prelude to a more mighty and terrible storm – General Govorov's massed artillery, with the addition of naval guns, firing on advance German positions outside the city. Wave after wave of heavy shelling, the intention of which was to 'soften' those lines – in many cases, softening them to pulp – and then to move in and overwhelm them decisively.

'The fate of Leningrad hangs on the speed of our advance,' General Govorov told his forces. 'If we are held up, the city will be subjected to such a terrible shelling that it will be impossible to stand it. So many people will be killed, so many buildings demolished.'[20] The Red Army now had emplacements on the Pulkovo Heights (a line of modest hills about twelve miles south of Leningrad): and from these, on 15 January 1944, an unimaginably vast bombardment against the Germans was launched, over half a million shells and rockets fired ceaselessly to create a monsoon of total destruction.

In the city, window frames trembled, and it was as though the earth itself was quivering. Govorov's plan was hardly a state secret, and the excitement ran through the city like electricity. In the days and nights to come, as the Red Army forces surged down from those heights, pointing west and south, firing endless ordnance as they pulsed across the land, and then firing more rockets in the dark, some Leningraders were convinced that they could see the aurora borealis. For the first time in over two years, the skies above the city were a source no longer of fear but rather of surging euphoria. In mid-January, in the brief daylight hours, Leningraders were out and about and going to work as usual; some found themselves hardly able to speak through the surge of emotions that they were feeling. The city's radio station gravely reported each fresh reclamation of the towns around the city. The Wehrmacht, which had been so viciously immoveable, had somehow instantly dissolved into thin air. Field Marshal von Küchler and the remnants of his Army Group North had by that stage pulled back about ninety miles west to the borderlands with Estonia, and to the remnants of defensive positions termed the Panther Line: in Küchler's wake lay countryside and small towns left in traumatized ruins. A further unimagined day came on 19 January 1944, when Krasnoe Selo and Peterhof were liberated. This 'liberation' took the form of slaughtered and captured Germans, and the discovery of all their desecrations: factories and clinics that had been turned into forts; roads and woods that had been transformed into death-traps, seeded with landmines by hurriedly retreating troops.

The great Peterhof Palace – outside which in the summer of 1941, on the day that the Great Patriotic War began, those twenty-four young graduates had promenaded, celebrating their degrees and the glittering prospect of the future – had been laid to waste by countless bombing raids. Fire had wholly gutted the building, leaving only its outer walls standing. The landscaped park was now bare – the Wehrmacht had hacked down most of the trees – and, once again, in attempting to evade their pursuers, they had planted the soil of the gardens with innumerable mines. Yet who could have stopped at that moment to mourn stucco and marble and stone? The absence of the enemy – and the visibility of dirty, frightened German prisoners – created further heart-leaping excitement.

Then, by 27 January 1944, in what was turning out to be a comparatively mild winter, the population of Leningrad were once more listening to the city's public speakers and their radio sets. This, then, was the moment of their deliverance: the reward for their faith. General Govorov had an announcement to make:

Citizens of Leningrad! Courageous and persistent Leningrad residents! Together with the troops of the Leningrad Front, you defended our home. With your heroic work and steely endurance, overcoming all the difficulties and torments of the siege, you forged a weapon of victory over the enemy, giving all your strength for the cause of victory. On behalf of the troops of the Leningrad Front, I congratulate you on the significant day of the great victory.[21]

That night, the winter sky glowed and growled as colours brighter and more dazzling than even the aurora borealis were traced across the heavens. There were twenty-four salvoes from 324 guns. Rockets were launched, filling the indigo sky with bright green. There was a dazzling bright white light, then dots of intense red, before a cascade of 'golden stars' streamed downwards. The fire from the guns on the Neva burned orange, and in addition to this unearthly incandescence – truly dazzling in a city that had been blacked out and darkened throughout the entire conflict – there were also mighty naval searchlights from battleships, now trained upon the historic survivors: the great eighteenth-century spire of the Peter and Paul fortress and the city's classical facades, creating what looked like solid bridges of angelic light. There were huge crowds on the Neva embankment and on the city's bridges. Some Leningraders were old enough to remember the St Petersburg that had been, the thick, sinister industrial fogs of winter combined with the natural Baltic mists, and the earliest days of electricity, when the streets were shrouded. To them, this wild defiance of the Petersburg night, their own faces glowing in the reflected golds and greens and reds, must have seemed miracle enough on its own. But then for all those people to know that they had food, and warmth, was also the perfectly commonplace made divine. The war was not over for Russia, nor would it be until the implacable Red Army had driven deep into Berlin in May 1945, creating its own atrocity and trauma for the German women there. But for Leningrad, the vast shadow of death that had darkened the city had finally lifted.

In the following month, February 1944, there was a general meeting of the surviving staff of the city's botanical gardens. The rich repository of seed specimens was examined and recatalogued; there were reports on the natural balsams that had been prepared for the hospitals throughout the siege; the flowers that had been grown for the wards, to provide visual and psychological cheer; the specialist vegetable growers who had distributed seedlings throughout the city, and who had given instructions on turning parks into farms; and on the tables of these botanical committees sat bowls filled with lily of the valley. There was white lilac too. In that botanical hothouse, the scent of the lilac was strong enough for all to smell.

26. 'Terror is still a necessity'

'Here lies half of the city,'[1] observed Sergei Davydov of the Piska-ryovskye Memorial Cemetery, where the uncountable bodies and bones of thousands lay bare, coffinless, pressed together in the black earth. The toll of the blockade had various estimates, ranging from 650,000 to over a million. Neither of these figures was fully com-prehensible in terms of envisaging the scale. It was not just resident Leningraders who had died but also great numbers of undocumented refugees, who had rushed into the city from Latvia, Estonia, Lithu-ania and the Russian countryside in that summer of 1941 in the hope of escaping the murderous Wehrmacht. Their names could never now be known. Their families – if any had survived – would never know where, when or even if their loved ones had died.

Those vast anonymous outdoor repositories could never be a site for mourning or a focus for family grief: the obscene pits were instead stark reminders of the dark depths of human possibility. But there was an intense drive throughout the final months of the war, with the Wehrmacht in giddying retreat, to ensure that Len-ingrad no longer resembled some terrible necropolis. There were propaganda photographs: well-fed young people up on the roof of the Kazan Cathedral, restoring it to its pre-war lustre; well-fed young people helping to rebuild apartments and apartment blocks; and, more coyly, well-fed young people walking romantically along the embankments of the Neva, bathed in the city's pearlescent light. This was about renewal and repopulation. In addition, many of the roughly one and a half million Leningraders who had been evacuated either via the Road of Life or by train were, when that passage was prised open, set to return. Those huge industrial citadels needed their workers. On top of this, the poets and the painters and the musicians were on their way back too, intent upon restoring the city's artistic heart. But there was also another, more personal undercurrent: the horror committed had been so vast that no one quite knew how to address it directly. Of course there was mourning; of course children were racked with grief. But grief for some took the form of a granite silence: a matter for the secret heart, their family ordeals not to be shared with the public realm but treated as though they were intensely private property. In the midst of all this, the city authorities in the shape of Zhdanov and Kuznetsov had resolved that the story Leningrad had to relate at this moment was one of intense heroism. Stalin himself would confer the honour of 'Hero City' upon Leningrad and its citizens at the end of the war. But underneath all this was a more complex series of violent repercussions. The cycle of destruction was not at an end, for all that the city wished to find new life.

Instead there would be vengeance, not against Germans but against selected Leningraders. A fresh purge, as though there was still a surplus of people that the city could spare. This new outbreak of death would seem subconscious, instinctive, the political authorities lashing out and finding that they in turn were to be condemned as transgressors. The city should have been at peace, but that peace could not quite be found, either individually or en masse. (In some curious way, this would remain true throughout the decades. Leningrad is now St Petersburg once more but it is yet to find true peace. This in part is a dark, distant echo of that murderous, implacable blockade; here is a city that still understands better than most the immanence of catastrophe.)

In mid-1944, the process of Leningrad's reconstruction began as the war's second front – the D-Day invasion of Europe – got underway in the west. On one street, Vera Inber was entranced by the spectacle of a man on a stepladder repairing one of the shattered public clocks. 'Time is coming back,' she wrote. 'It has come back!'[2] Yet there were others who were unsettled by the gaunt urban realm. For the internationally celebrated poet Anna Akhmatova, recently returned from her evacuee life in Tashkent, the city was now 'a terrible ghost that pretended to be my city'.[3] Her erstwhile lover, the art historian Nikolay Punin, was also returning, from his own exile in Samarkand. 'We brought a cat with us,' Punin wrote, 'knowing that in Leningrad, all the cats had been eaten and thinking that there wouldn't be any. We were amazed when we heard the feline concert in our garden.'[4] The cats had been introduced in great numbers in order to clear the city of rats. The more glaring absence was that of dogs; so many beloved family pets had been killed, and there was clearly no spirit or impulse to replace them. 'The longer you look at Leningrad, the more terrible it is,'[5] wrote Punin. Neither he nor Akhmatova could scent the danger: they were to find very soon that there was a latent nativist malignancy that would be aimed at them.

One of the first impulses of the authorities had been to open an exhibition, dedicated entirely to the city's recent ordeal. Like Tikhonov's propaganda volume, it was entitled 'The Defence of Leningrad'. And, rather like the film documentary about the city produced in 1942, it was intended to portray the city's people – and by extension the city's leaders Zhdanov, Kuznetsov and Popkov – as heroes. The exhibits were spread over several floors of a civic hall. There were piles of German helmets and captured German flame-throwers and artillery pieces. Spectacularly, there were the remnants of a downed plane. But there was also a 'public nutrition' section, with stark displays of albumin yeast, dextrin, flour and fish glue, as though any Leningraders might now care to gaze upon the grim ingredients that kept life ticking over at the barest minimum.

The theme was pride: the displays seemed to say, 'Look what we have been through. Look at what we had the power to endure. Look at the limitless possibilities of a society that can do without to such a degree in order to help the wider cause.' Marshal Govorov himself was minded to donate some military souvenirs to the exhibition: Leningraders were invited to witness their ordeals as the exploration of human potential. Admirers from outside Russia were also keen to pay tribute. Thus the freezing abyss into which a million victims had been cast was somehow reset to the valiant leitmotifs of Shostakovich's Seventh Symphony.

There had long been an interesting strain of Anglophilia about the city, and a little after victory in Europe was confirmed in May 1945, the brilliant English socialist playwright J. B. Priestley staged a theatrical coup in Leningrad: it was at the Theatre of Comedy (and in Moscow) where his play *An Inspector Calls* received its dual world premiere. The line with the greatest resonance, as uttered by the titular inspector, was: 'We don't live alone. We are members of one body. We are responsible for each other. And I tell you that the time will soon come when, if men will not learn that lesson, then they will be taught it in fire and blood and anguish.' The play (the title of which had to be changed to *This You Will Not Forget*, because the term 'inspector' carried echoes of Russian civil-service bureaucracy) was a roaring success. On the night, as Priestley's wife Jane told their children in a letter, 'Daddy made a speech, terrific applause, packed theatre stood and shouted.' She added that 'Daddy is adored here' and that his books 'sell like hot cakes'.[6]

There was another distinguished visitor from Britain that year: an academic/diplomat who himself had been raised in the city back in its pre-revolutionary days. Isaiah Berlin was a philosopher with an intense interest in (among a thousand other things) Russian poetry. His arrival in Leningrad in 1945 was to him a source of some awe and curiosity. Unlike Priestley, who had been feted with caviar, champagne and, reportedly, enough cigarettes to last for years, Berlin's progress was a little more discreet, but no less deeply felt – especially when he discovered that the great Anna Akhmatova had survived the cataclysm. He wrote:

> I had not seen the city since 1919. In Leningrad my recollections of childhood became fabulously vivid. I was inexpressibly moved by the look of the streets, the houses, the statues, the embankments, the marketplaces, the suddenly familiar, still broken, railings of a little shop, in which samovars were mended, below the house in which we had lived. The inner yard of the house looked as sordid and abandoned as it had done during the first years of the Revolution . . . The city had been greatly damaged, but still in 1945 remained indescribably beautiful. I made my way to the Writers' Bookshop in the Nevsky Prospekt. While looking at the books, I fell into casual conversation with a man who was turning over the leaves of a book of poems. He turned out to be a well-known critic and literary historian. We talked about recent events. He described the terrible ordeal

of the siege of Leningrad and the martyrdom and heroism of many of its inhabitants . . . Is Akhmatova still alive?' I asked. 'Why yes, of course. She lives not far from here on the Fontanka; would you like to meet her?' . . . He returned to tell me that she would receive us at three that afternoon.[7]

And together they crossed the Anichkov Bridge. Berlin, who knew nothing at that point of how the Soviet state had persecuted the poet and her son Lev, was greeted with a scene of mausoleum splendour:

> Fountain House, the palace of the Sheremetevs, is a magnificent late baroque building, with gates of exquisite ironwork for which Leningrad is famous, and built around a spacious court – not unlike the quadrangle of a large Oxford or Cambridge college. We climbed up one of the steep, dark staircases, to an upper floor, and were admitted to Akhmatova's room. It was very barely furnished – virtually everything in it had, I gathered, been taken away – looted or sold – during the siege. There was a small table, three or four chairs, a wooden chest, a sofa, and, above the unlit stove, a drawing by Modigliani. A stately, grey-haired lady, a white shawl draped about her shoulders, slowly rose to greet us.[8]

The young philosopher and the poet fell into intense discussion, and he was still there at 3 a.m. There was something almost holy about the encounter. She had risen briefly to prepare them both some food: all she could muster was a 'dish of hot potatoes'. Her poverty, after all those years of torment from the regime, was still acute.

And it was not long after that that Anna Akhmatova was once more targeted. This time it was an initiative from Andrei Zhdanov: the Zhdanov Doctrine. In essence, this engineer of human souls was once more setting to work: all artists and writers and poets and critics would have to submit to his vision, which was that of a pure Soviet art, untainted and uncontaminated by a wider European sensibility. At the beginning of this campaign, two of Leningrad's foremost literary and artistic journals, *Zvezda* and *Leningrad*, were targeted. And the attack on Akhmatova and her work was shocking. Her 'subject matter is . . . miserably limited', declared Zhdanov:

It is the poetry of an overwrought upper-class lady who frantically races back and forth between boudoir and chapel . . . A nun or a whore – or rather, both a nun and whore who combines harlotry with prayer . . . Akhmatova's poetry is utterly remote from the people . . . What can there be in common between this poetry and the interests of our people and our state?[9]

Here was the old tectonic tension of aristocracy; the sense that it had persisted spiritually and defiantly. There was a singularity about the fervour with which Zhdanov launched himself at his target. Anna Akhmatova was expelled from the Union of Soviet Writers: a sentence in effect making her poetry once more utterly forbidden, since anyone found with any of it would be regarded as a traitor. Akhmatova was not alone: her former common-law husband Nikolay Punin was also set upon by the authorities. He had been an object of suspicion since the 1930s and the great purges, an art historian steeped in love for the traditions of European work – especially that of Cézanne and Van Gogh – without displaying an even greater love for the new traditions of Soviet painting. Worse: he had opined that some portraits of Lenin had been rendered in a vulgar fashion. Here too, in the eyes of Zhdanov's deputies, was one of the old St Petersburg aristocrats: learned, superior, but most damningly, irredeemably cosmopolitan in outlook. In Punin's case, the punishment was breathtakingly harsh: a tribunal in Leningrad examined his work and sentenced him to the Gulag. He was sent to Abezlag, a camp in the Komi region above the Arctic Circle.

His fellow prisoners included other writers and economists. His surviving letters from the camp – he was only allowed to send a very limited number – were quite extraordinary, even given the strict censorship rules, in their quiet restraint and acceptance of his fate. He made simple requests for books, and small items of comfort. He insisted that in the summer months it was possible to work up quite a healthy tan. This was the face he had to present to his loved ones: any other would not have been permitted. Neither would he wish to endanger them by expressing any sentiments that the authorities might consider dangerous. For all of Leningrad's intensely learned atmosphere, this was the truth of the city under the Soviets: expressing a preference for a French Impressionist painting over a Soviet realist depiction of agriculture was enough to have life as you knew it snatched away, and to be sent to a purgatorial world from which one might never return. Punin certainly didn't: he died amid those endless forests, many thousands of miles from love and comfort. He had survived the siege of Leningrad, but not its rulers. Just a little later, the ban on European paintings – and the appreciation thereof – was equally arbitrarily lifted.

Zhdanov was perceived as the supreme Soviet leader-in-waiting: he too was showing steel, and unswerving fealty to the system engineered by Stalin, with whom he still enjoyed friendship. Zhdanov, Kuznetsov and Popkov held recovering Leningrad in an unbreakable grip, yet death was coming for them too. Like the pilot of a hot-air balloon, Zhdanov had risen higher and higher, but had no means of arresting his ascent into ever icier, ever thinner, air. His attack on Akhmatova was part of his new strategy – ordered by Stalin – of seizing control of the direction of Soviet art. This also involved summoning Shostakovich and Prokofiev to a special conference at which he humiliated the composers by lecturing them on the correct way to create Soviet music. He was also promoted to more international concerns, overseeing the development of socialism in Soviet satellite states in Europe. By 1948, Zhdanov's health appeared to be failing: a recurring heart problem. It was rumoured that – unusually – he had infuriated Stalin by not taking a hard enough line against the dissident state of Yugoslavia. His intense rivals Malenkov and Beria were watching closely. One of Zhdanov's doctors prescribed complete bed rest, concerned about the dangers of cardiac arrest. Zhdanov vanished from public view. Then, on 31 August 1948, came the news of his death.

The public mourning was extravagant: entire editions of *Pravda* devoted to Zhdanov's heroic life's work. Those senior rivals paid tribute of silent contemplation beside his body as it lay in state. But here too was the hallmark of Stalin's regime: a question that hung over the nature of Zhdanov's death. Was his death in fact murder? (A later malicious rumour – in a land where rumours could kill – suggested that his Jewish doctors had colluded to bring about his demise. This was the start of a new phase of anti-Semitism.) There was also an echo of the 1934 assassination of Kirov, which had lit the fuse for the first great purge. Leningrad was about to be targeted with a fresh round of political murders.

The most prominent figure to be stalked was Aleksei Kuznetsov, whose own rise within the Party had been as vertiginous as that of Zhdanov; Kuznetsov had become First Secretary of Leningrad in January 1945, and after that was also promoted to Secretary of the Central Committee, in charge of Party organization across the whole of the USSR. This still relatively young figure was also regarded in some circles as a potential successor to Stalin. He was loathed by Georgii Malenkov and by Lavrentii Beria. In the wake of Zhdanov's death, the jaws of a trap snapped shut on Kuznetsov: in early 1949 he was sacked for the 'crime' of having set up a trade fair in Leningrad and for boasting of the city's special status and heroism as a result of the war. Sharing in the blame was the city's hapless mayor Pyotr Popkov.

By summer 1949, Kuznetsov was under arrest, in the custody of Malenkov. He was pressured to sign a confession of anti-Bolshevik sentiments (the Leningrad trade fair recast as a plot to suck wealth from the rest of the country). He refused, but relented under torture. At his trial, he suddenly, vehemently recanted, proclaiming that he would remain a true Bolshevik despite this injustice. He was sentenced to death, even though the Soviet Union had abolished capital punishment in 1947. (His execution was permitted since the offence pre-dated the change.) It was said that his recantation so angered Stalin that the method used to kill him on 1 October 1950 was not a straightforward bullet but rather an extraordinarily brutal meat hook driven right through his neck.[10]

Trials and death also came in that year to Popkov and many other of Leningrad's high-ranking Party officials. This became another wave of executions, like those of the 1930s purges: a range not only of politicians, but of Leningrad academics too. The truly striking thing was that this was not an anomaly, or some symptom of post-war trauma: this was the true deathly essence of life under Stalin. All Soviet lives belonged to him, and all lives could be extinguished at his will. Thus it was that all the politicians from Leningrad's Smolny Institute, who had grimly held on through the cataclysm of Russia's war, found that their own deaths had merely been postponed. Kuznetsov and all his colleagues had been suspected of trying to elevate Leningrad's status to that of Moscow: first, the special exhibitions devoted to war heroism and then a glittering trade fair, filled with consumer goods, pointing to a brighter Leningrad future.

The city had overreached itself. Its own pride – that sense of exceptionalism, fostered in the effortless grandeur of the architecture, that had flowered in all its poets, composers and artists, stretching back to Pushkin – was anathema to Stalin. There was also that sense of aristocracy, of intellectual superiority; such things could not be tolerated. Murder was natural, and more than that: desirable. The purity of the revolution demanded it. 'They say the terror is going to end,' Victor Serge had written of Leningrad as long ago as 1931, adding prophetically, 'I don't think so. It is still a necessity. The storm must uproot the old trees, stir the ocean to its depths, wash clean the old stones, replenish the impoverished fields. The world will be new afterward.'[11] This was the continual story of the city under whatever name: effusions of blood, and then the blood washed clean from the stones. But in the wake of the war, what fresh form would this cycle of unease take?

27.   The Sense of the Human Nexus

There were corners of the post-war city not covered in the glamorous world-admired glories of ballet or literature: the drab, dark communal apartments where families put back together after the war had had to make ill-tempered accommodations with other residents, some freshly arrived from the countryside and quite unused, as one observer put it, to modern standards of urban hygiene. One Leningrad family had suffered the loss of their toddler son to starvation in that inhuman winter of 1941–2. The mother herself had come close to death; fainting in the street, she was almost mistaken for a corpse, about to be loaded on a sled to be taken to one of the city's mass graves. But now, with some semblance of secure life restored, she and her recently demobilized husband were ready to try again for a child. In 1952, the now forty-one-year-old woman gave birth in the Snegiryov hospital and her newborn son was swaddled in a basket dangling from the ceiling by ropes: a quaint Leningrad maternity practice. The mother's name was Mariya Ivanovna Putina; the father's name was Vladimir Spiridonovich Putin.

And so was the future President Putin born among the legions of the dead. His Leningrad upbringing would in its own way encapsulate the extremes and the possibilities of that extraordinary city. He and his parents lived in a communal apartment very close to the centre, though the block itself was austere and dowdy. There was no hot water, no indoor bath, and heating was via a wood-fired stove. There were cockroaches and rats. Keeping clean meant regular trips to the public baths and sauna. Putin's father was one of the many who had come to the city from the countryside in the 1930s; by the 1950s he was foreman at a railway works, while his wife worked night shifts in a bakery. In this sense, the small family was not particularly well off, and rather too busy to find the time for Leningrad poetry and dance; but Putin's father was a respected figure, there were books in the house, and there was stability, and plenty of food on the table. The young Putin's mother taught him to read, and gave him the basics of mathematics too.

He was an ill-behaved horror in primary education, possibly partly because his home education had given him a head start on many of the other children. But a tendency to get into fights with boys bigger than himself was tempered by the time he reached his Leningrad secondary school. While literature and history and German became Putin's academic passions, his inclination towards physical aggression found a valuable outlet in judo. He joined the Young Pioneers, but he also fixated quite early on another area of Leningrad life that he became convinced held one of the keys to history: espionage. A well-placed agent with the right timing might do more to affect the course of geopolitics than entire divisions of soldiers. Putin set his heart on joining the KGB. He was advised that studying for law would be one route in. In this sense, Leningrad – from its academia to its spies to its flourishing sporting and cultural life – offered Putin every possibility. Yet even here the essential paradox of the city became plain: as he studied law, he was acutely and painfully aware that the other students came from backgrounds that might be described as the intellectual and political Leningrad elite: parents of importance and some wealth. Unlike him, they were not brought up in shared apartments that lacked indoor lavatories. Leningrad still had its aristocracy: the form was a little different but the principle, and the nepotism, were exactly the same.

The city, on the face of it, was making the adjustments to a new generation that the entirety of Europe, west and east, seemed to be making too. But some transgressions could not be forgiven. Leningrad was once more a vibrant cultural centre, but two of its dancers – Rudolf Nureyev and, later, Mikhail Baryshnikov – were to find global fame as defectors who rejected the clammy embrace of communism. Nureyev became – for the West – a modern emblem of the city's ungovernable artistic spirit: on tour in France in 1961, he slipped away from his KGB escorts. In his absence, Nureyev was put on trial in Leningrad in 1962, labelled 'Traitor 50,888' and sentenced to seven years' imprisonment.[1] By this stage he was dancing with the Royal Ballet in London. He had yearned to dance for George Balanchine, the emblematic figurehead of the New York Ballet.

Others of Leningrad's young people made their own accommodations. There were pop bands in the city in the 1960s (the proximity to Finland, and the all-conquering musical aesthetic of Elvis Presley and the Beatles, meant that such forbidden tunes were more easily available in Leningrad than in any other Soviet city). Two popular Leningrad bands at that time had names that carried curious echoes of the city's more numinous past: one was called Forest Brothers and another The Scythians.[2] Music, even in the form of three-minute songs on acoustic guitar, was layered and deeply felt and sometimes secretly, slyly subversive. But there were limits, on this and all other forms of public discourse.

And beneath all of this there ran a concern with remembrance: how might the memory of the siege be marked for the future? Appropriately, it was another of the city's poets – Mikhail Dudin – who suggested a series of memorials to be placed around the city on sites that marked the front lines. These would form inner and outer rings of commemorative monuments. Work began in 1958 and was complete by 1964. But the city itself still required a site of central focus, and by 1975, work was completed in Victory Square, to the south of the city, on the vast Monument to the Heroic Defenders of Leningrad. The centrepiece was a towering obelisk, standing over a large circular enclosure, accessed by a ramp leading downwards, and the perimeter of this enclosure broken, to symbolize breaking through the ring of the blockade. Within this huge monument was an underground memorial hall, filled with art and relics and eternal flames; on the ground level above were a series of sculptures – of soldiers, of pilots, of factory workers and, perhaps most strikingly, of a young soldier and a young woman deep in a tender embrace. The city never lost sight of its sensuality.

The siege had left its mark intellectually as well. Writer and essayist Lidiya Ginzburg – whose own *Blockade Diary* was published much later, in the mid-1980s, had observed back in the 1950s that 'the age old argument about the futility of life has come to an end, to be replaced with another – how to survive without losing one's human image'. It was the siege, she contended, that revived 'the sense of the human nexus'.[3] Yet in terms of diaries and letters, there were continuing waves of uncertainty – partly in the wake of the old Stalinist anger, but also in terms of what constituted a proper public response to atrocity – about what should and should not be seen. There were huge numbers of diaries that had been submitted to city committees. They were lodged within archives, but not registered. And it was only years after communism collapsed that experts such as Alexis Peri, following paper trails, managed to gain access to these long-neglected materials.

There were medical and scientific departments by the 1970s that were also carrying out investigations into long-term health: how had the survivors fared and had the 'dystrophy' caused long-term problems? They were expecting to find increases in complaints such as heart disease; what they actually found pointed to an increased disposition towards strokes, with marked abnormalities of blood pressure. Between 1975 and 1982, thousands of men and women were surveyed. Professor Dmitrii Shestov, conducting the studies, had himself been a boy during the siege, so his fascination was personal as well as clinical. But what of the survivors' mental health? Although the city was never short of psychiatric and psychological facilities (for a dark time, sometimes deployed as weapons against political dissenters, who were hauled off to their wards), it was not until comparatively recently that a psychoanalytic study of Petersburgers who had been children throughout the siege was conducted, by Professor Marina Gulina. The findings from these surviving *blokadniki* were both moving and rather surprising. These people, by now elderly, retained the most piercingly terrible memories: of naked corpses, of the deaths of parents and siblings. 'I still cry at night,' said one. 'I am still hungry,' said another. Yet the wider survey found that, among those who had suffered, later life had brought a 'higher level of stress resilience', and in many, a 'lower level of depression'.[4] As Lidiya Ginzburg had written, they had never lost their 'human image';[5] some of them were reported to have higher levels of emotional sensitivity and empathy.

It would have been difficult to make any such claims, though, for Vladimir Putin, whose career progressed through the 1980s. He was the most perfect exemplar of the KGB ethic: not merely ruthless and icy when it came to the interests of the state, but also efficiently ascetic: no one who knew him was ever quite sure what he thought, and unlike many of his colleagues, he stayed clear of the tongue-loosening pleasures of strong drink.

And in time, Putin rose to conquer his own home city, triumphing over the Soviet Leningrad aristocrats, the sons of the Party officials. After serving as a KGB officer in East Germany (uncharacteristically growing a little tubby on the beer in Dresden), he was caught, like all other Russians, in the vortex that came with the collapse of the USSR and the communist system in 1989. In 1990, he was an adviser to Leningrad's mayor; within months, he himself was deputy mayor and head of the Committee for Foreign Economic Relations. This was rather more ambitious than anything that his predecessors Aleksei Kuznetsov or Pyotr Popkov could have dreamed. The city was honeycombed with corruption, and local businessmen required licences to trade with a new and rapacious Western market; Putin was in charge of granting those licences. He was also claiming a commission on each of them. By this time, by popular vote, the city was once more called St Petersburg – the name of 'Lenin' resolutely jettisoned. One of St Petersburg's oldest abiding sins, in the eyes of the Communists, was its instinct for trade. Putin took this instinct and welded it to the most cynical appetite for riches. He was now an aristocrat.

Yet across the years, and throughout the aggression that he inflicted upon others, from Georgia to Ukraine, he never lost sight of all that the city had suffered. President Putin attended a special ceremony in 2011, seventy years after the siege of Leningrad began, at the Piskaryovskoye Memorial Cemetery. He gazed out across the plots and mounds that marked the mass graves. Flowers had been laid everywhere; so too, apparently, had slices of bread. Putin made a striking and piercingly personal speech concerning his own older brother Viktor – the baby who had died of starvation in 1942. 'I don't even know where my own brother is buried, whom I never saw, never knew,' he said. 'It is very likely that he is buried here somewhere.'[6] And in that uncertainty, in that horrible ambiguity that could forestall full and proper mourning and remembrance, lay another manifestation of the city's uncanny borderlands: the line between the living and the dead; the ghosts beyond number who were simultaneously present and yet obliterated, as though they had never existed.

There are young couples still walking those wide, and now ostentatiously wealthy, boulevards under the unending sun of summer nights, the city's pavement tables still crowded with diners. Apartments that were once shared by several families now command gigantic sums. The city's museums and theatres continue to reign from their lofty peaks of aestheticism. There are those in Russia who continue to find St Petersburg rather full of itself in these terms: a friend of mine from Samara has a temperamental preference for the more straightforward life alongside the wide Volga. But there is something she does rather love about Petersburg: its sense of the numinous, the eerie. That awareness of living history pressing in on every street she walks down. It remains even under the commercialized glitz. Fyodor Dostoevsky, in *Notes from Underground*, describing darker, more desperate thoroughfares, declared St Petersburg 'the most abstract, pre-meditated city on earth'.[7] And yet that impossible, haunted city, conjured from the imagination of Peter the Great, somehow survived one of the most terrible atrocities of the twentieth century. The fogs and the ghosts abide.

Acknowledgements

It is no exaggeration to say that history has been co-opted into the current Russian conflict. The regime has a paranoid sensitivity to any areas of study that might show the nation or its past rulers in an unflattering light: tell what is perceived to be the wrong story and you are a traitor. For this reason – and even though there is nothing they have done that could be construed as remotely hostile to the memory of the people of Leningrad, quite the reverse – I shall not name the Russian friends and acquaintances who have given me invaluable guidance and advice throughout. But my gratitude is deep.

In terms of historical insight, depth and experience, I am very much in the debt of Andy Willimott and Abigail Karas, who were good enough to read the manuscript and whose forgiveness I now ask for any mistakes or errors of judgement that stubbornly remain.

I want to pay tribute to Connor Brown, Viking editorial director, for his driving enthusiasm and wise judgements. My sincere thanks also to Trisha Mendiratta for sharp ideas and suggestions across the project; and to Olivia Mead (publicity), Annie Lucas (campaigns), Emma Brown (editorial management), Annie Underwood (production), Georgia Sibbitt (inventory management) and all the wonderful sales team for their perennial brilliance. Plus a deep bow of admiration – as always! – to Viking's head of nonfiction, Daniel Crewe, overseeing all.

Huge gratitude is also due to Anthony Hippisley and Robert Drew for the expertise and knowledge they brought to the proofreading of the text.

Copy-editing is an art – and Trevor Horwood is a master. As ever, my profound thanks for his highly tuned ear for language and his piercing eye for clarity and detail. And a deep bow to my always fantastic agent Anna Power, who made it all happen, and Helene Butler, who sent it around the world.

Selected Bibliography

Ales Adamovich and Daniil Granin, *Leningrad Under Siege: First-Hand Accounts of the Ordeal* (Pen and Sword, 2007)

Anna Akhmatova, *Selected Poems*, intro. Carol Ann Duffy (Penguin Vintage Classics, 2009)

Andrei Bely, *Petersburg* ([1905] Penguin Classics, 2011)

Olga Berggolts, *Daytime Stars*, trans. Lisa A. Kirschenbaum (University of Wisconsin Press, 2018)

Richard Bidlack and Nikita Lomagin, *The Leningrad Blockade, 1941–1944: A New Documentary History from the Soviet Archives* (Yale University Press, 2012)

Jeffrey Brooks, *Thank You, Comrade Stalin! Soviet Public Culture from Revolution to Cold War* (Princeton University Press, 2001)

A. G. Bulakh, N. B. Abakumova and Iosif Vladimirovich Romanovsky, *St Petersburg: A History in Stone* (St Petersburg University Press, 2010)

Lidiya Chukovskaya, *The Akhmatova Journals: 1938–1941* (HarperCollins, 1994)

Katerina Clark, *Petersburg: Crucible of Cultural Revolution* (Harvard University Press, 1995)

J. M. Coetzee, *The Master of Petersburg* (Vintage, 2004)

Marquis de Custine, *Letters from Russia* ([1839] Penguin Classics, 2014)

John Langdon Davies, *Invasion in the Snow: A Study of Mechanized War* (Houghton Mifflin, 1941)

Fyodor Dostoevsky, *Crime and Punishment* ([1866] Penguin Classics, 2003)

———, *Demons* ([1871–2] Penguin Classics, 2008)

———, *The Idiot* ([1868] Penguin Classics, 2004)

———, *Memoirs from the House of the Dead*, trans. Jessie Coulson ([1861–2] Oxford University Press, 2008)

———, *Notes from Underground* ([1864] Penguin Vintage Classics, 2004)

Julie Draskoczy, *Belomor: Criminality and Creativity in Stalin's Gulag* (Academic Studies Press, 2014)

Helen Dunmore, *The Siege* (Viking, 2001)

Ralph Dutli, *Osip Mandelstam: A Biography*, trans. Ben Fowkes (Verso, 2023)

Sergei Eisenstein, *The Film Sense* ([1943] Faber, 1986)

Gennady Estraikh, *Rehabilitation: Jews in the Soviet Union* (New York University Press, 2022)

Orlando Figes, *Natasha's Dance: A Cultural History of Russia* (Allen Lane, 2002)

Georgii Apollonovich Gapon, *The Story of My Life* (Chapman & Hall, 1905)

Lidiya Ginzburg, *Blockade Diary* (Harvill Press, 1995)

Joseph Goebbels, *The Goebbels Diaries 1939–1941*, trans. Fred Taylor (Hamish Hamilton, 1982)

Nikolay Gogol, *The Collected Tales of Nikolay Gogol*, trans. Richard Pevear and Larissa Volokhonsky (Vintage Classics, 1999)

Jeffrey K. Hass, *Wartime Suffering and Survival: The Human Condition Under Siege in the Blockade of Leningrad* (Oxford University Press USA, 2021)

Gotthard Heinrici, *A German General on the Eastern Front: The Letters of Gotthard Heinrici*, ed. and intro. Johannes Hurter (Pen and Sword, 2015)

Vera Inber, *Leningrad Diary* (Hutchinson, 1971)

Michael Jones, *Leningrad: State of Siege* (John Murray, 2010)

Simon Karlinsky, *Freedom from Violence and Lies: Essays on Russian Poetry and Music* (Academic Studies Press, 2013)

Daniil Kharms, *Today I Wrote Nothing: The Selected Writings of Daniil Kharms* (Duckworth, 2007)

Nikita Khrushchev, *Khrushchev Remembers* (Little, Brown, 1970)

Wilhelm Lübbecke writing as William Lubbeck, *At Leningrad's Gates: The Combat Memories of a Soldier with Army Group North* (reissued edn, Casemate Publishers, 2007)

Curzio Malaparte, *Kaputt* ([1944] NYRB Press, 2005)

Witold Wojciech Mędykowski, *Macht Arbeit Frei? German Economic Policy and Forced Labor of Jews in the General Government, 1939–1943* (Academic Studies Press, 2018)

Brian Moynahan, *Leningrad: Siege and Symphony* (Quercus, 2013)

Vladimir Nabokov, *Speak, Memory* (Weidenfeld and Nicolson, 1967)

Alexis Peri, *The War Within: Diaries from the Siege of Leningrad* (Harvard University Press, 2017)

Anita Pisch, *The Personality Cult of Stalin in Soviet Posters, 1929–1953: Archetypes, Inventions and Fabrications* (Australian National University Press, 2016)

Nikolay Punin, *The Diaries of Nikolay Punin, 1904–1953*, trans. Jennifer Greene Krupala (University of Texas Press, 1999)

Alexander Pushkin, *Eugene Onegin* (Oxford World Classics, 2009)

———, *Novels, Tales, Journeys: The Complete Prose* (Penguin Classics, 2017)

Erhard Raus, *Panzer Operations: The Eastern Front Memoir of General Raus, 1941–1945* (Da Capo Press, 2013)

John Reed, *Ten Days that Shook the World* ([1919] Communist Party of Great Britain, 1926)

Roberta Reeder, *Anna Akhmatova: Poet and Prophet* (Allison and Busby, 1995)

Anna Reid, *Leningrad: Tragedy of a City Under Siege, 1941–1944* (Bloomsbury, 2011)

Harrison E. Salisbury, *The 900 Days: The Siege of Leningrad* (Secker & Warburg, 1969)

Gordon F. Sander, *The Hundred Day Winter War: Finland's Gallant Stand Against the Soviet Army* (University Press of Kansas, 2013)

Victor Serge, *Conquered City* (first published in 1932 in Paris as *Ville conquise*, NYRB Classics, 2011)

Victor Seroff, *Sergei Prokofiev: A Soviet Tragedy* (Frewin, 1969)

Dmitri Shostakovich, *Testimony: The Memoirs of Dmitri Shostakovich* (Hamish Hamilton, 1979)

Cynthia Simmons and Nina Perlina, *Writing the Siege of Leningrad: Women's Diaries, Memoirs, and Documentary Prose* (University of Pittsburgh Press, 2005)

Aleksandr Solzhenitsyn, *The Gulag Archipelago* ([1973] Penguin Vintage Classics, 2018)

Yngvar Bordewich Steinholt, *Rock in the Reservation: Songs from the Leningrad Rock Club 1981–86* (Mass Media Music Scholars Press, 2005)

Nikolay Tikhonov, *The Defence of Leningrad: Eyewitness Accounts of the Siege* (Hutchinson, 1944)

Leo Tolstoy, *Anna Karenina* ([1877] Penguin Classics, 2000)

———, *The Death of Ivan Ilyich and Other Stories* (Penguin Classics, 2008)

———, *War And Peace* ([1869] Vintage Penguin Classics, 2008)

William Trotter, *The Winter War: The Russo-Finnish War of 1939–40* (Aurum Press, 1991)

Ivan Turgenev, *Virgin Soil* ([1877] NYRB Classics, 2000)

Alexander Tvardovsky, *Vasilii Tyorkin: A Book About a Soldier* ([1942–5] Smokestack Books, 2019)

Solomon Volkov, *St. Petersburg: A Cultural History* (Sinclair-Stevenson, 1996)

Frances Welch, *Rasputin: A Short Life* (Short Books, 2015)

H. G. Wells, *Russia in the Shadows* ([1921] Faber Finds, 2008)

Alexander Werth, *Leningrad* (Hamish Hamilton, 1944)

Yevgenii Zamyatin, *We*, trans. Hugh Aplin ([1921] Alma Books, 2017)

Georgii K. Zhukov, *The Memoirs of Marshal Zhukov* (Cape, 1971)

Notes

1. The World Will Tremble

1 'The Great Adventure of Sergei Diaghilev', by Arlene Croce, *New York Review of Books*, January 2011, is a marvellous essay about the sensuous aesthetic world of Diaghilev and how both he and wider Petersburg developed in modernism.

2 Yevgeniya Aluf, interviewed for the Blavatnik Archive. This archive is an extraordinary enterprise devoted to Jewish voices across Russia and eastern Europe and can be viewed at www.blavatnikarchive.org. It is a non-profit project founded by the businessman Len Blavatnik and is in many ways a profoundly beautiful treasure house of memories, of images, and of thought-provoking essays, on a dazzling range of subjects. One striking element in the Petersburg/Leningrad accounts is how Judaism – although naturally vital to the lives of the interviewees – was simultaneously not quite at the forefront of their experiences either in the city or out on the battlefields.

3 The White Nights as poetically summoned in *Kaputt* ([1944] NYRB Press, 2005), a powerful memoir/novel by Curzio Malaparte (the pseudonym of Kurt Erich Suckert, an Italian). Malaparte, a correspondent who was at liberty to move around the Eastern Front, and who met with senior Wehrmacht figures, blended his eyewitness observations of horror and decadence with lightly fictionalized scenes; so while it cannot be taken as any kind of historical source, there is none the less vivid verisimilitude when he summons the landscapes around Leningrad, among others.

4 Natalya Uskova, quoted in *The War Within: Diaries from the Siege of Leningrad*, by Alexis Peri (Harvard University Press, 2017).

5 Moisei Frid, interviewed for the Blavatnik Archive, as above.

6 From Victor Serge's perceptive novel *Conquered City* (first published in 1932 in Paris as *Ville conquise*, NYRB Books, 2011). As with Curzio

Malaparte, this is not in any sense an historical source; yet the city that
it summons has its own intense truth.

7 *Letters from Russia*, by the Marquis de Custine ([1839] Penguin Classics,
2014).

8 From *The Bronze Horseman (A Tale of St Petersburg)*, by Alexander Pushkin.

9 From 'Nevsky Prospekt', by Nikolay Gogol, first published 1835, in
Gogol, *Petersburg Tales*, trans. Dora O'Brien (Alma Classics, 2017).

10 Malaparte, *Kaputt*.

11 Edith Matus, interviewed (and all her brilliant vivacity captured) by Ed
Vulliamy for the *Observer*; www.theguardian.com/theobserver/2001/
nov/25/features.magazine27.

12 From *Speak, Memory*, by Vladimir Nabokov (Weidenfeld and Nicolson,
1967) – not just one of the great memoirs of the twentieth century, with
some of the most exquisite sentences, but also a vivid, sensual and often
howlingly funny evocation of Nabokov's privileged childhood in and
around St Petersburg.

13 The legend lovingly retold in a variety of locations, including the *Wall
Street Journal* and all sorts of blogs and websites: but there is more in-depth
detail of the tomb itself, and the troubling history of Soviet appropriation, to be found in 'The Gur-i Amir Mausoleum and the Soviet Politics
of Preservation', by Charles Shaw, in *Future Anterior: Journal of Historic
Preservation, History, Theory, and Criticism*, Summer 2011.

14 Ibid. The essay also recounts the early Soviet attempts to suppress devout
Islam in Uzbekistan, and the way, in 1941, that archaeologists took samples
from Timur's (Tamerlane's) skull and skeleton – including hair fragments –
and bagged them up in preparation for analysis in a Samarkand laboratory.

2. Time and the Bolsheviks

1 These haunting images from *The Times*, 8 April 1921. The piece, by-lined
'From Our Special Correspondent', carried the sub-heading 'Petrograd
Under the Reds', suggesting a rather less forgiving editorial line than
the one taken by author H. G. Wells for the *Daily Express* on the occasion of his 1921 visit to Russia, where, having interviewed Lenin, he
found himself open to some of the possibilities of Bolshevism.

2 Ibid.

3 From Nikolay Punin, *The Diaries of Nikolay Punin, 1904–1953*, trans. Jennifer Greene Krupala (University of Texas Press, 1999) – an intense and in many ways rather beautiful memoir of aesthetic life in the jagged and brutal turmoil of revolution.

4 Andrei Bely, *Petersburg* ([1905] Penguin Classics, 2011) – a novel that still beguiles with its many-layered modernist sensibility. Here, the terrorist-haunted city is conjured in the manner of a suffocating bad dream.

5 Fyodor Dostoevsky, *Demons* ([1871–2] Penguin Classics, 2008).

6 From an illuminating monograph, 'Fear and Belief in the USSR's Great Terror', by Robert Thurston, *Slavic Review*, Summer 1986.

7 This poster is available on commercial websites, but, more importantly, its vibrant modernism raises a question about the Stalinist approach to jazz (which famously the Nazis had banned). In the late 1920s there had been efforts within Russia to control and censor fast syncopated music, but by the 1930s the authorities had relaxed to the extent that 'central policy permitted people to enjoy the fox-trot, tango, Charleston, lindy-hop, rumba, and jazz played both by amateur ensembles and by professional jazz stars'. This from a fascinating essay: 'Jazz, Power, and Soviet Youth in the Early Cold War, 1948–1953', by Gleb Tsipursky, *Journal of Musicology*, Summer 2016.

8 From a marvellous essay, 'Stumbling Toward Socialist Realism: Ballet in Leningrad, 1927–1937', by Carolyn Pouncy, *Russian History*, Summer 2005.

9 From Thurston, 'Fear and Belief in the USSR's Great Terror'.

10 Ibid.

11 Ibid.

12 There is a moving website put together by photographer Vladimir Pomortzeff featuring images of the Levashovo cemetery, and of the pictorial memorials attached to trees by families of the many victims. It can be viewed at https://pomortzeff.com/eng/levashovo. For a wider overview of the commemoration of silenced victims of the purges and others, there is a haunting monograph: 'Exhuming the Bodies of Soviet Terror', by Irina Paperno, *Representations*, Summer 2001.

13 A typically arresting passage in *Daytime Stars*, Olga Berggolts's poetic memoir of the siege and of wider Leningrad life, trans. Lisa A. Kirschenbaum (University of Wisconsin Press, 2018).

14 There is a truly immersive (in all senses!) essay by T. Vujosevic on saunas in Stalinist Leningrad and Moscow to be found in an online journal called *Architectural Histories* at journal.eahn.org/article/id/7457/.

15 *Sergei Prokofiev: A Soviet Tragedy*, by Victor Seroff (Frewin, 1969).

16 Adding layers of depth to an already mazy episode of history is a review entitled 'Did Stalin Kill Kirov and Does It Matter?', by Matt Lenoe, *Journal of Modern History*, June 2002.

17 Cited in the monograph 'Another Kind of Fear: The Kirov Murder and the End of Bread Rationing in Leningrad', by Lesley A. Rimmel, *Slavic Review*, Autumn 1997.

18 Lenoe, 'Did Stalin Kill Kirov and Does It Matter?'

19 Ibid.

20 Ibid.

21 Helpfully reproduced online by the Marxists Internet Archive – the speech can be found at www.marxists.org/subject/art/lit_crit/ sovietwritercongress/.

22 The reality-inverting nature of Yagoda's show trial was analysed almost contemporaneously, and with some wonder, in 1938 in an essay entitled 'Totalitarian Justice: Trial of Bukharin, Rykov, Yagoda', by lawyer Harvey T. Mann ('Member of the New York Bar') in *American Bar Association Journal*. Yagoda's trial also exposed his own methods of terror: focusing threats not merely upon his victims, but also upon their families.

23 As an extraordinary postscript, Dora Lazurkina, fully rehabilitated, and attending a 1961 conference, eight years after Stalin's death, told the delegates: that 'Lenin's ghost' had spoken to her. Lenin had told her that it was 'unpleasant to be [in the mausoleum] next to Stalin, who did so much harm to the Party'. From *Rehabilitation: Jews in the Soviet Union*, by Gennady Estraikh (New York University Press, 2022).

24 *The Leningrad Blockade, 1941–1944: A New Documentary History from the Soviet Archives*, by Richard Bidlack and Nikita Lomagin (Yale University Press, 2012).

25 As cited in 'Stalin at War 1918–1953: Patterns of Violence and Foreign Threat', by David Shearer, *Jahrbücher für Geschichte Osteuropas* 66 (2018).

26 Ibid.

27 As mentioned in Bidlack and Nikita Lomagin, *The Leningrad Blockade*.

28 As cited in Shearer, 'Stalin at War 1918–1953'.

3. The Haunted Forests

1 From Nikita Khrushchev, *Khrushchev Remembers* (Little, Brown, 1970), serialized at length that year in *The Times*.

2 There is a fascinating essay, 'Stalin at the Movies', by Stephen Kotkin, *New York Review of Books*, October 2017, which explores Stalin's growing engagement and involvement with the 1930s Soviet film industry (and his delight in a 1934 jazz-infused comedy called *Jolly Fellows*).

3 Bertha Gutkina, interviewed for the Blavatnik Archive.

4 Shostakovich's *Suite on Finnish Themes* went missing for many years (he was said to have lent the score to a friend), but it surfaced at the turn of the millennium, and – naturally – was performed. There is an interesting review in the journal *Tempo* by Martin Anderson (October 2001).

5 *The Hundred Day Winter War: Finland's Gallant Stand Against the Soviet Army*, by Gordon F. Sander (University Press of Kansas, 2013).

6 There is an interesting piece by tank expert Peter Samsonov at www. tankarchives.ca/2021/08/chief-designer-of-1930s. html.

7 Ibid.

8 *The Winter War: The Russo-Finnish War of 1939–40*, by William Trotter (Aurum Press, 1991).

9 *Invasion in the Snow: A Study of Mechanized War*, by John Langdon-Davies (Houghton Mifflin, 1941).

10 Ibid.

11 Yakov Elner, interviewed for the Blavatnik Archive.

12 Ibid.

13 As perhaps might be expected, there are many profiles (some breathlessly admiring); this, slightly more considered, is from the BBC's history magazine website: www.historyextra.com/period/second-world-war/worlds-deadliest-sniper-simo-hayha-finnish-white-death-winter-war.

14 This and other startling sauna and reindeer images from the war can be found at www.life.com/history/the-coldest-front-lifes-coverage-of-the-winter-war.

15 There is a beguiling essay, 'Across the Moominverse', by Frances Wilson, *New York Review of Books*, December 2023, that discusses the wartime genesis of the Moomins.

16 This and other arresting images of the Winter War can be viewed at www. rferl.org/a/finlands-winter-war-with-the-soviet-union/80280490.html.

17 Trotter, *The Winter War*.

18 Images at www.rferl.org/a/finlands-winter-war-with-the-soviet-union/ 80280490.html.

19 The full speech – given in a broadcast in January 1940 can be read at winstonchurchill.org/resources/speeches/1940-the-finest-hour/ the-war-situation-house-of-many-mansions.

20 Henrikh Dudnik, interviewed for the Blavatnik Archive.

21 Bidlack and Lomagin, *The Leningrad Blockade*.

22 A rich overview of his life, his work and his Scottish ancestry (Lermontov/Learmonth) can be read in the essay 'Lermontov's Demon', by Henry Gifford, *New York Review of Books*, May 1984.

23 There is an absorbing (and very much of its time) obituary of Krupskaya which traces her educational passions and work with evening schools' written by Louis Segal for the *Slavonic and East European Review*, July 1939.

24 All this was part of a genre of immense Soviet pride in industrial progress: there is a range of images of hydroelectric works to be found at museum.power-m.ru/en/stories/2017/volkhovskaya.

25 *Vozhdi naroda*, cited in Bidlack and Lomagin, *The Leningrad Blockade*.

26 From 'Us Against Them: Social Identity in Soviet Russia', by Sarah Davies, *Russian Review*, January 1997.

27 Ibid.

28 As cited in Bidlack and Lomagin, *The Leningrad Blockade*.

29 Ibid.

30 Anna Novikova, interviewed for the Blavatnik Archive.

4. *'Flung myself at the hangman's feet'*

1 *Anna Akhmatova: Poet and Prophet*, by Roberta Reeder (Allison and Busby, 1995).

2 *We*, by Yevgenii Zamyatin, trans. Hugh Aplin ([1921] Alma Books, 2017).

3 A long (and poetic) appreciation of Mandelstam's work, and his courage, can be found in 'Osip and Nadezhda Mandelstam', by Seamus Heaney, *London Review of Books*, August 1981.

4 Fyodor Dostoevsky, *Memoirs from the House of the Dead* (first published 1861–2), trans. Jessie Coulson (Oxford University Press, 2008).

5 Sometimes translated as 'soul-strangling gremlin'; there is a moving essay about Mandelstam's lethal taunting of the authorities to be found at www.poetryfoundation.org/poets/osip-mandelstam. In addition, there was a scholarly piece: 'Into the Heart of Darkness: Mandelstam's Ode to Stalin', by Clarence Brown, *Slavic Review*, December 1967.

6 In 'Reading Mandelstam and Stalin', by novelist and translator José Manuel Prieto in the *New York Review of Books*, June 2010, there is a little more on the psychological to-and-fro: Stalin wanting to know if Mandelstam was 'a master'.

7 A haunting essay on this subject, by Eimear McBride for *New Statesman*, May 2017, can be read at www.newstatesman.com/long-reads/2017/05/it-gets-people-killed-osip-mandelstam-and-perils-writing-poetry-under-stalin.

8 Reeder, *Anna Akhmatova*.

9 Ibid.

10 Ibid.

11 An interesting illustrated essay, 'From Africa to Acmeism: Nikolay Stepanovich Gumilev (1886–1921)', can be found at blogs.bl.uk/european/2016/04/from-africa-to-acmeism.html.

12 Reeder, *Anna Akhmatova*.

13 Ibid.

14 Ibid.

15 Berggolts, *Daytime Stars*.

16 Ibid.

17 Ibid.

18 Ibid.

19 Ibid.

20 Ibid.

21 Ibid.

22 The horror of the construction of the White Sea Canal – and the selective vision of those writers who were permitted to observe this enterprise – is discussed in *Belomor: Criminality and Creativity in Stalin's Gulag*, by Julie Draskoczy (Academic Studies Press, 2014).

23 Inber's favoured position within the regime as an artist – extending out from that 1934 Nordic tour – is tangentially explored through the lens of Soviet cultural exchanges in the Stalinist period in 'VOKS, Cultural Diplomacy and the Shadow of the Lubianka: Olavi Paavolainen's 1939 Visit to the Soviet Union', by Ville Laamanen, *Journal of Contemporary History*, October 2017.

24 Vera Inber, *Leningrad Diary* (English edition first published by Hutchinson in 1971 with – strikingly – an introduction by erstwhile Bletchley Park codebreaker Edward Crankshaw, himself posted to Moscow for diplomatic purposes later in the war).

5. New Gods and Old Believers

1 Stalsky's poetry is still admired in Russia: an exhibition devoted to his work recently opened in St Petersburg's National Library. His praise is cited in a fascinating work: *The Personality Cult of Stalin in Soviet Posters, 1929–1953: Archetypes, Inventions and Fabrications*, by Anita Pisch (Australian National University Press, 2016).

2 More on Stalin's Georgian roots and layers of local creation myths in 'Stalin, Man of the Borderlands', by Alfred J. Rieber, *American Historical Review*, December 2001.

3 Cited in *Thank You, Comrade Stalin! Soviet Public Culture from Revolution to Cold War*, by Jeffrey Brooks (Princeton University Press, 2001).

4 As cited in Bidlack and Lomagin, *The Leningrad Blockade*.

5 As cited in 'From "Counter-revolutionary Monuments" to "National Heritage": The Preservation of Leningrad Churches, 1964–1982', by Catriona Kelly, *Cahiers du Monde Russe*, January–June 2013.

6 Ibid.

7 For more, see 'Forced Secularization in Soviet Russia: Why an Atheistic Monopoly Failed', by Paul Froese, *Journal for the Scientific Study of Religion*, March 2004.

8 Cited in Pisch, *The Personality Cult of Stalin in Soviet Posters*.

9 The stubborn persistence of religious belief across the country and also the subversive celebration of religious holidays, to the extent that the League of the Militant Godless tried to stage their own secular versions

of Christmas, with home-made ornaments, is fascinatingly mapped in 'Soviet Atheism and Russian Orthodox Strategies of Resistance, 1917–1932', by William B. Husband, *Journal of Modern History*, March 1998.

10 Punin, *The Diaries of Nikolay Punin*.

11 Ibid.

12 Cited in Bidlack and Lomagin, *The Leningrad Blockade*.

13 Ibid.

14 The ending of Mussorgsky's opera *Khovanshchina* was said to have been based upon an Old Believer melody.

15 From 'Socialist Churches: Heritage Preservation and "Cultic Buildings" in Leningrad, 1924–1940', by Catriona Kelly, *Slavic Review*, 2012.

16 Cited in 'The Great Terror in Leningrad: A Quantitative Analysis', by Melanie Ilic, *Europe-Asia Studies*, December 2000.

17 A deeply evocative piece by Elif Batuman, 'The Bells', *New Yorker*, April 2009, can be found at www.newyorker.com/magazine/2009/04/27/the-bells-6.

18 Ibid.

19 Ibid.

20 Some mesmerizing images may be found at scientificinquirer.com/2024/01/04/the-big-picture-the-glorious-architecture-and-design-of-the-saint-petersburg-mosque/.

21 From Bidlack and Lomagin, *The Leningrad Blockade*.

22 Cited in Davies, 'Us Against Them'.

23 Ibid.

24 Ibid.

25 Ibid.

26 Henrikh Dudnik, interviewed for the Blavatnik Archive.

27 Bely, *Petersburg*.

6. The Blood of Saint Petersburg

1 George Steiner, writing of Pushkin in the *Observer*, 14 March 1999, adding that this 'conscience' also informed Dostoevsky and Joseph Brodsky.

2 Excerpt from Pushkin, *Eugene Onegin* (Oxford World Classics, 2009).

3 As cited in 'Soviet Social Mentalité and Russocentrism on the Eve of War, 1936–1941', by David Brandenberger in *Jahrbücher für Geschichte Osteuropas* 48 (2000).

4 Ibid.

5 Ibid.

6 An interesting essay on the philosophy of Narodnaya Volya, on the terrible aftermath, and on Petersburg assassins in 'Raskolnikov into Pnin: Betraying the People's Will in Tsarist Russia', by Tony Wood, *London Review of Books*, February 2010.

7 There is also absorbing detail about the assassination, and of some of the other key figures in the group, and their focus on making just one man – the Tsar – the repository of all evils, in 'The Making of a Revolutionary Icon: Vera Nikolaevna Figner and the People's Will in the Wake of the Assassination of Tsar Aleksandr II', by Lynne Hartnett, *Canadian Slavonic Papers*, June–September 2001.

8 Ibid.

9 Ibid.

10 Father Gapon's autobiography, published in 1906, can be found in PDF form on the Marxists Internet Archive website at www.marxists.org/ archive/gapon/1906-story-of-my-life.pdf. Gapon – or perhaps his writing collaborator – has filled this account with colour and drama.

11 Nicholas II and his imagined holy bond with the ordinary people is analysed in *Russian Monarchy: Representation and Rule*, by Richard Wortman (Academic Studies Press, 2013).

12 Cited in 'The Blessed Fools of Old Russia', by Natalya Challis and Horace W. Dewey in *Jahrbücher für Geschichte Osteuropas* 22 (1974).

13 Yusupov wrote his memoirs in 1927. Russian authority Orlando Figes explores layers of rich (and eye-poppingly lurid) detail in the Rasputin legend in 'A Very Close Friend of the Family', *New York Review of Books*, December 2016.

14 *Lost Splendour and the Death of Rasputin*, by Prince Felix Yusupov ([1927] Adelphi, 2016).

15 From Berggolts, *Daytime Stars*.

16 From Punin, *The Diaries of Nikolay Punin*.

17 *The Times*, 8 November 1917.

18 The full text is reproduced by the Marxist Internet Archive at www. marxists.org/archive/martov/1918/07/death-penalty.htm.

19 This pronouncement was made in August 1918 following the assassination of Cheka leader Moisei Uritsky.

7. 'Life has become merrier'

1 Yakov Pikus, interviewed for the Blavatnik Archive.

2 Later compiled as *Vasilii Tyorkin: A Book About a Soldier*, by Alexander Tvardovsky ([1942–5] Smokestack Books, 2019).

3 Mikhail Zhvanetsky would also write comic monologues for Raykin in later years: the two had a strong affinity (as well as matching wit).

4 Cited in 'Laughing with Comrade Stalin: An Analysis of Laughter in a Soviet Newspaper Report', by Natalya Skradol, *Russian Review*, January 2009.

5 Ibid.

6 Cited in 'Sanctioning Laughter in Stalin's Soviet Union', by Jonathan Waterlow, *History Workshop Journal*, Spring 2015. As mentioned, one of Stalin's favourite films – which he was instrumental in commissioning – was the musical *Jolly Fellows* (1933), about a Crimean shepherd mistaken for a sophisticated concert conductor, and intended as a pure escapist answer to American cinema (Charlie Chaplin and Buster Keaton feature in the opening credits as NOT appearing in the film).

7 Ibid.

8 Cited ibid.

9 Ibid.

10 Ibid.

11 Cited ibid.

12 The fate of Nikolay Chelyapov was even grimmer: denounced and named as an 'enemy of the people' – and then 'disappearing', never to be heard of again; the fear experienced by so many Soviet musicians is explored in 'Soviet Musicians and the Great Terror', by Caroline Brooke, *Europe-Asia Studies*, May 2002.

13 As cited in Seroff, *Sergei Prokofiev*.

14 From a thirteenth-century text – *Tales of the Life and Courage of the Pious and Great Prince Alexander*.

15 Much as Parisian aesthetes revelled in Diaghilev's vision, there was a sense among Western critics that the early productions were 'exotic' and even 'barbarous' – condescending views of Russian artistry that Petersburgers found intensely disagreeable and racist. Explored in: ' "The Russian Barnum": Russian Opinions on Diaghilev's Ballets Russes, 1909–1914', by Hanna Järvinen, *Dance Research*, Summer 2008.

16 Lopukhov's efforts to absorb and express pure ideological truth through dance are explored in 'Fedor Lopukhov: A Soviet Choreographer in the 1920s', by Elizabeth Souritz, trans. Lynn Visson, ed. Sally Banes, *Dance Research Journal*, Autumn 1985.

8. 'Germany has declared war on us!'

1 Yura Riabinkin's diaries, recovered by Ales Adamovich and excerpted in *Leningrad Under Siege: First-Hand Accounts of the Ordeal*, by Ales Adamovich and Daniil Granin (Pen and Sword, 2007).

2 Molotov lived until November 1986 (he was ninety-six when he died, in the Gorbachev era of perestroika); the line was quoted in his obituary in the *Washington Post*.

3 Henrikh Dudnik, interviewed for the Blavatnik Archive.

4 Ibid.

5 Georgii K. Zhukov, *The Memoirs of Marshal Zhukov* (Cape, 1971).

6 Elya Gendelevich, interviewed for the Blavatnik Archive.

7 Rahewin, a twelfth-century poet and chronicler, writing in volume 3 of *Gesta Friderici*.

8 The barbaric and lethal use of the cangue was an adaptation of an older Chinese restraint used like the European yoke, worn (non-lethally) around the neck for a short period and intended as penance and punishment.

9 *A German General on the Eastern Front: The Letters of Gotthard Heinrici*, by Gotthard Heinrici, ed. and intro. Johannes Hurter (Pen and Sword, 2015).

10 This report – and others – are quoted in a sumptuously illustrated article to be found at www.popularmechanics.com/military/weapons/a32439030/

t-34-soviet-tank-history/. There are accompanying photographs of tank assembly lines, and cross-sections of their workings and interiors.

11 Yura Riabinkin's diaries, reproduced in Adamovich and Granin, *Leningrad Under Siege*.

12 Ibid.

13 Samuil Hedekel, interviewed for the Blavatnik Archive.

14 Ibid.

15 As quoted in a detailed wartime history of the Mariinsky (Kirov) Theatre on the theatre's own Petersburg website: www.mariinsky.ru/en/about/ww2/1941/.

16 Georgii Knyazev's diaries, reproduced in Adamovich and Granin, *Leningrad Under Siege*.

17 Ibid.

18 Cited in Bidlack and Lomagin, *The Leningrad Blockade*.

9. Safeguarding the Treasure

1 Sofiya Mirskaya, interviewed for the Blavatnik Archive.

2 Cited in Bidlack and Lomagin, *The Leningrad Blockade*.

3 The text of the speech has been reproduced on the Marxist Internet Archive at www.marxists.org/reference/archive/stalin/works/1941/07/03.htm.

4 Ibid.

5 Daniil Kharms and his sexual judgements, delivered in poetic form, may not find widespread favour today; none the less, these and other of his works can be studied in *Today I Wrote Nothing: The Selected Writings of Daniil Kharms* (Duckworth, 2007).

6 There is an hypnotic and illuminating monograph focusing on Kharms and Stalinism – absurdist philosophy in a time of totalitarianism – interweaving such ideas as the mechanized human and erotic fixation. 'Daniil Kharms and the Liquid Language of Stalinism', by Maya Vinokour, *Slavic and East European Journal*, Winter 2016.

7 www.marxists.org/reference/archive/stalin/works/1941/07/03.htm.

8 Ibid.

9 Bertha Gutkina, interviewed for the Blavatnik Archive.

10 Leonard Polyak, interviewed for the Blavatnik Archive.

11 Yura Riabinkin's diaries, in Adamovich and Granin, *Leningrad Under Siege*.

12 From *Virgin Soil*, by Ivan Turgenev ([1877] NYRB Classics, 2000).

13 From Berggolts, *Daytime Stars*.

14 As quoted in *Leningrad: State of Siege*, by Michael Jones (John Murray, 2010).

15 Georgii Knyazev's diaries, in Adamovich and Granin, *Leningrad Under Siege*.

16 Ibid.

17 'Protecting the Art of Leningrad: The Survival of the Hermitage During the Great Patriotic War', by Lane Bailey, Honors Thesis, Ouachita Baptist University, 1997.

18 There are some arresting images of the evacuation to be found at www.dailyartmagazine.com/saving-art-during-the-world-war-ii/.

19 Mariya Vasilyevna Motkovskaya, as quoted in Adamovich and Granin, *Leningrad Under Siege*.

20 Georgii Knyazev's diaries, ibid.

10. World Without End

1 *At Leningrad's Gates: The Story of a Soldier with Army Group North*, by William Lubbeck (pen name of Wilhelm Lübbecke) (reissued edn, Casemate Publishers, 2007).

2 That terrible period is examined further in *Macht Arbeit Frei? German Economic Policy and Forced Labor of Jews in the General Government, 1939–1943*, by Witold Wojciech Mędykowski (Academic Studies Press, 2018).

3 'Finland's Foreign Policy 1940–1941: An Ongoing Historiographic Controversy', by Kent Forster, *Scandinavian Studies*, Spring 1979.

4 Ibid.

5 'Russia and the Russians in the Eyes of Spanish Blue Division Soldiers, 1941–4', by Xosé Núñez Seixas, *Journal of Contemporary History*, April 2017.

6 Ibid.

7 Ibid.

8 Lubbeck, *At Leningrad's Gates*.

9 Núñez Seixas, 'Russians in the Eyes of Spanish Blue Division Soldiers'.

10 Kluge appeared to be articulating a dark variation of St Paul in 1 Corinthians, 15:31: 'I die daily. If after the manner of men I have fought with beasts at Ephesus, what advantageth it me, if the dead rise not?'

11 Lubbeck, *At Leningrad's Gates*.

12 Nabokov, *Speak, Memory*.

13 Leonard Polyak, interviewed for the Blavatnik Archive.

14 Ibid.

15 'Life and Death in the Demiansk Pocket: The 123rd Infantry Division in Combat and Occupation', by Jeff Rutherford, *Central European History*, September 2008.

16 Cited in *Leningrad: Tragedy of a City Under Siege, 1941–44*, by Anna Reid (Bloomsbury, 2011).

17 'Germany's Staatssekretäre, Mass Starvation and the Meeting of 2 May 1941', by Alex J. Kay, *Journal of Contemporary History*, October 2006.

18 Ibid.

19 *The Goebbels Diaries 1939–1941*, by Joseph Goebbels, trans. Fred Taylor (Hamish Hamilton, 1982).

20 Hitler, talking to the German ambassador to Vichy France on 16 September 1941, from 'Hitler and Stalin in Perspective: Secret Speeches on the Eve of Barbarossa', by Jürgen Förster and Evan Mawdsley, *War in History*, January 2004.

11. 'The first herald of the hungry plague'

1 Georgii Knyazev's diaries, in Adamovich and Granin, *Leningrad Under Siege*.

2 Ibid.

3 Berggolts, *Daytime Stars*.

4 From Punin, *The Diaries of Nikolay Punin*.

5 Natalya Uskova, quoted in Peri, *The War Within*.

6 A fragment from the life of Yura Riabinkin, excerpted in Adamovich and Granin, *Leningrad Under Siege*.

7 From Inber, *Leningrad Diary*; what makes this a particularly gripping document is the fact of Inber's close relations with the authorities: while (as in the case of the 1930s White Sea Canal and its slave labour) this led

her to omit any details that might bring discredit upon the regime, it also enabled her to travel to the front line and to hospitals.

8 As cited in Bidlack and Lomagin, *The Leningrad Blockade*.

9 Quoted by St Petersburg local historian Alexander Shmidke (passionate on the subject) on the site histours.ru/news/now-and-then-occupation-Krasnoe-selo. Histours – aimed at foreign visitors – is run by Shmidke, who conducts tours personally. The site features a large range of 'then and now' photographs, and articles about key locations in the siege.

10 Quoted in Peri, *The War Within*.

11 Berggolts, *Daytime Stars*.

12 There is a short film as well as excerpts from Zinaida Fedyushina's diaries to be found on a site hosted by the Administrative Department of the President of the Russian Federation – or the Presidential Library – at www.prlib.ru/en/catalog. In the current climate, this Russian government site is naturally to be approached with a careful eye: but there are digitized Leningrad diaries and memoirs, as well as intriguing contemporaneous art.

13 Berggolts, *Daytime Stars*.

14 Inber, *Leningrad Diary*.

15 Ibid.

12. *'Wait for the silver night'*

1 *Testimony: The Memoirs of Dmitri Shostakovich*, by Dmitri Shostakovich (Hamish Hamilton, 1979).

2 It was Shostakovich himself who applied this label.

3 A recording of the broadcast is available at www.youtube.com/watch?v=N-lNbbYXj8Y.

4 The brilliant Russian historian Sheila Fitzpatrick wrote a wide and compelling account of Shostakovich and his torments in 'Voldemort or Stalin?', *London Review of Books*, December 2011.

5 Reeder, *Anna Akhmatova*.

6 Georgii Knyazev's diaries, in Adamovich and Granin, *Leningrad Under Siege*.

7 Ibid. The State Museum of the History of St Petersburg has exhibited a tribute to Betty and other of the zoo's animals.

8 Inber, *Leningrad Diary*.

9 Davies, 'Us Against Them'.

10 As quoted in Peri, *The War Within*.

11 Georgii Knyazev's diaries, in Adamovich and Granin, *Leningrad Under Siege*.

12 Ibid.

13 Cited in Bidlack and Lomagin, *The Leningrad Blockade*.

14 Ibid.

15 Punin, *The Diaries of Nikolay Punin*.

16 Ibid.

17 Berggolts, *Daytime Stars*.

18 Ibid.

19 Ibid.

20 Ibid.

21 'Gatchina – October 1917 Reminiscences', by Count Valentin Zubov, *Russian Review*, July 1969.

22 As quoted in local tour guides.

23 Yura Riabinkin's diaries, in Adamovich and Granin, *Leningrad Under Siege*.

24 Ibid.

25 Ibid.

26 Inber, *Leningrad Diary*.

13. 'They do not leave our earth in peace'

1 Another translation of this Daniil Kharms poem may be found at allpoetry.com/poem/11967757--This-is-the-onset-of-hunger...--by-Daniil-Ivanovich-Kharms.

2 Inber, *Leningrad Diary*.

3 The precise quantity of 200 grams of bread is exhibited at the Museum of the Defence and Siege of Leningrad, Solyanoy Lane. The day will come when this – and other exhibitions of the city's history – will be available for everyone to explore once more.

4 Yura Riabinkin's recollections of a surfeit of cabbage in Adamovich and Granin, *Leningrad Under Siege*.

5 Cited in Peri, *The War Within*.

6 Georgii Knyazev's diaries, in Adamovich and Granin, *Leningrad Under Siege*.

7 Berggolts, *Daytime Stars*.

8 Ibid.

9 Ibid.

10 Ibid.

11 Inber, *Leningrad Diary*.

12 Ibid.

13 *Russia at War: 1941–45*, by Alexander Werth (Barrie and Rockliff, 1964).

14 As cited in Bidlack and Lomagin, *The Leningrad Blockade*.

15 There are some striking images of the palace in its inter-war years on a curious site devoted to Nicholas – 'Emperor; Tsar; Saint' – at tsarnicholas.org/2019/08/08/the-alexander-palace-as-a-museum-1918-1951/.

16 Ibid.

17 Cited in Peri, *The War Within*.

14. 'The terrible wonders we saw that night'

1 Yura Riabinkin's diaries, in Adamovich and Granin, *Leningrad Under Siege*.

2 Punin, *The Diaries of Nikolay Punin*.

3 Yakov Pikus, interviewed for the Blavatnik Archive.

4 Ibid.

5 Ibid.

6 Abram Sapozhnikov, interviewed for the Blavatnik Archive.

7 Ibid.

8 Cited in Bidlack and Lomagin, *The Leningrad Blockade*.

9 Ibid.

10 Yura Riabinkin's diaries, in Adamovich and Granin, *Leningrad Under Siege*.

11 Ibid.

12 Inber, *Leningrad Diary*.

13 Punin, *The Diaries of Nikolay Punin*.

14 Georgii Knyazev's diaries, in Adamovich and Granin, *Leningrad Under Siege*.

15 Ibid.

15. *Primeval*

1 Quoted in many local tour guides.

2 Lubbeck, *At Leningrad's Gates*.

3 Ibid.

4 Among many works on the subject is *Hitler's Army: Soldiers, Nazis, and War in the Third Reich*, by Omer Bartov (Oxford University Press, 1994). Here, Bartov introduces and analyses the interlocking threads and myths of Wehrmacht motivation, and the extent to which certain soldiers might imagine themselves as comrades serving military tradition rather than as agents of the Nazi regime – despite the lines continually overlapping.

5 There is a haunting essay – 'Repress, Reassess, Remember: Jewish Heritage in Lithuania', by Vytautas Toleikis and Mark Belcher, *Osteuropa*, 2008 – concerning how the memory of these and other horrors were subsequently smothered and erased by the Soviet authorities; the victims were designated not as Jews, but as 'Soviet citizens'. This coincided with a post-war erasure of the visible tokens of Jewish culture in Lithuania. It was only with 1980s perestroika that the past was properly excavated.

6 The Russian Orthodox cathedral in London's Knightsbridge has a lovely illustrated essay concerning the icon, which can be read here: holytrinitycathedral.net/tikhvinicon. According to this site, the Soviets did not remove it to a museum – it was the Nazis who stole it directly from the monastery.

7 'Hitler's Strike for Tikhvin', by Gerald R. Kleinfeld, *Military Affairs*, October 1983.

8 Ibid.

9 A short but admiring profile (and handsome colour portrait) can be found on the site of the Russian Presidential Library at www.prlib.ru/en/history/685603.

10 Ibid.

11 There is an hypnotic essay on the important effect that rainfall (and glutinous mud) had on the course of the war: 'Great Historical Events that Were Significantly Affected by the Weather: Part 8, Germany's War on the Soviet Union, 1941–45. I. Long-Range Weather Forecasts for

1941–42 and Climatological Studies', by J. Neumann and H. Flohn, *Bulletin of the American Meteorological Society*, June 1987. There is a section devoted to the part played by lethal bogs and swamps in the struggle for Leningrad and Moscow.

12 Yakov Pikus, interviewed for the Blavatnik Archive.

13 *War and Peace*, by Leo Tolstoy (Penguin Vintage Classics, 2007), vol. 3 part 2, ch. 34.

16. Trances and Fevers

1 Reeder, *Anna Akhmatova*.

2 *The Akhmatova Journals: 1938–1941*, by Lidiya Chukovskaya (Harper-Collins, 1994).

3 As cited in Peri, *The War Within*.

4 As cited in Bidlack and Lomagin, *The Leningrad Blockade*.

5 Yura Riabinkin's diaries, in Adamovich and Granin, *Leningrad Under Siege*.

6 Ibid.

7 Ibid.

8 Leonard Polyak, interviewed for the Blavatnik Archive.

9 Ibid.

10 Ibid.

11 Bidlack and Lomagin, *The Leningrad Blockade*.

12 Ibid.

13 Ibid.

14 Ibid.

15 Elizaveta Zinger, interviewed for the Blavatnik Archive.

16 'The Diaries of Besieged Leningraders, 1941–44', by Sarah Gruszka, *Literature and Medicine*, Spring 2022.

17 Cited in Bidlack and Lomagin, *The Leningrad Blockade*.

18 Ibid.

19 'The Political Mood in Leningrad During the First Year of the Soviet–German War', by Richard Bidlack, *Russian Review*, January 2000.

20 As cited in Peri, *The War Within*.

21 Ibid.

17. The Fear of Mirrors

1 Gruszka, 'The Diaries of Besieged Leningraders'. Incidentally, St Petersburg today has a special memorial to the city's cats, in the form of two statues at Malaya Sadovaya Street; these are to celebrate the vital role the animals played much later in the siege: brought into the city to deal with the rat population.

2 'Norms and Survival in the Heat of War: Normative Versus Instrumental Rationalities and Survival Tactics in the Blockade of Leningrad', by Jeffrey K. Hass, *Sociological Forum*, December 2011.

3 Cited in Bidlack and Lomagin, *The Leningrad Blockade*.

4 Valerii Sukhov's siege diary – plus photographs – are in the St Petersburg Museum of the Defence and Siege of Leningrad.

5 Hass, 'Norms and Survival in the Heat of War'.

6 Ibid.

7 Peri, *The War Within*.

8 *John Donne: Selected Poetry* (Oxford World's Classics, 1996). Joseph Brodsky, born in Leningrad in 1940, almost died of starvation as a baby in the siege. As a young poet in the 1960s he met Anna Akhmatova and entered her circle. He was denounced as a dissident in the early 1960s and sentenced to five years' hard labour in the northern wilderness. His discovery of Donne was transforming.

9 Peri, *The War Within*.

10 Bidlack and Lomagin, *The Leningrad Blockade*.

11 Peri, *The War Within*.

12 Inber, *Leningrad Diary*. Additionally, there is some extraordinary visual material from the period – performances, tickets, etc. to be found on the Mariinsky Theatre website at www.mariinsky.ru/en/about/ww2/1941/.

13 Ibid.

14 Jones, *Leningrad: State of Siege*.

15 Ibid.

16 Bidlack, 'The Political Mood in Leningrad'.

17 Ibid.

18 Ibid.

19 *Writing the Siege of Leningrad: Women's Diaries, Memoirs, and Documentary Prose*, by Cynthia Simmons and Nina Perlina (University of Pittsburgh Press, 2005).

20 *Wartime Suffering and Survival: The Human Condition Under Siege in the Blockade of Leningrad*, by Jeffrey K. Hass (Oxford University Press, 2021).

21 Peri, *The War Within*.

22 Hass, *Wartime Suffering and Survival*.

23 Nikolay Gogol, *The Collected Tales of Nikolay Gogol*, trans. Richard Pevear and Larissa Volokhonsky (Vintage Classics, 1999).

24 Elizaveta Zinger, interviewed for the Blavatnik Archive.

25 Leonard Polyak, interviewed for the Blavatnik Archive.

26 Peri, *The War Within*.

27 Anna Novikova, interviewed for the Blavatnik Archive.

28 Bertha Gutkina, interviewed for the Blavatnik Archive.

29 Punin, *The Diaries of Nikolay Punin*.

30 Ibid.

31 Ibid.

32 Ibid.

18. This is My Blood

1 *Blockade Diary*, by Lidiya Ginzburg (Harvill Press, 1995); Ginzburg's memoirs are focused not just on events, but also on fascinating observations of human nature and the use of language in times of mortal crisis (e.g. the commonplace expression 'I'm ravenous', used by the mildly hungry, disappeared throughout that terrible winter: when people started using it again, it was clear that renewal and regeneration were underway).

2 See 'The Siege of Leningrad', by Constantine Krypton, *Russian Review*, October 1954.

3 Peri, *The War Within*.

4 Ibid.

5 Ginzburg, *Blockade Diary*.

6 Bidlack and Lomagin, *The Leningrad Blockade*.

7 Ibid.

8 *Blockade Diary*, by Yelena Kochina (Harry N. Abrams, 2014).

9 'The Siege of Leningrad as Sacred Narrative: Conversations with Survivors', by James Clapperton, *Oral History*, Spring 2007.

10 *The Defence of Leningrad: Eyewitness Accounts of the Siege*, by Nikolay Tikhonov (Hutchinson, 1944). What makes this a valuable document in its own right is its publication as the war was still raging; and at the point at which the UK and the USSR were firm allies. In this sense, much of it is fervid propaganda; yet wade through the treacly sentiments and there are gripping and valuable details.

11 Ibid.

12 Ginzburg, *Blockade Diary*.

13 'Lifting the Siege: Women's Voices on Leningrad (1941–1944)', by Cynthia Simmons, *Canadian Slavonic Papers*, March–June 1998.

14 Samuil Hedekel, interviewed for the Blavatnik Archive.

15 Hass,'Norms and Survival in the Heat of War'.

16 Dmitri Likhachev, a linguist and historian who was ardent in his love for Petersburg, was already familiar with the extremes of human nature, having been sentenced in the 1930s to penal servitude in the Arctic north. There he had made a popular study of prisoners' slang. By the time of the siege he was studying medieval Russian chronicles while the streets around him reverted to pre-modern darkness.

17 Hass, *Wartime Suffering and Survival*.

18 Ibid.

19 Bidlack and Lomagin, *The Leningrad Blockade*.

20 Ibid.

21 Ibid.

22 Ibid.

23 Yura Riabinkin's diaries, in Adamovich and Granin, *Leningrad Under Siege*.

24 Ibid.

25 Berggolts, *Daytime Stars*.

19. *The Children Who Could Not Grieve*

1 There is a fascinating nineteenth-century monograph: 'Hydrographical Survey of Ladoga Lake', by A. Andreyeff, trans. E. Delmar Morgan,

Proceedings of the Royal Geographical Society of London, 1868–69. But there are also some beguiling (and nicely illustrated) modern geographical essays, including 'Changing Waters of Lake Ladoga', by Alfred Colpaert and Augustine-Moses Gbagir in *Lake Ladoga: The Coastal History of the Greatest Lake in Europe* (Finnish Literature Society, 2023).

2 A website called 'Russia Beyond' has an entire illustrated section on the efforts to create the 'Road of Life': the pictures alone are stark and haunting. You can find it at www.rbth.com/history/334919-how-road-of-life-saved-leningrad.

3 Ibid.

4 Ibid.

5 Ibid.

6 Ibid.

7 Ibid.

8 Ibid.

9 Dora Fagina, interviewed for the Blavatnik Archive.

10 Ibid.

11 Ibid.

12 Erhard Raus, *Panzer Operations: The Eastern Front Memoir of General Raus, 1941–1945* (Da Capo Press, 2013).

13 Zhukov, *The Memoirs of Marshal Zhukov*.

14 Yura Riabinkin's diaries, in Adamovich and Granin, *Leningrad Under Siege*.

15 Ibid.

16 Ibid.

17 Ibid.

18 Ibid.

19 Hass, *Wartime Suffering and Survival*.

20 Ibid.

21 Ibid.

22 Peri, *The War Within*.

23 This diary is also reproduced in stone at the St Petersburg 'Flower of Life' memorial to the city's children: and an asteroid discovered by a Soviet astronomer was named '2127 Tanya' in her honour.

24 Peri, *The War Within*.

20. Scythians So Embellished With Nature's Pride

1 There are many translations available, some online. One such can be found at www.poetryintranslation.com/PITBR/Russian/BronzeHorseman.php.

2 Bidlack and Lomagin, *The Leningrad Blockade*.

3 Georgii Knyazev's diaries, in Adamovich and Granin, *Leningrad Under Siege*.

4 Inber, *Leningrad Diary*.

5 Bidlack and Lomagin, *The Leningrad Blockade*.

6 Ibid.

7 There are many appreciative essays about Kharms and his work now: one of the most striking is where he was shown to have chillingly anticipated, in some ways, the shape his fate would take. 'The Rudiments of Daniil Kharms: In Further Pursuit of the Red-Haired Man', by Neil Cornwell, *The Modern Language Review*, January 1998.

8 From a mesmerizing online essay to be found at balticworlds.com/books-and-their-owners-in-the-siege-of-leningrad/.

9 Ibid.

10 'The Spectacle of the Besieged City: Repurposing Cultural Memory in Leningrad, 1941–1944', by Polina Barskova, *Slavic Review*, Summer 2010.

11 Punin, *The Diaries of Nikolay Punin*.

12 Peri, *The War Within*.

13 Ibid.

14 Ibid. Yelena Martilla's art, capturing the haunted faces of the starving city, now stands as a powerful historical testimony. Some examples – which featured in an exhibition at Darwin College, Cambridge – can be viewed online at www.artandendurance.org.

15 Peri, *The War Within*.

16 Ibid.

21. 'The air was ripped like silk'

1 Lubbeck, *At Leningrad's Gates*.

2 Ibid.

3 Ibid.

4 Ibid.

5 Ibid.

6 Henrikh Dudnik, interviewed for the Blavatnik Archive.

7 Ibid.

8 Ibid.

9 A remarkable historical artefact in its own right (the aesthetics of Soviet montage applied to human calamity), this appears on and off on the streaming site MUBI but can also be viewed at www.youtube.com/watch?v=Ydz42545OmU.

10 Inber, *Leningrad Diary*.

11 Georgii Knyazev's diaries, in Adamovich and Granin, *Leningrad Under Siege*.

12 Leonard Polyak, interviewed for the Blavatnik Archive.

13 Ibid.

14 Elizaveta Zinger, interviewed for the Blavatnik Archive.

15 Ibid.

16 Tikhonov, *The Defence of Leningrad*.

22. Lilac

1 As well as a piercing analysis of the scene where Sonya reads the story of Lazarus to Raskolnikov, drawing him closer to confession, there is a fascinating study of Raskolnikov's relationship to Petersburg itself – a city that seems as fevered as his oppressive, frightening dreams – in 'Deferred Senses and Distanced Spaces: Embodying the Boundaries of Dostoevsky's Realism', by Sarah J. Young in *Dostoevsky at 200: The Novel in Modernity*, ed. Katherine Bowers and Kate Holland (University of Toronto Press, 2021).

2 'Where, how, and when had this little countess . . . sucked this spirit in from the Russian air she breathed?' This passage occurs in Tolstoy, *War and Peace*, vol. 2, part 4, ch. 7.

3 Georgii Knyazev's diaries, in Adamovich and Granin, *Leningrad Under Siege*.

4 Anna Novikova, interviewed for the Blavatnik Archive.

5 Ibid.

6 Ibid.

7 *Music During the Siege*, by A. Kryukov (Leningrad Sovietsky Kompositor, date unknown), quoted on the Mariinsky Theatre website at www.
mariinsky.ru/en/about/ww2/1942/.

8 This account from the distinguished linguist and academic Dmitri Likhachev features in his memoirs, published in Russia in 1995 and quoted at
www.mariinsky.ru/en/about/ww2/1942/.

9 Nadezhda Velter, *About the Opera House and Me* (Leningrad Sovietsky
Kompositor, 1984), quoted at www.mariinsky.ru/en/about/ww2/1942/.

10 Simmons, 'Lifting the Siege'.

11 Tikhonov, *The Defence of Leningrad*.

12 Ibid.

13 Much of this art – plus also some of the Nazi propaganda leaflets rained
down on the city – have been exhibited in the St Petersburg State
Museum of the Defence and Siege of Leningrad. But there is also an
illuminating online display of Leningrad postcard art from the time of
the siege to be found at the Blavatnik Archive.

14 Inber, *Leningrad Diary*.

15 Ginzburg, *Blockade Diary*.

23. 'Listen, comrades!'

1 Von Küchler addressing his divisional commanders on 25 April 1941.
cited in Jones, *Leningrad: State of Siege*. For a range of pre-invasion rheto-
ric see 'Hitler and Stalin In Perspective: Secret Speeches on the Eve of
Barbarossa' by Jürgen Förster and Evan Mawdsley, *War in History*, January 2004.

2 Tikhonov, *The Defence of Leningrad*.

3 Ibid.

4 As relayed in interviews with his son Vladimir, who himself rose to be a
senior military commander; 'How an Enemy of the Bolsheviks Became
One of the BEST Soviet Commanders', www.russiabeyond.com/
history/334519-enemy-of-bolsheviks-became-marshal.

5 'Tsarist Officer, Soviet Marshal. The Mysterious Fate of the Commander
of the Leningrad Front, Leonid Govorov'; en.topwar.ru/38922-carskiy-

oficer-sovetskiy-marshal-zagadochnaya-sudba-komanduyuschego-leningradskim-frontom-leonida-govorova.html.

6 'How an Enemy of the Bolsheviks Became One of the BEST Soviet Commanders',www.russiabeyond.com/history/334519-enemy-of-bolsheviks-became-marshal.

7 Anatoly Kibrik, interviewed for the Blavatnik Archive.

8 Tikhonov, *The Defence of Leningrad*.

9 Bidlack and Lomagin, *The Leningrad Blockade*.

10 Ibid.

11 There was a marvellous two-part essay by Ed Vulliamy in the *Observer*, 25 November 2001, about Eliasberg and the efforts of the Leningrad Philharmonic: www.theguardian.com/theobserver/2001/nov/25/features.magazine27.

12 A statement that, with a few adjustments, Shostakovich subsequently had published in *Pravda*, 29 March 1942.

13 Olga Kvade interviewed by the BBC for a piece published on 2 January 2016; www.bbc.co.uk/news/magazine-34292312.

14 This introduction, widely quoted since, also features heavily in an entire book devoted to the life of this symphony: *Leningrad: Siege and Symphony*, by Brian Moynahan (Quercus, 2013).

15 Berggolts, *Daytime Stars*.

16 A story relayed by musician Semyon Bychkov in a piece about the symphony, 2 January 2016. One version of the story can be found at www.bbc.co.uk/news/magazine-34292312.

24. The Fuse of Vengeance

1 Abram Sapozhnikov, interviewed for the Blavatnik Archive.

2 www.mariinsky.ru/en/about/ww2/1942/.

3 Ibid.

4 Tikhonov, *The Defence of Leningrad*.

5 Anna Novikova, interviewed for the Blavatnik Archive.

6 Tolstoy, *War and Peace*, vol. 3, part 2, ch. 39.

7 Ibid.

8 Ibid.

9 Lubbeck, *At Leningrad's Gates*.

10 Ibid.

11 Moisei Malkis, interviewed for the Blavatnik Archive.

12 Ibid.

13 Ibid.

14 Ibid.

25. *Golden Stars Streamed Downwards*

1 *Leningrad*, by Alexander Werth (Hamish Hamilton, 1944).

2 Ibid.

3 Ibid.

4 Ibid.

5 Ibid.

6 Berggolts, *Daytime Stars*.

7 Ibid.

8 Inber, *Leningrad Diary*.

9 Berggolts, *Daytime Stars*.

10 Werth, *Leningrad*.

11 Ibid.

12 Ibid.

13 Ibid.

14 Ibid.

15 Ginzburg, *Blockade Diary*.

16 Bidlack and Lomagin, *The Leningrad Blockade*.

17 Werth, *Leningrad*.

18 Ibid.

19 Ibid.

20 Jones, *Leningrad: State of Siege*.

21 This public pronouncement is also cited by his son Vladimir in interviews on Russian websites. For the fascinating 'through a glass darkly' Russian angle, see www.prlib.ru/en/history/618980, where the speech is quoted, together with a rather intriguing coda: in October 2022 (with the assault on Ukraine well underway) the St Petersburg City Court ruled the siege by the 'German-Fascists' to have been an act of genocide.

26. 'Terror is still a necessity'

1 As quoted mournfully on the city's own (now 'not secure') historical website. The poem is quoted in full at m.vk.com/wall-5197510_177461?lang=en.

2 Inber, *Leningrad Diary*.

3 'Anna Akhmatova: The Stalin Years', by Roberta Reeder, *New England Review*, Winter 1997.

4 Punin, *The Diaries of Nikolay Punin*.

5 Ibid.

6 There was an absorbing piece on the subject by Valerie Grove in the *Guardian*, 29 August 2015: www.theguardian.com/stage/2015/aug/29/how-jb-priestley-inspector-calls-ussr.

7 From a majestic essay by Isaiah Berlin in the *New York Review of Books*, November 1980; as well as this encounter with Akhmatova, the young Berlin also got to meet Boris Pasternak; despite the death, the suffering, the terror and oppression, here was a sense of poetry as the nation's lifeblood.

8 Ibid.

9 There is a terrible moment, cited in *Freedom from Violence and Lies: Essays on Russian Poetry and Music*, by Simon Karlinsky (Academic Studies Press, 2013), when several years after the 'half-nun, half-whore' denunciation, a delegation of visiting English students met Akhmatova in the presence of the Writers' Union and asked for her reaction to it. She had no alternative – given that she was being observed – but to respond that it was 'correct', thus compounding the humiliation.

10 Khrushchev, *Khrushchev Remembers*.

11 Serge, *Conquered City*.

27. The Sense of the Human Nexus

1 'No Beast More Refined', by James Davidson, *London Review of Books*, November 2007.

2 For further reading on the evolution of Leningrad pop – and the fury of the authorities, including Khrushchev's reference to dancing involving 'indecent wriggling of certain parts of the anatomy' – there are

the early chapters of *Rock in the Reservation: Songs from the Leningrad Rock Club 1981–86*, by Yngvar Bordewich Steinholt (Mass Media Music Scholars Press, 2005).

3 Ginzburg, *Blockade Diary*.

4 An absorbing introduction can be found at psychologyinrussia.com/volumes/index.php?article=2603.

5 Ginzburg, *Blockade Diary*.

6 Putin has visited the cemetery regularly, and these occasions have been marked on the official Kremlin website (warning: now deemed 'not secure') and on the news agency Tass.com.

7 Fyodor Dostoevsky, *Notes from Underground* ([1864] Penguin Vintage Classics, 2004).

Index